Mac OS X Keyboard Shortcuts

Learning and using keyboard shortcuts is the key to efficiency on a computer. Although most of the tasks in this list can be accomplished easily using your mouse alone, you can perform them more quickly if you don't lift your hands from the keyboard. Some of them require you to use both the keyboard and mouse, allowing you to do things with this combination that the mouse just can't do by itself.

tear here

General Shortcuts

Select all objects or text	Cmd+A	Maximize window	Option+click Zoom button
Copy selected text or object	Cmd+C	Move window without making it active	Cmd+drag
Cut selected text or object and place it on the Clipboard	Cmd+X	Minimize current window	Double-click its title bar
Paste text or object on Clipboard into current document	Cmd+V	Close current window	Cmd+W
Display contextual menu	Ctrl+click	Hide current application or Finder	Cmd+H
Cancel an action	Cmd+.	Shut down or restart	Power key
Undo last action	Cmd+Z	Force your Mac to restart	Cmd+Ctrl+power key
Quit current program	Cmd+Q		
Switch to another application and hide all others	Option+click another program's window	Force Quit	Option+Cmd+Esc
Minimize all open windows	Option+click minimize button or Option+double-click any window's title bar	Get help	Cmd+?

D1317959

Dialog Box Shortcuts

Go to next entry field	Tab	Select folders above or below current item in Save/Open dialog boxes	Up and down arrows
Click default button	Return or Enter		
Close dialog box	Cmd+. or Esc	Scroll list down or up	Page Down or Page Up

Dock Shortcuts

Turn Dock hiding on or off	Option+Cmd+D	Reveal original Finder icon for a Dock icon	Cmd+click Dock icon
Minimize window in slow button	Shift+click minimize motion	Switch to an application and hide all others	Option+Cmd+click its Dock icon
Minimize window in super slow motion	Shift+Ctrl+click minimize button	Place selected file or folder in folder whose icon is in the Dock	Cmd+drag file or folder over Dock icon
Restore minimized window in slow motion	Shift+click its Dock icon	Open selected file with an application whose icon is in the Dock	Option+Cmd+drag file over Dock icon
Restore minimized window in super slow motion	Shift+Ctrl+click its Dock icon		
Select each Dock item in succession	Cmd+Tab		

Finder Shortcuts

Go to your Home folder	Option+Cmd+H or Cmd+up arrow	Duplicate selected file or folder	Cmd+D
Go to Applications folder	Option+Cmd+A	Make alias of selected file or folder	Cmd+L
Go to Computer window	Option+Cmd+C	Copy name of selected object	Cmd+C
Go to your iDisk	Option+Cmd+I	Add selected file or folder to Favorites	Cmd+T
Go to your Favorites folder	Option+Cmd+F	Move selected file or folder to Trash	Cmd+Delete
Open the folder containing icons for items on Desktop	Cmd+down arrow	Eject selected disk	Cmd+E
Connect to server	Cmd+K	Copy and move selected file	Option+drag
Empty Trash	Shift+Cmd+Delete	Create and move an alias of the selected file	Cmd+Option+drag
Empty Trash with no dialog box	Press Option and choose Finder, Empty Trash	Show original of the selected alias	Cmd+R
Open new Finder window	Cmd+N	Select all objects in current window	Cmd+A
Minimize window	Cmd+M	Select next icon in window	Arrow keys
Close all open windows	Option+click close button or Option+Cmd+W	Select an icon by first letter of its name	Type name
See window hierarchy pop-up menu	Cmd+click title bar	Select next icon alphabetically	Tab
Hide Toolbar and switch to multiwindow mode or show Toolbar and switch to single-window mode	Cmd+B	Select more than one item	Shift+click
		Select adjacent items in list view	Click on first and Shift+click on last
Stack all open windows	Press Option and choose Window, Arrange in Front	Select or deselect nonadjacent items in list view	Cmd+click
Align icons	Cmd+drag	Select name of icon for editing	Click, then press Return or Enter
Create new folder	Shift+Cmd+N	In list view, open selected folder	Cmd+right arrow
Show Info about selected file or folder	Cmd+I	In list view, close selected folder	Cmd+left arrow
Show View Options for current folder	Cmd+J	In list view, open selected folder and all folders it contains	Option+right arrow
Move or remove an item in Toolbar	Cmd+drag		
Edit Toolbar	Shift+click top-right button in any Finder window	In list view, close selected folder and all folders it contains	Option+left arrow
Open selected file or folder	Cmd+O	Search for files or search the Internet with Sherlock	Cmd+F
Open selected folder in separate window	Cmd+double-click		

ALPHA

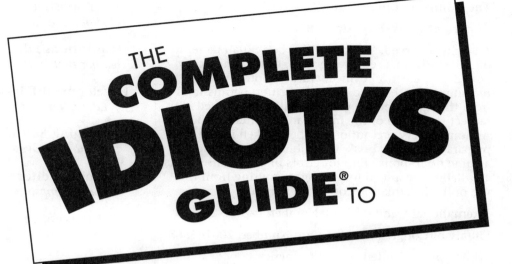

Mac™ OS X

by Kate Binder

ALPHA

201 West 103rd Street, Indianapolis, Indiana 46290

The Complete Idiot's Guide® to Mac™ OS X

Copyright © 2002 by Alpha Books

All rights reserved. No part of this book shall be reproduced, stored in a retrieval system, or transmitted by any means, electronic, mechanical, photocopying, recording, or otherwise, without written permission from the publisher. No patent liability is assumed with respect to the use of the information contained herein. Although every precaution has been taken in the preparation of this book, the publisher and author assume no responsibility for errors or omissions. Nor is any liability assumed for damages resulting from the use of the information contained herein.

International Standard Book Number: 0-7897-2528-2

Library of Congress Catalog Card Number: 200186868

Printed in the United States of America

First Printing: August 2001

04   03   02   01   4   3   2   1

Trademarks

All terms mentioned in this book that are known to be trademarks or service marks have been appropriately capitalized. Alpha Books cannot attest to the accuracy of this information. Use of a term in this book should not be regarded as affecting the validity of any trademark or service mark.

Mac is a trademark of Apple Computer, Inc.

Warning and Disclaimer

Every effort has been made to make this book as complete and as accurate as possible, but no warranty or fitness is implied. The information provided is on an "as is" basis. The author and the publisher shall have neither liability nor responsibility to any person or entity with respect to any loss or damages arising from the information contained in this book.

Publisher
Robb Linsky

Acquisitions Editor
Heather Banner Kane

Development Editor
Laura Norman

Managing Editor
Thomas F. Hayes

Project Editor
Tonya Simpson

Copy Editor
Kay Hoskin

Indexer
Chris Barrick

Proofreader
Maribeth Echard

Technical Editor
Ilene Hoffman

Illustrator
Judd Winick

Team Coordinator
Cindy Teeters

Interior Designer
Nathan Clement

Cover Designer
Michael Freeland

Page Layout
Cheryl Lynch
Mark Walchle

Contents at a Glance

Part 1: Getting Started   **5**

This part covers the Mac basics: What Mac OS X is and how it works, as well as a look at ways to get help when you're using Mac OS X and how the new system will interact with the rest of your hardware.

1 Meet the New Mac   7
Getting to know all about the new system—and inviting it into your Mac.

2 Making Friends with Mac OS X   23
What's new—and what's not—about Mac OS X.

3 Help! Getting It When You Need It   37
How to access Mac OS X's built-in help system, good places to find Mac help on the Web, and ways to get help when you're not online.

4 No Mac Is an Island   45
Peripheral devices to keep your Mac company, from multi-button mice to dye-sub printers.

Part 2: Getting Things Done   **57**

In these chapters, you'll learn how to organize your Mac and set it up for multiple users, as well as learn about Mac OS X's bundled free software, third-party programs, multimedia software, and games.

5 Managing Your Files   59
How your Mac's hard drive is organized under Mac OS X—and what you can do about it.

6 Sharing Your Mac with Multiple Users   75
Sharing your computer with other users while maintaining everyone's privacy and preferences.

7 Free Software! (Using Mac OS X's Built-In Apps)   81
Find out about all the cool programs that come already loaded on your Mac OS X hard drive—free.

8 Using Third-Party Applications   89
Three different kinds of Mac programs, and some useful apps for you to download.

9 Working with Audio and Video   97
Creating your own masterpieces of sound and vision with Apple's multimedia software.

10 The Games People Play   105
With the advent of Mac OS X, the coolest new games are going to be on your Mac.

Part 3: Getting Connected   **115**

*Meet the Internet—and the intranet: How to set up a local
network, print, hop on the Internet, and make your presence known on the Web.*

11 How to Succeed in Networking Without Even Trying   117
*Setting up your own network for file, printer, and Internet
sharing.*

12 Printing Up a Storm   129
*Managing fonts, setting up printers, and printing from
Mac OS X apps.*

13 Getting Online   141
*Whether you're using a phone modem or have high-speed
access, Mac OS X can get you online in no time.*

14 Nothing but Net   155
*Making use of the best the Web has to offer, including
searching with Sherlock.*

15 Publishing on the Web   173
*How to create and publish your own Web site on your
Mac.*

Part 4: Talking to Other Platforms   **185**

*Sharing space with users of other systems—can't we all
just get along? You can, and here's how.*

16 Interacting with Earlier Versions of Mac OS   187
*Making sure your Mac OS X can still share files and print-
ers with its less advanced Mac cousins.*

17 Interacting with Windows   195
*Keeping on good terms with the Windows side of the
family—and its files and printers.*

18 Interacting with Unix   203
*Teaching your Mac to share files and printers with its
Unix brothers under the skin.*

Part 5: Tweaking Mac OS X   **213**

*Here's the fun stuff: making your Mac look and act the
way you want it to.*

19 Setting System Preferences   215
*All the info you need to master Mac OS X's System
Preferences—from Startup Disk to Speech.*

20 The Desktop and the Dock As You Like Them   229
*What's in the Dock and how to use it, as well as how the
new Mac Desktop is different from the old one.*

21 File and Folder Boot Camp   241
    How to view your windows, rearrange your folders, and
    take control of your files.

22 Making Mac OS X More Familiar   253
    If you're nostalgic for the glories of Mac systems gone by,
    don't worry—your OS X Mac can act just like your OS 9
    Mac.

Part 6: Becoming a Mac OS X Power User   261
    When you're ready for the next level, turn here to discover
    the powerful potential of Mac OS X's Unix layer,
    AppleScript, and other Mac-first technologies.

23 Automating Your Work with AppleScript   263
    Mac OS X and AppleScript combine to help you get your
    work done faster and more accurately.

24 Using Mac Technology to the Max   271
    Color management, talking to your Mac, and getting it to
    talk back to you—it's all here.

25 Harnessing the Power of Unix   281
    You can ignore it or you can take advantage of it, but Mac
    OS X's Unix underpinnings are a powerful thing.

Part 7: Keeping Mac Happy   291
    Macs are easy and fun to use, but even they have bad
    days on occasion. Here's how to keep your Mac healthy
    and humming along.

26 Good MacHousekeeping   293
    Keeping your disks clean, your system running smoothly,
    and your files in good shape.

27 Preparing for the Worst   303
    Eventually your hard drive will crash, or you'll accident-
    ally trash a file you need. Be ready for it.

28 Troubleshooting   309
    When things go wrong, you'll need to know where to look
    and what to do about it.

A   Useful Web Sites   319
    Mac resources from all over the world are at your finger-
    tips on the World Wide Web.

    Glossary   327
    Technical terms defined for the nongeeks among us.

    Index   335

Contents

Part 1: Getting Started   **5**

1 Meet the New Mac   **7**

What Is Mac OS X? 8

Multifaceted, Multitasking 9

Roots: The Mac OS X Family Tree 11

Why You Need Mac OS X 11

Installing Mac OS X 12

The Countdown's On: Preparing Your Computer 13

Running the Installer 14

Setting Up Mac OS X 16

Starting Up Mac OS X 16

Shutting Down Mac OS X 17

Bipolar Shift: Switching Between Mac OS X and Mac OS 9 17

2 Making Friends with Mac OS X   **23**

Face to (Inter)face with Mac OS X 23

Watching Windows 23

Ordering from the Menus 24

Keyboard Shortcuts: In the Fast Lane 25

Just Your Type: Dialog Boxes 25

Contextual Menus—À la Carte 27

What's New in Mac OS X 27

Looks Like Aqua 27

Quartz Movement 27

Sittin' on the Dock of the Mac 28

The Finder 29

How It All Works (Candy-Coated Unix) 32

Application Madness: Classic, Carbon, and Cocoa 33

Classic: Old School 33

Cocoa: New School 34

Carbon: Having Your Cake and Eating It, Too 34

3 Help! Getting It When You Need It   **37**

What's on the (Help) Menu 37

Asking Questions 38

Getting Answers 39

Late Breaking News 40

Getting Help Offline 41

A Big Helping of the Web 42

4 No Mac Is an Island   45

Printer Mania 46
  Ink Versus Toner Versus Dye 46
  Getting Hooked Up 47
Seeing Through Scanners 48
  What Kind to Get 48
  Scanner Slang 48
Getting Input from Mice and More 50
  The Mouse Replacement 50
  Tablets and Styli 51
  Gaming Controllers 51
Zips, Hard Drives, and All That Jaz 51
  Removable Drives 52
  Portable Drives 53
Making Connections 53

Part 2: Getting Things Done   57

5 Managing Your Files   59

Your Drive's Built-In Folders 60
  Applications: The Engines 60
  Library: Where the Wild Settings Are 62
  Mac OS 9: Oldie von Moldies 62
  System: Your Mac's (Off-Limits) Control Center ..64
  Users: Storage for You and Me 64
Let There Be Files and Folders 65
  Surprise! When Folders Just Appear 65
  Mixing Your Own Folders 66
Moving, Copying, and Renaming Files and Folders ..67
  Move It Out! 67
  Makin' Copies 67
  Naming Names 68
Living Under an Alias 69
  Creating Aliases 69
  Advanced Alias-Making 201 70
But I Can't Find Anything! 70
  What's in a Name? 71
  It's the Content, Stupid 72
  Customizing Your Searches 72
  What to Do with the Files You Find 74

6 Sharing Your Mac with Multiple Users   75

Logging In, Logging Out 76
Here a User, There a User 77
Setting Up Users *77*
The User at the Root of It All *78*
Playing Well with Others 79
Separate Folders Make Good Neighbors *79*
Practice Safe Sharing *79*

7 Free Software! (Using Mac OS X's Built-In Apps)   81

Everything but the Stapler 82
Calculator *82*
Clock *83*
Key Caps *83*
Stickies *84*
Writing the Great American Memo 84
Move Over, Michelangelo 85
Preview *86*
QuickTime Player *86*
Image Capture *86*

8 Using Third-Party Applications   89

Carbon Fibers 90
Cocoa Loco 91
Jurassic Classic 93
Can I See Some ID? *93*
A Classic Installation *94*
What's New, Dock? 95
Wild Wild Web *95*
Keeping In Touch *95*
Modern Design *95*
At the Office *96*

9 Working with Audio and Video   97

The DJ on Your Desktop 98
Let's Go to the iMovies 100
Getting Video into Your Mac *101*
Editing Video and Adding Cool Effects *101*
Getting Your Opus Out There *102*
The Hardware You'll Need 102
The Fine Print 103

10 The Games People Play   105

The Mac's Classic Games 106
Made for Mac OS X 107
   Logic/Puzzle *107*
   Strategy/Simulation *108*
   Arcade *109*
   Action *109*
   Real-World Games *110*
Freaky Machines: Gaming Hardware 111
   Controlling the Game *112*
   Gaming Accessories *112*

Part 3: Getting Connected   115

11 How to Succeed in Networking Without Even Trying 117

Building a Hard-Wired Network 118
   Cable Me When You Get There *118*
   The Hub of Your Universe *119*
   Speed Trap *120*
   Mixing and Matching *120*
   Hooking It All Up *121*
Out of the Ether 121
Sharing Files 123
   Making the Macintosh Connection *123*
   Controlling Access *125*
Sharing Internet Access 126
Printing 127

12 Printing Up a Storm   129

Managing Those Funky Fonts 130
   Installing Fonts *130*
   Genuine Font Paneling *131*
Exercising Your Printing Options 133
   Introducing Mac OS X to Your Printer *134*
   Playing with Page Setup *134*
Getting Down to Printing Business 136
   Time to Print *136*
   Previewing Print Jobs *137*
   Keeping an Eye on Print Jobs *138*

13 Getting Online 141

Phone Modems: Dial Me Impressed 142
   Eating Your PPPs *142*
   Connecting with a Modem *144*
   When Good Modems Go Bad *145*
High Times with High-Speed Access 145
   Get Ready… *146*
   PPPoE for Thee *148*
Think Globally, Act Locally 149
   The Softer Side of Internet Sharing *149*
   Doing It the Hard Way *150*
   Taking Off from the AirPort *150*
Hello, Central 151

14 Nothing but Net 155

Surf's Up! 156
   Just Browsing *156*
   Browsers That Try Harder *158*
   Browsing the Way You Prefer *158*
Searching the Web with Sherlock 160
   Change the Channel *160*
   Taking Sherlock New Places *162*
Using E-Mail 163
   Setting Up E-Mail *164*
   Receiving E-Mail *165*
   Sending E-Mail *166*
   The Little Black (Address) Book *167*
Other Internet Applications 169
Apple Makes It Easy 169

15 Publishing on the Web 173

Creating a Site with iTools 173
   Setting Up iTools *174*
   Creating a Page with HomePage *175*
Home Cooking: Doing It Yourself 178
   Creating Content *178*
   Graphic Facts *180*
   Getting It Out There *181*
Hey! Free Stuff! 182
   Clip Art *182*
   Counters *183*

Part 4: Talking to Other Platforms   185

16 Interacting with Earlier Versions of Mac OS   187

Sharing Files with Sneakernet 187
Drive, She Said *188*
You Can Get There from Here *188*
Mary Had a Little LAN 189
Speaking the Same Language *190*
What's the IP Address, Kenneth? *190*
Finally! Getting Connected *191*
Going the Other Way *192*
Vintage Mac Software 193

17 Interacting with Windows   195

Moving Files with Sneakernet 196
Moving Files Across a Network 197
Peer-to-Peer with Windows *197*
On a Server-Based Network *198*
File Format Compatibility *199*
Printing Both Ways 200
Without a Network *200*
On a Network *201*
Running Windows Software 202

18 Interacting with Unix   203

Sharing Files with Sneakernet 204
Exchanging Files over a Network 206
Mount Disk *206*
FTP *207*
File Formats 208
Sharing Printers 209
Running Unix Software 209
Unix by Remote Control *210*
Keeping It Local *210*

Part 5: Tweaking Mac OS X   213

19 Setting System Preferences   215

Getting Going 216
Startup Disk *216*
Energy Saver *217*
Screen Saver *217*

Nuts and Bolts 218
   General 218
   Dock 219
   Software Update 219
   Classic 219
   Users 220
   Date & Time 220
   International 221
Keeping Connected 222
   Internet 222
   Network 223
   Login 224
   Sharing 224
Playing with Peripherals 225
   Mouse 225
   Keyboard 225
   Displays 225
Messing with Multimedia 226
   Sound 226
   Speech 227
   QuickTime 227
   ColorSync 228

20 The Desktop and the Dock As You Like Them 229
Hickory Dickory Dock 230
   What Can You Put in the Dock? 230
   Having the Dock Your Way 233
   Dock Strategy 234
Desktop Decisions 236
   Finding the Way 236
   Appearances Count 237
   Digging Deeper 238
Juggling Disks 239

21 File and Folder Boot Camp 241
Here a Window, There a Window 241
   One Window or Many Windows? 242
   Icons, Columns, and Lists, Oh My 244
We Do Windows 245
   Custom Windows 245
   Off the Shelf 246
Info Overload 247

22 Making Mac OS X More Familiar 253

Getting Things Back Where They Belong 254
   Drive Icons and the Trash *254*
   Missing Menus *255*
More Third-Party Help 256
   Dock Alternatives *257*
   Missing in Action *258*
Familiar Faces, New Names 259

Part 6: Becoming a Mac OS X Power User 261

23 Automating Your Work with AppleScript 263

Why Should You Care About AppleScript? 263
Cooking Up Scripts 264
   Writing Scripts in Script Editor *265*
   Recording Scripts *267*
   Saving Scripts *267*
Putting Your Scripts to Work 268
   Using Scripts Within Applications *268*
   Dragging with Droplets *269*
   Creating Login Items *270*

24 Using Mac Technology to the Max 271

Color Management: Not Labor-Intensive 271
   Color Whatsis? *272*
   Making Color Management Work for You *273*
   Mixing Your Own *274*
Speaking in Tongues 275
Talking Back to Your Mac 276
   Speak to Me *276*
   Cutting New Orders for Your Mac *278*

25 Harnessing the Power of Unix 281

What's Unix, Anyway? 281
Using a Command-Line Interface 282
   Peeking Under the Hood *283*
   Turning Commands into Scripts *284*
   Turning a Script into a Reusable Command *285*
Using Unix Applications 287
   What Can Unix Do for Me? *287*
   How to Use Unix Apps *288*
   Where to Find Unix Software *289*

Part 7: Keeping Mac Happy   **291**

26 Good MacHousekeeping   **293**

Periodic Mac Maintenance 293
Update Your System 294
Update Other Software 295
Check for Viruses 296
Take Good Care of Classic 297
Defragment Your Hard Drive 298
When It's Time to Go 299
A Few Useful Tools 299

27 Preparing for the Worst   **303**

Backup Strategies 304
Backing Up on a LAN 305
Backing Up to the Net 307

28 Troubleshooting   **309**

Analyzing the Problem 310
What Goes There? 311
Your Mac Won't Boot 311
Unexpected Quits or Freezes 314
Erratic Behavior 315
Missing or Jumbled Files 315
Missing or Malfunctioning Peripherals 316
Other Helpful Resources 316

A Useful Web Sites   **319**

The Best Mac Sites 319
TidBITS: www.tidbits.com 319
MacInTouch: www.macintouch.com 320
MacFixit: www.macfixit.com 320
MacCentral: maccentral.macworld.com 320
Macworld: www.macworld.com 320
MacSpeedZone: www.macspeedzone.com 320
EveryMac: www.everymac.com 321
Low End Mac: www.lowendmac.com 321
MacNN: www.macnn.com 321
MacAddict: www.macaddict.com 321
Clan MacGaming: www.clanmacgaming.com/macosx.php 321
dealmac: www.dealmac.com 321
Macintosh Products Guide: guide.apple.com 322
Apple Support: www.apple.com/support/ 322

Mac Software Archives 322
  VersionTracker: www.versiontracker.com 322
  MacDownload: www.macdownload.com 322
  The Mac Orchard: www.macorchard.com 322
  MacScripter.net: www.macscripter.net 323
Learning About Unix 323
  Unix Primer: www.hearsay.demon.co.uk 323
  Resources for Newbies: www.freebsd.org/
    projects/newbies.html 323
  GNU Project: www.fsf.org 323
  Tao of Regular Expressions: sitescooper.org/
    tao_regexps.html 323
  sed FAQ: www.cornerstonemag.com/sed/sedfaq.html 324
  Coping with Unix: nacphy.physics.orst.edu/
    coping-with-unix/book.html 324
  X.org: www.x.org 324
All-Around Useful Sites 324
  Google: www.google.com 324
  AltaVista: www.altavista.com 325
  Outpost.com: www.outpost.com 325
  PDFZone: www.pdfzone.com 325
  Tao of Backup: www.taobackup.com 325
  Coalition Against Unsolicited Commercial E-Mail:
    www.cauce.com 325

Speak Like a Geek   **327**

Index   **335**

About the Author

A desktop publishing geek from New Hampshire, **Kate Binder** is the author of *Sams Teach Yourself QuarkXPress 4 in 14 Days* and *Easy Adobe Photoshop 6*. In addition to writing books and magazine articles about desktop production tools and techniques, Kate has helped produce hundreds of books, magazines, and other publications. Her ventures into the online world include acting as co-editor of PDFzone.com and Web mistress of bluesreviews.com. When not debating the relative merits of Illustrator and FreeHand or FrameMaker and QuarkXPress, she enjoys hanging out with her four retired racing greyhounds (see www.adopt-a-greyhound.org for more info) and avoiding the many chores to be done in her 100-year-old home. A partner in Prospect Hill Publishing Services, Kate makes her home on the Web at www.prospecthillpub.com.

Dedication

To Dr. Henry Vittum—"a scholar, and a ripe and good one; exceedingly wise, fair-spoken, and persuading."

Acknowledgments

As always, thanks are due to my long-suffering husband and partner Don Fluckinger, who tolerated much crankiness during the writing of this book. I'd also like to thank my friends and editors at Que Publishing for their calm guidance and support, especially Beth Millett, Laura Norman, and Heather Banner Kane, who together received the majority of my panicked phone calls.

Many, many thanks are due to Richard Binder and Paul Sihvonen-Binder: the geek corps upon whom I called while writing this book. Their patience and wisdom are much appreciated.

Also much appreciated are the efforts of Steve Jobs, the man who loves Macs most and who brought Mac OS X to fruition. Long may he live!

Introduction

From some people's perspective, I came late to the world of Macintosh. I'm not a Mac pioneer, or a Mac software developer, or even a Mac hacker.

I just love my Mac.

I love my Mac (currently a very shiny Power Mac G4/450) so much that you couldn't pay me enough to give it up. Nope, not gonna happen. And that's why I was so glad to be able to write this book. Mac OS X is another in a long line of reasons to love your Mac.

With this brand-spanking-new operating system, Apple has put a new face on the Mac—and given it new legs. Mac OS X makes your Mac stronger, faster, and easier to use, and the new system reaches out to the Internet and to other computer platforms as well. Everything you do on your Mac will go faster, do more, and work better with Mac OS X.

What's in This Book

In this book, I'll tell you what you need to know to use Mac OS X from day to day, as well as introduce you to some cool things you can do with your Mac that you might not have known about before. Here's a quick preview of what you'll find in these pages:

➤ **Part 1: Getting Started**

These four chapters get you up and running on your new system. You'll install and set up Mac OS X, learn how to get help using it, and make sure your computer is complete with all the peripheral devices you need.

➤ **Part 2: Getting Things Done**

In this part, you'll move on to getting some work done—and maybe some playing, too. You'll organize your files, learn about sharing your Mac with others, install and use new software, and explore the multimedia side of the Mac, as well as check out Mac games.

➤ **Part 3: Getting Connected**

Here you'll move on to connecting with other people and computers via local networks and the Big Kahuna Network: the Internet. These chapters talk about local networks, file sharing, printing, using the Internet, and publishing your own Web content.

➤ **Part 4: Talking to Other Platforms**

Let's face it: Not everyone is smart enough to be using a Mac. Because you have to interact with other people using other kinds of computers, this part explains how to share files and resources with users of Windows, Unix, and previous versions of the Mac OS.

➤ **Part 5: Tweaking Mac OS X**

You can have your Mac your way, today and every day. Here are a few chapters on ways to be sure your Mac acts the way you want it to—from files, folders, and the Dock to utilities that make Mac OS X look more like Mac OS 9.

➤ **Part 6: Becoming a Mac OS X Power User**

With Mac OS X, you have more ways to expand the power of your Mac than ever before. In this part, we'll look at AppleScript, a way to write Mac programs without being a programmer, move on to some other cool Mac technologies, such as color management, and finish up with a brief look at what the Unix underneath Mac OS X can do for you.

➤ **Part 7: Keeping Mac Happy**

When your Mac starts up, it smiles at you. This part explains ways to keep your Mac smiling, including performing regular maintenance, backing up your important files, dealing with any problems that arise, and getting rid of software you no longer want.

How This Book Works

You'll want to know a couple things about this book before you start reading. First of all, there are at least two ways to do almost everything you do with your Mac. You're probably more familiar with using menu commands than with keyboard shortcuts, but I'm a big fan of shortcuts, and I've sprinkled them throughout the book. For the most part, they involve holding down one of four keys (the Command, Option, Shift, or Control keys) while you press another key (usually a letter). For example, "Press Cmd+S" means to hold down the Command key while pressing the S key.

Next, I've stuck all sorts of information in boxes along the margins of these pages. Some of this information is important and some of it is just for fun. The book still makes sense if you skip the text in these boxes, but you'll get a whole lot more out of it if you read them. Examples are shown on this page.

Finally, I hope you enjoy reading this book almost as much as you enjoy using your Mac. Let me know what you think by e-mailing me at kbinder@mac.com. I might not be able to write back right away, but I'd love to hear your stories about how you use this book—and how much you love your Mac.

What Does It Mean?

Throughout the book, where I've used a technical term that you might not already know, I've added a definition in a box out in the page's margin, named *Show Info* after the new version of Mac's Get Info box. These words are *italic* in the text, and they also appear in a glossary at the end of the book.

You Might Want to Know This...

Information that you might find interesting or useful appears in boxes marked *Read Me*. You can skip these if you're in a hurry, but stopping along the way to read them will make you a more educated Mac user.

Watch Out!

If I want to tell you about a problem that you might run into or offer a caution, I've put this information into boxes labeled *OS Tension*. It's not the greatest pun you've ever heard, I'm sure, but it's probably also not the worst!

Take Off, Eh!

When I want to send you off to another part of the book or to another resource such as a Web site for more information, I've added pointers in boxes called *Go To*. When you get started using Mac OS X, you'll find that this concept is borrowed from the new system's Go menu, which allows you to jump instantly to the place you want to be.

Part 1
Getting Started

Whether you ordered the Mac OS X CD-ROM or bought yourself a new Mac with Mac OS X installed, you're about to enter a whole new Macintosh world. Mac OS X combines the traditionally friendly Mac experience with a whole new set of technologies that make it more powerful, more stable, and more versatile than any Mac system before it.

In this part, you'll see how the Mac OS X installation process works in Chapter 1. Then, in Chapter 2, you'll go on to learn what's new (and what's not) about Mac OS X and what that means to you. In Chapter 3, you'll find out how to get Mac OS X help when you get stuck, and Chapter 4 covers ways to make sure your printers, scanners, and other peripherals work with Mac OS X.

Meet the New Mac

In This Chapter

➤ What Mac OS X is and where it came from

➤ Why Mac OS X makes a difference to you

➤ Getting Mac OS X up and running

➤ Moving from Mac OS 9 to Mac OS X and back again

In 1984, when Apple Computer released the original Macintosh, it was something completely new for the computer-using public. It used little pictures instead of text commands, it had this strange thing called a mouse, and—most bizarre of all—it smiled at you when you turned it on (see Figure 1.1). Over the next few years, though, people got used to the Mac's appealing *GUI*, its ease of use, and its friendly attitude. The Mac's friendliness made it the favored computer in schools and publishing companies, and its power and flexibility brought it into laboratories and movie studios.

Today's Mac is still found in all those places—and Mac OS X is a big part of why Macs still stand out from the personal computer pack as both fun to use and ready to tackle the most demanding tasks. This chapter introduces you to Mac OS X, shows you how to get started with it, and explains why you'll want to.

Figure 1.1

*Your Mac, my Mac—
they're all happy Macs.*

Gooey GUI

GUI stands for graphical user interface. It's the term for a computer interface that uses icons instead of just text. In a GUI, you can open a file by manipulating the file's icon on the screen; in a traditional text-based interface, you must type in a command and the file's name to open it.

Operating on the System

A computer's **operating system** (sometimes called system software) is the software that enables you to communicate with the computer: to give it commands and to enter data. An operating system also governs how the computer responds to your instructions. Unix, Windows, and Mac OS X are all different operating systems.

What Is Mac OS X?

Mac OS X is the latest generation of the Macintosh *operating system*. The "X" is the Roman numeral for 10, because this is the tenth major version of the Mac's system software. This new version of the Mac OS is completely new, instead of just being a revision of the previous version—it's built on a foundation of *Unix*, an extremely powerful and stable operating system used for large mainframe computers and for powerful work-stations. Added to that powerful foundation is a completely new user interface, which is what you see when you start Mac OS X.

If you've bought a new Mac since this book was published, it almost certainly came with Mac OS X installed. If you're using Mac OS 9, the previous version, you might be able to upgrade to Mac OS X, depending on which Mac model you have. Because you're reading this book, I'll assume that's what you're going to do. The following sections explain what Mac OS X does, where it came from, and why you should or shouldn't be using it.

Caveat Mactor

Apple has designed Mac OS X to run only on its newer Mac models. Here are the Macs on which you can install Mac OS X: Power Mac G3s (beige and blue models), Power Mac G4s, iMacs, iBooks, some PowerBook G3s, and PowerBook G4s (as well as any Mac models released after July 2001). If you have another Mac (such as a Power Mac 8500, 9500, or 9600), you might be able to get Mac OS X up and running, but that's not recommended by Apple, and you won't be able to get technical support from the company. The same is true if you have an older Mac that contains a G3 or G4 processor upgrade card.

Multifaceted, Multitasking

When Apple designed Mac OS X, the company was trying to create an operating system that would be easy for new users to learn, would look enough like previous systems that it wouldn't scare off longtime Mac users, and would be built from the ground up to be more stable, faster, and more flexible. We'll take a look at Mac OS X's interface in Chapter 2, "Making Friends with Mac OS X"; here, let's investigate what makes Mac OS X such a powerhouse.

To start with, Mac OS X is designed to be more stable than other operating systems. It has *protected memory*, which means that the part of the system that's devoted to running each program you're working with at any given time is walled off from the rest of the system. So, if one of your programs crashes, it won't take the whole system down with it. Mac OS X's memory setup also frees you from having to decide how much *RAM* to allocate to each program before you run it—the operating system allocates memory to each program as required, hands out more when necessary, and takes back memory that isn't being used.

Speed is another advantage of this new OS. By using *preemptive multitasking*, Mac OS X enables programs to work more efficiently simultaneously.

RAM for Remembrance

RAM (random access memory) is a computer's equivalent of your conscious mind—the part you use to hold the information you're thinking about at any given time. When your Mac is running, the operating system, any active programs, and the contents of any open documents are all being stored in RAM. That's why you need more RAM if you want to run more programs or open more documents at the same time.

While your Web browser is downloading a file, you can still print, copy files to a removable disk, and resort your address database—all at the same time. All your applications will feel more responsive as you work, and you'll spend less time waiting for your computer to catch up with you.

Similarly to multitasking, *multithreading* enables one program to do more than one thing at a time. So, you can save one file, search another, and print a third without having to wait for each process to end before going on to the next. Meanwhile, Mac OS X is built to use *symmetric multiprocessing*, or the use of more than one processor chip in one computer at the same time. The new OS can hand one program to the first processor and another program to the second processor in one of today's multiprocessor Macs. This way, your Mac's processing power—and its speed—gets a huge bump.

Best of all, if you happen to be a Unix geek, is that behind Mac OS X's pretty interface is a system that runs on Unix, the same system that runs the world's largest and fastest computers. If you choose, you can bring up a *command-line interface (CLI)* and delve into the depths of the Unix underneath. Although that might not sound very exciting at first, any geek will tell you that the CLI enables you to customize your computer to the nth degree, as well as use tons of software (much of it free) that won't run on older Macs—or on Windows. Check out Chapter 25, "Harnessing the Power of Unix," for a quick introduction to what Unix is and what you can do with it.

Jargon Alert

Whew! When you're talking about the guts of an operating system, there's a lot of jargon to get through. Let's start with ***protected memory***. This means that the system software sets up an area in its memory for each program you start up. Although the OS can resize that area of memory to give you more memory if you need it, no other program is affected by what goes on inside the partition. So, if that program crashes, it doesn't affect the rest of what's in memory at the time—any other programs and, best of all, the system software itself. Everything just goes right on working. Meanwhile, ***preemptive multitasking*** enables the system to allocate processing power for each task as it comes up, alternating jobs so quickly that it seems as though everything's happening at once. ***Symmetric multiprocessing*** allows the system to use two processors (the brains of your Mac) at the same time to accomplish work faster.

Finally, a ***command-line interface*** is what you see when you turn on a DOS or Unix computer: no icons and no mouse, just a blinking cursor where you type in commands for the computer. A CLI forces you to get things just right—no typos allowed—but it also enables you to use shortcuts and scripts to get things done quickly, such as enabling you to write the name of an object more quickly than you can draw a picture of it.

Roots: The Mac OS X Family Tree

For genealogy buffs and real Mac-heads, here's a quick rundown on how Mac OS X came to exist. Although this info might seem obscure if you just want to jump in and get started using Mac OS X, there are two points you should consider. First, knowing where Mac OS X came from can help you understand why it works the way it does. And second, you are free to skip right on down to the next section!

Okay, now that everyone who's not interested has moved on, I can tell the story. Listen up, gang.

It all started in 1984, when Apple released the first Macintosh. Although that small, smiling computer seems woefully underpowered to us today, for its time it was something special. And over the next few years, Apple kept introducing new features in both its hardware and its Mac system software that made Macs easier to use than any other computer. For years, Macs have had built-in printing and networking capabilities. They've been able to read disks formatted for DOS and Windows computers. And they've always been extremely backward-compatible, meaning that newer machines could coexist with older ones—they could run the same programs and use the same peripheral devices.

Eventually, though, that very backward compatibility became an anchor holding the Mac system software back. Because Apple was committed to supporting all kinds of older hardware and software, many new technologies just couldn't be incorporated into new versions of the Mac system software. Finally, Apple decided that for its computers to move forward, some radical changes had to be made.

Meanwhile, Apple cofounder Steve Jobs was off starting up NeXT, a company that designed and sold another computer with a proprietary operating system. Although NeXTSTEP, the Unix-based operating system for Jobs' spiffy-looking black computers, was technically quite advanced, NeXT's sales were never very good.

After Apple, spent time floundering financially in the mid-1990s, Jobs ended up back at the company in 1996, pledging to bring Apple back to profitability. One of his first moves was to merge NeXT into Apple and announce that the NeXTSTEP operating system would form the basis for a new operating system for the Mac. Although the new system would leave some older Macs behind, its advantages would outweigh that one disadvantage—Apple hoped.

What with, the, typical delays and a long, careful development cycle, it's been several additional years before this long-heralded operating system has seen the light of day. But it's here now, and it's everything Jobs hoped it would be—so let's get into it!

Why You Need Mac OS X

The reasons you'll benefit from running Mac OS X on your Mac fall into two categories: practical and frivolous.

The practical reasons are fairly apparent. If you want to keep up with current technology, you need to install the current operating system for your computer. Using Mac OS X enables you to use the most recent application software, it ensures compatibility with upcoming hardware, and it allows you to continue exchanging files with other Mac users who have upgraded. In the meantime, you'll still be able to run Mac OS 9 in the Classic environment (see Chapter 2, "Making Friends with Mac OS X," for more info), so you can stay compatible with users of older Macs who can't upgrade to Mac OS X.

As well as compatibility, Mac OS X helps make you more productive. As you learned earlier in this chapter, Mac OS X is designed to be more stable, easier to use, and extremely customizable. All this has the potential to save you a lot of time as you work on your Mac.

And if it's frivolity you're looking for, welcome to the fun side of Mac OS X. As well as powerful, Apple wanted its new operating system to be attractive, and it is. It has huge, scalable file icons, stunning motion effects, and "lickable" candylike buttons. It feels bright, shiny, and new, and that counts for something—doesn't it?

Now, before this starts to sound like an ad for Apple, you need to be aware that using a first-generation operating system like Mac OS X has its downside, too. For starters, the earlier you get in on the Mac OS X game, the more likely it is that your favorite Mac programs haven't yet been released in Mac OS X–compatible versions. Although you should be able to run just about any Mac program in Mac OS 9 using Classic, it's possible that some programs won't work under these circumstances. And you should also know that some hardware might not work right away with Mac OS X. These problems will be solved over time, but as with any new software, it's virtually certain that not everything will work right the first time you try it.

Go To

A Bridge over Troubled Macs

Troubleshooting is still, unfortunately, a fact of life for computer users. For information on figuring out any problems you might run into with Mac OS X, see Chapter 28, "Troubleshooting."

Installing Mac OS X

If you bought a Mac with Mac OS X installed, you're all set—you can skip this section. If you're installing Mac OS X on an older Mac, the following sections will tell you how to set up your Mac beforehand, how the installation works, and how to use Mac OS X side by side with Mac OS 9.

The process of installing Mac OS X is both strange and familiar. It's familiar because the installer looks pretty much like any other Mac installer, but it's strange because it actually runs in Mac OS X. The Mac OS X CD contains a Mac OS X system, and you must reboot from the CD before the installer will run. So, running the installer itself provides your first taste of the new OS.

The Countdown's On: Preparing Your Computer

Here are a few things you'll need to take care of before you run the Mac OS X installer:

➤ Your Mac should have at least 128MB of RAM. You can install and run Mac OS X with less memory, but it will be slow and you might not be happy. Trust me.

➤ Be sure you have at least 1.5GB of available space on your hard drive.

➤ Because Mac OS X doesn't support some third-party video cards, you should be sure your monitor is connected to the internal video port on the back of your Mac (check the manual that came with your Mac if you're not sure which port this is). Or, if your Mac includes an Apple-supplied video card from IXMicro, ATI, or NVidia, you can use that video connection.

➤ Your Mac must have the most recent *firmware* update. Use the Software Update control panel to see whether there's a firmware update available for your Mac.

➤ If you plan on running Mac OS 9 in the Classic environment, Mac OS 9 will need to be installed on your drive already, or on a SCSI external drive that you can use with this Mac. You can't install Mac OS X on a FireWire or USB drive.

➤ You'll also need to be sure that the drive you want to install Mac OS X on is formatted using the Extended format (HFS Plus). To make sure your drive is formatted in this way, click its icon on the Desktop and press **Cmd+I** or choose **File, Get Info**. In the Info box, look for Mac OS Extended next to Format—that's what you need. If you see Mac OS Standard instead, you'll need to reformat your hard drive before you can proceed. You can do this as part of the installation process; just be sure you back up all your files first, because reformatting your hard drive erases all the files it contains.

➤ If your Mac is a G3 PowerBook without USB, a beige Power Mac G3, or a Rev.A, Rev.B, Rev.C, or Rev.D iMac, and the hard disk is larger than 8GB and has more than one partition, you must install Mac OS X on a partition that is within the first 8GB on the disk.

➤ Finally, be sure your current version of Mac OS 9 is the most recent (that's 9.1 as I write this).

Show Info

Hardware, Software, Jelloware?

Although most of us think of computers as having pretty obvious lines between hardware (the equipment) and software (the programs), they also have software embedded in their hardware. Because it falls between software and hardware, it's called *firmware*, and it's what enables the computer to start up to the point where the software installed on a hard drive can take

Update Now

Mac OS 9's Software Update control panel can make sure your Mac and its system software are completely up to date before installing Mac OS X (or any time). Choose **Control Panels, Software Update** from the Apple menu, click **Update Now**, and check the box next to each update that the control panel finds. You might need to allow one or two items to download and install, and then restart. When your Mac is finished rebooting, go back to the Software Update control panel, click **Update Now** again, and repeat the process until you see a dialog box that says, "Your software doesn't need updating." Now you're totally current.

Depending on the computer you're using, you might run into other issues with installing Mac OS X. When you pop in the CD, you'll see a file called READ BEFORE YOU INSTALL.pdf; double-click this document to see any late-breaking news about installing the version of Mac OS X that you've purchased.

Running the Installer

Okay, you're ready to go. Insert the Mac OS X CD-ROM, double-click the installer icon, and follow instructions from there. The installer will reboot your computer into Mac OS X from the CD-ROM and then start up a second installer program that will actually perform the installation. All you need to do is follow the prompts; here's what you'll be doing, step by step, in each screen of the installer:

Reformat with Caution

Reformat your drive only if you're installing Mac OS X on a secondary hard drive or on a new computer—reformatting a disk erases all the files it contains, so you must be sure you're not erasing your important data.

1. If you feel the need, prepare your hard drive for installation by using First Aid (to detect and repair any formatting problems) or Drive Setup (to reformat the disk).

2. Choose a language for both the installer and the installed software to use.

3. Read a Read Me file that lets you know about any vital issues you might encounter while installing and using Mac OS X.

4. Agree to Apple's legal license agreement for Mac OS X.

5. Choose a hard drive on which to install the system (see Figure 1.2). At this point, the installer can erase and reformat the drive before installing Mac OS X if you choose.

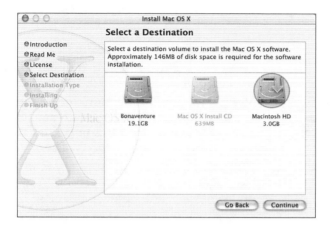

Figure 1.2

The Mac OS X installer doesn't ask you to make many decisions, but you do need to let it know on which hard drive you'd like the new system installed. On my Mac, the internal drive is called Bonaventure and the external one is called Macintosh HD.

6. Decide whether to perform a basic installation or a custom installation. (Most of the time, you'll need all the components available in a custom installation, so you should just do a basic installation.)

7. Wait while the installation proceeds. When the installation's done, your Mac restarts automatically so that you can set up Mac OS X.

Problems using the installer can take one of two forms:

➤ The installer tells you it won't install Mac OS X (for example, if your hard drive is too small) and you can just quit it.

➤ The installer crashes your computer (this is much less likely).

If, for whatever reason, your computer does crash and won't reboot correctly, you can boot the Mac from the CD that came with it. Insert the CD and hold down the C key on your keyboard as the computer restarts; this ensures that the computer will reboot from the System Folder on the CD. When your Mac is back up, running from the CD, you can use the troubleshooting tools on the CD to fix any problems resulting from the failed installation.

Try, Try Again

If you had trouble installing Mac OS X, here are a few things to remember when you're ready to try again. First, review the requirements for installing Mac OS X, and then be sure your Mac's hardware is working correctly, and disconnect any third-party peripherals (such as scanners and external drives) to make sure they're not interfering with the installation.

15

Setting Up Mac OS X

When the Mac OS X installer is finished putting Mac OS X on your hard drive, it restarts your Mac. This first restart includes some extra steps to set up Mac OS X that you won't see during subsequent restarts. Here's what will happen in each successive screen:

Using User Accounts

For more information on Mac OS X's multiple user features, including how and why to set up more than one user account, turn to Chapter 6, "Sharing Your Mac with Multiple Users."

1. Choose the country you live in.
2. Choose the keyboard layout you want to use for your language.
3. Enter registration information, including your name and address. If you're concerned about what Apple will do with this info, click Privacy to read the company's privacy policy.
4. Answer two questions about how you use your Mac and choose whether to receive promotional info from Apple and other companies.
5. Create a user account that Mac OS X can use to identify you when you start using it. You'll enter your name, a short version of your name, a password, and a password hint (in case you forget your password).
6. Choose whether to use your current Internet connection. If you don't have an Internet account, you'll skip the Internet setup screens that follow.
7. If you want to use your current Internet account, specify how you connect to the Internet (with a phone modem, through a network, with a cable modem or DSL line, or using AirPort).
8. Enter the settings for your Internet account.
9. Create an iTools account or, if you already have one, enter your member name and password.
10. Select your time zone.
11. Click **Go** to get started using your Mac.

Now the Mac OS X Desktop appears. The Software Update utility runs right away to update your software, if needed. You'll see its icon pulsing in the Dock; click it to see the results of its check. If it suggests downloading and installing an update, click Install to proceed. You might need to restart your Mac when the update is installed; if so, Software Update will let you know.

Starting Up Mac OS X

After Mac OS X is installed and set up, your Mac starts up pretty much as it always has. The first thing you see on subsequent restarts is that legendary "Happy Mac" smiling at you.

Then, a "Welcome to Mac OS" screen appears. Although you won't see a series of icons appearing below the Welcome box, as you would in Mac OS 9, you will see a progress bar as the system loads. In Mac OS X, the progress bar has handy notes below it about what part of the system is loading at any given moment.

When the system is finished loading, the screen changes to show a Desktop picture, the new Mac OS X menu bar, and the Dock (see Figure 1.3). As the system finishes loading and any startup applications get going, you'll see their icons bounce up and down in the Dock. While all this is happening, the mouse cursor is a spinning rainbow-colored disk; when the startup process is finished, the cursor changes to the familiar black arrow.

Figure 1.3

Here's what you'll see when you start Mac OS X.

Shutting Down Mac OS X

Shutting down or restarting your Mac works the same way under Mac OS X as it always has. To shut down, choose **Apple menu**, **Shut Down**. Each application will quit, and if you have any open, unsaved documents, you'll be asked whether you want to save changes. After everything has quit, the system turns off the Mac.

If you just want to restart, choose **Apple menu**, **Restart**.

Bipolar Shift: Switching Between Mac OS X and Mac OS 9

Mac OS X is a truly cool operating system, but it's a fact that any new OS can have some problems and might not yet run all the software you want to use. If you're not ready to plunge into Mac OS X full time, you can set up your computer as a *dual-boot* system.

Two Feet, Two Boots

A ***dual-boot*** system can boot, or start up, from either of two complete sets of system software installed on its drives. In this case, a dual-boot system is one that can boot from either Mac OS X or Mac OS 9.

There are two ways to do this:

➤ If you installed Mac OS X on the same drive as an existing Mac OS 9 system, use Mac OS X's Startup Disk preference pane to designate the Mac OS 9 System Folder as the system from which you want to boot. The next time you reboot, you're right back in Mac OS 9.

➤ If you prefer not to mix the two systems, you can install Mac OS X on a separate hard drive from Mac OS 9. This ensures that your Mac OS 9 files aren't affected at all by the Mac OS X installation, and your Mac OS X files aren't affected by anything you might do while you're running Mac OS 9.

Which way to go? That depends on how much insurance you want. If you're the kind of person who worries a lot, install the two systems on separate hard drives. That way, if one develops problems, you'll still be able to run the other.

On the other hand, Mac OS X doesn't make any changes to your Mac OS 9 system other than to drop in a couple of invisible files that don't do anything whatsoever when you're running your Mac OS 9 system. So, it's usually safe to install Mac OS X on top of Mac OS 9.

The Latest and Greatest

To run in Classic, your Mac OS 9 system folder must be version 9.1 or later; earlier versions of Mac OS 9 won't work with Classic. However, if you have an earlier version of Mac OS 9 on a separate hard drive, you can restart your Mac using that system. After doing this, you'll need to use the special version of the Startup Disk control panel on the Mac OS X installation CD to reboot into Mac OS X.

Either way, you can use your current Mac OS 9 system within Classic, meaning that you can run Mac OS 9 within Mac OS X. You should be aware, though, that some of the software add-ons your system might have (such as fax software) won't work in Classic, and others may crash Classic. Usually, these are system components that talk directly to hardware, such as drivers for modems or scanners.

For the best of both worlds, the safest possible way to set up a dual-boot system is to install a clean Mac OS 9 system on a second hard drive and then install Mac OS X on that same drive. This gives you a trouble-free version of Mac OS 9 that you can use with Classic, as well as the ability to reboot using your old Mac OS 9 system any time you want.

Regardless of which way you set up your dual-boot system, the way you switch from one operating system to the other is the same.

In Mac OS 9, you'll need to use the Startup Disk control panel to switch systems. Choose **Apple menu**, **Control Panels**, **Startup Disk** to open the control panel. When you open it, the control panel scans your system for any working system software and displays an icon for each system it finds (see Figure 1.4). Click the one you want to use, close the control panel, and choose **Special**, **Restart**. In Figure 1.4, the icon that says Mac OS X 10.0 represents the Mac OS X system that will load when the Mac is restarted; it's located on a hard drive named Polycarp.

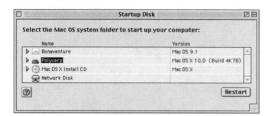

Figure 1.4

Here's where you let Mac OS 9 know that you'd like to reboot using Mac OS X.

Startup System Switchback

Versions of Mac OS 9 before 9.1 had a Startup Disk control panel that couldn't always recognize the Mac OS X system. If you're currently using one of these versions and you want to boot from your Mac OS X system, you'll need to use the Startup Disk utility in the Utilities folder on your Mac OS X installation CD-ROM. It works similarly to the Startup Disk control panel.

After you're in Mac OS X, the procedure for switching back to Mac OS 9 is similar, except that you might need to know the user name and password for your Mac's Administrator. This is the first user account created in Mac OS X's setup routine, which appears the first time you boot in Mac OS X. If you're the only person using your Mac, you can just enter your own user name and password; if your Mac is administered by someone else who has locked this setting, you'll need to have that person authorize this change. You'll need to worry about this only if the startup disk setting has been locked.

Learning to Share Your Mac

To learn about how Mac OS X works with multiple users, see Chapter 6, "Sharing Your Mac with Multiple Users."

First, click anywhere on the Desktop and choose **Apple menu**, **System Preferences**, and then click the Startup Disk icon. This pane of the System Preferences dialog box works just like the System Disk control panel (see Figure 1.5). If the lock button at the bottom of the dialog box shows a locked padlock, click it, enter an Admin user name and password, and click **OK**. Then, click the icon for the one you want to reboot from (in Figure 1.5, it's the one called Bonaventure). Now you can close the dialog box and choose **Apple menu**, **Restart**.

Figure 1.5

The System Preferences dialog box might require you to enter a user name and password before you can switch systems.

She Sells Switched Systems by the Seashore

Here's a tip that might come in handy if your computer is completely shut down and you want to start it with Mac OS 9, but you shut down without switching systems in Mac OS X's System Preferences. (Whew! Got that?) Press the Option key right after you press the power key to turn on your Mac, and keep holding it down. After a few seconds, you'll see a screen that shows an icon for each bootable system—much like the System Disk control panel or the Startup Disk preferences pane. Click the icon for the system you want to use, and then click the right-arrow button. Unfortunately, if you shut down in Mac OS 9, this trick won't display the system for Mac OS X; it works only going from Mac OS X to Mac OS 9.

The Least You Need to Know

➤ Mac OS X is technically advanced over previous versions of the Mac system software. It's completely modern, rebuilt from the ground up to be more stable, more efficient, easier to use, and more attractive than any other Mac OS. And if you have a new Mac, or one bought in the last couple of years, you can install Mac OS X and try it out for yourself.

➤ Installing Mac OS X is a simple procedure that's directed by the installer on the Welcome to Mac OS CD. In fact, it looks pretty much like the installer that came with the last several versions of the Mac OS.

➤ You have two choices when you install Mac OS X: whether to install it all by itself or on the same drive as a version of Mac OS 9. If you retain your Mac OS 9 system, you can run it in the Classic environment within Mac OS X, or you can reboot with the Mac OS 9 system.

➤ After you've installed Mac OS X—or if your Mac came with it already installed—you're ready to move on.

Chapter 2

Making Friends with Mac OS X

In This Chapter

➤ Interacting with your Mac through Mac OS X's interface

➤ What's new and different in Mac OS X

➤ The three different kinds of Mac OS X applications

Although Mac OS X is designed to be easy to use, it's still a completely new operating system. Both experienced Mac users and those new to the Mac will have a few things to learn before jumping into the deep end of the Mac OS X pool. This chapter explains how Mac OS X is both the same as and different from its predecessors.

Face to (Inter)face with Mac OS X

It's easy for computer users to forget that computers are still new to many people. For those who haven't spent the last few years with their heads buried in their computers, this section explains how the basic elements of the Mac OS X interface work. Most of these mechanisms are the same on other Mac systems and even Windows, so, if you're used to using one of these you can skip right down to the next section.

Watching Windows

There are several kinds of windows that you'll encounter as you use Mac OS X, but most often what you'll see are Finder windows and document windows.

To keep the files on your Mac organized, they're stashed in various folders. The operating system and other programs create folders that they require, and you can create folders in which to store your own files. Regardless of what's in a folder or how it was created, though, folders and their contents are displayed in Finder windows (see Figure 2.1). Within each window are icons that represent files and other folders.

Figure 2.1

File folder icons represent folders that can contain files and other folders.

To open a folder or a file, double-click it. When you open a file, assuming it's a file that you're able to edit, the appropriate program starts up and opens the file in its own window. When you open a folder, on the other hand, its contents are displayed in another Finder window. You can move either kind of window around on your screen by clicking and dragging the title bar at the top.

For more about how the Finder works, see "The Finder" later in this chapter.

Ordering from the Menus

You tell your Mac what you want it to do by giving it commands, and those commands are located in menus that drop down from the menu bar at the top of the screen when you click each menu's name.

Any time you see a menu, it's a way for you to choose from different options. The menu choices that are light gray aren't available to you in the current situation. You can choose only the commands that are black. To choose a command, hold down the mouse button as you slide the arrow cursor down the menu. Each command is highlighted in a band of color as the cursor passes over it; when you get to the command you want, release the mouse button. Some menu commands have arrows that indicate submenus that open up to the right or left. To use a submenu command, slide the cursor to the side where the submenu extends and release the mouse button when the command you want is highlighted.

Show Info

Menus Popping Up All Over

Pop-up menus get their name from the fact that they can pop up from almost any location rather than descend from the menu bar at the top of the screen.

Menus can show up in other places, too. For example, each Finder window contains a hidden *pop-up menu* that shows the pathname (folders within folders, all the way back to the hard drive) of the folder that contains the items you're looking at. Hold down the Command key and click the folder's name at the top of the window to see this menu.

Keyboard Shortcuts: In the Fast Lane

Next to many of the commands in Mac OS X's menus are letters and symbols indicating the keyboard shortcuts for those commands. If you're good with a keyboard, it's almost always faster to use a keyboard combination to execute a command than to mouse your way up to a menu. By putting keyboard shortcuts in menus, Apple and other software developers make it easier for you to learn them—any time you want to know what the keyboard shortcut is for a command, just look at that command in the menu.

Most keyboard shortcuts consist of a combination of keys; for example, to open a new Finder window on the Desktop, hold down the Command key (which has a little cloverleaf symbol) and press the N key at the same time. When you release the N key, the new window appears. Keyboard shortcuts can also use the Control key, the Option key, the Shift key, or any combination of these four *modifier keys*. Except for the Command key, the modifier keys are labeled with their names on your keyboard, but the keyboard commands in the menus use symbols to save space. In this book, keyboard shortcuts are written like this: Ctrl+Cmd+Option+Shift+O means to hold down the Control, Command, Option, and Shift keys while typing O.

Keyboard shortcuts are also available for some functions that aren't strictly commands. For example, if you're typing an e-mail in Mail, you can select the word to the left of the text cursor by holding down Shift and Option and pressing the left arrow key. After the word is selected, you can delete it by pressing Delete or replace it by just typing something else over it.

Show Info

Making a Few Slight Modifications

A keyboard shortcut usually uses a letter key that has some relation to the name or function of the command. To open a file, you press Cmd+O—O for Open. Because some programs have more than one command that uses the same letter, you can modify the shortcuts with different combinations of modifier keys.

Just Your Type: Dialog Boxes

Whereas menu commands tell your Mac what to do, dialog boxes tell it how and where to do it. They enable you to have a dialog with the computer: It asks you for details about what you want to do, and you provide the information it needs. In Mac OS X, a dialog box that applies to an individual document is attached to that window's title bar to ensure you know which document you're dealing with.

Read Me

To Dialog or Not to Dialog

You can always spot menu commands that require you to make dialog box choices—they're followed by an ellipsis (such as Open...).

Open and Save are probably the most common dialog boxes. They allow you to open documents and save them, respectively. In each case, you'll use most of the space in the dialog box to tell the computer where to get the file (if you're opening it) or where to put it (if you're saving it). Depending on the program you're using, you might be able to choose other options as well.

Dialog boxes can contain a variety of controls (see Figure 2.2).

Figure 2.2

This dialog box contains several different ways for you to make choices.

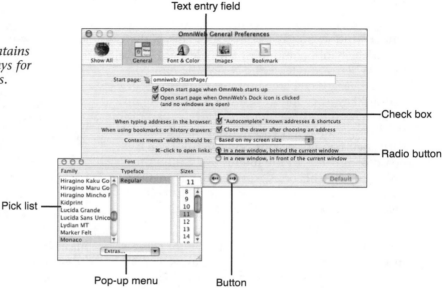

➤ **Pop-up menus**—These work just like the menus in the menu bar.

➤ **Buttons**—Press these by clicking them. If one button is glowing blue (often the OK button), pressing Return (above the Shift key) or Enter (on the numeric keypad, if your keyboard has one) is the same as clicking it.

➤ **Check boxes**—Check off each choice; you can usually check more than one box.

➤ **Radio buttons**—Click next to your choice; you can usually click only one radio button per option.

➤ **Text entry fields**—Enter the information requested (such as the name you want to assign a file you're saving).

➤ **Pick lists**—Choose the file, folder, or other option from the list. Often, double-clicking your choice selects it and simultaneously takes you out of the dialog box and back to what you were doing before.

➤ **Tab**—Different groups of settings in some dialog boxes are placed on different tabs, similar to the tabs at the top of file folders. Click a tab's name to see which settings it contains.

Contextual Menus—À la Carte

Watch out—there's yet another kind of menu (see Figure 2.3). To see a contextual menu, hold down the Ctrl key and click the Desktop (or right-click if your mouse has more than one button). Now click a file or folder icon, and then Ctrl-click or right-click it. See how the menus that pop up are different? That's because their context was different. Contextual menus change depending on what you're doing when you invoke them. Contextual menu commands also appear elsewhere—in the menu bar, usually—but it's generally quicker to use the contextual menu.

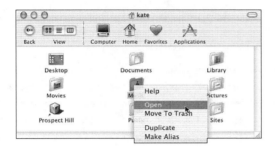

Figure 2.3

Clicking this folder produces a contextual menu that includes commands relating to folders.

Now that you've discovered contextual menus, feel free to spend some time Ctrl- or right-clicking on everything in sight. Clicking on an item in a program window gives you commands specific to that program; there's a different set of useful contextual menus for each program.

What's New in Mac OS X

Now that the novices have their fill of Mac information for the moment, this section is for long-time Mac users who want to know exactly how much their world is about to be rocked. Just about everything in Mac OS X is new, which means there's a lot to get used to if you're familiar with earlier Mac systems.

Looks Like Aqua

The way Mac OS X actually *looks* is called Aqua because it has so many transparent, shiny, and droplet-shaped elements, bringing to mind water. Although it's supposed to make Mac OS X easier for you to use than other operating systems, it's also supposed to make the new system easier on the eyes.

Quartz Movement

Quartz is the basis for most of the new visual effects you'll see as you work on a Mac OS X–equipped Mac. It uses Adobe's PDF image format to create all the images displayed on the screen—including dialog boxes, icons, and windows. This means that objects can be transparent or translucent, they can be animated, and they can have sophisticated effects such as the soft drop shadows you'll see under every window on the Desktop.

Quartz also allows you to save any printable document as a PDF file (regardless of whether you have a printer). PDF files can be read on any computer that has Adobe's free Acrobat Reader installed, and the files will display and print the same as they did on your computer.

A Handy Freebie

Acrobat Reader is just about the handiest piece of software you'll ever run across. If you don't already have it, you can download a free copy at **www.adobe.com/products/acrobat/readstep2.html**. With Reader, you can open, view, and print any PDF file and it will look just like the original. The reproduction is so good, in fact, that if you find you're missing any vital forms at tax time, you can download them from the IRS's Web site—in PDF format—and print as many copies as you want.

Sittin' on the Dock of the Mac

It only makes sense that if you're swimming around in Aqua, you'll want to keep stuff on the Dock. In the case of Mac OS X, the Dock sits at the bottom of your screen and holds icons for frequently used programs, all programs that are currently running, and files or folders that you want to be able to get to quickly (see Figure 2.4). The other thing you'll find in the Dock is *minimized* windows.

Figure 2.4

One way to use the Dock efficiently is to decrease the size of its icons (so that more will fit) and turn on its Magnification feature to enlarge icons as you move the mouse cursor over them.

As you drag your mouse across the Dock, each item's name pops up. To open any program, file, or folder, just click its icon. A black triangle below an icon indicates a program that's already running, and clicking that icon brings the program to the front. Clicking the icon for a minimized window unfurls it to its full size.

Minimized Windows, Minimal Hassle

Suppose you're surfing the Web and your phone rings. It's your mom, and she wants to know your favorite dry cleaner's phone number. So, you minimize the Web page you're looking at by either double-clicking the window's title bar or clicking the yellow button next to the title, and the window is sucked down into the Dock as you watch. Now you can go find that number in the Address Book, and when you're ready to return to the Web page, you can just click its icon in the Dock to bring it back to life.

The Dock comes loaded with the icons Apple thinks you'll find useful, but you can add and remove stuff to make the Dock more efficient for you. To get rid of icons on the dock, just click and drag them off the Dock (and then watch them go poof). To add icons to the Dock, drag any file or folder over the Dock and along it to the point where you'd like the icon to sit.

Doctoring the Dock

Everyone works differently, so it's only reasonable that you can customize the Dock to act in the way that makes sense for you. Chapter 20, "The Desktop and the Dock As You Like Them," explains ways you can change the Dock's appearance and behavior.

The Finder

The changes that are most likely to trip up longtime Mac users are in the Finder (see Figure 2.5). In Mac OS X, as in previous versions of the Mac OS, you use the Finder to access the files stored on your computer. Unlike earlier Mac systems, the new Finder enables you to navigate throughout your hard drive in a single window. A toolbar at the top of each window contains buttons that take you to frequently used folders on your Mac. Other elements in each window include

➤ A title bar that displays the name of the folder; click and drag the title bar to move the window around.

➤ A hidden pop-up menu that can take you to any level between the folder you're looking at and the top level of your computer. In other words, the first entry on the menu is the name of the current folder, and that's followed by the folder in which the current folder resides, and so on up to the level of the computer itself. To see this menu, Cmd+click the name of the folder in the title bar.

Figure 2.5

Here's a closer look at Mac OS X's new Finder windows.

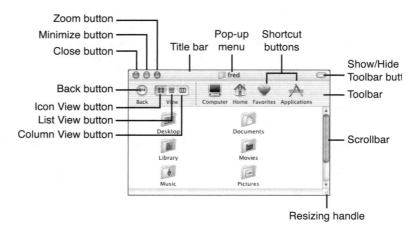

➤ Three colored buttons at the top left: a red one to close the window, a green one to enlarge it to show all its contents, and a yellow one to minimize it and move it into the Dock.

➤ A clear button that shows or hides the folder's toolbar and switches the Finder from single-window mode to the multiwindow mode and back again. If you want a new window to open each time you double-click a folder, click the clear button to hide the toolbar.

➤ In the toolbar, a back-arrow button that takes you to the folder window that preceded the one you're looking at.

➤ Buttons for the three different views: icons, a text list, and a column view that shows multiple levels of folders between the folder you're looking at and the top level of your computer.

➤ Scrollbars that allow you to view all the folder's contents.

➤ A resizing handle at the lower-right corner of the window—click and drag to resize the window.

To open a Finder window, click on the Desktop and choose **File**, **New Finder Window** or press **Cmd+N**. If you can't see the Desktop at the moment, you can both get there and open a Finder window by clicking the Desktop icon at the left end of the Dock. Then, to get to the folder you're looking for, you can use one of these methods:

➤ Double-click to open a folder that contains what you need.

➤ Use the pop-up menu at the top of the window to move up to a higher level in your computer's organization, and then double-click to open the folder you're looking for.

➤ Click on one of the toolbar buttons to go straight to frequently used folders. If you don't see the toolbar, choose **View, Show Toolbar** or click the clear button in the window's top-right corner.

➤ Choose an an option from the **Go** menu: **Go to Folder** to search for the folder by typing its name, **Recent Folders** to access folders you've been using in the last little while, **Connect to Server** to communicate with another computer on your network, or a list of commonly used folders, such as **Home** and **Applications**.

What's Where and Why

Now that you've seen how folders and the Finder work in Mac OS X, you're probably starting to wonder about the folders that are already in place. What are they for, and where can you put your stuff? Chapter 5, "Managing Your Files," explains the structure of the Mac OS X hard drive, including where you're supposed to stash your own files.

Mac OS X's single-window interface is designed to eliminate the mess your Desktop turns into when you open multiple folders in quick succession. When you want to copy or move items from one folder to another, using multiple windows can make your task easier. So, if you're in single-window mode, just choose **File, New Finder Window** or press **Cmd+N** to pop up another window.

Changing How Mac Does Windows

When Apple first started talking about what Mac OS X would be like, many users were upset at the idea of being stuck in single-window mode all the time. It's just not the way Mac users are used to doing things. In response, Apple made it an option that can be turned off and on. For more on this and other Finder options, see Chapter 20, "The Desktop and the Dock As You Like Them."

How It All Works (Candy-Coated Unix)

For all its beauty, Aqua is just the surface of a very powerful system. That's the case with Windows and with previous Mac systems, too, but the difference with Mac OS X is that now you can dig under the surface. What you'll find there is *Unix*. Here are some of the reasons why that is a good thing:

➤ Unix is more stable than other operating systems because its core functions are more clearly separated from the programs you're running. In Unix, you can crash a program, but you generally can't crash the whole computer.

You Need Unix

Originally written in 1969 at Bell Labs, Unix is used all over the world to run both large and small computer systems. It has been modified and mutated by many people, resulting in an operating system that's adaptable to almost any purpose. Many Unix variants and many Unix programs are open source, meaning that they're free to anyone who wants to use, modify, and redistribute them.

➤ There's a huge range of free software already written for Unix that you can run—assuming you have a little know-how—on your Mac OS X–equipped Mac.

➤ Unix, in its myriad variations, has a long history and a large user base, which means that many potential problems have been thought of and dealt with long before you'll have to worry about them.

The Geek End of the Pool

If you are already familiar with Unix, all you need to know to get started using it in Mac OS X is that the Terminal application is located in the Utilities folder within the Applications folder. If you haven't used Unix before, turn to Chapter 25, "Harnessing the Power of Unix," for a primer on how Unix works and what you can do with it—as well as what you shouldn't do with it.

Application Madness: Classic, Carbon, and Cocoa

All this is very nice, but when do we get to do something with our newly Mac OS X–equipped Mac? Real soon now, I promise. Applications are the programs we use to actually accomplish stuff, and Mac OS X divides them into three kinds. For the most part, you won't need to worry much about which category a particular program falls under, but there are a couple of differences in how things work in each category.

Classic: Old School

By now, it should be apparent that Mac OS X is very different from earlier versions of the Mac system. It's so different, in fact, that many programs that run in Mac OS 9 won't run in Mac OS X. But that doesn't mean you can't use them. To accommodate these programs, Mac OS X comes with an environment (actually a program) called Classic that starts up a little Mac OS 9 bubble within your Mac OS X system (see Figure 2.6). Within this environment, Mac OS 9 applications can run quite happily, without your having to restart your computer using the Mac OS 9 system. The best part is that after Classic has started up, you can start up and work with Mac OS 9 programs, just the same way you do with Mac OS X ones, and you can use the Dock to switch back and forth between Mac OS 9 programs, Mac OS X programs, and the Mac OS X Finder.

A Helping Hand

For info on using Mac OS X's built-in help, and other ways you can get help with your Mac, turn to Chapter 3, "Help! Getting It When You Need It."

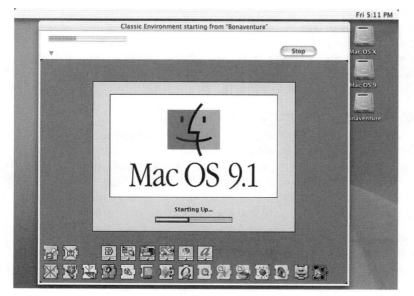

Figure 2.6

The first time you double-click a Classic application, the Classic environment takes a few minutes to start up.

Switch Hitting

If you've been using Macs for a while, you're probably accustomed to using the old Application menu to switch from one program to another. This menu is located in the far-right end of the menu bar in Mac OS 9 and earlier—and you'll still see it when you're working in a Classic application. It still works, too, showing all the Mac OS 9 and Mac OS X applications that you're currently running. Just choose one from the menu to switch to it. If you switch to a Mac OS X program, you'll need to use the Dock (or click on an open window) to move back to a Mac OS 9 program running in Classic.

When you're working in a Classic application, you'll see a Mac OS 9 menu bar across the top of the screen. If you choose an option from the Help menu, you'll get Mac OS 9 help instead of the Mac OS X Help Viewer. And you'll see your old friends the Apple menu and the Application menu on the left and right sides of the menu bar, respectively. Dialog boxes will look as they do on a Mac running Mac OS 9, rather than having the clean, white Aqua appearance. Don't worry—they still work just fine.

Cocoa: New School

All Mac OS X's promise is being packed into the slew of new applications written for the new system. These programs are written in Cocoa, the development environment for Mac OS X, and they take advantage of all Mac OS X's features. Those include the Help Viewer and the Services menu option, which enables you to access other programs' features from within the application you're using. See Chapter 7, "Free Software! (Using Mac OS X's Built-In Apps)," for examples of what you can do with Services.

Carbon: Having Your Cake and Eating It, Too

It is possible to have the best of both worlds. When Apple was designing Mac OS X, the company knew it would be hard on developers to have to build Mac OS X software from scratch. To make software development for Mac OS X easier, Apple created Carbon, a collection of system elements that work the same way in Mac OS 9 and Mac OS X. Applications that have been reworked to use Carbon elements work well in both Mac OS 9 and Mac OS X, without your having to use the Classic environment.

When Carbon apps are running in Mac OS 9, they use the Mac OS 9 menu bar and dialog boxes. When they're running on your Mac OS X Mac, though, they look just like any Mac OS X application.

Why Carbon?

There's a simple answer to that question. All life on earth is based on the element carbon—and all applications on your Mac are based on the Carbon system functions.

The Least You Need to Know

➤ Mac OS X looks new and different, with its clean, bright Aqua appearance. In some ways it works differently from previous Mac systems, although in other ways not much has changed.

➤ You'll still find windows, menus, and dialog boxes in Mac OS X, and they work much the same way they always have.

➤ New features include the Dock, which displays icons for programs, documents, and folders so you can open them quickly. The Dock always shows running programs; what else it shows is up to you.

➤ Applications in Mac OS X come in three kinds: Classic, Cocoa, and Carbon. Classic apps are the same ones you've used in Mac OS 9, Cocoa apps are written just for Mac OS X, and Carbon apps work in both Mac OS 9 and Mac OS X.

Chapter 3

Help! Getting It When You Need It

In This Chapter

➤ Accessing Mac OS X's built-in help

➤ Asking common questions

➤ Finding out more about a subject

➤ Getting help if you're not online

Despite their legendary ease of use, even Macs can befuddle their users sometimes. If you're dazed and confused about something your Mac is doing—or isn't doing— believe me, you're not alone. Fortunately, Apple has created an extensive help system that's always available via Mac OS X's Help menu. It's hooked up to Apple's Web site, so it always has the most current information. And it can walk you through tasks step by step, even opening the right dialog boxes for you at the right times in some cases.

In addition to basic instructions for using your Mac, Mac OS X's built-in help offers tips and techniques that benefit even power users. So, don't be afraid to ask for help— everyone does it!

What's on the (Help) Menu

Asking for help in Mac OS X is as simple as choosing a command from the Help menu. The command changes depending on which program you're using at the time; if you're in the Finder, working with files and folders, the Help menu's only option is Mac Help. When you're using Mail, on the other hand, the only command in the Help menu is Mail Help. So, before asking for help, you need to be sure you're using the program or tool you want help with.

When you're where you want to be, choose the appropriate command from the Help menu. This starts up the Help Viewer and opens it to the start page for the program you're working in (see Figure 3.1).

Figure 3.1

The start page for Mac Help offers several kinds of help.

Classic Help

If you're using a Classic application—in other words, one that doesn't run by itself in Mac OS X but must run within the Classic environment—you will probably see a Help menu in the menu bar, but its commands won't take you to the Mac OS X Help Center. Instead, they'll invoke whatever help options are available for that program under Mac OS 9, such as Microsoft Office's annoying Mac-with-legs. (If you don't know what I'm talking about there, count yourself lucky.)

Asking Questions

There is more than one way to start looking for information after you're in the Help Center. If you're at a main page (such as Mac Help), you can click one of the links under the search field to enter a help section. In each main page, such as Mac Help or AppleScript Help, clicking a Quick Clicks link takes you to a list of topics that covers the broad areas about which most users have questions.

You can search for the specific information you want on any page. To start a search in the main Help Center window or in a help section, enter words describing the information you're looking for in the search field and click Ask.

Whether you click through or search for a topic, you end up at a page listing Answers for your question (see Figure 3.2). There might be several pages of answers; if so, you'll see a link in the lower-right corner of the Help Center that says Next. Clicking this link takes you to the next page of answers.

As you click your way through the Help Center, you can use three buttons to get back to where you came from at any time. First, to return to the Help Center's opening screen, click the question mark button at the lower-left corner of the Help Center. Second, to move back and forward one screen at a time, click the arrow buttons in the lower-right corner. No matter in what order you view the screens, these buttons will take you back through the screens you've looked at, and then forward again, in the order in which you saw them.

Dead End

If clicking the right-arrow button doesn't do anything then you haven't been beyond this point in the Help Center yet. Click a link or make another search to keep homing in on what you're looking for.

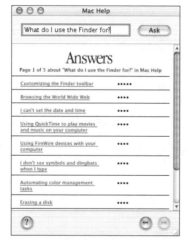

Figure 3.2

Each answer links to a page explaining that topic.

Getting Answers

After you've found some answers for your question, where do you go from there?

Obviously, the first thing to do is read an answer. To do this, just click on its name. Your Mac connects to Apple's Web site, downloads the information very quickly, and displays it for you.

Help in a Vacuum

There's just one flaw in Apple's snazzy Help Center system: It depends on your having an active Internet connection so it can download the information you need. Although this ensures that you'll always get the latest facts, it also means you're out of luck if you're not able to connect to the Internet. To learn about your options if you're not online, see "Getting Help Offline," later in this chapter.

In some cases, the answer you find in the Help Center is all you need to know. After you've read it, you're on your merry way. Other times, you need to know more about the topic in question. In these cases, you'll often see a "Tell me more" link at the bottom of the page. Clicking there takes you to a list of related answers. For example, one of the topics under the Quick Click for Printing is "Choosing your default printer." After you've read that answer, clicking "Tell me more" takes you to a list of answers based on the search terms "add" and "printer." Here you'll find out how to add a new printer to your system and how to install printer software.

Sometimes, just reading the answer doesn't solve your problem. If you need to take action to implement the answer, the Help Center often offers to give you a hand. If you're still looking for help with printing, for example, the answer page about "Choosing your default printer" also includes an "Open Print Center for me" link. Clicking this link takes you to the Print Center, where you can follow the instructions in the Help Center to choose a default printer.

And If That's Not Enough

If, after all this messing around with the Help Center, you're still mystified about printing, do what you should have done in the first place—turn to Chapter 12 in this book, "Printing Up a Storm."

Late Breaking News

To be sure you get the latest news about Mac OS X, Apple has put an icon called Late Breaking News in your Dock. Click Late Breaking News to see a list of topics that include the most recent information about using Mac OS X (see Figure 3.3).

Each Late Breaking News topic links to a list of answers that all fall into one of three categories: Updates, Tips, and Issues. Late Breaking News generally warns you about things that might not work as you expect because of conflicts with third-party hardware or software, bugs in Apple's software, or other unexpected circumstances. You'll also find suggestions under the Tips category for ways to use Mac OS X's new features.

News Flash

Even if your Dock doesn't have an icon for Late Breaking News, you can always find it in the Help Center by entering "late breaking news" in the search field and clicking Ask.

Getting Help Offline

All this help sounds just wonderful—unless you don't have an Internet connection, or if you're online but not all the time. Because so much of Mac OS X's built-in help depends on an Internet connection to get the information from Apple's Web site to you, you're pretty much out of luck under these circumstances.

You do have some options, though.

First, if your Mac came with Mac OS X, it also came with a manual that explains the basics of using Mac OS X, along with how to set up your hardware.

Your second option is to use Apple's phone support, which will cost you money each time you call. The number in the U.S. is 800-APL-CARE. If you live in another country, you can find the number in the documentation that came with your Mac.

If you have access to the Web at all (such as at the library or at work), you can use the support options explained in the next section.

And, finally, there's this book, which has a very complete index designed to help you find information on anything and everything discussed within these pages.

A Big Helping of the Web

Sometimes, the best way to get help is to help yourself. Even if you have full access to Mac OS X's built-in help, you'll find that the technical support information on Apple's Web site offers more comprehensive information that will come in handy for troubleshooting. The Support area of Apple's Web site is located at `www.apple.com/support/`. After you're there, you can access several help-related tools (see Figure 3.4).

Figure 3.4

Apple's Support site has several ways for you to get help.

More on the Web

The Web is a great place to look for help with your Mac, as well as for deals on hardware and software. For more great Mac resources on the Web, see Appendix A, "Useful Web Sites."

➤ Click Knowledge Base to search Apple's entire body of support information. The Knowledge Base first asks you what general area you want information about so that it can narrow the search and present you with the specific information you want.

➤ Apple's Technical Information Library (TIL) contains specific technical articles that can be extremely obscure or annoyingly general. It's searchable, too. The information here is considered the definitive data about how Apple products work.

➤ The Apple Web site is also a good place to hook up with other Mac users in the Discussions area. Here you can read people's posts about issues that interest you, check out the responses they got from other users, and post your own questions or comments.

➤ If it turns out that the answer to your question involves updating your software, you'll find what you need in the Software Updates area. Click Downloads in the navigation bar at the top of the main Support page to get there.

The Least You Need to Know

➤ The good news is that Mac OS X's built-in help is connected to the Internet, so it constantly updates itself to bring you the latest information on how to use your Mac.

➤ The bad news is that Mac OS X's built-in help is connected to the Internet— so if you're not online, it won't be much help to you.

➤ Apple's Web site also offers helpful information about Macs, various versions of the Mac OS, and other Apple products.

Chapter 4

No Mac Is an Island

In This Chapter

➤ Choosing a printer

➤ Getting started with scanners

➤ Looking into alternatives to mice

➤ Expanding your Mac's storage capacity with removables

➤ The different kinds of peripheral interfaces

If you do more with your Mac than just surf the Web, you're eventually going to install some *peripheral* devices. This chapter covers several different kinds of peripherals:

➤ Printers

➤ Scanners

➤ Mice and other input devices

➤ Storage devices

When you're shopping for peripheral devices, you'll need to consider more than just whether the device you're looking at can do the job. Speed often is a consideration, as is capacity—whether it's in terms of the number of pages that can be printed per minute, the number of images that can be scanned per hour, or the number of megabytes of data that can be stored.

Stuff Around the Edges

A ***peripheral*** is any piece of hardware you hook up to your Mac that isn't part of the original system.

The final section in this chapter covers the different ways you can hook up peripherals to your Mac—you don't want to buy a scanner, for example, and then find out that your Mac doesn't have a compatible port into which to plug the device. Most peripheral installations consist of plugging the device in and running a program that installs the device's drivers—software that lets your Mac use the device. Always read the installation directions that come with any device, though, to be sure you know what you're doing.

Printer Mania

Let's face it: No matter how much we keep hearing about e-books and the paperless office, we still need to print stuff. In fact, a printer often is the first "extra" device people usually get to go with their computers. Your printing options are limited only by the amount of money you have to spend.

Ink Versus Toner Versus Dye

Should you get a laser printer or an inkjet model, or maybe a dye sublimation printer? Your choice depends, first of all, on what you want the printer for. You can use printers to print your digital photos, to run off reams and reams of text pages, or to create your holiday newsletters and business communications.

Inkjet printers are the choice of most home users, and they come in both color and black-and-white versions. Color inkjets are so inexpensive these days, however, that there's not much point in buying black-and-white models. Most inkjet printers aren't network printers, which means they're designed to be connected to a single computer rather than shared on a network. Special photo inkjet printers can print photos that look almost like real photo prints. *Consumables* for inkjet printers are relatively inexpensive.

Conspicuous Consumption

Printer ***consumables*** are the paper and ink or toner that printers use up in the course of doing their jobs. The price of consumables has a major impact on the price of using a printer over time.

Laser printers are more expensive than inkjet printers, but their printouts are more durable and they print multipage documents faster. Although you can get a low-end black-and-white laser printer for about the same price as an inkjet photo printer, color laser printers and faster, networkable black-and-white models cost much more. For this reason, laser printers are generally used in offices rather than at home. Laser printer paper is quite cheap (you can use copier paper), but toner generally is expensive; fortunately, a toner cartridge usually lasts for thousands of pages.

P.S., I Love You

When shopping for printers, graphic designers will want to look for the PostScript label to be sure that a particular printer can process PostScript fonts and graphics with no trouble. Most inkjet printers don't have PostScript engines, but laser printers are more likely to use PostScript. Stay away from emulated PostScript and go for the real thing to help avoid annoying printer errors.

If you want the best-quality photo prints, and you don't care about printing text, a dye sublimation printer is your best bet. These devices really do produce photo-quality images. They're slow, and the consumables are quite expensive, but small models designed for home users have entered the market recently, and these are fairly affordable.

Getting Hooked Up

If you want to use a printer with a single computer, hooking it up is simply a matter of making sure it has at least one of the same interfaces that your Mac has. Local printers hook up to your Mac through the old-fashioned printer serial port or the newfangled USB port.

Network printers connect to your network, whether it's Ethernet or LocalTalk. Older printers might have a LocalTalk connector, which plugs into the round printer port on older Macs. To hook these up to newer Macs, which don't have printer ports, you'll need to do one of two things:

> ➤ If you have an Ethernet network, you can get a LocalTalk-to-Ethernet adapter for any printers or Macs that don't have Ethernet ports but do have LocalTalk ports.

> ➤ Otherwise, you can get a serial-to-USB adapter and use it to plug the printer into one of your USB ports.

Newer network printers have Ethernet connectors, which can plug right into your Ethernet network. See the "Making Connections" section at the end of this chapter for more on different ways to connect peripherals.

The Printer Connection

For more on interfaces between peripherals, including printers, and your Mac, see "Making Connections" at the end of this chapter.

Built for Networking

If you want to set up a small network, see Chapter 11, "How to Succeed in Networking Without Even Trying."

Seeing Through Scanners

Whereas printers are the way you get images *out* of your Mac, scanners are the way you get images *into* your Mac. They're not just for scanning photos, either—you can scan anything that you can get into your scanner. Here are some of the ways you can use a scanner:

➤ Turn photos and other artwork into electronic images that can be displayed onscreen, printed, or incorporated into other projects.

➤ Convert printed documents into electronic text with the use of OCR (optical character recognition) software.

➤ Make copies of printed documents without running out to the copy shop.

➤ Create images of small items you're selling on eBay to enhance your auction listings.

What Kind to Get

What kind of scanner you use depends on what kind of scanning you want to do—and how much money you want to spend. You want the most accurate color and the clearest images you can get, but there's no point in buying more scanner than you need.

Most people use flatbed scanners. Like photocopiers, they have glass beds on which you can scan anything that's flat enough. Some flatbed scanners have optional transparency adapters that let you scan film negatives and slides by shining a light through them toward the scanning mechanism.

If film negatives and slides are all you want to scan, you'd be better off with a slide scanner. These devices have a toaster-like slot into which you can insert a slide or a strip of negatives. The film is held inside the scanner, instead of just sitting on the glass scanning plate of a flatbed scanner, so the scans are bright and clear and the images are always straight.

Mac-compatible scanners can have USB, SCSI, or FireWire interfaces, and many have more than one kind of connector. Generally, the more money you spend, the more likely you are to get SCSI. The most expensive and newest scanners might have FireWire. (See the "Making Connections" section at the end of this chapter for more on different ways to connect peripherals.)

Read Me

Reality Check

Four trillion colors is many, many more colors than the human eye can see, so it's not as relevant as it might seem that a scanner can perceive that many colors. On the other hand, more colors certainly can't hurt!

Scanner Slang

When you're shopping for scanners, you're likely to run into some unfamiliar terminology. Here are a few scanner-specific words you'll want to know.

➤ **Color depth**—The number of different colors the scanner can perceive. The higher the number, the better quality scans you'll get. It's measured in bits, so the number of individual colors is actually 2 to the power of the number of bits. A 48-bit scanner can see more than four trillion colors.

➤ **Descreen**—A method of improving the quality of previously printed materials that you scan. Printed colors are made up of dots laid out in rows, and these often create a discernible pattern when you scan them. Descreening can minimize this pattern.

➤ **ppi**—Pixels per inch, referring to the resolution of a scanner or an image (see "Resolution," later in this list). Sometimes also called dpi, dots per inch, although that term is more correctly used to refer to dots produced by a printer.

➤ **Dynamic range**—The sensitivity of the scanner's capability to distinguish different brightness levels in an image. Dynamic range is measured on a four-point scale, with higher numbers indicating better-quality images.

➤ **Interpolate**—A method of creating new pixels when an image is enlarged or reduced (see "Pixel," later in this list).

➤ **Line art**—Black-and-white artwork with no gray tones or colors.

➤ **Pixel**—A tiny dot of color that combines with the pixels around it to produce an image. Most Web images are 72ppi (see "ppi," earlier in the list), which means that each inch of the image on your screen is 72 pixels square.

Read Me

Resolved: To Understand Resolution

Now that you know what resolution is, you might be asking yourself why you need to know about it. The answer has two parts: file size and image quality. The higher the resolution you use in creating an image, whether you scan it or create it from scratch, the larger its file will be. Image files that are larger than they have to be take more space on your hard drive and take longer to transmit when you're e-mailing them or waiting for them to download as part of a Web page. So, it makes sense to use a resolution that's appropriate for the image quality required in a given situation. Any image you're going to view onscreen, such as a Web page logo, should be created at 72ppi. However, images that you plan to print out should use a higher resolution, usually 300ppi or more.

➤ **Prescan**—A quick scan that shows you what's on the scanner's bed but doesn't save an image file. Working with the prescanned image, you can indicate the area you want to scan and make color and resolution settings for the image that will result from the final scan.

➤ **Resolution**—The number of times per inch the scanner stops and measures the color and brightness of the image. Each stop translates into a single pixel in the image (see "Pixel," earlier in the list). Resolution is measured in pixels per inch (see "ppi," earlier in the list).

Getting Input from Mice and More

At the birth of the Macintosh, in 1984, the mouse was a strange innovation. Now everyone's got one, and discussion has shifted to the burning question: One button or two? Macs still come with single-button mice, but you don't have to stick with that tradition. In the ongoing quest to avoid *RSIs* and become more efficient—or better at video games—you're aided by a host of alternatives to the humble mouse.

Older Macs have ADB ports on their backs and on their keyboards that mice plug into, whereas newer Macs have USB connectors for keyboards and mice. Other input devices, such as tablets, trackballs, and joysticks, use these same connectors. For more info on these and other connector types, see "Making Connections," later in this chapter.

Tunnel of Carpals

RSIs are repetitive strain injuries—in other words, the kind of owies you get from making small, repeated motions with your hands. Using a keyboard or a mouse all day is like asking to come down with an RSI, so be sure to take frequent breaks and use input devices that are comfortable for you.

The Mouse Replacement

There are many reasons you might want to use a mouse equivalent, or just a different mouse from the one that came with your Mac. You might be looking for a more ergonomic design, or you might want to have multiple buttons. Or maybe you just don't like mice!

Multibutton mice enable you to program the buttons for different functions. On a Mac, probably the most common practice is to set the right button to emulate a Ctrl+click, so that it can be used to display *contextual menus*. A third, smaller button or wheel in the center of the mouse is used to scroll through long documents, particularly Web pages. The more buttons you have, though, the more creative you can get—software included with most mice enables you to choose the functions each button performs and usually offers suggestions.

It's All in the Context

Contextual menus are menus that pop up from the point at which you're working, rather than within a dialog box or down from the menu bar. The commands they contain change depending on the program you're using and the task you're performing. On a Mac, you can Ctrl+click to bring up a contextual menu.

Trackballs and trackpads are alternatives to mice that are used primarily with laptops. They're both making inroads in the desktop computer market, however. A trackball is similar in function to a mouse, only upside down; instead of rolling the device along the table, you manipulate the ball directly with your fingers. Similarly, a trackpad enables you to drag a finger along a rubber pad to indicate the direction you want the cursor to take; current PowerBooks have trackpads. Whereas trackballs and trackpads have buttons, most trackpads can be set to generate a click with a simple tap of your finger on the pad.

Tablets and Styli

If you're an artist, you definitely need a pressure-sensitive tablet. These devices let you draw or paint onscreen with a penlike stylus—a much more natural way to draw than dragging a mouse around. Pressure sensitivity varies the width or color of each stroke as you make it, allowing you to reproduce the effects you'd get by using traditional artists' tools. Most tablets have plastic overlays under which you can tuck artwork that you want to trace.

Another use for graphics tablets is for signing documents electronically. And many artists who have tablets installed for their work also use them as a general-purpose mouse replacement—a tap of the stylus or a click of a button on its side acts as a mouse click.

The most expensive graphics tablets have integrated flat LCD monitors, so you can draw right on the screen as it sits on your desk or in your lap. Someday, your entire computer might be encapsulated in a device that looks like this. For now, these combination tablet/monitors are expensive luxuries for high-end artists and designers.

Gaming Controllers

If you're a hardcore action gamer, you might want to add a gaming controller to your Mac. Such devices don't make great mouse substitutes, but you can use one in addition to a mouse or trackball. They come in several varieties:

➤ Joysticks—Just like the ones used on coin-operated video machines and in airplanes, these devices enable you to control motion onscreen by tilting a stick back and forth.

➤ Gamepads—These are based on the controllers that come with standalone video game systems such as Nintendo. They have a plethora of buttons, lights, and other controls that are used for a variety of game functions.

➤ Flight controllers—Intended to mimic airplane flight yokes, these are designed to work with flight simulator games.

➤ Pedals and wheels—Steering wheels, accelerator and brake pedals, and other lifelike accessories are available for use with almost any game that has a real-life action component, such as auto-racing games.

Read Me

Maximum Joy

Most joysticks have a base that sits on your lap or on a desk, but the extremely cool Macally Airstick (www.macally.com) has a motion sensor and can be operated with one hand in midair.

Zips, Hard Drives, and All That Jaz

Hard drives just keep getting cheaper, faster, and bigger. Just 15 years ago, the 20-gigabyte (20GB) drive inside my Power Mac G4 would have cost thousands and thousands of dollars—except that you couldn't buy a 20GB drive back then.

The highest-capacity hard drive available 15 years ago held much less than a single gigabyte of data and was more than twice the size of my entire G4.

Now that we're done wandering down Memory Lane, let's get back to the point: getting you more storage. What kind of removable drive should you get? As always, that depends on what you want to do with it. The following are possible uses for removable storage devices:

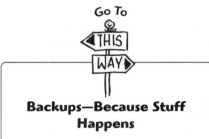

Backups—Because Stuff Happens

If your computer contains any information you don't want to lose—financial records, work projects, or the Great American Novel—you should be making backups. For information about backup software, hardware, and strategies, see Chapter 27, "Preparing for the Worst."

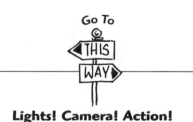

Lights! Camera! Action!

If you're interested in getting into the movie business—or the home movie business—check out Chapter 9, "Working with Audio and Video." You'll learn about Apple's multimedia software, including iMovie and iTunes, and about the hardware you need to start working with digital video.

➤ Backup storage for copies of your important data (for example, the data file from your money management program).

➤ Transport storage for large files (or large *numbers* of files) you need to move from one computer to another; this applies when the two computers aren't on a network together (or don't have Internet access) or when the files are too large to be moved across a network.

➤ Archiving storage for completed projects that you don't have room to store on your Mac's hard drive, such as digital video files you create with iMovie.

Removable Drives

When you're deciding what removable media format to go with, you must consider how much data you want to put on a disk, how long you need the data to be readable, and what systems are being used by people with whom you'll be exchanging data.

For lots of data, you'll want lots of space. Whether you need high speed depends on how much time you have. For unattended overnight backups, speed doesn't matter very much, but if you're going to be waiting as a file copies to the disk before you can grab it and run out to a client presentation then you'll want that device to be pretty speedy.

Table 4.1 compares the media costs and drive speeds of four kinds of removable media. SuperDisks, Zips, and Jaz disks all require special drives to read, whereas CD-Rs (CD-Recordable discs) and CD-RWs (CD-Rewritable discs) can be read in any CD-ROM drive but require special software to write.

Table 4.1 Removable Drive Comparison

Device	Data Transfer Rate	Media Capacity	Media Cost	Compatibility
SuperDisk	About 1MB/sec	120MB	$10 (8¢/MB)	Drive can also read floppy disks.
Zip	1.4MB/sec (100MB) or 2.4MB/sec	100MB or 250MB	$8 (100MB) or $11 (250MB) (8¢/MB or 4¢/MB)	250MB drives can also read 100MB Zip disks.
Jaz	5.5MB/sec	1000MB (1GB) or 2000MB (2GB)	$90 (1GB) or $120 (2GB) (8¢/MB or 6¢/MB)	2GB drives can also read 1GB Jaz disks.
CD-R/ CD-RW	Varies; 1.2MB/sec	About 675MB	$.85 (CD-R) or $1.75 (CD-RW) for 8x drive (.1¢/MB or .3¢/MB)	CD-Rs can be read in any CD-ROM drive and in most stereo CD players.

New SuperDisk, Zip, and Jaz drives use USB, while older versions use SCSI. CD-RW drives (which can write on both CD-R and CD-RW discs) can have USB, SCSI, or FireWire interfaces. See "Making Connections," later in the chapter, to learn about different peripheral interfaces.

Portable Drives

Portable hard drives are similar in function to regular hard drives, but they're small, light, durable and *hot-swappable*. They're designed both as accessories for laptop computers and as movable storage for people who work on more than one computer. Portable drives have strong cases and are designed to be moved around and even dropped occasionally. Because they have either USB or FireWire interfaces, they're not generally used with older Macs, but they offer fast, flexible, and reliable storage for users of newer Macs.

Show Info

Swap Meet

For a long time, it wasn't a good idea to disconnect a peripheral from your Mac without turning your system off. **Hot-swappable** devices, however, can be plugged in and unplugged without powering down your Mac. Believe me, this saves a lot of time in the long run.

Making Connections

The connection between a peripheral device and your Mac is called its *interface*. To some extent, the connectors available on your Mac determine which interfaces you should shop for in peripheral devices. On the other hand, adapters and add-on cards allow you to connect most devices to most Macs in one way or another.

The interface used depends on the requirements and price point of the device being connected (see Figure 4.1). For example, FireWire is expensive but fast, so it's used for hard drives, while USB is cheap but slow, so it's used for smaller-capacity removable drives.

Figure 4.1

This illustration shows the standard peripheral interfaces on an iMac.

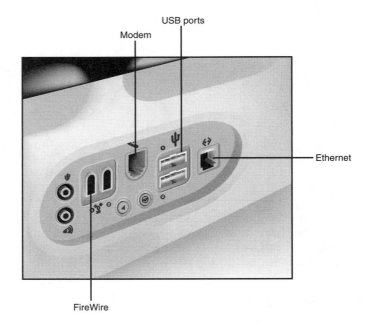

Here's a quick guide to the different peripheral interfaces used on Mac devices:

➤ **SCSI** (Small Computer System Interface) and **FireWire** are fast interfaces used for storage drives and for scanners. SCSI is an older standard, and FireWire is the up-and-coming interface. Both allow multiple devices to be connected to each other, with the one at the end connected to the Mac. FireWire is hot-swappable, whereas SCSI is not, and SCSI chains are more susceptible to mysterious ailments.

➤ **ADB** (Apple Desktop Bus) and **USB** (Universal Serial Bus) are the old and new standards, respectively, for Mac mice and keyboards. A lot of slower storage devices and low-end scanners also come with USB connectors these days. USB is a standard that's being adopted in the PC world, as well, so your newer Mac can use some USB PC devices as long as you can find software drivers to support them (see Figure 4.2). Adapters and add-on cards are available to connect ADB devices to USB-only Macs and vice versa.

Figure 4.2
The USB connector is thin and flat with no prongs or pins.

➤ **LocalTalk** and **Ethernet** are two different networking methods. For many years, Macs had built-in networking capabilities via LocalTalk, a slow but easy-to-use method that could run on standard telephone wire. Then Macs got Ethernet ports in addition to their LocalTalk network ports. Current Macs have only Ethernet ports; it's the standard for networking across platforms, so PCs and Unix computers can coexist on Ethernet networks with Macs. LocalTalk-to-Ethernet adapters allow you to connect older Macs and printers to Ethernet networks.

Read Me

Making a Baby Network

Older Macs have two matching round ports on the back, each labeled with a tiny icon. The modem port has a telephone icon and the printer port has a little printer next to it, although they're actually the same kind of connector. The important thing to know about the printer port, however, is that it's also the LocalTalk network port. You can connect the printer directly to the Mac with a serial cable. Alternatively, you can plug a LocalTalk adapter into the printer port, plug another one into the printer, and connect the two of them with a phone cable to form the simplest, smallest network of them all.

The Least You Need to Know

➤ Inkjet printers provide inexpensive color, whereas laser printers provide high speed and quality text printouts.

➤ Flatbed scanners are useful for scanning images, text, and even fairly flat objects, whereas slide scanners do a better job on slides and film negatives.

➤ Whatever the primary use for your Mac, there's an alternative input device for you. Trackpads and trackballs are commonly used to avoid RSIs, and multibutton mice are for power users. Artists can draw better with graphics tablets, whereas gamers get more excitement with joysticks and other gaming controllers.

➤ Removable media drives enable you to store more data and move it to where you want it. Which kind you choose depends on how much data you have to store, how much time you have to wait around while it copies, and how much money you can spend.

➤ Before you buy peripherals for your Mac, be sure you know what peripheral interfaces it has. If your Mac doesn't have an interface you want to use (such as the speedy FireWire for hard drives), you sometimes can buy an add-on card to install inside the Mac and provide the external connectors you need.

Part 2
Getting Things Done

Now that you're used to seeing Mac OS X's new look on your Mac's screen every day, it's time to get some work done—or some play, if you're so inclined. This part helps you get started using your new Mac, or your old Mac with its brand-new system.

In Chapter 5, you'll learn about Mac OS X's new folder structure—what you can do with it, what you can't, and why—as well as how to organize your own files and folders. Chapter 6 explains Mac OS X's multiuser orientation, which allows different people to experience completely different Macs on one computer, simply by logging in with their own user names. Next, Chapter 7 covers the software that is included with Mac OS X, and Chapter 8 talks about finding, using, and installing third-party software. In Chapter 9, we'll start having some real fun by learning how to make movies and mix your own music CDs on a Mac. Finally, Chapter 10 introduces some Mac OS X games and gaming hardware.

Chapter 5

Managing Your Files

In This Chapter

➤ Navigating Mac OS X's built-in folder structure

➤ Creating your own files and folders

➤ Manipulating files and folders in the Finder

➤ Finding stuff

➤ Saving time with aliases

In the early days of Macs, many things were much simpler. For one thing, because they didn't have hard drives, early Macs couldn't store any files or programs internally; everything had to fit on floppy disks, including the system software. Although this setup made for a lot of floppy-swapping, it kept users from wading through a swamp of mysteriously named files and disorganized folders.

You might have noticed that your real-life stuff expands to fill the rooms of your house, no matter how big a house you move into. The same is true of the stuff on your computer's hard drive. Like earlier versions of Mac system software, Mac OS X uses the metaphor of paper documents (files) and file folders as a way for you to organize the information you keep on your Mac. Unlike real-world file folders, the Mac OS lets you put folders within folders within folders... and so on. And also unlike the real world, there's little limitation on the number of documents you can cram into each folder.

With all this in mind, this chapter will show you how your drive is organized under Mac OS X and how you can keep the situation under control so you can find what you need, when you need it.

Your Drive's Built-In Folders

It used to be that there was only one folder on your hard drive that you were supposed to avoid messing with just for fun—the System Folder. Now, with Mac OS X, there is no System Folder. Nevertheless, there are several folders that are vital to the workings of Mac OS X: Applications, Library, System, and Users, along with the usual Mac OS 9 folders, if Mac OS X was installed on your computer over a version of Mac OS 9 (see Figure 5.1). These folders are created automatically when the system software is installed on your computer, and they're the starting point for getting a sense of what's where on your computer. The next few sections explain what these folders are, what is in them, and what you can and can't do with them.

Figure 5.1

The Documents, System Folder, and Applications (Mac OS 9) folders are part of the Mac OS 9 installation on this drive, whereas the others belong to Mac OS X.

Go To

Cool Stuff...and It's Free!

For the most part, the applications that come with Mac OS X are pretty utilitarian. There's an address book, a clock, and a calculator. But the Applications folder is also where cool stuff such as Sherlock, QuickTime Player, and Mail reside. For more about what apps you get with Mac OS X, see Chapter 7, "Free Software! (Using Mac OS X's Built-In Apps)."

Applications: The Engines

When you want to get some actual work done, you'll probably start here. This folder is where Mac OS X stores your applications—also known as programs or software. Some applications come with Mac OS X, and others might have been installed on your computer before you bought it (if it came with Mac OS X) or might have been installed in this folder by you or other users. Examples to of Mac OS X applications are Internet Explorer, Mail, TextEdit, and Key Caps.

Applications that are located in this folder can be used by anyone who logs on to your computer. If you have applications that you don't want other people to use, you can store them in your user directory.

To get to the to Applications folder quickly, open a Finder window (click the **Desktop** and press **Cmd+N**) and click the **Applications** button at the top of the window (see Figure 5.2). If you don't see the toolbar buttons, press **Cmd+B** or click the clear button at the top-right corner of the window to bring them back.

You can't to move, delete, or rename anything in the Applications folder unless you're logged in to Mac OS X as the system's Administrator. If you logged in using another account when you started your computer, dragging applications out of the Applications folder actually makes a copy of them in the folder where you drag them (or on the Desktop).

If you want to to store an application elsewhere for easier access to it, you can make an alias by holding down Cmd+Option and dragging the application's icon into another folder or onto the Desktop. See "Living Under an Alias," later in this chapter, for ways to use aliases.

Playing Nice with Others

In Mac OS 9, you had the option of setting up your computer to be used by more than one person. In the world of Mac OS X, you no longer have a choice—the system is designed from the inside out for multiple users. For more information on how this works, see Chapter 6, "Sharing Your Mac with Multiple Users."

Who's the Boss?

At this point, you might be saying, "Administrator? I don't remember naming an administrator for my computer." This is simpler than it sounds: Mac OS X treats the first user account that was created for a system as the system's first Administrator. To find out which login names are Administrators of your system, open the System Preferences (there's an icon for it in the Dock) and click the Users button. The first user in the list has the word "Admin" in the Kind column, letting you know that it's an Administrator account.

Library: Where the Wild Settings Are

The Library folder stores many of the items that used to live in the System Folder in earlier versions of the Mac OS. Most of the files in the Library folder are put there by either Mac OS X or an application that needs access to these files. In general, you won't work with the Library files from day to day; the times you're most likely to need to see what's hiding in there are when you're manually installing or uninstalling software or troubleshooting your system. Unless you're logged in to Mac OS X as an Admin user, you can't move, rename, or delete anything you'll find here.

Go To

Gettin' Rid of Programs... for Good!

Installing software is usually fairly easy in Mac OS X, but uninstalling programs isn't always a simple task. For more information about what to do when you want an application gone from your computer, check out Chapter 28, "Troubleshooting."

Here are some examples of the kind of files that are stored in the Library folder:

➤ Plug-ins, helper applications, templates, and other resources for applications

➤ Web browser plug-ins

➤ Help Center data files

➤ Fonts

➤ Preferences

➤ Sherlock plug-ins

➤ Sound files

➤ Printer definitions (in the Extensions subfolder)

➤ ColorSync profiles (also in the Extensions subfolder)

➤ Voices for applications that use speech

Mac OS 9: Oldie von Moldies

Mac OS X is a big step forward for Mac users—it's totally new technology, designed from the ground up to combine power with ease of use—all of which sounds just great, until you find out that some of your favorite programs haven't been released in Mac OS X–compatible versions yet. There's no need to panic, though. You can run Mac OS 9, the previous version of the Mac's system software, from within Mac OS X. That means you can run your Mac OS 9 versions of those applications.

To accomplish this, most people start with a computer that's already running Mac OS 9, and then install Mac OS X on that computer. When you do this, the contents of your pre–Mac OS X hard drive are all still there, right along with the Mac OS X system and other files.

You can go the other way, too. If your Mac came with Mac OS X installed, you can add Mac OS 9 by starting up using your Mac OS 9 CD. In both cases, you'll want to be sure you're using Mac OS 9.1; earlier versions of Mac OS 9 aren't compatible with the Classic component of Mac OS X.

After restarting from the CD, follow these steps to install Mac OS 9:

1. Choose **File**, **New Folder** to create a new untitled folder at the top level of your hard drive.

2. Move the Mac OS X Applications folder into the untitled folder.

3. Start up the Mac OS 9 Installer.

4. Choose the **Clean Install** option and continue with the installation.

5. Quit the Installer.

6. Move the Applications folder back to the top level of your hard drive and delete the untitled folder.

To access Mac OS 9, you have two options:

➤ Double-click any Mac OS 9 application (or click the **Classic** icon in the Dock) to start up the Classic environment using your Mac OS 9 System Folder. When Classic is running, you can move back and forth between Mac OS 9 applications and Mac OS X ones without restarting your computer.

➤ Use the System Preferences' Startup Disk pane to specify that the Mac OS 9 System Folder should be used when you restart your computer. When you restart, you'll see the Mac OS 9 Finder, although your hard drive will still be organized the way it needs to be for Mac OS X to work.

Read Me

Version Vision

The idea of using Mac OS 9 and Mac OS X at the same time, on the same Mac, sounds too good to be true, doesn't it? Well, there is one caveat—but it's a little one. To use Mac OS 9 within the Classic environment, you must have at least version 9.1, the latest version when Mac OS X was released. That's not so bad, is it?

Go To

Classic Is a Classic

Classic will remain an important part of the Mac OS for a few years, until the selection of Mac OS X applications widens to accommodate everyone's needs. For more about using Classic applications, see Chapter 2, "Making Friends with Mac OS X." In Chapter 19, "Setting System Preferences," you can find out how to specify a Mac OS 9 System Folder in Classic.

System: Your Mac's (Off-Limits) Control Center

The System folder is sort of, but not quite, like the old Mac OS System Folder. In it are files that are part of the system software or part of Apple-installed applications, and most of these reside in another Library folder within the System folder. Even an Admin user can't move, rename, or delete any of the files or folders in the System folder.

Users: Storage for You and Me

As a user, your true domain is the Users folder. Within this folder, Mac OS X creates a *home folder* for each registered user of your computer, as well as a Public folder in which you can keep items you want everyone to have access to. Your home folder is called by the user name you created for yourself when you first logged in to Mac OS X, and its icon is a house. Inside that folder you can keep whatever your heart desires—although your home folder, too, contains some special prefab folders created by Mac OS X.

Go Home

Your *home folder* is where Mac OS X stores any files that are for your use alone. You keep your own documents there, and the system keeps your preferences, special fonts, and personal items, such as e-mail boxes, there.

One of the toolbar buttons visible at the top of a Finder window takes you to your home folder inside the Users folder. After you get to your home folder, you'll notice that it already contains some folders, as follows:

➤ The *Documents* folder is where you'll keep most of the files you create: letters, artwork, or whatever. You can create subfolders to organize it any way you want. Although other users can see what's in this folder, they can't change any of the files or folders.

➤ The *Library* contains the same kind of items as the main Library folder, but things you put here in your home folder are available only to you. For example, if you have a custom font that you use for your signature, you might want to put it here so that no one else will be able to use it.

➤ Your *Public* folder has a *Drop Box* folder inside it. Items placed in the Public folder are accessible to any user, but other users can't remove or delete those files—only read or copy them. The Drop Box folder is where other users can put files they want to give you—putting files here is the only way another user can add anything to your home folder.

➤ The *Desktop* folder is where items that appear to be on the Desktop really live. It's been around for a while in earlier versions of the Mac OS, but it wasn't visible until now. You can safely ignore it most of the time.

➤ The *Music* folder is used with iTunes, Apple's new software for converting music to a form that you can store and play on your Mac, and the *Movies* folder is intended for use with iMovie, Apple's digital video editing program. See Chapter 9, "Working with Audio and Video," for more info.

➤ The *Pictures* folder contains images that you want to use for a custom screen saver that creates a slideshow from the images. See Chapter 19, "Setting System Preferences," for more info.

➤ The *Sites* folder is for your Web files. If you use Web Sharing to create a Web site accessible on your own intranet, the files to make up that site live in this folder. See Chapter 15, "Publishing on the Web," to learn more.

I Have My Rights!

If you can't open a folder you need access to, odds are you don't have the right access privileges. Use the Inspector to see which user owns the folder in question, and then have that user or an Admin user change the folder's access privileges. See Chapter 21, "File and Folder Boot Camp," for more about the Inspector; to learn more about folder access privileges, check out Chapter 6, "Sharing Your Mac with Multiple Users."

Let There Be Files and Folders

Now that you know how your hard drive is organized, and what's on it that the system software put there, it's time to start adding your own stuff! I tend to think of a new computer as my new home—when I move in, the first thing I do is put everything away, and then I start jazzing the place up a bit. Let's get started with the organization part, and we'll start putting up pictures and rearranging the furniture in Part 5, "Tweaking Mac OS X."

Surprise! When Folders Just Appear

As you work with Mac OS X and its programs, you may notice new folders and files appearing in your home folder. For example, after you start using Mail to send and receive e-mail, you'll see a new folder in your home folder's Library folder: Mail. This folder is where Mail stores the user names and passwords for the e-mail accounts you've set up as well as your e-mail messages, both sent and received.

Don't Randomly Reorganize

Don't rename, move, or delete folders unless you know who or what program created them. If they were created by a program, doing so can cause the originating application to lose track of them.

Other folders might appear in your home folder or its subfolders whenever you install or start using a program that can accommodate different users. Such programs need to keep your files—which may be preferences or documents—separated from those of other users, so the files are stored in your home folder for safekeeping.

Lookin' in Your Drawers

The **top level** of your hard drive is where the system displays the entire contents of the drive. If we go back to the file cabinet analogy for how your files are stored, the top level is like the file cabinet itself; the folders you can see at the top level are like the cabinet's drawers. Within them are folders, but you can't see those until you open the drawers.

Mixing Your Own Folders

Because of Mac OS X's insistence on maintaining the basic organization of your hard drive just the way it is, non-Administrator users can't create new folders at the *top level*, where the Applications, Library, Mac OS 9, Users, and System folders are stored. And unless you're an Administrator user, you also can't create subfolders inside any of those folders except the Mac OS 9 folder. The idea behind Mac OS X's multiuser setup is that you'll work within your own home folder, so you're restricted to creating folders only there and in Mac OS 9's domain, which isn't owned by any particular user and therefore isn't subject to the same rules.

Inside your home folder, you can make as many folders as you want, and you can call them whatever you want. Although the OS has created a Documents folder for you, you're not locked into using it for your documents, and you can even delete it if you don't want to use it. You can create folders with whatever names you want; Figure 5.3 shows one way you might organize your home folder with subfolders.

Figure 5.3

In this home folder, the user keeps different kinds of documents in separate folders.

So, how do you actually make a folder? First, open the window for the folder where you want to add a subfolder. Then choose **File**, **New Folder** or press **Cmd+Shift+N**. The new folder appears, with the name "untitled folder" highlighted, so that you can change its name right away by just typing. If you make more new folders before changing the first one's name, each subsequent folder has a number tacked onto its name: "untitled folder 2," "untitled folder 3," and so on.

Moving, Copying, and Renaming Files and Folders

One of the nice things about rearranging your Mac is that you can do it as many times as you want. Folders never get frayed or ripped, you don't have to use messy labels to give folders new names, and you can copy files and folders with no risk of traumatic paper jams. Here's a quick look at moving, copying, and renaming work in Mac OS X.

Move It Out!

Moving files and folders is about as simple as it seems: Click and drag the item into a new Finder window. There are two situations in which this won't work:

➤ If the item can't be moved from its folder (if you're trying to move a folder that belongs to another user, for example), the system makes a copy in the new location instead. There's no way around this.

➤ If you don't have the correct access privileges for the destination folder, you'll see a dialog box informing you of this fact (see Figure 5.4). If you run into this problem, you'll need to move the item somewhere else (such as your home folder) or have the destination folder's owner change its access privileges.

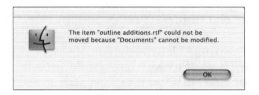

Figure 5.4

This message lets you know that you're trying to put a file someplace where you're not allowed to go.

Makin' Copies

If you wanted to, you could fill up your entire hard drive with copies of just one file—and you could do it in much less time than you probably think. Now, you're probably not going to want to do that, but making copies of a file is one of the most common tasks in using computers, and it's just as easy to do in Mac OS X as in earlier versions of Mac OS. Here are the three methods:

➤ If you want to make a copy of a file or folder in the same location as the original, choose **File**, **Duplicate** or press **Cmd+D**. The duplicate file has the word "copy" either at the end of its filename or just before the period if the file has a filename extension. You can then move the copy wherever you want it, or leave it there as a backup version.

➤ To copy a file or folder to another location on the same drive, hold down **Option** as you drag it to the new folder. Ordinarily, dragging an item moves it, but the Option key ensures the original item stays put while a duplicate is deposited in the destination folder. In this case, the copy has the same filename as the original.

➤ If you're copying the file to another disk, all you have to do is drag it to the disk's Finder window or on top of the disk's icon.

Naming Names

You can rename any file or folder for which you have the right access privileges. In practice, this means that you can't rename other people's files or folders, and you can't rename the files and folders your Mac's system software uses. When it comes to your own stuff, though, you can do it your way.

To rename an item, click the icon of the file you want to rename and either move the mouse slightly or press **Return**. The name of the file or folder becomes highlighted, and you can type to replace it or click anywhere in the name to place the text cursor there. Here are a few keyboard shortcuts you can use as you type a new file or folder name:

➤ **Cmd+C**—Copies selected text.

➤ **Cmd+X**—Cuts selected text.

➤ **Cmd+V**—Pastes copied text into the filename.

➤ **Cmd+Shift+left arrow**—Selects from the cursor to the beginning of the filename.

➤ **Cmd+Shift+right arrow**—Selects from the cursor to the end of the filename.

➤ **Option+Delete**—Deletes all text left of the cursor.

➤ **Option+Forward Delete**—Deletes all text right of the cursor up to the *filename extension* (if there is one) or the end (if there is no extension).

What's this about extensions, you're saying? Many fortunate Mac users have never seen or heard of *filename extensions*. Those of us who have to coexist with users of Windows computers, though, are familiar with the tricky buggers.

What's in a Name?

The idea behind *filename extensions* is that some computer systems don't know what program to open a document with unless the document has a two- or three-letter code tacked onto the end of its filename, separated from the filename by a period. Filename extensions are most common in the Unix and Windows worlds, but now that Mac OS X is built into a Unix base, Mac users will be seeing more of them.

For example, Web pages usually use a filename extension of .html, whereas Web graphics generally have .gif or .jpg extensions. Such extensions help ensure that all different computers will know what to do with a given file. Although Mac programs historically haven't needed filename extensions, Mac OS X uses them, and so does Windows, so it never hurts to use them, especially if you're planning to share files with someone who uses another computer platform. Often you'll find that the program you're using has tacked on a filename extension without even asking you; in this case, you're best off just leaving it to make sure that program can always identify the file as one of its own.

Living Under an Alias

Macs have used *aliases* for a while—no, not names like John Doe or Tokyo Rose, but small files whose only purpose is to point to other files. An alias is like a *Star Trek* wormhole: It takes you where you want to go without your having to travel through a maze of files and folders. Aliases are handy for organizing your hard drive, especially because Mac OS X doesn't allow you to move some kinds of files. With aliases, you can have access to any kind of file from within a single folder or from your Desktop.

For example, suppose you're writing a book. As you work on this project, you'll be creating artwork in Adobe Photoshop, writing text in Microsoft Word, and e-mailing the completed chapters and artwork to your editor. (All right, this isn't the most original analogy you've ever read, but stick with me a bit longer....)

So, you create a folder in your home folder—call it Book Project—that you'll use to store the documents that make up the book. In the Book Project folder, you'll save the artwork and the text files, and you might also add some aliases: one for Word and one for Photoshop, as well as one for an article you wrote on the book's topic last year. Finally, you add an alias to a folder of PDF documents you downloaded that document the software about which you're writing.

When you double-click any of these aliases, the corresponding document, program, or folder opens up, but that file or folder stays where it belongs. It's not copied to your folder; the alias in your folder just points the system to the correct file or folder when you want it.

Creating Aliases

Now that you know what they are, don't you feel the urge to create some aliases? The first way to make an alias of a file is the simplest: Click the file to select it, and then choose **File**, **Make Alias** or press **Cmd+L**. The alias appears next to the file. You can tell them apart in two ways (see Figure 5.5):

➤ The alias has a special icon with an arrow in the corner.
➤ The alias has the word alias at the end of its filename (before the period if you're using a filename extension).

Figure 5.5

Aliases have distinctive icons so they're easy to spot.

After you've created an alias, you can drag it into any folder for which you have access privileges.

Advanced Alias-Making 201

A faster way to make aliases is by dragging. Click the file to select it, and then hold down **Option+Cmd** as you drag it into another folder or onto the Desktop. Rather than moving or copying the file to the new location, Mac OS X makes an alias of it in that location.

Here are a few useful things to know about aliases:

➤ Any given file or folder can have as many aliases as you like.

➤ You can make an alias of any file, folder, or drive icon that you can see in the Finder.

➤ An alias has the same user privileges as its original file, so if you can't open the original (because it belongs to someone else), you won't be able to open it by double-clicking the alias, either.

➤ A copy of an alias points to the same file or folder as the first alias.

➤ An alias doesn't go away when you delete the file or folder to which it points.

➤ Deleting an alias doesn't affect the original file or folder.

But I Can't Find Anything!

If you've lost a file—you know it's somewhere on your hard drive, but you can't figure out where—the answer is easy: Call Sherlock.

No, not Sherlock Holmes, but Sherlock, Mac OS X's search utility. To get there, click on the Desktop or in a Finder window and press **Cmd+F**, or click the **Sherlock** icon in the Dock. Sherlock is a powerful tool for searching the Web, but it's also the way to locate anything you've lost on your own computer (see Figure 5.6).

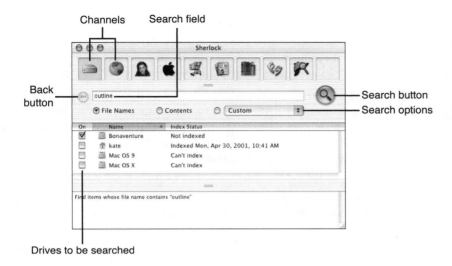

Figure 5.6
The Sherlock window contains multiple channels, but the Files channel is where you go to search your hard drive.

Restricting Sherlock for Your Own Good

If you know which folder a file is in, you can speed up Sherlock's search quite a bit and reduce the number of found files to review by dragging the folder into the drives area of the Sherlock window and clicking on only that folder's check box. This restricts the search to that folder.

What's in a Name?

The most obvious way to look for a file is by its filename, assuming you know what the file is called. To do this, be sure the File Names radio button is clicked, and then type the filename or any part of it into the search field. Click the check boxes next to the names of the disks you want to search and press **Return** or click the **Search** button. Sherlock searches for a few seconds and then either lists the found files in the bottom half of the window or displays a dialog box saying it can't find anything that matches the name you entered.

71

It's the Content, Stupid

If you know what text is in a file, but you don't know the name, you can search the contents of files by clicking the **Contents** radio button in the Sherlock window. Then, type a word or phrase into the search field and press **Return** or click the **Search** button.

For content searches to work, your drive must be indexed. In the indexing process, Sherlock creates a database of all the text contained in each file on your drive. Without an index, content searches would take so long that they'd be utterly impractical. You can create an index on-the-fly when you need one, or you can have Sherlock index your drives automatically and update the indexes regularly.

Read Me

Finding Faster

If you don't use content searches often, you can speed up Sherlock's launch by deselecting the two indexing options in Sherlock's Preferences dialog box. After you've turned these options off, you can index any item by clicking on it and choosing **Find, Index Now**.

To create an index on-the-fly, open **Sherlock**, select the drive or folder you want to index, and choose **Find, Index Now**. Sherlock immediately indexes the text contained in the files in that folder or drive and saves the index; when that's done, you can do content searches in that drive or folder. You'll be able to index folders only with access privileges that let you both read the files they contain and add, move, or copy the files.

To have indexes created automatically, open Sherlock and choose **Sherlock, Preferences**. In the Indexing Options area of the Preferences dialog box, check on "Automatically index items when Sherlock is opened" and "Automatically index folders when they're added to the Files channel," and then click **OK**. Doing this ensures that each drive has an up-to-date index each time you open Sherlock.

Customizing Your Searches

What do you do if you're really in a bind? You don't know a file's name, and it's not a text file with searchable contents. You do, however, know it's an Acrobat file that was last saved on December 12, 1999.

With Sherlock, you're all set. Start by clicking the **Custom** radio button; then click **Custom** and scroll down to Edit. Welcome to the More Search Options dialog box—this is where you can enter almost any search criterion you can imagine, including the following (see Figure 5.7):

➤ Name

➤ Contents

➤ Date created

➤ Date modified

➤ Size

➤ Kind

➤ File type

➤ File creator

➤ File version

➤ Folder status

➤ Comments contents

➤ File/folder locking status

➤ Name/icon locking status

➤ Custom icon

Figure 5.7

Sherlock's custom search options are extensive.

If you don't see all these options, click next to **Advanced Options** to display the more obscure choices. You can use any combination of these criteria for your search, and you can save criteria that you're likely to use again by clicking **Save As**. Just enter a name for the search in the Custom Settings dialog box (see Figure 5.8) and click **OK**. After settings have been saved, their names appear in the main Sherlock window's Custom menu above Edit; to use them, click the radio button next to the menu and choose the saved search from the menu.

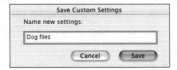

Figure 5.8

Entering a name in the Custom Settings dialog box saves a set of search criteria so you can use them again.

What to Do with the Files You Find

No matter what kind of search you do, the results appear in the lower half of the Sherlock window in a neat little list. Below the list, you can see the hierarchy of enclosing folders for any found file by clicking on the file. From here, there are a number of things you can do with a found file:

➤ **Open the file**—Double-click the file, choose **File**, **Open Item**, or press **Cmd+O**.

➤ **Open the file's folder in a Finder window**—Click the file, and then choose **File**, **Open Enclosing Folder** or press **Cmd+E**.

➤ **Print the file**—Click the file, and then choose **File**, **Print Item** or press **Cmd+P**.

➤ **Move the file to the Trash**—Click the file, and then choose **File**, **Move to Trash** or press **Cmd+Delete**.

➤ **Show the file's original, if it's an alias**—Click the file, and then choose **File**, **Show Original** or press **Cmd+R**.

➤ **Move the file to another location**—Drag the file into any Finder window, on top of any drive or folder icon, or onto the Desktop.

The Least You Need to Know

➤ Mac OS X is both very rigid and very flexible about how it lets you organize your computer's hard drive. The operating system has several built-in folders where it stores various items, but the one of these that most concerns you is your home folder, located in the Users folder and named with your login name. Here you can store anything you want, and you can create and name subfolders to organize your files as you want.

➤ One method of keeping your files organized is to use aliases. An alias is a small pointer file that refers to another file; if you double-click the alias, its original file opens instead. They're useful for providing access to a file or folder from more than one place in your drive's organizational structure.

➤ With the size of today's hard drives, it's easy to lose files, no matter how organized you get. Sherlock is a powerful search utility built in to Mac OS X that can search for files based on their names, their contents, or their file attributes, such as size or modification date. You can work with found folders in the Sherlock window by moving them, opening them, printing them, or locating them in a Finder window.

Chapter 6

Sharing Your Mac with Multiple Users

In This Chapter

➤ Why Mac OS X is designed for multiple users

➤ Logging in and out to change users

➤ Setting up new users and changing user settings

➤ Enabling the root user—and why you probably shouldn't

➤ Keeping your files in their place

➤ Sharing files with other users

Although previous Mac systems supported multiple users, Mac OS X is designed from the ground up to be used by more than one person (not at the same time, of course!). The very first time you start it up, you're asked to create a user name and password that you'll use to log in. It might seem strange at first to many users, but this setup has advantages you might not have considered. Mainly, it keeps each user's documents safe from other users, whether they're co-workers or just three-year-olds with sticky fingers.

Another advantage to Mac OS X's multiple-user scheme is that you can set up your Mac to look and work the way you want it to—and so can every other user of the same computer. When you log in, you'll see your Desktop picture, your version of the Dock, and your Home folder. Anyone else who logs in will see their own setup rather than yours. Here's how it all works...

Logging In, Logging Out

A multiuser system is like an automatic teller machine. People let the machine know who they are by entering their personal identification numbers, and then they can access their bank accounts. With a multiuser computer, you enter your name and your password to access your files. The first time you do this is at startup, when you see the login screen. Entering your user name and password lets the Mac know how it should start up: which desktop picture to display, and so on.

You can change users without restarting your Mac. To log out, click the Desktop and choose **Apple menu**, **Log Out**. Click **Log Out** (or press Return) and wait for a minute. The system quits all the active programs, including the Finder, and presents you with a new login screen. Enter a name and password to log in as another user. If the dialog box clears your entry and shakes back and forth, either you spelled the user name wrong or you entered the wrong password; try again.

You'll need to enter a user name and password in some dialog boxes, as well. For example, the Startup Disk pane in the System Preferences may require you to enter an Administrator name and password before you can make changes. The idea here is that if you're not an *Admin*, you shouldn't be changing certain things about how your Mac works.

Show Info

Admins Administer

The first login name and password you created are automatically made an **Admin** account. Any Admin user has access to most of the files on your Mac and can lock and unlock system-level settings such as which OS your Mac should use when it restarts. Initially, the only Admin user is the first user account created on the system, but any user can become an Admin user—see "Setting Up Users," in the following section.

Read Me

I Yam Who I Yam

As I write this, Mac OS X ships with the initial login screen turned off. If you find that your system is set up to present you with the login screen, and you are the only person who uses your computer, or you don't want to assign user accounts, you can bypass the login screen. In the Desktop, choose **Apple menu**, **System Preferences** and click the **Login** icon. In the Login pane, click the **Login Window** tab and check the **Automatically Log In** box. If the lock button shows a closed padlock, you'll need to click the padlock and enter an Admin user name and password before making changes here.

Here a User, There a User

If more than one person will be using your Mac, you'll probably want to set up an account for each person. Even if you're the only person using your Mac, you can set up different user accounts for different purposes. For example, if you were going to be scanning and adjusting photos for part of each day, you could set up a user account in which the Desktop is a neutral gray, Photoshop starts up automatically when you log in, and the Dock is hidden. When you're finished working on that project for the day, log out and back in with your regular user name, and your Desktop picture and other settings are back the way you like them.

Setting Up Users

The Users pane of the System Preferences allows you to add new users and change settings for existing users. Click the Desktop and choose **Apple menu**, **System Preferences**, or click its icon in the Dock.

When you open the Users pane, you see a list of the users that currently exist (see Figure 6.1). Before making changes, you might need to click the lock button and log in as an Admin user—at this point, that's the first user account you created (see "Adding Admins," next, to make other users Admins). You can make changes after you're logged in.

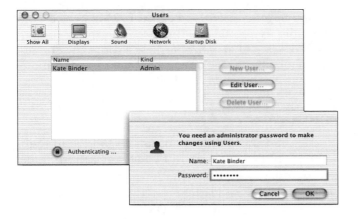

Figure 6.1

Before you can make any changes in Users, you might have to supply an Admin password.

> ➤ Click **New User** to add a user. You'll enter the user's full name, a short version he or she can use to log in, and a password (in two places to make sure you get it right). You can enter a password hint, too, to be displayed if the user enters an incorrect password.

> ➤ Click a user's name and click **Edit User** to change a user name or password.

> ➤ Click **Edit User** and click the **Allow User to Administer This Machine** box to make that user an Admin.

When you're finished adding and editing users, click the lock button if you don't want non-Admin users to be able to make further changes.

The User at the Root of It All

The only account that has enough privileges to do *everything* is one called *root*, a term that's obviously a hangover from Mac OS X's Unix background. It's not listed in the System Preferences' Users pane, but it exists regardless. However, the root account is disabled, so it doesn't come into play until you enable it. I'll explain how to do that in a minute, but first let's take a look at what root can do and why that's kind of scary.

The Best Password

When you choose a root password, make it a good one—use capital and lowercase letters, mix in some numbers with the letters, and don't use a word other people know, such as your mother's maiden name. Because the root account can access your entire computer, you don't want anyone to be able to guess your root password.

When would you need to use the root account? 99.99% of the time you won't need to use it at all. It has access to all the files and folders on your hard drive, including folders that are hidden when you're logged in as any other user. This means that you can use the root account to mess with Mac OS X's guts—which is not something most Mac users want to do because the system is much more complex and more esoteric than any previous Mac system. Being logged in as root also gives you access to other users' home folders. If you need to move or delete files or folders that belong to other users, you can either log in as each of the other users, one at a time, or you can log in as root and take care of all your business at once. Just be sure you remember to log out and log back in with another account when you're finished.

Now, here's how to enable the root account, if you need to do so:

Cutting Out the Root

If you decide to disable root access to your Mac—a good idea if you don't use the root account often—you can follow the same procedure you used to enable root access, except that you'll choose **Domain, Security, Disable Root User**.

1. Start up NetInfo Manager; it's located in the Utilities folder within your Applications folder.
2. Click the lock button in the NetInfo Manager window and enter an Admin user name and password, then click **OK**.
3. Choose **Domain, Security, Enable Root User**. If this is the first time you're working with root, you'll see a dialog box letting you know that you haven't set a root password; just click **OK**.
4. Enter a password for the root account.
5. Enter the password again and click **Verify**.
6. Click the lock button again to lock the root account so no one else can change its password.

I know I said this a few paragraphs ago, but I'm going to say it again. Don't enable the root account unless you need it, and don't log in with the root account unless you must. When you are logged in as root, do what needs doing and log out. Then, log back in as yourself. As my favorite Unix geek tells me, "Only a Windows user would be dumb enough to log in every day as root!"

Playing Well with Others

When you're sharing a computer with other people, there are two things everyone wants: to keep his or her own files safe and secure, and to be able to share files with others on occasion. Mac OS X makes it possible for you to accomplish both of these goals.

Separate Folders Make Good Neighbors

Imagine that you're sharing an apartment with two other people. The house rule goes like this: Be as messy as you want in your own room, but keep your personal stuff out of the living room, kitchen, and bathroom. This rule makes it easier to get along with your roommates, and Mac OS X has the same kind of rule to make it easier to get along with other users or your Mac.

Each user has a home folder, and your home folder is called by your user name. It's the first thing you see when you initially log in to your Mac—a Finder window showing the contents of your home folder. And you can always get back home again quickly by choosing **Go**, **Home** or pressing Option+Cmd+H. Here, you can be as messy as you want to be without bothering anyone else. You can create folders, delete and rename folders, and add or delete files. Go to town: It's your home folder, after all.

Go To

There are several folders already in your home folder before you move in. The Documents folder is where you're supposed to keep your files (like a closet), although you're not required to do so. The Library contains preference files that are tied to your user account. And the Public folder is where you put files that you want to make available to other users. Other preinstalled folders in your home folder have more specialized uses that you'll discover as you need them.

Rearranging the Furniture

For a look at how your Mac's entire hard drive is arranged under Mac OS X, as well as more info about what to do with your home folder, see Chapter 5, "Managing Your Files."

Practice Safe Sharing

All this protection sounds like a great idea—until you actually *want* another user to have access to your files. How do you accomplish that? Here's how.

Only you can change or delete files and folders in your home folder or in most of the other folders it contains (see Figure 6.2). But there's one exception: the Public folder. Any user of your Mac can read or copy the files in your Public folder. If you turn on File Sharing, these files are also available to users who are logged in over a network. But only you can delete items from your Public folder.

Figure 6.2

You'll see this warning if you try to move or delete a file that doesn't belong to you.

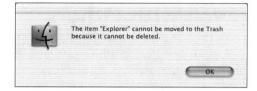

You can give files to another user by putting them in that user's Drop Box. To see another user's home folder, open a Finder window and click the Users button in the toolbar. All home folders are stored in the Users folder; double-click the one you want to open. The Drop Box folder is inside the Public folder. To add files, drag them onto the icon for the Drop Box, or open in a Finder window and drag files into the window. After a file is in there, though, you won't be able to get it back—you can't even see what files are in another user's Drop Box—so be sure you save a copy of the file in your home folder if necessary.

The Least You Need to Know

➤ Mac OS X is designed to make Macs easy for more than one person to use. The system protects your files from being deleted or changed by other users, while allowing you to exchange files with others when you want to.

➤ A Mac can have as many users as its owner wants. Any user can be designated as an Admin user, who can make changes to system settings, such as Startup Disk, even when they are locked. The most powerful user is one that doesn't appear in the Users window: root, an account that has access to all files on your Mac.

➤ Your home folder is where you can store all your files. Other users can't change the files in your home folder. If you want to share files with others, you can put the files in your Public folder. When you want to give a file to a specific person, you can put it in that person's Drop Box folder.

Chapter 7

Free Software! (Using Mac OS X's Built-In Apps)

In This Chapter

➤ Using desk accessory programs

➤ Using TextEdit for word processing

➤ Drawing pictures

➤ Working with sound and vision

When you think of the programs you're likely to use on your Mac, you probably think of applications such as Internet Explorer, Photoshop, or FileMaker. You probably don't think of TextEdit, PDF Compositor, or Address Book.

It's easy to overlook these small applications that come with Mac OS X; however, you might be surprised at how much you can accomplish using them. Here's your chance to take a look at some of the programs you already have installed on your computer—the ones you don't have to pay extra for.

You'll find icons for some of these programs in the Dock at the bottom of your screen, but all of them can be found in the Applications folder. To get there, just click anywhere on the Desktop and choose **Go**, **Applications** or press **Option+Cmd+A**. Some of the apps mentioned in this chapter are right in the Applications folder, whereas others can be found in the GrabBag and Utilities folders, lurking inside the Applications folder.

Besides the programs mentioned here, there's lots more cool stuff in your Applications folder, so be sure you explore!

Easy Access

If you find yourself using particular programs often, you'll probably get pretty sick of locating them in the Applications folder every time you want to use them. There are two ways around this. For programs you use all the time, just drag their icons into the Dock while they're not running. And for programs that you use only when you're working on a specific project, **Cmd+Option+drag** their icons into the project's folder to create aliases.

If You Like This

There isn't enough room here to go into every function of each of these programs, so I'll just try to give you the high points. For more info about getting stuff done with any program, start the program and head for the Help menu.

Everything but the Stapler

Once upon a time, the term desk accessory referred to objects people kept on their desks. Then Mac came along, and desk accessories became useful little programs found in the Apple menu. With Mac OS X, the Apple menu has a different function, but the desk accessory lives on—in the form of useful little programs that take over the functions of those objects you keep on your desk (see Figure 7.1).

Calculator

Need to add up some numbers? Whip out your Calculator (it's in the Applications folder) and get started. It works just like a real-world pocket calculator. You can either click the buttons on the calculator to enter numbers or functions, or you can use the equivalent keys on your keyboard. In fact, if you're used to using an adding machine, try using the numeric keypad with the Calculator and watch those numbers fly.

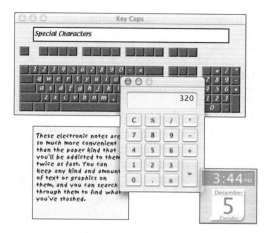

Figure 7.1

Mac OS X really does come with electronic equivalents of everything but your stapler.

Clock

The Clock displays the time and date in a floating window that you can position wherever you want it on your screen. The Clock preferences (choose **Clock**, **Preferences**) enable you to choose an analog clock (with hands) or a digital one and also enables you to restrict the Clock to the Dock. You'll find the Clock in the Applications folder.

Key Caps

Each font that your computer uses has many more characters than the basic numbers, letters, and punctuation. For example, you can type accented e's (é or è), currency symbols (£ or ¢), and math symbols (≤ or Δ). To see the different characters that each font includes, start up the Key Caps application. Choose the font you want to view from the Font menu, and the available characters appear. If you press any of the modifier keys (Shift, Option, and Command), or any combination of them, you'll see the characters each letter turns into when those keys are pressed. Key Caps lives in the Utilities folder within the Applications folder.

Read Me

Telling Time

If you like the Clock but you don't want it to take valuable space on your screen, drop it into the Dock—its Dock icon still shows the correct time.

Read Me

Running the Numbers

There are three big differences between Mac OS X's Calculator and your pocket calculator. First, you can't lose the Calculator. Second, its batteries never run out. And third, you can transfer the results of a calculation into another program. When you've finished doing your math, choose **File**, **Copy** or press **Cmd+C** to copy the number displayed. Click in the other program's window and choose **File**, **Paste** or press **Cmd+V** to paste the number.

Stickies

So, you're a stickies addict—it's time to admit it. The edges of your monitor are crusted with these handy slips of paper, and they keep unsticking themselves and fluttering helplessly to the floor. Fortunately, your Mac has the answer, and it's called…Stickies.

These electronic notes are so much more convenient than the paper kind that you'll be addicted to them twice as fast. You can keep any kind and amount of text or graphics on them, and you can search through them to find what you've stashed.

To start Stickies, locate it in the Applications folder. When Stickies is running, you can make a new sticky note by choosing **File**, **New Note** or pressing **Cmd+N**. Start writing, or copy and paste the text you want to save. To search your stickies, choose **Edit**, **Find**, **Find**, type the word or phrase you're looking for, and click **Find**. You can also enter text with which to replace the found text, and you have the choice of searching one sticky or all your stickies.

You can change the appearance of stickies, too. Each sticky can be any size you want; just click the lower-right corner and drag to resize it. To choose a color for a sticky, click it and make a choice from the Color menu. You can choose any font and color for selected text in a sticky; the options are all under the Note menu.

Sticky Service

Many applications in which you can select text have access to the Sticky service, which means that you can create a new sticky from selected text. Just click and drag to select the text you want to save, and then choose **Services**, **Make Sticky** from the application's main menu, at the left end of the menu bar.

Writing the Great American Memo

Although you probably won't choose to write the great American novel in TextEdit, it's a fine tool for cranking out a quick memo or letter (see Figure 7.2). It saves documents in RTF (Rich Text Format), which supports bold, italic, and other formatting, so you can open TextEdit files in more advanced word processors if you want to do things to them that TextEdit can't do, such as formatting them in multiple columns. You'll find TextEdit in the Applications folder.

TextEdit always starts up with a blank document window. After you've used that one, you can create a new document in TextEdit by choosing **File**, **New**. You can enter text by typing or by copying it from another application (such as from a Web page in Internet Explorer) and pasting it into your document. Then, you can apply formatting to selected text; here's how:

➤ To change the font, choose **Format**, **Font**, **Font Panel**. Pick a font from the Family list, choose a variation from the Typeface list, and specify a size from the Sizes list or enter a value in the Size field.

➤ To change the style, choose another option from the **Font** submenu under the **Format** menu: **Bold**, **Italic**, or **Underline**.

➤ To change the color, choose **Format**, **Font**, **Colors**. In the Colors panel, click one of the four buttons to use different methods of specifying colors: the standard color picker, grayscale or color sliders, a palette based on an image, or a list of standard colors. Or click the magnifying glass button to choose a color from anywhere on the screen—just poise the magnifying glass cursor over it and click. When you have a color you like, click **Apply** to change the text.

➤ To align text, choose an option from the **Format**, **Text** submenu: **Align Left**, **Center**, or **Align Right**.

Instant Text Formatting

You can save time in TextEdit by copying the font, style, and size of section of text to another section. Select the text whose attributes you want to copy and choose **Format**, **Font**, **Copy Font**. Then, select the text you want to change and choose **Format**, **Font**, **Paste Font**.

TextEdit has more options—it's actually pretty impressive for a freebie text editor. If you think you'll be using TextEdit, I encourage you to explore its menus and panels and try different things. Just remember that if you make a change you don't like, you can always choose Edit, Undo or press Cmd+Z to go back one or more steps.

Figure 7.2

When you're ready to write the great American memo, TextEdit is the tool for the job.

Move Over, Michelangelo

All right, so you're actually pretty unlikely to use these tools to create any artwork that will rival the Sistine Chapel's ceiling—but, hey, beauty is in the eye of the beholder. Mac OS X's built-in art and multimedia include a program for viewing images from your digital camera, the Web, or anywhere else; one for viewing movie files and video over the Internet; and one for managing images created with a digital camera.

Preview

Preview is a utility for quickly opening and viewing image files in formats including PDF, TIFF, PICT, GIF, and JPEG. You can resave any image opened in Preview as a TIFF file; choose **File**, **Save As**, enter a name, and click **Save**.

If you click the Preview button in the Print dialog box while printing from any application (other than Classic applications that use Mac OS 9), Preview opens and displays the page. From the preview, you can click Print to continue printing the file or choose **File**, **Save As PDF** to create a PDF file of the document.

Figure 7.3

Mac OS X's built-in programs allow you to work with digital camera images, play movies, and view graphic images in a variety of formats.

QuickTime Player

The QuickTime Player can handle downloaded movies or streaming video from the Web. To play one of the built-in channels, just click the TV button to see a list of them. Double-click on any one to see what it's broadcasting at the moment. To play a movie or sound file that you've saved on your hard drive, choose **File**, **Open Movie** and select the file you want to play. You can use the controls on the Player just like the ones on your VCR to rewind, play, and fast forward the movie or sound file, and there's a volume control to the left of the other buttons.

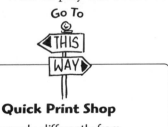

Go To

Quick Print Shop

Printing works differently from Classic applications that it does from programs that run directly under Mac OS X. To learn more about Classic applications and how Classic works, see Chapter 2, "Making Friends with Mac OS X." For more on how printing works in Mac OS X, turn to Chapter 12, "Printing Up a Storm."

Image Capture

The next generation of camera-using consumers will likely not even know what film is for. After all, who needs film when you can use a digital camera to capture an image, edit it, print as many copies as you like, e-mail it around the world, post it on the Web, or anything else you'd want to do with a picture?

Of course, with digital camera images the first step is getting the image out of the camera and into your computer. That's where Image Capture comes in. This handy little utility is designed for one purpose: to transfer images from any digital camera plugged into your computer's USB port to a designated folder on your hard drive. Along the way it can rename the images to your specifications and perform other tasks, such as uploading them to your iDisk (your free Web space on Apple's Web site).

Step into My Web Site

These days, everyone who's anyone is on the Web. To get your own site up (and learn about iDisk and the other cool Web tools Apple supplies free to Mac users), check out Chapter 15, "Publishing on the Web."

The Least You Need to Know

➤ Mac OS X comes with a multitude of applications—some simple utilities and others more sophisticated. Although third-party applications are still necessary, there's no point in overlooking the free software you already have.

➤ Desk accessories fill the same functions as their real-world counterparts, only more efficiently. And you'll never run out of stickies or lose your address book with the Mac OS X equivalents.

➤ For low-end word processing, consider TextEdit, Mac OS X's built-in text editor. Because it reads and saves files in RTF format, it's fully compatible with its more capable cousins, and it's always there when you need it.

➤ Art and multimedia tools such as Preview, QuickTime Player, and Image Capture enable you to express your ideas visually, work with your own and other people's images, and watch streaming video from the Internet.

Chapter 8

Using Third-Party Applications

In This Chapter

➤ The different kinds of Mac OS X applications

➤ How to run the Mac software you already have

➤ Installing new Classic software

➤ New programs on the horizon

While writing this book, I asked a few people to sit down at my Mac and take a look at Mac OS X so they could tell me what they thought of it. Mainly, what I found out was that, despite all the system's new features, what people really wanted was to *do* something. In other words, there's only so much time you can spend playing with the Dock and the Desktop before you go looking for some programs that will let you get some work (or some play) done.

Mac OS X runs a lot of software. To start with, it runs most of the applications people have been using with Mac OS 9. And added to those are the exciting new programs that are being written to run strictly on Mac OS X—new Web browsers, new graphics programs, and more. This chapter takes a look at the three categories of applications you can use with Mac OS X and spotlights a few new programs I think you're going to like—a lot.

More Apps Than You Can Shake a Mouse At

Apple maintains a page on its Web site that showcases applications written to work with Mac OS X. For the latest list on what third-party apps are available for Mac OS X, see **www.apple.com/macosx/applications/**.

Carbon Fibers

To give software developers a head start on creating software for Mac OS X, Apple created a group of system-level features that were planned to be the basis of software running in both Mac OS X and earlier versions of the system (Mac OS 8.1 and later). This group of system functions is called Carbon, because it was intended to be the basis for all software running on a Mac. What this means to you is that Carbon applications will run on either Mac OS 9 or Mac OS X, changing their appearance to match the system (see Figure 8.1).

Figure 8.1

On the top is StuffIt Expander's Preferences dialog box in Mac OS 9. The bottom dialog box is the same thing, only in Mac OS X.

Because Mac OS X is a brand-new operating system, the first applications released for it are likely to be Carbon programs that can be used on either Mac OS 9 or Mac OS X. As more people use Mac OS X, developers will release programs written just for the new system using the Cocoa development environment (see the next section, "Cocoa Loco").

Read Me

Two-Way Street

Technically, you can run the same Carbon program in Classic mode or in native Mac OS X mode. Most Carbon programs, however, don't supply a way to let your Mac know which way you want them to run. To see whether the software developer has given you this option, click the application and choose **File**, **Show Info**. If you see a check box labeled Open in the Classic Environment in the Info window, you can choose which way the program should run. I used this option when I found that an early Mac OS X release of my e-mail program was actually more stable under Classic than under Mac OS X.

Cocoa Loco

Like Carbon applications, Cocoa programs will run under Mac OS X—but they won't work in Mac OS 9, so they can't be used in Classic or on a Mac that has been started with Mac OS 9. These are the most advanced Mac OS X applications, with the coolest features. Many tools are the same across all Cocoa programs, such as

➤ **The Colors panel**—Any Mac OS X program can use the Colors panel, which incorporates several different standard color pickers that you can use to choose colors for text or graphic objects, depending on what program you're in (see Figure 8.2). TextEdit and Mail, for example, use the Color panel (see Chapter 7, "Free Software! (Using Mac OS X's Built-In Apps)," for more information).

➤ **The Font panel**—In the Font panel, you can specify fonts for selected text. You can organize fonts into collections—the fonts you use for a particular job, or your corporate fonts, for example. When you click on a collection in the left column, the middle column lists the font families in that column, while the next column shows the styles available within each font family and the right column lists font sizes (see Figure 8.3).

Figure 8.2

The Colors panel looks the same in any program in which it appears.

Figure 8.3

The Font panel enables you to group your favorite fonts into collections.

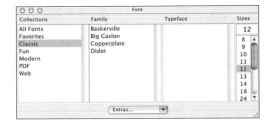

Oh, the Possibilities!

The extent of a software developer's creativity is the only limit on what you can do with Services. Take some time to explore the options in various programs' Services submenus—you'll be glad you did.

➤ **Services**—Using Services, you can use some tools from one application in other programs. For example, you can select a range of text in TextEdit and choose **TextEdit**, **Services**, **Stickies**, **Make Sticky**. This command creates a new sticky note that contains the selected text. You can also select text on a sticky and choose **Stickies**, **Services**, **Mail**, **Mail Text** to create a new e-mail message containing the selected text.

➤ **Print Preview**—You can see a preview of how any file will look when it's printed by choosing **File**, **Print Preview** or by choosing **File**, **Print** and clicking the **Preview** button. This is also the way to make an Acrobat PDF file from any file that you can print; after you look at the preview, choose **File**, **Save As PDF**.

Most of the applications that come with Mac OS X, such as TextEdit and Sketch, are Cocoa applications.

Jurassic Classic

Mac OS X's Classic utility sets up a protected area of the system in which Mac OS 9 is running. Classic applications are the same software Mac OS 9 users know and love, running within Classic on Mac OS X. If you're already using Mac OS 9, you'll be able to run the applications you have now within Classic.

Can I See Some ID?

How can you tell whether an application that's already installed is Classic? Here are a few clues:

➤ Its icon doesn't scale smoothly when you change the size of the Dock or mouse over it with magnification turned on (see Figure 8.4). Chapter 20, "The Desktop and the Dock As You Like Them," explains these Dock features.

Stickies   Stickies

Figure 8.4

The Mac OS X Stickies icon (left) is much smoother than the scaled-up Mac OS 9 Stickies icon.

➤ When you double-click its icon to start the program, you see the Classic window for a minute or two before the program finishes its startup.

➤ When you're using the program, the menu bar, windows, and dialog boxes are gray instead of white, and you see Mac OS 9's multicolored Apple icon in the menu bar instead of the blue Apple icon of Mac OS X.

Because Classic applications are really running in Mac OS 9, rather than directly in Mac OS X, they can't take advantage of Mac OS X's new features (such as Print Preview and Services). For the most part, they should work just as they would under a normal installation of Mac OS 9. You might find that programs that interact directly with hardware (such as scanners or tape drives) don't work as expected. In these cases, you'll probably need to find either an update to that program or a replacement program that *does* work correctly under either Mac OS X or Classic.

Read Me

Crashing in Classic

By now you've probably heard a lot about how Mac OS X is more stable—meaning, less likely to crash—than other systems (such as Mac OS 9 and Windows). There's just one exception: Classic and its applications. The Classic environment is really just Mac OS 9, and applications running in it are the old-fashioned kind as well. That means that they're just as likely to crash (or not crash) as they ever were. If an application is stable under Mac OS 9, it will probably do fine in Classic. Chapter 28, "Troubleshooting," has information on how to deal with crashes.

A Classic Installation

Apple does recommend that you reboot in Mac OS 9 before you install Classic applications. To change the system your Mac boots from, follow these steps:

1. Click the Desktop or the Desktop icon in the Dock and choose **Apple menu, System Preferences**.

2. Click **Show All**, and then click the **Startup Disk** icon. The program scans your hard drive to find bootable systems and displays an icon for each.

3. If the lock button shows a closed padlock, wait until you see a folder icon for each system and the mouse cursor returns to an arrow (instead of the spinning color wheel), and then click the lock button.

4. Enter a user name and password and click **OK**. It doesn't matter which account you use, as long as it's an Admin account.

5. Now click the icon for the Mac OS 9 system you want to use (see Figure 8.5), and then click the lock button again if you want to lock the Startup Disk setting.

6. Choose **Apple menu, Restart**.

Only Admins Allowed

Mac OS X's user accounts fall into two categories: regular and Admin. If you're logged in as an Admin user, you have access to a few more files and folders than other users, and you can make system-level changes in places like the Startup Disk pane when they're locked. To see which user accounts are designated as Admin accounts, check the Users pane of the System Preferences.

Figure 8.5

You can use Startup Disk to specify any system that's installed on your Mac as the one that should be used when you restart.

Your Mac will reboot from the Mac OS 9 System Folder you chose instead of the Mac OS X system. When you're ready to go back to Mac OS X, use the System Disk or Startup Disk control panel in Mac OS 9 (depending on which version of Mac OS 9 you're using) to specify the Mac OS X system, and restart again. For more information about the System Disk control panel, see "Bipolar Shift: Switching Between Mac OS X and Mac OS 9" in Chapter 1, "Meet the New Mac."

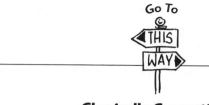

Classically Compatible

For a list of applications that Apple has tested with the Classic environment, go to **www.apple.com/macosx/applications/** and click the **Classic** icon on the right side of the page.

What's New, Dock?

After you get used to using Mac OS X, ideally you won't have to start up Classic to run every single application. The more apps you have that run native in Mac OS X—either Carbon or Cocoa—the happier you'll be. With that in mind, here's a look at some Mac OS X-native programs that should make you very happy indeed. There are lots more—the applications mentioned here are just a sampling intended to get you started.

Wild Wild Web

Mac OS X ships with Microsoft Internet Explorer, which is already one of the two standard Web browsers for Mac (along with Netscape Communicator). You don't have to stick with the Web browsers everyone else uses, though; Mac OS X users have alternatives that include iCab (www.icab.de), a speedy and efficient little browser from Germany, and OmniWeb (www.omnigroup.com), from an early and impressive Mac OS X developer.

Keeping In Touch

If you're online, chances are you're as addicted to e-mail as I am. And for those times when even e-mail isn't fast enough, there's instant messaging—a great way to keep in touch with friends, family, and co-workers at all hours of the day and night. E-mail and instant messaging clients available for Mac OS X include PowerMail (www.ctmdev.com), a fast and flexible e-mail client whose users have abandoned Mac standby Eudora in droves, and epicware's Fire (www.epicware.com), a multiplatform instant messaging client that's compatible with AOL Instant Messenger, ICQ, and Yahoo! Pager.

Modern Design

Design and graphics pros are excited about Mac OS X for several reasons. For one thing, it's gorgeous, which makes a designer's heart sing. And for another thing, its PDF-based imaging makes everything you create in it look gorgeous, too. Graphics applications are sure to be a popular category for Mac OS X developers.

Two programs stand out from the pack: TIFFany (www.caffeineSoft.com) and the Stone Super Seven Suite (www.stone.com). The former is an image processor with some advanced features even Photoshop doesn't have, whereas the latter is a group of applications that enable you to do graphic design with page layout and Web publishing features, manage digital photos, track time and bill clients, and produce PDF files.

At the Office

No matter what kind of work you do, chances are you need to use a word processor at least occasionally. The same probably holds true for other business applications such as databases and spreadsheets. Although Microsoft's Office package is quite popular in the business world, Mac users have another option: the AppleWorks integrated office application. Unless you're required to use Microsoft Office, AppleWorks is definitely worth a look (www.apple.com/appleworks/).

Like other office packages, AppleWorks is really several applications in one. It includes six modules: word processing, spreadsheet, database, presentation, drawing, and painting. AppleWorks doesn't take up nearly as much hard disk space as six applications, and it needs nowhere near as much memory.

The Least You Need to Know

➤ Mac OS X applications come in three categories: Classic, Carbon, and Cocoa. Classic apps are carryovers from previous systems that require the Classic environment to run. Carbon apps are rewritten to work in either Mac OS 9 or Mac OS X. And Cocoa applications are completely new programs, written specifically for Mac OS X, which take advantage of all Mac OS X's new features.

➤ To run Classic applications, you must have Mac OS 9 installed on your computer. The Classic environment, itself an application, starts up a Mac OS 9 system within which older programs can run. For the most part, Classic programs work the same way in Classic as they do on a Mac that's been booted from Mac OS 9.

➤ Carbon applications can run in Mac OS 9 or Mac OS X, taking on the appearance of the system under which they're running. When they're running under Mac OS X, Carbon apps can have access to most of the cool features of Mac OS X—if their developers have done the work to allow it.

➤ To get the most from Mac OS X, you'll want to run Cocoa applications. At first these might be harder to find than Classic or Carbon programs, but as more and more people use Mac OS X, more Mac programs will be written under Cocoa.

Chapter 9

Working with Audio and Video

In This Chapter

➤ Putting tunes on your Mac with iTunes

➤ Creating mix CDs from your favorite tunes

➤ Moving video from your camcorder to your Mac

➤ Editing video clips into a full-fledged movie

➤ Saving movies to the Web, to tape, or to DVD

Back in the 1980s, the original Macs—with their *WYSIWYG* interface and, later, laser printers—started the desktop publishing revolution. Suddenly, anyone could design, typeset, and print out anything from business cards to entire books. These days, Apple has laid the foundation for a digital multimedia revolution—one that will allow anyone to mix up confections of digital video and audio and share them with their friends.

What all this means to you is that your Mac enables you to play and burn your own music CDs and produce your own movies. This chapter will give you an idea of how these processes work and how easily you can get started. Believe me, you won't need any more information to get started playing tunes on your Mac, but if you want to delve more deeply into moviemaking, I recommend grabbing a copy of *The Complete Idiot's Guide to iMovie 2*, by Brad Miser.

Whizzy Wig?

WYSIWYG stands for "what you see is what you get." Old-style typesetting systems required the user to type in special codes for typeface, point size, and other settings, so you couldn't see what the final product would look like until you printed it. Modern desktop publishing software shows you right on your screen what your settings will produce, so what you see on your screen is really what you get when you print your work.

Can't Buy Me Tunes

One of the best things about Apple's iTunes software is that it's free. It comes installed on Macs sold in 2001 and later, and it's a free download for people using older Macs (`www.apple.com/itunes/`).

The DJ on Your Desktop

The stereo as a standalone system might be coming to the end of its lifetime—with the musical Mac, who needs it? Using iTunes, you can play digital music on your Mac, create mix CDs from your collection of tunes, and even listen to the radio over the Internet.

When you first start up iTunes, its Setup Assistant offers to look for *MP3* files on your hard drive and catalog them for you. When it's finished doing this, your iTunes library contains listings for any music files iTunes found. Now you can play them just by double-clicking their names in the list, and you can create playlists to play series of songs in any order you like.

Making Music Small

MP3 files are digital music files that have been compressed in size by removing the redundant sound information that human ears can't hear. A song from a CD-ROM can be reduced to one-twelfth its previous size by conversion to MP3 format. And because MP3 files are so small, they can be transferred over the Internet easily. You can play MP3s using your Mac or using a device such as the Rio Player (`www.riohome.com`).

Want more songs to choose from? Pop an audio CD into your CD drive, click the **Import** button, and iTunes copies the songs off the CD and saves them to your hard drive in MP3 format. As it goes, it can automatically add artist and title info to the files from the Internet's CDDB database (see Figure 9.1).

Figure 9.1

iTunes can keep track of the artist and performer for each tune you add.

Whenever you download MP3s, you can add them to your Library by dragging them into the Library window. You can search your Library collection by artist, album, genre, year released, title, sample rate, or comments. When you've found the songs you're looking for, you can add them to a playlist by dragging and dropping them on the playlist's name.

If you want to take your tunes with you (and you have a *CD-R* or *CD-RW* drive), click a playlist's name and click the **Burn** button to put the tunes on a CD that you can play in almost any CD player. If you have a personal MP3 player, you can hook it up to your Mac and drag tunes from the iTunes window to the device's icon on your Desktop (or in the Computer Finder window, if you don't have disk icons set to display on the Desktop).

Just for fun, iTunes provides a constantly changing light show that's synchronized with the music you're playing, as well as an Internet radio that can tune into Web stations from around the world. You can switch from playing MP3s to playing Internet radio by clicking **Radio Tuner** in the iTunes window's left column. Personally, I like the '80s Pop stations, but you'll find dozens of categories ranging from Blues to Electronica to Reggae/Island.

All this happens just as smoothly in the background as in the foreground, so you can truly listen while you work, and you can even keep on listening to new tunes while you're burning CDs.

CDs R Us

CD-R (CD-Recordable) and **CD-RW** (CD-ReWritable) are two varieties of CDs that you can create. Blank CD-R discs are inexpensive, but you can record on them only once; CD-RW discs cost more, but you can erase them and use them several times.

No Burning Allowed

The first Mac OS X version of iTunes did not support burning CDs. If you are using version 1.1 for Mac OS X, check the Apple Web site for an update (**www.apple.com/itunes/**).

The iTunes window has two modes: a full-fledged display and a miniaturized version with only the necessary controls to play tunes (see Figure 9.2). To minimize the window, or maximize it when it's in small mode, click the green button.

Smash Mouth
Elapsed Time: 0:21

Figure 9.2
The miniature version of the iTunes interface is perfect for when you just want to play music while you're working or surfing the Web.

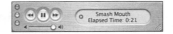

Let's Go to the iMovies

Have you always wanted to be Cecil B. DeMille (or perhaps Stephen Spielberg or Quentin Tarantino)? Now's your chance. With a camcorder, your Mac, and Apple's iMovie software, you can star in, direct, and produce your own movies.

iMovie 2 packs a lot of tools into an uncluttered workspace (see Figure 9.3). Its Monitor area is like a video monitor, where you view the video clips with which you're working. The Shelf holds video clips, special effects, titles, and audio clips that you can use in your projects. And at the bottom of the iMovie window, you'll find a Timeline and a Clip Viewer, where you can string together the different elements that you're using to construct a movie.

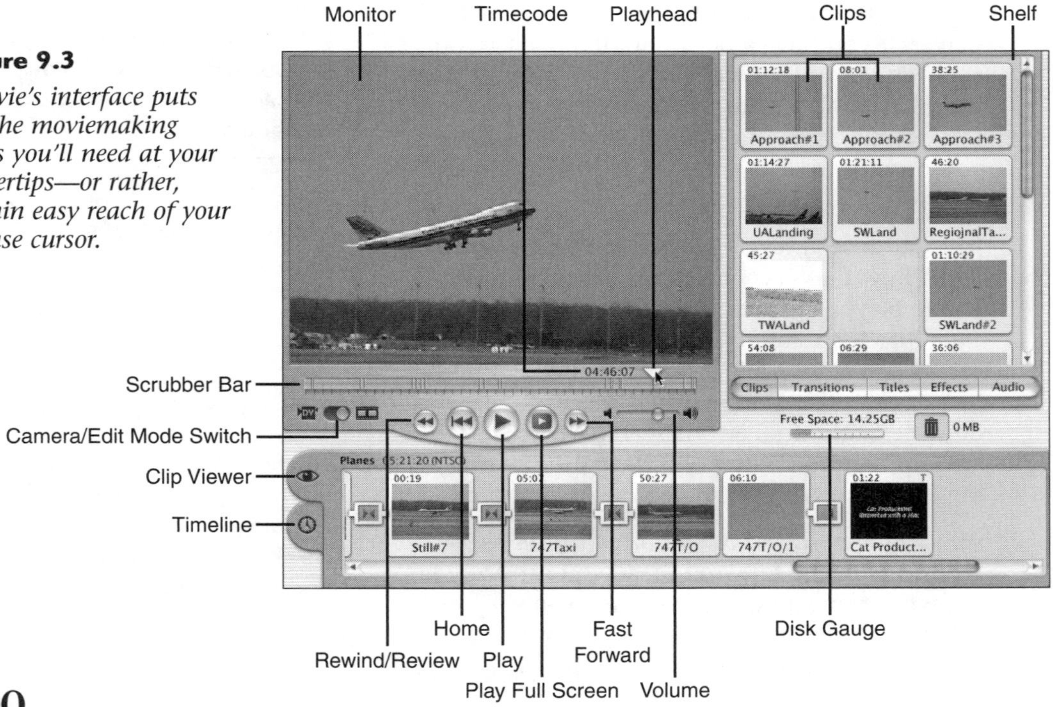
Monitor
Timecode
Playhead
Clips
Shelf
Scrubber Bar
Camera/Edit Mode Switch
Clip Viewer
Timeline
Home
Rewind/Review
Play
Play Full Screen
Fast Forward
Volume
Disk Gauge
Clips
Transitions
Titles
Effects
Audio
Free Space: 14.25GB
0 MB

Figure 9.3
iMovie's interface puts all the moviemaking tools you'll need at your fingertips—or rather, within easy reach of your mouse cursor.

Getting Video into Your Mac

The first step in making a movie is to transfer the footage ("clips") to iMovie. To accomplish this, you'll set your camera to its VCR setting (it might also be marked VTR) and connect the FireWire cable to the camera and your Mac. Start up iMovie.

If your camcorder is iMovie-compatible, you can click iMovie's Play, Stop, and other buttons to control the camcorder. Otherwise, you'll need to use the buttons on the camcorder. Click or press **Play** to start viewing the footage. When you see a section you want to import, click the **Import** button below the Monitor screen, and then click **Import** again or press the spacebar to stop importing. Or just let iMovie keep importing. All the clips are placed on the Shelf, ready to be edited.

Editing Video and Adding Cool Effects

After you've collected all the video clips you want to assemble into a movie, you can edit them down to just the sections you want to use by dragging crop markers along a slider. From there, assembling your movie is a simple matter of dragging and dropping each clip into the Clip Viewer area in the order you want to use them, and then dragging transitions between clips if you want. You can record your own sound effects with a microphone attached to your Mac, or import sound files you've downloaded and add them to the movie by dragging them to the Clip Viewer.

At any time, you can click **Play** to see how your movie is taking shape in the Monitor window, or you can click **Play Full Screen** to see the movie without any distraction from the iMovie window. If you want to experiment with more transitions, title formats, background images, and sound effects, you can download lots of each from the Apple Web site (`www.apple.com/imovie/`)

Read Me

The Best Things in Life

iMovie is free for a lot of people—Apple bundles it on all new Macs, and the Mac OS X version was a free download when Mac OS X first came out. For others, it's just $49 to download it from the Apple Store (`store.apple.com`).

Read Me

Film Festival

To see a few examples of what others have done with *iMovie*, check out the *iMovie* Gallery (`www.apple.com/imovie/gallery/`). My favorites include a dramatic depiction of a pet toad eating his dinner and a miniature opus called *Go Fetch!*, in which a dog named Glen fetches his tennis ball from a *long* way away.

Read Me

Let the Software Do the Work

If your preferences are set to allow it, iMovie will automatically create a new clip each time the scene changes on the tape.

Getting Your Opus Out There

When your movie is complete, you have three options for exporting it:

➤ Save it onto a videotape using your camcorder.

➤ Export it as a QuickTime movie that you can post on the Web or e-mail to your friends.

➤ Save it in a format that you can put on a DVD using Apple's iDVD software.

The best part is that you can make as many copies of your movies as you want, and each one will be just as clear as the original because they're digital files rather than data stored on fragile analog tapes.

Read Me

Tools for iMovies

If you want to put your iMovie projects on the Web, check out Apple's free iTools service. You can use it to set up a Web page featuring your movies, complete with a vintage television, drive-in screen, or other cool image framing the movies as they play.

The Hardware You'll Need

To use all the fun software covered in this chapter, you'll need to make sure your hardware is up to date, starting with your Mac itself.

To use iTunes to import music from CDs and play downloaded MP3s, you'll need any Mac with built-in USB ports, such as G4s, iBooks, recent PowerBooks, and iMacs. To burn CDs, you'll need a supported CD-R or CD-RW drive; see www.apple.com/itunes/compatibility/ for a list of third-party drives that work with iTunes. Of course, iTunes supports all internal Apple CD-RW drives.

You can run iMovie on just about any Power Mac, but you need a FireWire port to hook up a DV (digital video) camcorder and transfer footage to your Mac. You can add a FireWire port to an older Mac with an add-on card, but older Macs are also likely to be too slow to handle the high demand video processing places on the system.

Make Way for Movies

You will need lots and lots of disk space to create digital movies. Today's Macs come with large hard drives, and you'll need that space—trust me. iMovie constantly monitors your hard drive and displays the amount of free space; if you find yourself running out of room too often, you might want to buy a FireWire hard drive to plug in to your computer and store video clips on.

Of course, you'll also need a video camera, or camcorder. If you have an analog camcorder, you can buy a PCI digitizer card that will enable you to transfer footage to your Mac and export your movies to analog videotapes. You can also use a digital video (DV) camcorder hooked up to a VCR to transfer analog footage to your Mac for editing.

Finally, if you want to create DVDs, you'll need one of Apple's high-end Macs with a built-in DVD burner.

Some Cameras Are More Equal Than Others

Some camcorders work better with iMovie than others. Apple maintains a list of these models on its Web site (`www.apple.com/imovie/`).

The Fine Print

You've been waiting for this, right? It's the obligatory intellectual property rights lecture. Here goes:

When you write an article for publication or scan one of your photos to share with others, you want to be sure that it's not used in a way you wouldn't approve of and that you get the credit for creating it, right? Well, the same goes for anyone who records a song or makes a movie. Such things are called "intellectual property" because, although they don't have a physical form, they still belong to their creators.

What this means to you is that you must be aware of who owns the legal rights to a piece of intellectual property before you "borrow" it to use in one of your own projects. Many of the MP3 music files floating around the Internet, for example, have been copied illegally. Their creators don't get a share of the sales of the music because it's not being sold—it's being traded by people who have no right to do so. All of which doesn't give musicians much incentive to go on making new music, does it?

Bottom line: It's okay to, for example, use iTunes to listen to music imported from your CDs. It's not okay to take that music and give it to anyone who asks for it. And it's also not okay to use other people's movies or images in your iMovie projects without their permission.

The Least You Need to Know

➤ Apple's iTunes software provides you with a stereo system inside your Mac; it can import music from CDs, play downloaded MP3 files, and tune in to Internet radio stations. You can combine imported songs in any order you want and burn them to CDs, or you can transfer them to portable MP3 players.

➤ iMovie, on the other hand, is a movie studio inside your Mac. You can hook it up to a digital camcorder and edit video footage into movies, complete with soundtracks, special effects, and titles, with a minimum of effort.

➤ After you've created your movie, you can send it back to your camcorder, turn it into a small QuickTime file for e-mailing or posting on the Web, or put it on a DVD.

Chapter 10

The Games People Play

In This Chapter

➤ Playing your favorite Classic Mac games in Mac OS X

➤ Stocking up on the latest and greatest Mac OS X games

➤ Using gaming hardware devices to enhance your gaming experience

With a completely retooled imaging engine and sophisticated built-in 3D graphics support, Mac OS X has the potential to offer gamers the best-looking games they've ever played. Meanwhile, Mac OS X's preemptive multitasking ensures that game play continues to be smooth while your Mac does other things in the background (such as printing, running backups, and checking e-mail).

Using Mac OS X's Classic environment, you'll be able to continue playing your old favorites—and the new Mac OS X games are guaranteed to knock your socks off.

Making a List and Checking It Twice

Clan MacGaming, a Web site offering information, tips, and reviews of Mac games, is also keeping track of which games run under Mac OS X and how—in other words, whether they run only under Classic or have been released in Mac OS X–native versions. You can see their list at **www.clanmacgaming.com/macosx.php**.

The Mac's Classic Games

One of the nice things about Mac OS X is that you don't have to go out and get all new games to run with it, because it runs Mac OS 9 within the Classic environment. Pretty much any game you could play on your Mac before Mac OS X should run in Classic. Of course, these games won't be capable of taking advantage of Mac OS X's cool graphics and other new features, but they'll keep you going while you build up your library of Mac OS X–native games (see "Made for Mac OS X," later in this chapter, for a few suggestions to get you started).

Administrative Changes

Because Mac OS X is designed to allow a Mac to be used by more than one person, the System Preferences can be locked so that changes that affect all users must be made by an *Admin* user. The first user account you created when you set up Mac OS X is automatically designated an Admin user, and you can make other users Admins if you want. For more information, see Chapter 6, "Sharing Your Mac with Multiple Users."

If you want to install new Classic games, Apple recommends that you reboot in Mac OS 9 to do so. To change the system from which your Mac boots, follow these steps:

1. Click the Desktop or on the Desktop icon in the Dock and choose **Apple menu**, **System Preferences**.

2. Click **Show All**, and then click the **Startup Disk** icon. The program scans your hard drive to find bootable systems and displays an icon for each.

3. When you see a folder icon for each system and the mouse cursor returns to an arrow (instead of the spinning color wheel), check the lock button, and if it shows a locked padlock, click it.

4. Enter a user name and password. It doesn't matter which account you use, as long as it's an *Admin* account.

5. Now click the icon for the Mac OS 9 system you want to use.

6. Choose **Apple menu**, **Restart**.

When you restart, the Mac boots from the Mac OS 9 System Folder you specified instead of the Mac OS X system. To go back to Mac OS X, use the System Disk control panel in Mac OS 9 to choose the Mac OS X system and restart by choosing **Special**, **Restart**.

Made for Mac OS X

Although most gamers will be looking for Mac OS X versions of their favorite games as they switch systems, the more intrepid ones will be wondering what brand-new games they're likely to find on this side of the fence: maybe even some games that are available *only* for Mac OS X. If you're in this group, you're keeping a weather eye out for those *Cocoa* and *Carbon* games that will really let your Mac shine. This section offers a sneak peek at what you'll find.

Now, there are gamers and then there are gamers. Some people are happy to play Hearts all day long, while others want the fastest, most heart-pounding action shoot'em-ups available. Never fear, though, there's something here for everyone. Here are a few of the games you'll find for Mac OS X if you go looking. Lots more are out there, but this list of commercial, freeware, and shareware games will give you a taste.

Logic/Puzzle

Logic and puzzle games sharpen wits and relieve stress at the same time. Ask any Windows user—a few games of MineSweeper really clear one's head. Fortunately, we have MineSweeper on the Mac, as well as a passel of other "think-it-through" games. Here are two games you might want to check out:

Go To

How to Make the Switch

For more information about the System Disk control panel, see "Bipolar Shift: Switching Between Mac OS X and Mac OS 9" in Chapter 1, "Meet the New Mac.")

Show Info

Carbonized Cocoa, Anyone?

You might think that **Cocoa** and **Carbon** constitute a snack that includes burnt toast and hot chocolate. You'd be right, but in the context of Mac OS X, Cocoa and Carbon also refer to different kinds of programs. Cocoa applications are built to run only on Mac OS X and take advantage of all its new features, whereas Carbon programs can run on both Mac OS X and Mac OS 9. You'll find more details in Chapter 8, "Using Third-Party Applications."

➤ **MegaMinesweeper** (Carrot Software, www.tcnj.edu/~nowalk2/carrot/) is a modern version of MineSweeper that supports extreme field sizes, plug-in–based themes and sounds, the capability to save and open games, and much more. In this game, players try to clear a field of mines by clicking to remove what they think are "defused" mines—click in the wrong place, and your game goes up in smoke.

➤ **Down & Out** (Tobias Peciva, www.peciva.com) is a board game in which players try to clear a grid of colored pebbles. To win by clearing the entire board, you must think several moves ahead. Watch out, though—this game is so addictive that you could wind up losing entire workdays to its multicolored temptations.

Strategy/Simulation

These games simulate real-word experiences, both large and small. The best games offer the kind of detail that really makes you feel as though you're immersed in the game. Here are two for you to try:

➤ **Tropico** (PopTop Software, www.poptop.com) takes place on a remote Caribbean island where the player is the newly installed dictator. Your job is to bring peace and prosperity to your new country by building hotels, mines, factories, and other structures. Meanwhile, you must deal diplomatically with various political factions in your country, as well as threats from the outside world.

➤ **FLY! II** (Terminal Reality, fly.godgames.com) is an aviation simulation in which you can fly any of an extensive collection of airplanes all over the world while viewing true satellite terrain imagery. This is a sequel to the original Fly!, and it includes more and better 3D models, high-resolution images, and elevation scenes, as well as ultra-realistic cockpit and avionics systems.

➤ **Clan Lord** (Delta Tao Software, www.deltatao.com) is a multiplayer high-fantasy role-playing game whose online characters heal the wounded, study magic, and solve puzzles. The play emphasizes cooperation rather than competition.

➤ **Diablo II: Lord of Destruction** (Blizzard Entertainment, www.blizzard.com) offers a darker version of fantasy role-playing. The scenario in this sequel to the original Diablo: "After possessing the body of the hero who defeated him, Diablo resumes his nefarious scheme to shackle humanity into unholy slavery by joining forces with the other Prime Evils, Mephisto and Baal. Only you will be able to determine the outcome of this final encounter...."

Learning to Share

Shareware? Great, free stuff! Well, not exactly. Shareware programs are released for free distribution by their authors, who hope that people who use the programs will send in a small registration fee. If users don't pay for shareware, authors stop writing it. So, if you use shareware games or other programs, be sure to pay your shareware fees and help keep the Mac shareware market alive.

The Right Tools for the Job

If you're a big fan of driving simulation games—whether they're about cars, trucks, boats, or airplanes—be sure you check out the "Freaky Machines: Gaming Hardware" section at the end of this chapter to learn about game controllers designed just for this kind of game.

Arcade

Way back a long time ago, when people didn't have personal computers in their homes and before video game consoles were invented, video game fans had to go out and pump quarters into arcade machines to get their kicks. These days you can have that experience right in your own home—and you don't need to go to the change machine first. Give some of these a try:

➤ **Native Assault** (Adrenaline Entertainment, www.adrenalineent.com) is a new take on the classic fast-paced arcade game Missile Command that offers state-of-the-art graphics and sound effects as well as what the developers call "numerous enemies to challenge your skills."

➤ **TheCowCatchingGame** (homepage.mac.com/mwengenm) is a very silly game in which the player is the pilot of a UCCO (Unidentified Cow Catching Object) whose mission is to catch as many cows as possible within three minutes. No explanation is offered as to why the cows are falling from the sky or why it's your job to catch them—but then again, no explanation is needed. Get out there and catch those cows!

➤ **SNES9X** (John Stiles, www.snes9x.com) is a Super Nintendo Entertainment system emulator; using this program, you can play Super Nintendo games on your Mac.

Better Than the Real Thing

To play console games on a personal computer, you must have the ROMs (data from game cartridges) for the games you want to play. Some game fans distribute ROMs on the Internet, although doing so is a copyright violation. It's perfectly legal for you to make ROMs from your own games. For more information about SNES9X and other game console emulators that you can use on your Mac, go to Emulation.Net (www.emulation.net).

Action

If you love Chuck Norris, Bruce Lee, and Arnold Schwarzenegger at the movie theater, you doubtless crave action in your computer games as well. These games will serve it right up to you, with extra helpings and a dessert of even more action.

➤ **Oni** (Bungie, www.bungie.com) is a 3D shoot'em-up (also known as an action/adventure game). The player has a third-person perspective on the main character, an elite cop and one-woman SWAT team named Konoko. She's a crime fighter who is haunted by oni ("ghosts" or "demons" in Japanese). The game features hand-to-hand martial arts combat and gunplay.

➤ **Quake 3 Arena** (id Software, www.quake3arena.com) comes to Mac OS X courtesy of the Omni Group (www.omnigroup.com; download the game at www.clanmacgaming.com/files.php), which ported the game to the new OS with the blessing of its developers. This is a first-person shoot'em-up, meaning that all action is displayed onscreen from the viewpoint of the main character.

109

This is the third in a series of games in the Quake universe, Quake being a multiplayer game with a grungy, industrial look whose original release included a Nine Inch Nails soundtrack. 'Nuff said.

➤ **4X4 EVO** (Terminal Reality, www.terminalreality.com) is a down-and-dirty offroad car-racing game with fantastic graphics. It offers players cross-platform networking between Mac, PC, and Sega Dreamcast console platforms.

Gaming Networks

If you haven't been paying attention to computer games for a while, you might be wondering what the fuss is about multiplayer games. After all, any game can be multiplayer, right? The players just wait around and take their turns. Um, not exactly. Modern multiplayer games can be played over a network, either the Internet or a local network, so that more than one person can play the same game at the same time. If your Mac is already set up on a local network or on the Internet, you're ready to play network games—check the instructions for each game to find out how to hook up with other players.

Chess Genealogy for Geeks

You don't need to know this to play Chess, but just in case you're interested: The look of Chess is based on the Chess game included in NextStep (one of Mac OS X's operating system parents), and the program itself is a front end for gnuchess (a familiar program for Unix, Mac OS X's other parent).

Real-World Games

Why get up from your computer and venture out into the real world when all the real-world games you'd ever want to play are available for your Mac? Playing games such as pool and poker on your Mac means you don't have to find room in your house for a real pool table, and you never have to try to round up enough other people to play, because your Mac is always ready and waiting for you.

➤ **Maximum Pool** (Sierra Attractions, www.maximumpool.com) includes Eight Ball, Nine Ball, Cutthroat, Rotation, Pocket Billiards, Snooker, and Carom, as well as five new pool games that could exist only on a computer. It also comes with five different computer opponents to challenge.

➤ **Klondike** (www.casteel.org) is for nostalgic Mac lovers—this is the same Klondike that originally came out in 1984 for the first *128K Macintosh*. If you haven't played Klondike in a few years, you'll be surprised to see that it now has color face cards, four different Solitaire games, and 256 levels of Undo "for those who get carried away," as its developer says. If all this doesn't appeal to you, you haven't been using a Mac long enough.

Blast from the Past

If you were paying attention to the personal computer market in January 1984, you would have seen the beginning of a revolution. The original **128K Macintosh**, which didn't have a model number, was introduced that month with 128KB of RAM (yes, that's kilobytes), a 3.5-inch 400KB floppy drive (whose disks would hold less than half of one percent of the data that fits on a Zip disk), a tiny black-and-white monitor, a mouse, and a couple applications, including MacWrite and MacPaint. Wimpy as this configuration might sound, it's important to remember that the first Mac had two times as much memory as the Commodore 64, used floppies that held two and a half times as much data as the IBM PC's single-sided 5.25-inch disk, included two serial ports (and could accommodate a network with no extra hardware), and had an innovative graphical operating system.

➤ **VideoPoker** (Mactelligence, www.mactelligence.com/software/VideoPoker.html) is a simple poker game that follows the rules of Video Poker machines (meaning that you can draw five cards and jacks or better are required to win). Its cards are beautifully drawn and very realistic.

➤ **Chess**, which is included with Mac OS X in the Applications folder, is a lovely three-dimensional chess game that really shows off Mac OS X's new graphics system.

Freaky Machines: Gaming Hardware

Being serious about gaming means you want the right hardware as well as the right software. Of course, you'll start with the speediest Mac you can round up, but there's a lot more to it than that. You can choose from a wide range of gaming hardware, from inexpensive mouse replacements to high-end machinery designed to give you the ultimate gaming experience.

111

Controlling the Game

The first and most important piece of hardware you'll need to play a game—pretty much any game at all—is a controller. This device enables you to give the game instructions, whether you want to say "Move right really fast!" or "Create a new character with the following attributes." Most games work with the same controllers you use for the other things you do on your Mac: a keyboard and a mouse. Others work better with more specialized devices.

If your games don't require much in the way of specialized controls, you might consider a gamer's mouse, such as the WingMan Gaming Mouse (Logitech, www.logitech.com). It's an ergonomic three-button mouse with ultra-precise movement.

The next step would be to choose one of the many gamepads or joysticks on the market. These devices look more like the controllers used with standalone video game systems such as Nintendo. Joysticks have several buttons and vertical sticks that can be moved from side to side or back and forth to move elements on the screen, whereas game pads stick to buttons but have a wide variety of them. A good example of this kind of controller is the GamePad Pro USB (Gravis, www.gravis.com), a 10-button controller with a digital directional pad and a detachable joystick handle. It looks like the controller used with the Sony PlayStation.

Hardcore gamers can even get controllers designed just for their favorite games. Most of these are flight controllers, such as the Flight Sim Yoke USB LE (CH Products, www.chproducts.com/macgear/), which is a flight yoke featuring pitch, roll, and throttle controls as well as 14 buttons of various kinds. There are also pedal setups that can be used for flight simulators and racing games, such as the Pro Pedals (also CH Products). It has sliding forward/backward motion, heel-toe control, and three axes of control.

And if you want to get really funky, there's the PoolShark (Miacomet, www.miacomet.com), which is a special controller designed exclusively for pool and billiards games. It has a cue stick holder that senses forward and backward motion.

Read Me

Win Friends and Influence People

If you really want to impress your friends, check out the new P5 game controller. It's a glovelike device that enables you to manipulate game objects just as you would in real life, by maneuvering your hand. The P5's developer (Essential Reality, www.essentialreality.com) calls this innovation "gesture-based communication."

Gaming Accessories

If you still have money in your pocket after stocking up on the latest Mac games and snazzy controllers with which to play them, take a look at these cool devices:

➤ For the serious racing game fan, there's the Racing Simulator (SP Engineering, www.slponline.com; search for part number 72500), a chair and attached computer desk that simulate the feel of sitting in a race car. Yes, it will run you several hundred dollars, but isn't it worth it?

➤ If you require visual *and* audible perfection in your accessories, the Harman/Kardon SoundSticks (www.harman-multimedia.com) are just what you need. These external speakers are just about the coolest-looking peripheral money can buy, and the sound quality's pretty darn good, too.

Other hardware many gamers like to add to their Mac systems includes speaker sets (including subwoofers, for those really rumbly lows) and video acceleration cards, to speed up graphics rendering.

In Search Of...

If you're looking for hardware to expand your Mac system, start at the Macintosh Products Guide (**guide.apple.com**), which lists thousands of hardware and software products that are made to work with Macs.

The Least You Need to Know

➤ Most of the games you know and love will still run on your OS X Mac, using the Classic Mac OS 9 environment. If you run into games that don't work correctly, check the game developer's Web site for updates.

➤ A slew of favorite Mac games of the past and exciting new games are being released in Mac OS X versions that take advantage of the new operating system's stability, speed, and graphics power.

➤ Gaming hardware is designed to enhance your gaming experience by providing controls that work with the weapons, vehicles, and other objects in Mac games. You can choose from a wide range of devices, from simple mouse replacements to specially designed gaming desk-and-chair combos.

Part 3
Getting Connected

Macs have always been easy to network, from the early days when they were the only personal computers that came with built-in networking. Today's Macs are no exception, and they also have Internet capabilities early Mac users could only dream of. This part introduces you to network and Internet connections and what you can do with them.

In Chapter 11, you'll learn how to network your Mac with other computers, Mac and non-Mac alike. Chapter 12 makes sure you know how to set up a printer with Mac OS X, whereas Chapter 13 gets you online in a hurry. After you're there, you'll want to know what you can do on the Internet, so Chapter 14 covers the Web, e-mail, and other Internet applications. Finally, Chapter 15 offers Web publishing techniques and tips.

Chapter 11

YEAH!!

How to Succeed in Networking Without Even Trying

In This Chapter

➤ Setting up a network with cables and a hub

➤ Setting up a wireless network

➤ Sharing printers and an Internet connection

➤ Connecting Ethernet and LocalTalk networks

➤ Sharing files after you've set up your network

➤ Controlling access to your files over a network

If one Mac is great, two Macs are better, and three or more are really the bee's knees, right? And if you have all those Macs floating around, wouldn't it be great if they could communicate with one another and share the same printers and Internet connection? That's what networks are for.

If you haven't done it before, building a computer network can seem pretty intimidating—it certainly did to me at first. After you've built a *LAN*, though, you'll realize that networking is just one more thing that Apple has made easy for us fortunate Mac users. All the software you'll need is included in Mac OS X, and most of the hardware already exists in your computer as well. This chapter will look at the software and hardware requirements to set up a small network in your home or office and explain how to share Internet access among all the computers on a network.

Can't We All Just Get Along?

To learn about sharing files and printers with other computers on a network, turn to one of the chapters in Part 4, "Talking to Other Platforms." Chapter 16 covers connecting with other Macs, Chapter 17 goes into how to hook up with Windows PCs, and Chapter 18 explains how to integrate a Mac into a Unix network.

Are You a LAN/WAN Man?

A **LAN** is a local area network, meaning one that's set up within a single building or in buildings quite close to one another (within half a mile or so). WANs (wide area networks) are networks that span larger distances, and a MAN (Metropolitan Area Network) covers an area the size of a small city.

Building a Hard-Wired Network

The most important piece of hardware needed to connect your Mac to a network is a network interface card that goes inside the Mac. Here's some good news: Modern Macs, without exception, have built-in network interfaces, so you're all set on that count. What hardware you'll need to build the network itself depends on whether you want a traditional cabled network or a newfangled wireless network.

Cable Me When You Get There

The physical manifestation of a computer network consists, for the most part, of a whole lot of cables. Apple's original network technology, LocalTalk, ran on telephone wiring and was daisy-chained, meaning that each computer or other network device was connected to the next in a long line. Ethernet, on the other hand, is what's used by modern Macs, and it usually uses a "star" layout in which each computer or peripheral is connected to a central *hub*.

Untangling the Cable Nest

Oh, great, you're saying—just what I needed, more cables. Apple has done its best with the latest iMacs to reduce the number of cables required to set up a Mac, but a conventional network puts you right back in the middle of a tangle of wires again—unless, that is, you opt for a wireless network. Check out the "Out of the Ether" section later in this chapter for information on AirPort and other wireless networking options.

The cables you'll need are twisted-pair Ethernet patch cables with RJ-45 connectors. These connectors look like giant telephone jacks, which makes sense, because telephone jacks use RJ-11 connectors. You'll pay several dollars apiece for Ethernet patch cables, which come in a variety of lengths from 3 to 100 feet and even longer. Be sure you buy the shortest cables that will bridge the distance from each device to your hub without straining; there's no sense in making your data travel a longer distance than necessary. And buy at least Category 5 or 6 cables; the higher the category number, the higher the maximum speed of your network, and the price difference isn't great enough to warrant buying cheaper cables.

The Hub of Your Universe

Your next purchase should be a hub. No, you Bostonian readers, I'm not talking about Beantown (also known as The Hub). I'm talking about the network hub that goes at the center of a LAN. It's a small box with several ports for Ethernet cables that look just like the port on the back of your Mac, and it makes the connections between your Mac and the other devices on your network.

Get the fastest hub you can afford, and one with as many ports as possible. Trust me—you might think a four-port hub will be enough when you get started, but after you find out how easy Mac networking is, you'll want to be able to expand your network. Because of this, it's also important to buy a hub with an uplink port, which enables you to link one hub to another. Hubs have come down quite a bit in price in the last few years—an eight-port 100Mbps hub costs less than $50. You can find a good selection at Mac hardware retailers, such as Outpost.com (www.outpost.com).

Hub to Hub

Another kind of hub you might use is a USB hub, a device that enables you to connect several USB peripherals (such as disk drives, printers, or modems) to your Mac. USB hubs aren't interchangeable with network hubs—they're no good at all when it comes to setting up your network.

Speed Trap

As you learn about networking, you're likely to start running into numbers that represent the amount of data that can be transferred over a network in a given time—in other words, the network's speed. Each piece of networking hardware has a maximum speed at which it can work.

Read Me

Theory Versus Real Life

Why do I keep saying "in theory"? Because any file transfer, whether it's over the Internet or just within your LAN, includes "overhead" data that the system includes to be sure the data being transferred gets where it's going without error. This data takes time to transfer, too, so it increases the total transfer time for your original data.

Older Macs with Ethernet interfaces, for example, can transfer data at a rate of 10Mbps. That's 10 megabits per second, or more than 1 megabyte. So, transferring the entire contents of a Zip disk over a 10Mbps network takes (in theory) a minute and a half or so. Of course, the transfer rate from the Zip drive itself is much slower than 10Mbps, but you get the idea.

More recent Macs, such as iMacs, have 100Mbps Ethernet interfaces—in theory, 10 times as fast as 10Mbps interfaces. Then there's Gigabit Ethernet, the latest and greatest, which has a transfer speed of 1,000Mbps. Each component in your network can restrict the speed of data moving over the network. For example, if your Mac has a Gigabit Ethernet interface (1,000Mbps) but your hub is only 100Mbps, data will be transferred at the slower speed of the hub.

Your network will get by if you set it up at 10Mbps; although you might wait a little while for large file transfers (such as network backups), this speed is fine for Internet sharing. For example, as I write this, the fastest DSL connection you can get in my area (the relatively wired Northeastern U.S.) is 7.1Mbps, so a 10Mbps network is plenty fast enough to accommodate Internet data transfer. On the other hand, if you move a lot of large files from one system to another within your network, you'll want at least 100Mbps. Plus, it's a good idea to build for the future. If I were setting up a network from scratch today, I'd use 100Mbps hubs and Category 6 cabling.

Mixing and Matching

Depending on your networking needs, there are two other pieces of hardware you might want to add to your LAN:

➤ LocalTalk-to-Ethernet adapters enable you to integrate older Macs that don't have Ethernet interfaces, as well as older printers, with your Ethernet network. These devices are small boxes that cost between $50 and $100 and have a LocalTalk port in one end and an Ethernet port in the other end. No software is involved—just plug them in and go.

➤ Internet routers provide Internet sharing for all the computers on a LAN—Macs, Windows PCs, whatever. You plug your modem (phone, cable, or DSL) into the router, plug the router into your hub, follow simple configuration instructions, and that's it. Which router you buy depends on what kind of network and what kind of Internet connection you have.

These devices are easy to install, and they usually don't require you to pay any attention to them after you've hooked them up. You can find a selection of both LocalTalk adapters and routers at Mac retailers, both online and local.

Route Softly

A software router is a program that runs on your Mac and accomplishes the same thing as a hardware router. It's less expensive and more customizable, but it (obviously) works only when the "gateway" Mac on which it's installed is turned on and the program is running. For more info, turn to Chapter 13, "Getting Online."

Hooking It All Up

Here's the really easy part. You have all the pieces of your LAN; now you just have to plug everything in. Here's what you need to do:

1. Plug the hub in (using a good surge suppressor or battery backup, if possible).
2. Connect each Mac to a port on your hub with a patch cable.
3. Connect any Ethernet-ready printers and any devices for which you've purchased LocalTalk-to-Ethernet adapters in the same way.
4. If you're using more than one hub, connect them with a patch cable that runs from the uplink port of one hub to a regular port on the other hub.
5. If you're using an Internet router, plug your modem into the router, and then use another patch cable to plug your router into the hub. Follow the instructions that came with the router; you might need to plug the cable into the uplink port on the hub.

That's it—you're good to go! Now you can move on to "Sharing Files" and "Sharing Internet Access," later in this chapter, to make a few software settings.

Out of the Ether

Besides the factthat you must go out and buy more cabling every time you want to add a computer to your LAN, traditional cabled networks have another big disadvantage: Access to the network exists only at certain points, namely where the cables are run. If you want total freedom to move around within the area occupied by your network, you should consider creating a wireless network.

The Middle Way

There is a compromise between using a wireless network and creating a whole new system of cables running around your home or office. You can use your existing phone lines to carry data across a LAN. The disadvantage is that transfer rates on a phone line LAN are about 1Mbps, quite a bit slower than 10Mbps Ethernet. Data is transferred at a different frequency than voice communications, so you can use your network and place phone calls at the same time. Available systems include HomeFree (Diamond Multimedia, `www.diamondmm.com`) and HomeLine (Farallon, `www.farallon.com`).

Using AirPort is similar to using a cordless phone. The system has two components:

➤ **The AirPort base station**—This device combines a router, a network hub, and a phone modem that you can use if you don't have high-speed Internet access. When it's running, any computer within its range can connect to your network just as though you'd hooked it up with network cabling.

➤ **An AirPort card for your computer**—This is the hardware that allows your computer to talk to the AirPort base station. Apple's AirPort card works only with iBooks, iMacs, recent PowerBooks, or Power Mac G4s, but you can buy third-party cards that work with older Macs, such as the Skyline card from Farallon (`www.farallon.com`).

AirPort has several advantages over traditional wired networks:

➤ It makes your laptop computers truly portable—you don't have to put your laptop down and plug it in anywhere to get online or to share files with your other computers.

➤ It allows Internet connection sharing right out of the box, with no additional hardware or software needed. And it works with any kind of connection—phone modem, DSL, cable modem, whatever.

➤ It's quick and easy to set up, with no need to go crawling around the attic to run wires.

To create an AirPort network, you purchase an AirPort card for each computer that you want to be able to move around, as well as an AirPort base station. You can set the base station up to connect to the Internet with its included phone modem, or you can use it with a high-speed connection simply by plugging it into your network hub. Install the AirPort cards in your Macs, set up the Macs' network software ("Sharing Files" and "Sharing Internet Access," next), and you're online and on the move.

What a Wonderful (Wireless) World

Just to give you an idea of the trouble you can avoid by using AirPort, I offer a list of some of the features of my home office's network. First, there's the stovepipe jammed through my office's closet wall, which routes the network cable to my server Mac and the printer's power cable to the outlet in the closet (don't ask). Then there are the "extra" holes in the upstairs hallway's ceiling, which provide an example of what kind of mistakes you can make with a power drill when stringing cabling. Finally, there's the 100-foot cable that I string from the dining room through the kitchen, past the back door, and into the family room when I want to use my PowerBook while I'm watching TV. That's called a disaster waiting to happen. Take my word for it—wireless is worth it.

Sharing Files

Mac OS X uses TCP file sharing, which means that if you want to share files over your LAN, you'll need to give your Macs IP addresses. These are numbers that identify your computer to other computers on a network, both the Internet and your local network. An IP address has four segments, separated by periods, like this: 192.168.0.1. You can use any numbers between 0 and 255 for the third and fourth segments, but good numbers to use for the first and second segments are 192 and 168, respectively; those numbers signify that this is a local address rather than an Internet one.

To assign an IP address, choose **Apple menu**, **System Preferences**. Click the **Network** button and fill in the IP Address field in the TCP/IP tab of the Network pane (see Figure 11.1).

Making the Macintosh Connection

Now you're ready to start sharing files by connecting to other Macs. By default, you can access any Public folder on another OS X Mac, and you can access other users' home folders if they allow you to. Here's how to connect to folders for which you have *access privileges*:

Access Is a Privilege

Access privileges are settings for each folder that determine who can see what's in it and add or change files in it. See "Controlling Access," next, to learn how to set access privileges for your folders.

Figure 11.1

Assigning your Mac an IP address allows other computers to locate it on a network.

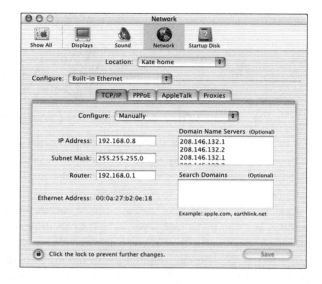

1. To share your files with other Macs, click the Desktop and choose **Apple menu**, **System Preferences**.
2. Click the **Sharing** button and click **Start** to turn on File Sharing.
3. To connect to other Macs, be sure the owners of these Macs have turned on File Sharing (steps 1 and 2 above). Then click the Desktop and choose **Go**, **Connect to Server**.
4. Click **Local Network** in the first column; a list of Macs that you can access appears in the next column (see Figure 11.2).

Figure 11.2

Connect to a server by locating its name; here I'm connecting to "Boston," another Mac on my network.

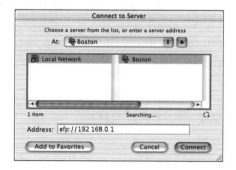

5. Navigate to the Mac and shared folder to which you want to connect.
6. Click the **Connect** button.
7. Enter your user name and password to log in to the other Mac.

When you log in, you'll see an icon for the shared folder appear on your Desktop. You can double-click it to open a window, from which you can browse its contents just as you would those of your own Mac. Your access privileges are the same as they would be if you sat down in front of that Mac and logged in to it that way.

Controlling Access

You can decide which other users get access to your files by setting access privileges; these settings enable you to control access to your home folder and to any subfolder within it. By default, only your Public folder is shared, but you can change the privileges for any folder in your home folder. Here's how:

1. Click the folder and press Cmd+I or choose **File**, **Show Info**.

2. From the Show pop-up menu, choose **Privileges**.

3. In the bottom pop-up menu, labeled "Everybody else can," choose a level of access:

> ➤ **Read and Write**—Allows another user to work with these files as though they were his or her own.

> ➤ **Read Only**—Prevents other users from modifying files (although they can open them) and adding files to the folder.

> ➤ **Write Only (Drop Box)**—Allows users to add files but not to see what's in the folder.

> ➤ **None**—Prevents other users from opening the folder at all.

Read Me

Share and Share Alike

To share files with other users, put them in your own Public folder within your home folder. You can view your home folder by clicking on the desktop and pressing Cmd+ Option+H or choosing **Go**, **Home**.

Read Me

Drop by Drop

Write Only (Drop Box) is the default privileges setting for the Drop Box folder inside your Public folder.

These settings affect other users' access to your folders in the same way regardless of whether they're logging in over the network or sitting at your computer.

Sharing Internet Access

Sharing Internet access is even simpler than sharing files over a LAN. Most routers, hardware and software alike, use a system called Dynamic Host Configuration Protocol (DHCP) to point your computer in the direction of the Internet. This means that you don't have to worry about IP addresses; all you have to do is let your Mac know you're using DHCP. Follow these steps:

1. Choose **Apple menu**, **System Preferences**.
2. Click the **Network** button (if you don't see it, click **Show All**).
3. From the top Configure pop-up menu, choose **Built-in Ethernet**; this lets your Mac know you want it to connect through the network.
4. Click the **TCP/IP** tab and choose **DHCP** from its Configure pop-up menu (see Figure 11.3).
5. Click **Save**.

That's it—you're online!

Figure 11.3

Specify DHCP in the TCP/IP tab to get in touch with your router.

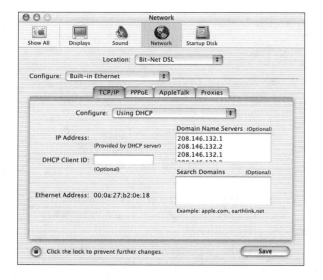

Printing

Printing over a network requires two things: a networked printer and the correct network protocol on your Mac. If your printer works over a network, it's likely to use either TCP/IP or AppleTalk.

If you have a TCP/IP printer, all you need to do is specify your Ethernet connection in the Network tab of the System Preferences (see "Sharing Internet Access," the previous section). If your printer talks only AppleTalk, which is likely unless it's fairly new and fairly expensive, then you'll need to enable AppleTalk. Go back to the Network tab of the System Preferences and click on the **AppleTalk** tab. Check the box labeled Make AppleTalk Active, and you're all set.

Checking for Prints

To begin printing, you'll need to set up your printer in the Print Center. To learn how to do this, see Chapter 12, "Printing Up a Storm."

The Least You Need to Know

➤ Most Mac networks use Ethernet cable and network hubs to connect multiple computers for file sharing and printing. Other devices enable you to integrate older LocalTalk networks and share Internet access across a network.

➤ AirPort and similar wireless systems help you create a network without any cables, working similarly to cordless telephones.

➤ After your Macs are connected on a local access network, users on one computer can access shared folders and files on another computer. Access privilege settings control whether other users can see your files and make changes to them.

Chapter 12

Printing Up a Storm

In This Chapter

➤ Installing and using fonts

➤ Setting up printers

➤ Selecting printer-specific options

➤ Printing documents

➤ Previewing and monitoring print jobs

Chapter 4, "No Mac Is an Island," talks about hooking up a printer to your Mac under Mac OS X. Now it's time for the fun part—in this chapter, we'll get to the actual printing.

Mac OS X's printing system and its onscreen display system use the same data, which means that anything you can see on your screen can be printed (theoretically, anyway), and everything you print should look exactly the same as it does onscreen. And not only should your printouts look good, you should have an easier time creating them, because Mac OS X has a completely redesigned printing system that's much simpler than Mac OS 9's.

A Printer of a Different Color

Classic applications can print, for the most part, but they don't use the interface and options described in this chapter. To set up printers and print documents from Classic applications, follow the same procedures you normally would in Mac OS 9.

Managing Those Funky Fonts

Mac OS X comes with a selection of useful and not-so-useful TrueType fonts for you to use when printing text documents. Mac OS X can use the following kinds of fonts:

Just the Outlines, Ma'am

Outline fonts are defined in terms of mathematical descriptions of their shapes. That means that you can view and print them at any size and they'll look the same. Bitmap fonts, on the other hand, don't have scalable outlines, so they look good only at predetermined sizes; they're usually used only in onscreen applications where you're restricted to using those specific sizes.

➤ TrueType
➤ PostScript Type 1
➤ OpenType
➤ Bitmap

The first three are *outline font* formats, whereas bitmap fonts are intended only for use onscreen and with low-resolution impact printers such as Apple's old ImageWriters.

Installing Fonts

One of the cool advantages of Mac OS X's multiuser nature is that you have two places you can install fonts. If you want to allow everyone who uses your computer to have access to your fonts, put them in Library/Fonts—that's the main Library folder on your hard drive. But you have your own Library folder in your home folder, and the Fonts folder in that Library folder is where you can stash fonts that you want to keep all to yourself.

To install a font, drag it into either Fonts folder. After they're installed, you can access fonts in the Font panel of any Mac OS X application.

Classic Fonts

Okay, I admit it: I left out another place you can install fonts. That's in the Fonts folder in the Mac OS 9 System Folder that you use with Classic. Fonts installed there are available to Mac OS X, but Mac OS X fonts aren't available in Classic applications. And fonts activated in Classic using **Suitcase**, **Font Reserve**, or another font management program, are not available in Mac OS X applications.

For more info about using Classic and Classic programs, turn to Chapter 8, "Using Third-Party Applications."

Genuine Font Paneling

The Font panel is new in Mac OS X. Mac OS 9 applications simply list fonts in a Fonts menu, but Mac OS X–native applications use the Font panel. It offers multiple ways for you to view the fonts you have installed and to organize them for quick access. The Font panel's main interface has four columns (see Figure 12.1).

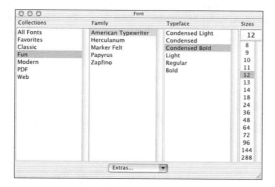

Figure 12.1

The Font panel has a lot of functions packed into its compact interface.

➤ **Collections**—The first collection, All Fonts, lists all the installed fonts. You can create other collections that include groups of fonts you need quick access to, such as corporate fonts or project-related fonts. Click a collection to see the fonts it contains.

➤ **Family**—This list shows the font families included in the selected collection. Click a font family to see its members.

➤ **Typeface**—Here you see the individual fonts contained in the selected font. For example, if you select Helvetica in the Family column, the Typeface column shows the Regular, Oblique, Bold, and Bold Oblique fonts. Click the typeface you want to use.

➤ **Sizes**—The text entry field at the top of this column displays the current size. Choose a size from the list or enter a new size in the Size field.

Ch-ch-ch-changes

Changes you make in the Font panel are applied immediately to selected text. If no text is selected, the changes take effect as soon as you start typing new text.

An Extras pop-up menu at the bottom of the Font panel contains several useful commands:

➤ **Add to Favorites**—If you're not interested in making different named collections, but you do use a few fonts frequently, you can designate them as Favorites, and they'll appear in a new set called Favorites in the Collections column. Select any font and size in the Fonts pane and click **Add to Favorites** to see the font listed here. To delete a Favorite, click its name here and choose **Extras, Remove from Favorites.** You can also double-click the Favorite's name (by default, the font and point size) and give the combo a custom name to indicate what you'll use it for, such as "Bike shop logo" or "Personal letters."

➤ **Edit Collections**—Here's where you can create font collections of your own (see Figure 12.2). Click the plus button to add a collection, and then type a name for your new collection. Click a font family in the All Families column and click the left-arrow button to add the family to the new collection. To remove a family, click it and click the right-arrow button. Click **Done** to return to the Font panel's main interface.

Figure 12.2

Font collections enable you to view only the fonts you know you need for a particular project.

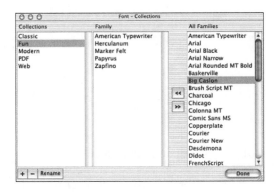

➤ **Edit Sizes**—Choose this command to edit the list of preset font sizes displayed in the Font panel's main interface. Click a size in the list, and then click the minus button to remove it; enter a new size and click the plus button to add it. Click **Done** to return to the Font panel's main interface.

➤ **Color**—This command displays Mac OS X's standard color picker so that you can set the font color.

➤ **Get Fonts**—If you're connected to the Internet, this command opens your Web browser to a page on Apple's Web site where you can buy new fonts from the Apple Store.

Unlike many dialog boxes in Mac OS 9 programs, the Font panel doesn't have to be closed before you can continue editing the document you're working on. If you're changing fonts or type sizes a lot as you work, you can leave the Font panel open for easy access (just move it aside so you can see your document).

Exercising Your Printing Options

Most of the time, printing in Mac OS X is as simple as pressing Cmd+P and then pressing Return (or choosing **File**, **Print** and clicking **Print**, if you're more a mouse type than a keyboard type). If you want to, say, print multiple copies or print at a different size, though, you'll need to explore Mac OS X's printing options. They're located in three different places:

➤ **Print Center**—This is the central location from which you control all printer functions, including monitoring print jobs and setting up printer options. You'll find it in the Utilities folder within the Applications folder.

➤ **Page Setup dialog box**—You can control paper size and orientation here, as well as enter a size percentage for the printout itself. Some applications might include other controls here—usually, those would be programs that produce designs or graphics specifically intended for printing.

➤ **Print dialog box**—Here's where you actually tell your computer to print something. Here you can specify the number of copies and the page range you want to print.

The next sections will take you through the process of setting up a printer, choosing print options, and printing a document.

Read Me

A Printer by Any Other Name

The options in the Print Center, the Page Setup dialog box, and the Print dialog box can vary depending on what type and brand of printer you're using. For example, a color printer's Print dialog box is likely to have color settings that you won't see if you're using a black-and-white printer.

Introducing Mac OS X to Your Printer

The first step toward printing is—you guessed it—to set up a printer. Here's how it's done:

1. Open the Print Center (see Figure 12.3). It's in the Utilities folder within the Applications folder; to get there, click on the Desktop and press Cmd+4.

Figure 12.3

The Print Center is where Mac OS X gets cozy with your printer (or printers).

2. Click **Add Printer**.

3. From the pop-up menu at the top of the dialog box, choose the kind of printer connection you have. The Print Center lists all the printers it finds on the network or plugged directly into your Mac.

4. Click the name of the printer you want to set up, and then click **Add Printer**.

5. To make the new printer your default printer, select it and choose **Printers, Make Default**. A dot in that column indicates the default printer: the one that's automatically chosen for you when you print a document.

After a step printer is set up, you can choose it from the pop-up list at the top of the Print dialog box when you're printing a document. Before you can use printer capabilities such as extra paper trays, though, you must complete another phase of the setup process:

Playing with Page Setup

After you have your printer set up and you're ready to print a document, take a second to be sure your Page Setup options are set correctly. Choose **File, Page Setup** while the document is open to see the Page Setup dialog box (see Figure 12.4).

Read Me

Anticipating Your Every Need

If no printers have been set up on your system before, the Print Center might ask you immediately if you want to add a printer. If so, click **Add Printer** and move straight to step 3.

Go To

The Printer Connection

The kind of printer connection you have depends on the kind of printer you're using and which Mac model you're using. To review the possible kinds of printer connections, see Chapter 4, "No Mac Is an Island."

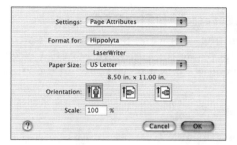

Figure 12.4

The Mac OS X Page Setup dialog box looks reassuringly like the one from Mac OS 9.

Making It Stick

If you want to use a particular combination of Page Setup options for all your new documents, close all open documents and choose **File**, **Page Setup**. Any changes you make here while no documents are open are applied to all documents you create after this point.

The Page Setup dialog box can have different panes in different applications (to switch panes, choose an option from the Settings pop-up menu). You'll always see a Page Attributes pane and a Summary pane (as shown in Figure 12.5). The former enables you to choose different paper sizes and different paper orientations and adjust the printing size percentage. You can enter any percentage; if you enter a size that makes the document larger than the selected paper size, the printer will print the document on multiple sheets of paper.

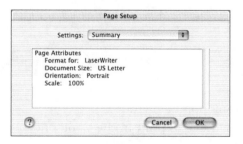

Figure 12.5

The Page Setup dialog box groups different settings onto separate panes, each accessed through the Settings pop-up menu.

Getting Down to Printing Business

Some applications don't support printing—you can't print from the Calculator, for example. Those that do, however, all operate the same way, with the exception of a few application-specific options that can show up in a special pane in the Print dialog box.

Printing with No Print Command

If you need to print from an application that doesn't print, there *is* a workaround (you didn't think I'd leave you hanging, did you?). Start up Grab (it's in the Utilities folder inside the Applications folder). With Grab, you can take screen shots—images of what's on your screen. Choose **Capture**, **Selection**, and then click and drag around the area of the screen you want to print. The screen shot opens in a new, untitled window, which you can then print, save as an image file, or save and then print.

Time to Print

Here's how to get that document printed:

1. Choose **File**, **Print** to display the Print dialog box (see Figure 12.6).

Figure 12.6

The Print dialog box is attached to the title bar of the window containing the file you're printing.

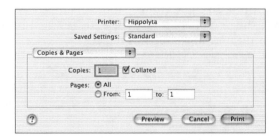

2. Choose a printer from the Printer pop-up menu.
3. Enter the number of copies you'd like to print in the Copies field.
4. Click **All** to print the entire document, or **Page Range** to print just part of it.
5. If you choose Page Range, enter the numbers of the first and last pages you want to print.
6. To print multiple copies of the document's pages, enter the number of pages to print.

7. To choose options specific to the application you're using, switch to the Application pane from the Layout pane and make your choices. For example, in Internet Explorer you can choose to print headers and footers or leave them off the printout.

8. Click **Print**.

Previewing Print Jobs

If you want to see what a document will look like when it's printed—before you actually print it— click the Print dialog box's Preview button. This creates a new print file from your document and opens it in the Preview application (see Figure 12.7). From here you have two choices:

➤ You can page through the document to see it all by clicking the arrow buttons at the bottom-left corner of the window. Continue the printing process by clicking **Print**.

Read Me

Micro-Mini-Printouts

A fun—and paper-saving—print option is the ability to print smaller versions of a document's pages. To make mini-printouts, switch to the Layout pane and click an icon to indicate the order in which you want the pages laid out on the paper. Then, choose an option from the Border pop-up menu.

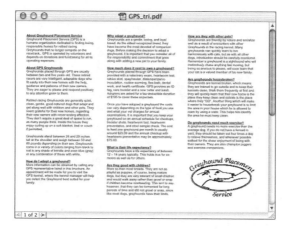

Figure 12.7

Preview was created specifically to show you what your documents will look like when they come out of the printer.

➤ Save the document as a PDF file by choosing **File, Save As PDF**. After it's a PDF, you can give the file to other people and they can view it onscreen or print it. This is a good way to be sure that files you exchange with other people print as they should, regardless of whether those people have the same fonts—or even the same operating system—as you do.

Keeping an Eye on Print Jobs

After you've sent a document to the printer, how can you keep track of its printing progress? Simple: Monitor the print job in the Print Center. Any time a document is being printed from your Mac, the Print Center is running, which means its icon is visible in your Dock. Click the Print Center icon to view its window, which shows a list of the printers you have installed.

Next to each printer, in the Status column, the Print Center lets you know whether that printer is active or idle. To see what's happening with a particular printer, double-click its name in the list to open a window displaying its queued jobs (see Figure 12.8). In this window you can

➤ Put a print job on hold by selecting it and clicking **Hold**.

➤ Restart a print job that's on hold by selecting it and clicking **Resume**.

➤ Cancel a job by selecting it and clicking **Delete**.

Go To

Info on PDF, PDQ!

For more information about PDF—what it is, what it's good for, and Acrobat software designed for working with PDFs—go to Adobe Systems' Web site (`www.adobe.com/products/acrobat/`).

Figure 12.8

The first job in the list is currently printing, while the others are waiting their turn.

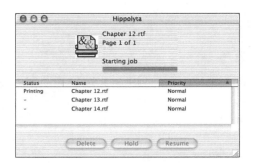

To change the order in which print jobs are listed, click one of the column headers (Status, Name, or Priority). This doesn't change the order in which documents will be printed, but it's useful for figuring out just what you've already sent to the printer when you're printing a lot of documents at one time.

The Least You Need to Know

➤ Before you can print text, you'll need to have some fonts installed. Mac OS X can use TrueType, PostScript Type 1, OpenType, and bitmap fonts. Mac OS X's Font panel enables you to make collections of fonts you use often so that you can access them easily.

➤ To use printers, you must set them up in the Print Center. There you can set up both basic connectivity and specific features for AppleTalk, LPR, USB, and other printers. All the printers you've set up appear in a pop-up menu in the Print dialog box.

➤ Print options are set in the Page Setup and Print dialog boxes. You can preview documents before they're printed, and you can monitor the progress of print jobs in the Print Center.

Chapter 13

Getting Online

In This Chapter

➤ Connecting to an ISP with a phone modem

➤ Using cable modems and DSL

➤ Sharing one ISP account across a LAN

➤ Setting Internet preferences

In the 21st century, more and more of the things we do every day take place online. With Mac OS X, that's even more true than ever before, because the new system relies on Internet connections to work at its best. For example, with Mac OS X, your Mac can connect to a *timeserver* as needed to be sure its clock is always set correctly. And the Mac OS X Help Center downloads the latest information on a topic whenever you need assistance.

When you first install Mac OS X on your Mac or start up your new OS X Mac, the Setup Assistant asks you for the connection information you need to get online. If you switch connection methods or need to change this information for any other reason, this chapter can help you get your Mac connected to the Internet again so that all your online dreams will be fulfilled.

What Time Is It Again?

Timeservers are computers that keep track of the time and supply it to other computers that ask for it. Apple operates its own timeservers around the world, so your Mac can set its own clock whenever you want it to.

Phone Modems: Dial Me Impressed

Despite the popularity of high-speed access, most people are still connecting to their *ISPs* with a good ol' telephone line and an analog *modem*. Although connection speeds are relatively slow using this technology, it's available almost everywhere—you can even use an analog modem with a cell phone or satellite phone. And these days, almost every Mac comes with a built-in 56K modem, the fastest kind.

Call Me Any Time

Internet service providers (**ISPs**) provide the link between your computer and the Internet. To get there, you can use an analog **modem**, a device that translates the digital information your Mac supplies into analog sounds that can be transmitted over a phone line. When the information gets to the other end of the phone line, another modem translates it back into digital terms and it goes sailing away across the Internet to its destination.

Eating Your PPPs

To connect to an ISP over a phone line, Macs use a method called PPP: *Point-to-Point Protocol*. Here's how to set up your Mac to get online:

1. Click the Desktop and choose **Apple menu**, **System Preferences**.

2. Click the **Network** icon to display the Network pane, and then choose **Modem Port** from the upper **Configure** menu.

3. If the padlock button in the lower-left corner of the System Preferences window is locked, click it and enter an Admin user name and password to authorize the changes you're about to make.

4. Click the **PPP** tab (see Figure 13.1) and enter a name in the Service Provider field for the configuration you're about to create.

5. Enter your ISP's phone number (and an alternative number, if you like).

6. Enter your user name in the **Account Name** field, and then enter your password.

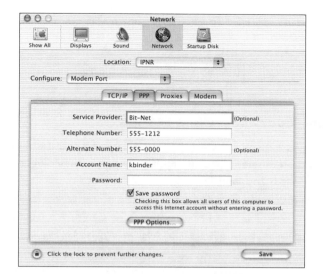

Figure 13.1

The information that enables you to connect with your Internet service provider goes in the PPP tab.

7. Click **Save Password** if you don't want to enter your password every time you connect.
8. Click the **Modem** tab to specify your modem.
9. Choose your modem model from the **Modem** pop-up menu.
10. Click **Tone** or **Pulse**, depending on what kind of phone service you have.
11. Click **Save** to save your changes.

For Grown-Ups Only

Like many System Preferences panes, the Network pane enables you to lock its settings so that an Admin user must authorize changes before you make them. This can be a very useful option, because these are not the kind of changes you want your three-year-old to make for you.

Any Modem Port in a Storm

The modem ports available to you depend on which Mac model you have and what kind of modem you're using. For info on different kinds of modems and how they plug in to your Mac, see Chapter 4, "No Mac Is an Island."

Read Me

Don't Dream Online, Be Online

If you want to connect automatically any time your Mac tries to access the Internet, click **PPP Options** at the bottom of the PPP tab and check **Connect Automatically When Starting TCP/IP Applications**.

Read Me

A PPP Shortcut

If you connect to your ISP every time you start up your computer, consider adding Internet Connect to your Login Items.

Connecting with a Modem

Now you're ready to get online. Mac OS X includes a little program called Internet Connect whose sole function is to get you connected through PPP. Here's how:

1. Start up Internet Connect (see Figure 13.2). It's located in the Applications folder, so you can find it by clicking the Desktop and pressing Cmd+Option+A or choosing **Go, Applications**.

2. Choose **Modem Port** from the **Configuration** pop-up menu.

3. If you want to change any of the settings or you need to enter your password, click the triangle next to the Configuration pop-up menu to display the rest of the dialog box. Otherwise, skip to step 6.

4. Choose a telephone number.

5. Enter your password, unless you elected to save it in the PPP tab of the Network preferences, in which case it's already there.

6. Click **Connect**.

When you click Connect, the system displays the status of your connection while it dials and hooks up with your ISP. If you change your mind about connecting (for example, if you find out that someone's on the phone in the next room—oops!), click **Cancel** to stop the Mac from trying to connect.

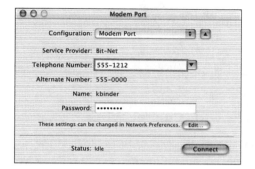

Figure 13.2
Internet Connect is your route to getting online with your local ISP.

When Good Modems Go Bad

If the Mac isn't able to connect, it will let you know what it thinks the problem is, such as that it can't recognize the modem. Here are a few connection problems you might run into:

➤ The information entered in Internet Connect is incorrect. This can include your user name, password, or the phone number. Remember that your account with an ISP can have a different user name and password from the ones you use to log in to your Mac.

➤ If you're using an external modem, the modem isn't plugged into your Mac. If you have cats or kids, someone might have crawled behind the computer and accidentally disconnected the modem. Check all the physical connections between your modem and the Mac, as well as the phone line from the modem to the wall outlet.

➤ The wrong modem type is selected in the Modem tab of the Network preferences. Choose **Apple menu**, **System Preferences**, click the **Network** button, and double-check your settings.

In Case of Emergency

Hayes Compatible is a fairly generic setting that should work with any modem model, so try that if the modem type you selected doesn't work.

High Times with High-Speed Access

If you're an early adopter of cable modem or DSL access—lucky you! These high-speed Internet access services don't keep your phone line busy while you're online, and they're always on (or close to it), so you don't have to wait around to connect. Then there's the speed advantage—you're really surfing now.

Cool Tricks with Copper Wires

DSL stands for *digital subscriber line*, and it's a very cool technology. If you have DSL service, your Mac can use your existing phone line for Internet access without tying up the voice part of the line—you can still fax or talk on the phone while you're online. The most common kind of DSL service is **ADSL**, which stands for *asynchronous digital subscriber line*; the asynchronous part means that you can download information much, much faster than you can upload it. This isn't a problem for most consumers, because they download much more information than they upload.

TC-What?

TCP stands for Transmission Control Protocol, and **IP** stands for Internet Protocol. These two protocols allow your computer to connect to other computers in such a way that messages can pass back and forth and arrive in the correct order, uncorrupted.

Get Ready...

If you selected DSL or cable modem access when the Mac OS X Setup Assistant ran, and you can't get connected, you must enter your connection settings manually. Here's what to do:

1. Track down the information in the following list. If you are still able to connect using Mac OS 9, you can get this info from the TCP/IP control panel in Mac OS 9 (see Figure 13.3); otherwise, you can get it by calling your DSL or cable modem service provider.

   ➤ IP address
   ➤ Subnet mask
   ➤ Router address
   ➤ Name server address

Figure 13.3

Mac OS 9's TCP/IP control panel is equivalent to Mac OS X's TCP/IP Preferences pane.

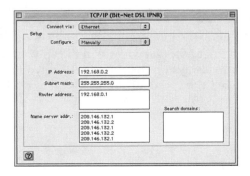

146

2. Start up in Mac OS X.

3. Click the Desktop and choose **Apple menu, System Preferences**.

4. Click the **Network** icon to display the Network pane, choose **Built-In Ethernet** from the upper Configure menu, and click the **TCP/IP** tab (see Figure 13.4).

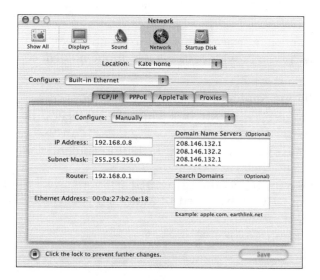

Figure 13.4
TCP/IP settings are used to set up both local networks and Internet access.

5. If the lock button shows a closed padlock, click the button and enter an Admin user name and password, and then click **OK**.

6. From the Configure pop-up menu, choose **Manually**, and enter the IP address, subnet mask, and router information in the appropriate fields.

7. In the Domain Name Servers field, enter the domain name server (*DNS*) addresses.

8. Click **Save** and close System Preferences.

When you make changes to your TCP/IP settings, you should be back online without a hitch. If not, double-check the settings you've entered with your ISP's tech support people—they should be able to help you track down the source of any problems you're having.

Show Info

411

DNS servers (domain name servers) are the computers that tell your Mac where to find the Web pages it's looking for. They're kind of like phone books—they take the text address you type in, such as **www.apple.com**, and convert it into a numerical address that your Web browser can locate.

PPPoE for Thee

Some DSL services use PPPoE (PPP over Ethernet) to connect. With these services, you must use dialer software that logs you in to the service; with PPPoE, you're not online the minute the hardware is connected, as you would be with other DSL services. In the case of Mac OS X, your dialer is Internet Connect, just as it is for a PPP connection over a regular phone line.

Before you can connect using PPPoE, however, you need to set up PPPoE with some basic information similar to what you provide for a regular phone modem connection. Here's how:

1. Click the Desktop and choose **Apple menu**, **System Preferences**.
2. Click the **Network** icon to display the Network pane, and then click the **TCP/IP** tab.
3. If the lock button shows a closed padlock, click the button and enter an Admin user name and password, and then click **OK**.
4. From the Configure pop-up menu, choose **Using DHCP** if you have a regular Internet account, or **Using DHCP with Fixed IP Address** if your Internet provider gives you a fixed IP address.
5. Click the **PPPoE** tab (see Figure 13.5).

Figure 13.5

PPPoE settings enable you to transmit your user name and password to a DSL provider.

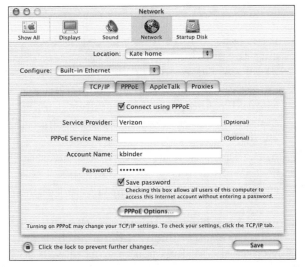

6. Enter the name of your ISP.
7. Enter your user name in the Account Name field.
8. Enter your password. Click **Save Password** if you don't want to enter the password again every time you connect.
9. Click **Save** and close System Preferences.

Now you're ready to connect to your ISP. This works the same way as using an analog modem, and you use the same utility: Internet Connect. You'll find it in the Applications folder.

1. Start up Internet Connect.

2. Choose **Built-In Ethernet** from the **Configuration** pop-up menu.

3. If you want to change any of the settings or you need to enter your password, click the triangle next to the Configuration pop-up menu to display the rest of the dialog box. Otherwise, skip to step 5.

4. Enter your password, unless you elected to save it in the PPP tab of the Network preferences, in which case it's already there.

5. Click **Connect**.

You don't need to set up your system for PPPoE unless you're sure that your DSL provider requires it; many DSL providers are switching to a PPPoE-free service.

Think Globally, Act Locally

If you have more than one computer, you've probably thought how nice it would be to be able to get online with multiple computers at the same time. It turns out that setting this up is a simple task, especially if you're a Mac user. Two issues are involved: getting the computers connected, and getting your ISP to talk to both of them. Internet sharing solutions are available as both software and hardware.

The "getting connected" part of Internet sharing requires you to set up a *LAN*, a local area network. That's generally just a question of plugging a few cables into the back of your Macs and then into a network hub. For more information, see Chapter 11, "How to Succeed in Networking Without Even Trying."

The Softer Side of Internet Sharing

The least expensive way to share one Internet connection is to buy a program that does *NAT*—network address translation. This software runs on one Mac that's connected to the Internet and enables any other computer (Mac or PC) that's networked with the first one to piggyback on its Internet connection.

Read Me

Addresses, but No Zip Codes

When you connect to your ISP, you're allotted one IP address, a numerical code that identifies your computer to the other computers on the network. All the information you request is routed to this address—that's how it gets to you instead of to someone else. But to use more than one computer, you'd need more than one IP address, right? That's where the *translation* part of NAT comes in. Using NAT, all your requests seem to the outside world to come from one computer, but when the information gets back to your location, the NAT software routes all the requests to the individual computers on your network.

Here are two excellent Mac programs for NAT:

➤ **SurfDoubler** (Vicom Technology, www.vicomsoft.com) allows two or three computers to get online at once. It also enables you to use more than one modem and phone line to increase the speed of your connection.

➤ **IPNetRouter** (Sustainable Softworks, www.sustworks.com) is a simpler product that can be used to provide Internet access to an unlimited number of computers. It costs slightly less than SurfDoubler and is extremely stable, but it's a bit more complicated to set up.

Getting In Touch with Your Inner Mac

For information about Mac hardware, software, and the Mac marketplace, Macintouch is the place to go: **www.macintouch.com**. Included on this site at **www.macintouch.com/ accessrouters.html** is a great collection of reader reports about hardware routers.

Doing It the Hard Way

Although using a software router is inexpensive, it means that the computer where the software is running must be powered up to allow the other computers to get online. You'll need to be sure that computer has enough RAM to run the router software in addition to the other programs being used, and any time you restart it, the Internet connection for the rest of the network is lost. Hardware routers are a way for you to avoid all these potential pitfalls, and they've become quite affordable in the last couple of years.

You set up a hardware router by plugging your modem (whether phone, DSL, or cable) into one side and your Macs' network hub into the other side. Some routers have built-in modems, and some have built-in hubs as well.

If you have DSL service and need a PPPoE-savvy router, Linksys (www.linksys.com) and MacSense (www.macsensetech.com) are two companies whose DSL routers work with PPPoE.

Coming In for a Landing

For more information about AirPort, see Chapter 11, "How to Succeed in Networking Without Even Trying." You can also check out Apple's Web page on AirPort, at **www.apple.com/ airport/**.

Taking Off from the AirPort

If you want to connect to the Internet and to your other Macs from anywhere in your home or office, without wires, AirPort is the product for you. It's Apple's wireless networking system, and it allows both Internet sharing and file sharing among computers connected to it. For small networks, AirPort is a bit of an investment ($300 for the base station and at least $100 per connected computer), but it's definitely the coolest way to connect.

Hello, Central

Do you get tired of filling out preferences dialog boxes in triplicate? I do—some days it seems that every single program I install wants to know what my e-mail address is. Fortunately, Mac OS X can keep track of information such as this in a central repository where any application that wants it can find it. Here's what you do:

1. Click the Desktop and choose **Apple menu**, **System Preferences**.
2. Click the Internet icon to display the Internet pane (see Figure 13.6).

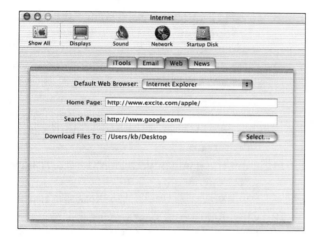

Figure 13.6

The Internet pane of the System Preferences contains information that's needed by all your Internet programs.

3. In the iTools tab, enter your iTools member name and your password if you have an iTools account. If you don't have one, you can click **Free Sign Up** to get one.

4. In the Email tab, first choose the program you want to use to send and receive e-mail. This is the program that will be opened when you click on an e-mail link in a Web browser or other program. If you don't see the program you want, choose **Select**, and then locate your e-mail client in the dialog box and click **Select**.

5. In the other fields in the Email tab, enter the information your ISP provides: your e-mail address, your incoming and outgoing mail servers, your user name, and your password.

iTools of the Trade

iTools is a set of Web-based utilities Apple provides free to Mac users. You can put up your own Web page, back up important files to an "iDisk" on Apple's servers, get a free e-mail address, and more. For more info, go to the iTools home page at **itools.mac.com**. Chapter 15, "Publishing on the Web," walks you through the iTools sign-up process.

Dual Identity

Remember that your e-mail user name and password might not be the same as the ones you use to log in to your Mac.

All the News That's Fit to Post

Usenet is a huge collection of *newsgroups*, public bulletin boards where anyone can post messages on a specific topic. For more information, see Chapter 14, "Nothing but Net."

6. Click a radio button to choose the kind of e-mail service you have: POP or IMAP. If you connect to the Internet through a local ISP, you probably have POP e-mail. If you get online at work using a large network, or if you're setting up your Mac.com address, you might be using IMAP e-mail.

7. In the Web tab, first choose the Web browser you want to use. Any time you click a Web link in another program, this browser will start up.

8. In the Home Page and Search Page fields, enter URLs for your preferred home page and search engine page.

9. Click **Select** to choose a folder in which to place downloaded files.

10. In the News tab, first choose the news reader program you want to use. Any time you click a Usenet link in another program, this program will start up.

11. Enter the name of your news server. This can be a server operated by your ISP or the company where you work, or it can be a public news server.

12. Click **Registered User** or **Guest**; if you choose Registered User, enter your user name and password.

If you enter your e-mail address and other Internet settings in the System Preferences, with luck you'll never have to enter this information again.

The Least You Need to Know

➤ No matter what Internet access method you use, Mac OS X asks you about it when it first sets itself up for you. If you have trouble connecting after this, you can change your settings yourself to what they're supposed to be. You might need to contact your ISP or go back to your Mac OS 9 settings to find out how to configure your Mac OS X settings.

➤ Although high-speed access is becoming more common for home and small business computer users, most people still get online using an analog modem and a regular phone line. Mac OS X's PPP Connect program is what you use to get connected if you fall into this category.

➤ If you have high-speed access, Mac OS X's TCP/IP Preferences pane contains the settings you'll need to work with. PPPoE users will need to locate a Mac OS X–compatible PPPoE dialer program.

➤ Sharing one Internet connection among several computers can be accomplished with hardware or software, but no matter which method you choose, you'll need to network the computers together, which you can do with conventional cabling or Apple's AirPort system, a wireless networking setup.

➤ The Internet Preferences pane is a central repository for information about your identity and the servers you use that might be required by various Internet programs.

Chapter 14

Nothing but Net

In This Chapter

➤ Getting on the Web

➤ Setting up to use e-mail

➤ Filtering e-mail into folders

➤ Searching the Web with Sherlock

➤ Using other Internet services: chat, instant messaging, Usenet, FTP, and telnet

This is truly the age of the Internet. Just about any information you can think of is online, just a *search engine* query away. You can use the Net for entertainment, shopping, keeping in touch with friends and family, working, researching—you name it. Your Mac is ready to go online—and take you along for the ride!

Looking for Mr. Goodweb

A *search engine* is a Web site that searches the Web or parts of the Web for the information you want. AltaVista (**www.altavista.com**) and Google (**www.google.com**) are two of the largest search engines. To find information using a search engine, you type in words that describe what you want and the search engine locates Web pages that contain those words.

Surf's Up!

If you're like me, you head out on the Web at odd moments of the day, almost every day. Need to look up a business phone number or a mail order returns policy? Wondering what countries border Kenya, or just looking for the latest news and weather? It's all on the Web.

Just Browsing

Whether you're looking for something specific or just browsing, the program you use to surf the Web is called a Web browser. Each Web page is actually made up of at least one *HTML* file, perhaps some graphic files, and multimedia files, such as animations, sound, or video. A browser reads all those files and uses them to build the Web page you see (see Figure 14.1).

The Web was created as a way to link information to related data. Clicking on a Web link, whether it's part of a Web page or in an e-mail or other file, usually displays a different Web page. Links on *that* page take you somewhere else, and so on. But you have to get started somewhere. You can begin surfing the Web in several ways:

Surfing the Efficient Way

You can save yourself some time by setting Web surfing preferences in the Internet pane of System Preferences. You can specify a default Web browser, a home page and a search page, and a folder location for files you download. See "Hello, Central" in Chapter 13, "Getting Online," for more information.

➤ Start up a Web browser and type in the *URL* of the Web page you want to view. This is similar to dialing a phone number to call a friend. Like phone numbers, URLs must be entered correctly or you'll either go somewhere you didn't mean to go or get an error page.

Show Info

Duke of URL

URLs (Uniform Resource Locators) are a way of identifying the locations of objects on the Internet. Usually, those object are Web pages, but they can also be other kinds of files. The part of the URL before the colon indicates what kind of link the URL is. **http** indicates a Web link; **ftp** refers to a file transfer link; **news** means a Usenet newsgroup; and **mailto** specifies an e-mail address. The rest of the URL is the actual location. For example, **http://www.apple.com/** is a Web link to Apple Computer's home page, whereas **mailto:kbinder@mac.com** is a link to my e-mail address. Although some people pronounce URL as "earl," the term is more commonly spoken spelled out, as "U-R-L."

➤ Choose a page from the Bookmarks or Favorites menu in your Web browser, just as you would push an autodial button on your phone to call a number you've programmed in. To bookmark a page that you want to come back to, choose the appropriate command at the top of the Bookmarks or Favorites menu in your browser.

➤ Click a link in another kind of document, such as an e-mail message.

A Little Hyper

Every country has its own language, and in the land of the Web, that language is HyperText Markup Language, or **HTML**. It's a system of tags (such as <H1> for a first-level heading) that allows a Web browser to display different kinds of information in visually appropriate ways.

Start Your Day Off with the Web

You can have your Web browser display a specific page every time you log in to your Mac by creating a URL clipping file. Then, choose **Apple menu, System Preferences** and click the **Login** button. Click **Add** and locate the URL clipping file to add it to the list of items that are opened when you log in, or just drag the file into the list of Login items.

➤ Double-click a URL "clipping" file on the Desktop or in a folder. You can make your own URL clippings by selecting a URL from the Location field at the top of a Web browser window and dragging it onto the Desktop. These files don't contain any data; they're just links in the form of files that you can move around, rename, and copy.

➤ Set a start page in your browser preferences. Or, set it in the System Preferences Internet pane to make it the start page for all your browsers, if you have more than one installed.

Browsers That Try Harder

For several years, the two most popular browsers have been Netscape Communicator (or Navigator; www.netscape.com) and Microsoft Internet Explorer (www.microsoft.com). These two are still around, but a couple of interesting competitors are closing in on them. Internet Explorer ships with Mac OS X—you'll find it in your Dock when you start up for the first time—but you might want to take a look at these two alternatives:

➤ iCab—This German product is small, fast, and sleek—it doesn't include extra features such as e-mail and news support. The developers place a strong emphasis on supporting Web standards rather than coming up with their own ways of doing things, as Microsoft often does. You can find out more at www.icab.de.

➤ OmniWeb—A slicker browser that's more focused on user enjoyment than efficiency is this new product from the Omni Group, one of the first Mac OS X software developers. OmniWeb has a lot of nice details and a lovely interface. It's downloadable at www.omnigroup.com.

Browsing the Way You Prefer

Although the preferences available to you depend on which Web browser you're using, some preferences are common to all browsers. You'll find the preferences for your Web browser (and those for almost every other program) in the application menu; for example, choose **Explorer, Preferences** to open Internet Explorer's preferences dialog box. Here's a list of things you'll want to consider customizing in your browser:

➤ **Colors**—You can set the background color for Web pages that don't specify their own, and you can determine the colors for text, links you haven't clicked on, and links you've already clicked on. Some browsers let you specify that your choices here should override the choices coded into the Web pages you view.

➤ **Fonts**—Web browsers choose one or more fonts in which to display text, and you can control this choice. Ordinarily, you'll specify a proportional font, such as Times, for normal text and a monospaced font, such as Courier (which looks like a typewriter font), for text that is aligned using multiple space characters. Sometimes you can choose other kinds of fonts; for example, Internet Explorer enables you to specify *serif* and *sans serif* fonts as well as a cursive font and a "fantasy" font.

➤ **Downloads**—If you want to be able to find the files you download (such as sound files, images, and software updates), it's a good idea to specify a folder in which they should be deposited on your computer. Otherwise, they can end up on your desktop or in your home folder, but you'll need to go looking for them.

➤ **Identity**—Web browsers usually have one or more preference panels in which you can enter information about yourself: your name, e-mail address, company name, and so on. This information is to identify you online, such as when you submit e-mail forms from a Web page. You can save time by entering personal information in one place: the Internet pane of the System Preferences (see "Hello Central" in Chapter 13, "Getting Online"). In Explorer, you can use the AutoFill Profile section of the preferences to instantly fill out forms with this kind of information.

➤ **Helper applications**—Software developers keep trying, but they haven't yet come up with a Web browser that can do it all. Applications that perform special functions while you're on the Web are called helper applications, and they can include programs that decompress file archives (such as StuffIt Expander), play multimedia files (such as the QuickTime plug-in), or open file formats that aren't supported by your browser. If you find yourself presented with a dialog box indicating that your browser doesn't know what to do with a particular file type, take the time to add the appropriate entry for a helper application in its preferences. That way the browser will send the file directly to the correct application the next time.

Go To

Venturing Deeper into Cyberspace

If you need to set your Mac up for Internet access, see Chapter 13, "Getting Online." To delve more deeply into what the Web has to offer, consult a book such as *The Complete Idiot's Guide to the Internet*.

Show Info

With or Without Serifs

Serifs are the small doglegs at the ends of type characters, such as the short stroke at the bottom of a lowercase "i." Typefaces that have serifs are referred to as **serif** faces, and faces without them are called **sans serif**.

Eating from the Apple Tree

A great place to find Mac Internet applications (some for Mac OS X, some not) is the Mac Orchard (`www.macorchard.com`). As the site's maintainer says, "The Mac Orchard is a carefully cultivated list of the most vital Internet applications and links for Macintosh Internet users, along with Internet software reviews contributed from The Mac Orchard's audience." So, if you want to try something new or are looking for the right helper application, check out the Orchard.

Searching the Web with Sherlock

Both the Web and your own computer have so much space to store stuff that you probably spend an ever-increasing amount of time just looking for what you want. That's why Apple created Sherlock a few years back and includes an improved version with Mac OS X.

Change the Channel

To start Sherlock, click its icon in the Dock or click the Desktop and press Cmd+F. Across the top of the Sherlock window (see Figure 14.2) are buttons representing channels, each of which enables you to search a different area of the Internet (or your computer).

Searching the Neighborhood

This section shows you how to use Sherlock to search the Internet. If you're looking for something on your own computer, you'll find instructions for searching your files with Sherlock in the section "But I Can't Find Anything!" in Chapter 5, "Managing Your Files."

➤ **Files**—The first channel is selected when you start up Sherlock. Using the Files channel, you can search your hard drive, removable drives mounted on your computer, and network drives to which you're connected.

➤ **Internet**—In this channel, you'll find mostly search engines and Web directories.

➤ **People**—Here you'll find directories of people on the Internet so you can look up e-mail addresses and personal home pages. The search results display e-mail addresses right in Sherlock's window.

➤ **Apple**—Search Apple's product listings and technical information with the sites listed under the Apple channel.

Figure 14.2
The icon to the left of each listing indicates what search site it comes from.

➤ **Shopping**—The E-commerce sites listed here enable you to search for books, music, and other merchandise being sold online. The search results include the items' prices.

➤ **News**—This channel includes technology, sports, financial, and entertainment news sites.

➤ **Reference**—Who needs a printed dictionary or encyclopedia when you can fire up Sherlock and search either one or both?

➤ **Entertainment**—This channel comes with plug-ins for E! Online, the Internet Movie Database, and *Rolling Stone* magazine.

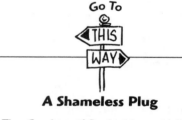

A Shameless Plug

The Greyhound Project is a real-life organization dedicated to helping people learn how to adopt and care for retired racing greyhounds. You'll find it on the Web at **www.adopt-a-greyhound.org**.

Now that I've piqued your interest, let's take a look at how you actually use Sherlock. The first step is to choose a channel and to check off the search sites you want to include in your search. To check off all the sites, press Cmd+T. If sites were already checked, this unchecks them; press it again to check all the sites.

Now take a minute to choose search terms that describe what you're searching for. If you're looking for something concrete, search terms are generally easy to come up with. For example, if I'm using the Shopping channel to look for a carpet steamer, I'll just type "carpet steamer" in the text field under the channel buttons. If my desire is to find out how to adopt a retired racing greyhound, however, I'll probably want to enter more than just "greyhound"—I'll get better results by entering something like "adopt racing greyhound." And if I don't find what I want, I'll add more terms and try the search again.

Choosing Your Windows

In addition to double-clicking, you can drag a site listing to a Web browser window to open the site in that window. This is useful if you keep multiple windows open at the same time. For example, as I write this I'm monitoring football scores in one window that I want to keep open, so I'll drag my site listings to another window so my sports scores don't disappear.

After entering search terms, click the **Search** button to the right of the text field. A progress bar at the bottom of the window lets you know that Sherlock is searching, and sites start popping up in the list window as the search continues. In the case of my greyhound search, the Greyhound Project is the very first link. It turns out to be a central repository for information on racing greyhounds and local adoption group listings—just what I want.

When the search is finished, you have a list of sites that you can sort several ways by clicking on the column headers at the top of the list. Which column headers you see depends on the channel you searched; for example, the Shopping channel brings back price information (see Figure 14.3), whereas the Internet channel includes a relevance rating. If you see a site that you think is what you want, click it to see a summary of its content at the bottom of the Sherlock window. And if it *is* what you want, double-click it to open it in your Web browser.

Figure 14.3

Here are the results of my search on the Internet auction site eBay for a blueberry iBook, sorted by price (which is the current high bid in the case of eBay). $217.50—wow!

Taking Sherlock New Places

You're not restricted to using Sherlock's built-in channels and search sites. You can download Sherlock *plug-ins* and create your own channels to search your own favorite sites.

Many Web sites offer Sherlock plug-ins that you can download and add to Sherlock's built-in sites. For example, if you want to search the free online classified ads at YardSale.net, you can download the site's Sherlock plug-in (www.YardSaleNet.net/sherlock/) and do your searches from Sherlock.

One way to find plug-ins is to search the Internet channel for the text "Sherlock plug-in." Another way is to check out the Apple Donuts site, where Mac OS add-ons are collected for you to download. The Apple Donuts Sherlock page (www.apple-donuts.com/sherlocksearch/) catalogs about 300 different plug-ins for Sherlock—everything from online auction giant eBay to Amherst College in Massachusetts.

After you've downloaded a Sherlock plug-in, you can add it to any channel you want. Click the button to open the channel, and then drag the plug-in from the Desktop or folder window into the list of search sites.

Plugging In and Turning On

A **plug-in** is a piece of software that adds capabilities to another program. In the case of Sherlock, plug-ins allow Sherlock to search additional Web sites that are not part of the default set.

Creating your own channels enables you to organize your search sites in a way that makes sense to you. To create new channels:

1. Choose **Channels**, **New Channel**.
2. Type in a name for the channel.
3. Choose a Channel type from the pop-up menu. This choice determines what information appears in the search results list window.
4. Click the up and down arrows next to the Icon window to pick a picture for the new channel's button.
5. Click **OK**.

Picture This

You can use any picture you like for channel buttons; just drag a picture file from the Desktop or folder window onto the Icon window.

You can go back and edit your custom channels in the same way; click the channel's button and choose **Channels**, **Edit Channel**. The built-in channels can't be edited or deleted.

Using E-Mail

It's not as flashy as the Web, but e-mail is really the killer app of the Internet. It's quick, it's easy, and it comes to you—you don't have to go looking for it. You can sign up for e-mail newsletters and discussion lists related to your interests, and then wait for the information to come rolling into your mailbox. Of course, you can also use e-mail to keep in touch with friends, relatives, customers, co-workers, and just about everyone else.

163

Read Me

Lovely Spam! Wonderful Spam!

Where there's e-mail, there's spam—that is, unsolicited commercial e-mail, AKA electronic junk mail. The more you use the Internet, the more you're likely to receive spam, and it can get pretty annoying. Fortunately, you're not powerless to fight spam. CAUCE, the Coalition Against Unsolicited Commercial Email, offers information and resources for dealing with junk e-mail at its Web site: **www.cauce.com.**

Setting Up E-Mail

Mac OS X comes with a compact e-mail application called, naturally, Mail. Although Mail probably won't be the power user's choice, it does the job just fine. Here are a few things you'll need to know to use Mail.

After you start up Mail, you can set up e-mail accounts in the Preferences dialog box. Here's how:

1. Choose **Mail**, **Preferences** and click **Accounts**; you can create as many accounts as you have e-mail addresses.

2. Click **Create Account** to set up a new account (see Figure 14.4).

3. Choose the type of account you're using. If you're a home or small business user with an ISP connection, choose **POP Account**; at a large company, check with the IT staff to see which type you should use. The rest of these steps assume you're setting up a POP account.

4. Enter a name for the account, and then enter the e-mail address and your name.

Figure 14.4

You'll need to know the names of your ISP's mail servers to set up new e-mail accounts.

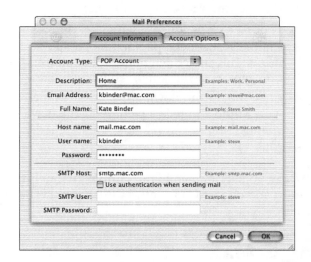

5. Enter the incoming mail server in the Host Name field, and then add your user name and password.

6. Enter the outgoing mail server in the SMTP Host field. Both this server name and the incoming server name (also called a POP server) are available from your ISP.

7. Click the **Account Options** tab and check **Include This Account When Checking for New Mail** and **Delete Messages on Server After Downloading**. This second setting deletes mail permanently from the server, making sure that your mailbox there doesn't fill up.

8. Click one of the two radio buttons. Show This Account Separated in Mailboxes Drawer gives you a separate In Box for this account, whereas Download Messages from This Account Into Folder enables you to specify a folder other than your main In Box for messages received by this account.

9. If you don't want to receive large attachments, enter a message size over which to skip.

10. Click **OK** to return to Mail Preferences, and click the close button.

Read Me

There's Always an Exception

The only time you don't want to check *Delete Messages on Server After Downloading* is if you're setting up e-mail on a laptop or other computer that isn't your main computer, and you want all your e-mail to be duplicated on another computer.

Receiving E-Mail

After your accounts are set up and you're connected to the Internet, you can begin receiving and sending e-mail with Mail. To check your e-mail, be sure you have a viewer window open (choose **File**, **New Viewer Window** if you don't see one). Then, click the **Get Mail** button at the top of the window.

Go To

Making the Connection

Turn to Chapter 13, "Getting Online," to learn how to set up your Mac to connect to the Internet.

All your new mail is dropped into the Inbox for the e-mail address to which it is addressed, but you can create other mailboxes into which to sort your e-mail. To see your mailboxes, click the **Mailbox** button at the top of the viewer window. A drawer pops out to the side of the window (see Figure 14.5). Listed in the drawer are all your e-mail accounts, as well as an item called Personal Mailboxes. Within Personal Mailboxes are mailbox folders labeled Drafts, Personal, and Sent Messages. To these you can add mailboxes and submailboxes to help you keep your e-mail organized.

For example, I have a personal mailbox called Mailing Lists, and within that mailbox folder are submailboxes for each mailing list to which I subscribe. I use another Mail feature, rules, to have e-mail from those lists filed in these folders as I receive it, rather than having to sort through it and move it into the folders myself.

To sort e-mail automatically, choose **Mail**, **Preferences** and click **Rules**. Click **Create Rule** to make a new sorting rule, and then type a name for it in the Description field. Then enter the new rule's parameters below:

Figure 14.5

You can have all your e-mail deposited into your In Box, where this message ended up, or you can set up a separate mailbox for each kind of mail you receive.

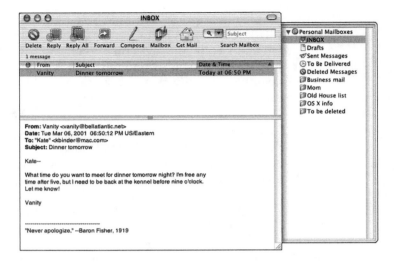

1. In the Criteria area, choose a header field, such as From.

2. Choose an option, such as Contains or Does Not Contain, and then enter the text that you want Mail to look for when sorting mail (for example, choose **Contains** and enter mom@mac.com to pick out mail from Mom).

3. Then, choose the action that you want Mail to take when it receives mail that fits your criteria. In this case, all mail from my mother gets automatically filed in the "Mom" mailbox as it comes in, and Mail plays the Submarine alert sound to let me know it has arrived.

4. Click **OK** to return to the mail viewer window.

Sending E-Mail

You can write e-mail from scratch, forward messages, or send replies to messages that you've received. To forward e-mail, click the **Forward** button in the viewer window. To reply to e-mail, click **Reply** or **Reply All**, which sends your reply to all the original message's recipients as well as to the sender. To write an e-mail from scratch, click **Compose**.

If you click Forward or Compose, you'll see a message window with a blinking text cursor in the To field. Here's where you enter the names or e-mail addresses of the people to whom you want to send the message. If you've created entries in the Address Book, you can just type the names of your recipients and Mail fills in their e-mail addresses. Or click **Favorites**; a drawer slides out to the side of the window listing the names of people who are in your address book. Double-click a name to add it to the To field, or click it and click **To**, **CC** (carbon copy), or **BCC** (blind carbon copy; other recipients won't see this recipient listed in the e-mail).

For people who aren't in your address book, type the e-mail addresses themselves. Then, if you've set up more than one e-mail account in Preferences, choose which account to send the mail from. Finally, add a subject for the e-mail in the Subject field, type your message in the main body of the window, and click **Send** to mail it (see Figure 14.6).

Figure 14.6

Clicking Send will get this message on its way back to my friend Vanity.

The Little Black (Address) Book

Address book, you say? What address book?

Address Book is another useful little program included with Mac OS X. In it you can store not only e-mail addresses, but also Web page URLs, phone numbers, *snail mail* addresses—even birthdays. To get there, create a new e-mail message and click the **Address** button.

Choose a category from the Show pop-up menu to view people in that category. The All option shows addresses in all categories, and the Temporary Cards option displays addresses harvested from e-mails you've received since you logged in.

To add an entry to the Favorites address book, click **Edit** at the top of the Address Book window, and then click **Categories**. Click **Favorites** in the Categories list, and then click **OK**. After you've entered someone in your Favorites address book, that person's name shows up in the Favorites list you see when you're composing an e-mail message.

Mail à l'Escargot

If you've been using e-mail for any length of time, it's hard not to become frustrated with the slower real-life version. This leads to an obvious name for the letters and packages delivered by your local postal carrier: *snail mail*.

Making New Friends

You can copy an entry from Temporary Cards into Favorites by clicking **Edit**, adding any other info you want to include in the listing, and clicking **Categories** to change the contact's category from Temporary to a regular category.

Each entry looks like a Rolodex card. In addition to e-mail addresses, you can enter other information on each "card" (see Figure 14.7):

➤ The top area of each person's card contains his or her first name, last name, and company.

➤ Below that, you can enter the person's address, phone numbers, fax number, and e-mail address.

➤ The bottom area of the card contains four custom fields. You can click **Customize** to enter names for these four fields; for example, you might use these fields to store pets' or children's names, birthdays, or shipping account numbers.

Show Me a Picture

You can add a picture to an Address Book entry by dragging an image file from the Desktop or a folder window into the white square at the upper-right corner of that card. If you receive e-mail from a person whose picture is in the Address Book, the picture is displayed in the e-mail message.

Figure 14.7

Address book entries can contain a variety of useful contact information.

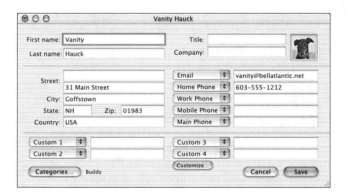

Other Internet Applications

Go To

Branching Out

You can find software for just about any Internet application at the Mac Orchard (www.macorchard.com).

Despite appearances, there's a lot more to the Internet than e-mail and the Web. Here's a quick look at some of the other ways the Internet can entertain, assist, and enlighten you.

➤ Instant messaging is like instant e-mail—you type a message, hit **Send**, and it appears on the recipient's screen, and only there. Chatting, on the other hand, is more like having a conversation at a party or the dinner table. Multiple people can participate in a chat simultaneously, and every participant can see what all the others are saying. Each company that offers a chat or instant messaging service also provides software to access the service.

➤ Usenet is an Internet service that's much, much older than the World Wide Web. It's a collection of *newsgroups* with topics ranging from the obscure to the bizarre and everything in between. Some newsgroups are moderated, meaning that posts are vetted for relevance and good manners before being posted, while others are unmoderated, meaning that things can get pretty wild and woolly. You can read and post to newsgroups on the Web at sites such as Deja.com (www.deja.com) and Liquid Information (www.liquidinformation.com). It's much faster, though, to use a dedicated application called a newsreader to read and post to Usenet newsgroups.

➤ File Transfer Protocol (FTP), a standard way of moving files from one Unix workstation to another, is also the standard way to move files around on the Internet. If you maintain your own Web site, chances are you use FTP to upload the HTML and graphics files that the site contains.

➤ Like FTP, telnet has Unix roots. It's a way of opening a Unix terminal window for another computer on your own computer, either over a local network or over the Internet. You can use telnet directly from the command line in Mac OS X's Terminal application, but if you telnet more than just occasionally, you'll want a telnet application.

Apple Makes It Easy

Mac OS X makes heavier use of Internet services than any other operating system, with features like Software Update, Network Time, and the online Help system. Apple expects that most Mac users either are online now or will be soon, and the company wants the Mac to help make the Internet easier to use. That's the reasoning behind iTools, Apple's free set of Web-based tools and services (see Figure 14.8).

Figure 14.8

iTools is free for Mac users.

You'll find instructions for signing up with iTools in the next chapter. Here's a look at what you'll find when you start using iTools:

➤ **iCards**—Electronic postcards that you can e-mail to all your friends.

➤ **KidSafe**—A list of Web sites reviewed and approved by educators for kids.

➤ **iDisk**—Storage space on Apple's Internet servers that you can use to back up files, store Web pages, or share images or movies with your friends.

➤ **E-mail**—A free e-mail address at the Mac.com domain.

➤ **HomePage**—The easiest way to create your own Web site.

Keep reading—the next chapter contains more information on how to create a Web site with iTools.

The Least You Need to Know

➤ The Web is where it's at, and Mac OS X is on the Web. Although Microsoft Internet Explorer ships with Mac OS X, you can use any browser you prefer, including OmniWeb (which is Mac OS X–only).

➤ Using Sherlock, Mac OS X's built-in search engine, you can search your computer or the Web. Sherlock's Web search capabilities can look for specialized information such as e-mail addresses and retail prices.

➤ Mac OS X comes with an e-mail program called, strangely enough, Mail. Using Mail, you can receive e-mail at multiple addresses, organize messages using a hierarchical folder system, and filter incoming mail into selected folders automatically.

➤ The Internet is more than just the World Wide Web. Other Internet services that you might find entertaining and/or useful include e-mail, FTP, chat, instant messaging, telnet, and Usenet. Software exists to let you use all these services on your Mac and you get access to iTools free.

Chapter 15

Publishing on the Web

In This Chapter

➤ Signing up for iTools

➤ Using iTools to build your Web site

➤ Creating a Web site on your own

➤ Saving images for the Web

➤ Finding a home for your pages on the Web

➤ Finding free Web design resources

These days, everyone's gotta be on the Web. It's a great way to keep in touch with your family, promote your business, and share party invitations and photos with your friends. Apple gives you an easy way to put up a good-looking Web site quickly with iTools, and if you're ready to learn a little HTML, you can create your own Web page designs from scratch.

Creating a Site with iTools

Apple's free Mac-only iTools give you 20MB of space on the Apple Web site, your own e-mail address at mac.com, and the opportunity to create your own Web site with no special tools required—just a Web browser and an Internet connection.

Setting Up iTools

Before you can use iTools, you need to create an account and enter your account settings in the System Preferences. You had the opportunity to do both of these things when you set up Mac OS X for the first time. If you didn't (or if another user of your Mac created an account at that point and you want your own), you can sign up (if necessary) and enter your settings now.

iTools, Not iTools

The iTools Web site at **www.itools.com** has nothing to do with Apple's iTools—be sure you go to **itools.mac.com** to use the iTools we're talking about in this chapter.

Choose **Apple menu**, **System Preferences** and click the **Internet** button, and then click the **iTools** tab. First things first: If you don't yet have an iTools account, click **Free Sign Up** to go to the sign-up form on Apple's Web site (see Figure 15.1).

After you complete and submit the sign-up form, the next page shows you your account settings. It's a good idea to print a copy of this page and stash it somewhere where you won't lose it. The information shown includes your member name, your password (so don't leave the page lying around!), your e-mail address, and the incoming mail server name, which you can use to collect your mac.com e-mail using Mac OS X's Mail or another e-mail program.

Figure 15.1

The iTools sign-up form requires your name and address; you also must create a member name and a password.

The next screen contains a form where you can enter your friends' e-mail addresses to send them an electronic change-of-address card letting them know your new e-mail address. After that's taken care of, you can begin creating Web pages right away by clicking the **Start Using iTools** button to begin using the iTools services.

To access your iTools e-mail account with Mail and your iDisk storage space, you'll need to go back to the System Preferences and enter your member name and password.

After you've entered this information, you can access your iDisk by clicking the Desktop and choosing **Go, iDisk**. The iDisk appears on the Desktop or in a Finder window along with your Mac's local drives. To copy files to the iDisk, just drag them to the icon as you would with any other disk; to see the iDisk's contents, double-click it to open a Finder window.

If you've entered your iTools member name and password in the Internet pane of the System Preferences, Mac OS X's built-in e-mail program, Mail (located in the Applications folder), automatically sets up your mac.com e-mail account the first time you run it, so you don't have to do a thing.

Go Go Go!

If you're in a hurry to get started creating your Web page, you can skip this step (click **No Thanks!**) and send a card later by clicking the **iCards** button on the main iTools page.

Creating a Page with HomePage

To begin setting up your iTools Web site, click the **HomePage** button on the main iTools page (`itools.mac.com`). You'll need to log in with your new member name and password. Remember to use your iTools member name and password, which don't have to be the same as the ones you use to log in to your Mac. Then you can follow these steps:

1. Click to choose a type of page to create, such as an invitation, a résumé, or a photo album.
2. Choose a theme—these are predesigned templates for your page (see Figure 15.2).
3. Click the **Edit Text** buttons to edit the heading and text on the page.
4. Click the **Edit Link** buttons to add links to the page; these can be e-mail addresses or Web links.
5. If your template has places for images, click **Choose** to pick an image to use. You can choose images from Apple's Image Library or use any GIF or JPEG image files stored in the Pictures folder of your iDisk. (See "Graphic Facts," later in this chapter, to learn about the kinds of image files you can use on the Web.)

HomePage Trivia

If you choose the Newsletter theme for your page (it's in the Personal category), you'll see a typical newspaper layout, with a volume and issue number below the "Newsletter" title. The numbers start counting from the debut of the Macintosh in the winter of 1984—the first "edition."

Figure 15.2

iTools includes profession-ally designed templates for your Web pages.

6. Click the **Preview** button at the top of the page to see what your page will look like (see Figure 15.3).

Figure 15.3

You can preview your page at any time, even if you know you're not finished editing it.

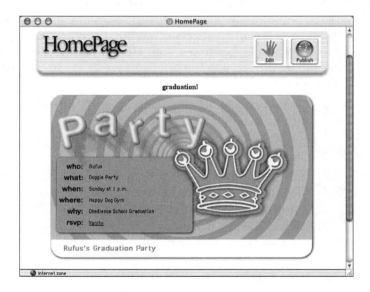

7. If you want to make changes, click the **Edit** button and go back to step 3.

8. When you're satisfied with the page, click the **Publish** button to put your page on the Web. The next screen shows you the page's *URL* and enables you to send an iCard to give your friends the new link (see Figure 15.4).

9. Click the link to go to the page and see how it looks in your Web browser.

Figure 15.4
You can use iCards to notify your friends about your new page, or you can just e-mail the URL to them yourself.

10. Click the **Build Your Own Web Site** button to go back to HomePage's starting point and create another page.

The finished pages are stored in your iDisk storage area. To open it, click the Desktop and choose **Go, iDisk** (Option+Cmd+I). You'll find the files that make up your Web pages in the Sites folder. If the iTools templates are too limiting for you, you can create your own pages and put them in your iDisk's Sites folder to publish them. Read the next section, "Home Cooking: Doing It Yourself," to learn how.

Show Info

U R Your URL

A **URL** is an alphanumeric address that indicates a specific page on the Web. For example, the URL for Apple's Web site is **www.apple.com**.

Read Me

A Good Starting Point

Your Web site needs a start page, the first page people see when they go to your main URL. If you have only one page, or you don't specify a start page, the first page you create will automatically be designated the start page. You can choose which page should be used as your Web site's starting point by logging in to iTools and clicking the **HomePage** button. After you've created a page, the main HomePage page includes an area marked Edit a Page, where you can choose a page to modify and specify which page should be your start page.

Home Cooking: Doing It Yourself

If you're the DIY type, you're going to love the Web. You'll need to learn a few simple skills to create your own Web pages, but you can get started quickly and get into more complicated Web designs as your knowledge grows. This section covers creating Web pages, creating Web images, and publishing your files on the Web.

Creating Content

Web pages are written in a coding language called *HTML*. The files are plain text, easy to read, and the HTML codes are simple—in fact, one good way to learn how HTML works is to use your Web browser's View Source command to see the HTML behind a page that you like the looks of.

Here's an example of the HTML for a simple Web page (see Figure 15.5):

```
<HTML
<HEAD>
<TITLE>Kate's Page</TITLE>
</HEAD>
<BODY BGCOLOR="#FFFFFF">
<P>Hello, world!</P>
<P>Click <A HREF="http://www.apple.com/">here</A> to go to Apple's Web
➥site.</P>
</BODY>
</HTML>
```

Figure 15.5

It takes just a few lines of code to create this Web page.

The <HTML> tag lets a Web browser know that this is—surprise!—a Web page, and the <HEAD> and <BODY> tags divide the document into information about the document and information that should appear on the page, respectively. <P> is the tag for a paragraph, and <A HREF> is the tag for a hyperlink; clicking on the word "here" inside the <A> tags takes you to the URL specified by the HREF code: www.apple.com. Each tag requires a beginning and an end, and the end tags are the same as the beginning tags with the addition of a /.

178

Where to Learn More About HTML

Webmonkey offers a good HTML tutorial that will teach you the standard HTML tags and how to use them, how to insert special characters, how to keep your HTML files as small (and therefore as fast-loading) as possible, and more. You'll find it at `hotwired.lycos.com/webmonkey/authoring/html_basics/`.

You can write HTML from scratch in any program that can produce a plain text file, including Mac OS X's built-in TextEdit. But HTML editors, programs designed for creating Web pages, offer features that simplify the job.

Create (Stone Design, `www.stone.com`) is an example of a *WYSIWYG* Web page design application for Mac OS X. You can place text and images anywhere on the page, just the way you would in a page layout program (see Figure 15.6), and turn the whole assemblage into a Web page simply by choosing **Web**, **Create Web** pages and giving the resulting HTML file a name.

Hyper Text

HTML stands for HyperText Markup Language, a system of inserting codes within text files to indicate how a Web browser should display the file.

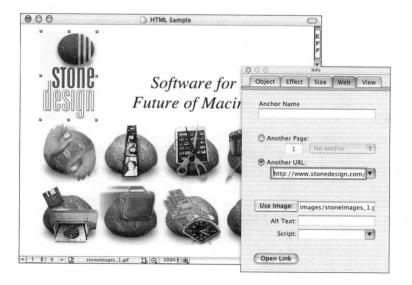

Figure 15.6

You don't have to know a word of HTML to use a WYSIWYG HTML editor such as Stone Design's Create.

What You See...

...is what you get with a **WYSIWYG** program, whether it's for designing printed pieces or Web pages. The idea is that what you see on the screen as you work is exactly what the final product will look like.

Avoiding a Loss

For GIF and PNG images, compression is almost always lossless, meaning that no image quality is sacrificed for the sake of compression.

A third option is to create your pages in a program that you already use, such as Microsoft Word, and use the program's HTML export feature to turn your files into Web pages. Not all programs have such a feature, but enough do that it's worth looking at your favorite page layout program or word processor to see whether it can do this.

Of course, in addition to text, you're going to need pictures to put on your pages. The next section explains how to turn your photos and artwork into Web-ready graphics.

Graphic Facts

To be displayed on the Web, your images should use one of two different file formats:

➤ GIF—This is the right format to use for simple graphics such as logos.

➤ JPEG—Use this format for photos.

Most painting or drawing programs can save images that you scan in or create yourself in at least the first two of these formats, which is really all you need. The object when creating Web images is to make the files as small as possible without affecting how they look, because smaller files download faster. So, most programs that can save images in Web formats offer you a couple of options when you save, as follows:

➤ **How much compression do you want to use?**—When you're saving a JPEG image, you get to choose how much the image will be compressed to reduce its file size. The catch is that JPEG compression is "lossy," meaning that it can create little glitches in an image. So, you need to balance the amount of compression you use with the quality you want for the file; in fact, many JPEG options dialog boxes (see Figure 15.7) offer a quality slider instead of a compression slider. The thing to remember is that higher quality means less compression and a larger file, whereas lower quality allows the image to be compressed more for a smaller file. You might want to experiment with different quality levels to get a feel for the results of the different settings.

➤ **How many colors should the image contain?**—GIF image files can be smaller if fewer colors are present in the image, and often you have the option of choosing the number of colors used when saving the file (see Figure 15.8). Higher-end graphics programs include a preview area that shows you how the image changes as you reduce the number of colors, so you can pick the smallest number that doesn't affect the way the image looks.

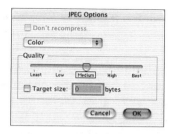

Figure 15.7

Higher quality means larger JPEG files; lower quality means smaller files.

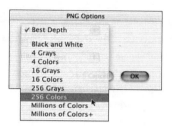

Figure 15.8

The number of colors you allow the image file to contain affects the file size.

Another optional setting you might run into is "interlaced" (for GIF files) or "progressive" for JPEG files. Saving a file in this way makes it display right away at low resolution when the Web page is first accessed, even before the entire image file is downloaded to the user's computer. The image is gradually displayed more clearly until the entire file is downloaded. Using this option doesn't affect the file's size and is a boon to your Web page's readers.

Getting It Out There

Of course, creating a Web site doesn't stop with making the graphics and the HTML files—you must get your work out on the Web where people can see it. One way to do this is to put your files on your iDisk (HTML files in the Sites folder and image files in the Pictures folder). Another way is to use a Web hosting service.

Hundreds, maybe even thousands, of companies provide varying levels of Web hosting services, offering everything from free Web pages all the way up to setting aside an entire computer to serve your Web site exclusively. Your ISP probably includes free space on its server in the price you pay for your Internet access.

If you're ready to move up to the big time, you might want to purchase your own domain name, such as (in my case) www.prospecthillpub.com. That's the Web site I use to promote my business. To set it up, I did the following:

It's the Little Extras That Make the Difference

The advantage of putting your Web page up using the server space your ISP provides instead of your iDisk is that you might be able to enhance your pages with special programs hosted by your ISP, such as counters and guestbook programs.

What's FTP?

FTP stands for File Transfer Protocol, and it's a standard way of copying files across a network, either locally or over the Internet. It's used quite commonly to copy files from one Unix computer to another, and it's the most common way to transfer files over the Internet.

Musically Speaking

There's a lot of other stuff you can incorporate into your Web sites, including animations and music. Using music on your Web site is a good news/bad news situation. The good news is that you'll have fun picking it out, the music might be very appropriate for your subject matter, and many of your site's visitors will love it. The bad news is that many of your site's visitors will hate it.

➤ Registered the domain name for $35 per year; see www.internic.net for information on how to do this.

➤ Signed up for a hosting service, which costs me about $20 per month (although rates start at just a few dollars a month); my provider's own Web page is at www.hostme.com.

➤ Created my HTML and image files; I use an HTML editor called PageSpinner (Optima System, www.optima-system.com) and the industry-standard image editor Adobe Photoshop (Adobe Systems, www.adobe.com).

➤ Transferred the files to the hosting service's computer using an *FTP* client called Transmit (Alsoft, www.panic.com).

I had instructions to follow every step of the way, so the whole procedure was quick and easy. If you decide to go this route, don't be afraid to call your hosting provider and ask for help with registering your domain name and uploading your files.

Hey! Free Stuff!

I wouldn't be a true New Englander if I didn't appreciate a bargain when I found one. The resources listed here offer the best kind of bargain: free stuff. In this case, "stuff" refers to cool artwork and counters you can use on the Web pages you create.

Clip Art

The term "clip art" refers to small pieces of artwork that can be used as part of logos or as incidental artwork. You'll find a huge selection of clip art at the following sites:

➤ Barry's Clipart Server (www.barrysclipart.com)

➤ Clips Ahoy! (www.clipsahoy.com)

➤ ClipArtConnection (www.clipartconnection.com)

➤ AAAClipArt.com (www.aaaclipart.com)

➤ GifArt.com (www.gifart.com)

You'll also find that these sites tend to all link to each other, so if you visit a couple of them you'll be able to find lots more. Happy surfing!

Counters

If you like to keep track of how many people visit your Web site, you'll want to get a counter. These little features display a "hit counter" on your Web page so you (and everyone else) know just how much traffic your site is getting. Counters come in all different styles, and there are a ton of free ones. Here are a few you might want to try:

➤ **Hitometer** (www.hitometer.com)

➤ **theCounter** (www.thecounter.com)

➤ **Zcounter.com** (www.zcounter.com)

➤ **Beseen** (www.beseen.com/beseen/free/counters.html)

➤ **Admo.net** (www.admo.net/counter/)

You can find reviews of these and many more counters, both free and commercial, at CounterGuide (www.counterguide.com).

The Least You Need to Know

➤ Apple's free, Mac-only iTools offers an easy, convenient way to create your own Web pages. Using the supplied templates, you can have a Web page up in just a few minutes with no special software required to create it.

➤ If you prefer, you can build your Web site from scratch using an HTML editor and images you create or find in clip-art archives.

➤ You can put your Web pages on your iDisk, on the free space provided by your Internet service provider, or on a Web server that allows you to have your own domain name.

➤ When it comes to free artwork, counters, and other "extras" you can use on your Web pages, there are hundreds, maybe even thousands, of sources.

Part 4
Talking to Other Platforms

It's a rare Mac user who never has to share files with users of other computer systems. This part offers advice on getting along in a world where—sad but true—many people don't have Macs.

In Chapter 16, you'll learn what you need to know about working with other Mac users who might not be using Mac OS X yet, from sharing files to using a network and running older Mac programs. Chapter 17 covers similar ground for Windows users: transferring files from Mac to Windows and back, using the same printer, and running Windows software—without a Windows PC. And for those Mac lovers who hang out with Unix users, Chapter 18 offers ways to exchange files, share printers, and use Mac OS X's Unix underpinnings to run Unix programs on your Mac.

Chapter 16

Interacting with Earlier Versions of Mac OS

In This Chapter

➤ Transferring files using removable disk drives

➤ Setting up file sharing with other Macs

➤ Assigning IP addresses for TCP/IP file sharing

➤ Making sure others can read your files and vice versa

Hey, just because *you're* hip and cool and have a Mac with Mac OS X doesn't mean that all your friends or co-workers are running Mac OS X on *their* Macs. So, if you want to coexist with all those other Mac users, you'll need to learn how to get along with them—in computer terms, of course.

Macs have always had built-in networking, and Mac OS X is no exception. Because of the new system's revamped architecture, though, your networking options are a little more limited than they used to be—meaning you might just have to go back to the old standby method of putting files on removable disks to move them around.

Besides moving files around between your OS X Mac and Macs running older systems, you'll also want to be sure those files can be read on both systems. This chapter briefly reviews some ways to keep your files compatible.

Sharing Files with Sneakernet

If you don't have a real network, you're stuck with sneakernet: putting files on a disk and walking them over to the computer you want to share with. That's sneakernet, and it's certainly a viable option with Mac OS X. You will need to figure out what disk formats your OS X Mac has in common with the other Mac, though.

What's in a Name?

Trust Apple to muddy the waters with its product-naming conventions, just when we all thought the Mac product line was being streamlined. The SuperDisk mentioned here is *not* the same thing as the SuperDrive Apple announced in 2001, which is for burning CDs and DVDs but won't help you a bit when it comes to reading SuperDisks or floppies.

Pop It In, Pop It Out

For more details about the different kinds of removable disk drives you can use with Mac OS X, and the different kinds of interfaces they can have, see Chapter 4, "No Mac Is an Island." And to learn what kind of disk drives you have in your own Mac, use System Profiler—you'll find instructions in Chapter 26, "Good MacHousekeeping," in the "A Few Useful Tools" section.

Drive, She Said

Because Mac OS X runs only on newer Mac models (primarily G3 and G4 models and iMacs), you probably don't have a floppy disk drive. Here are some other options that may work for you:

➤ **SuperDisk**—These small disks are the same size as 3.5-inch 1.4MB floppy disks, but they hold 120MB. The Mac version of the SuperDisk drive has a USB connector, and the drive also reads floppy disks.

➤ **Zip**—Zip disks hold 100MB or 250MB, depending on the age of your Zip drive. The current version uses USB. Built-in Zip drives are an option on Power Mac G4s and many earlier Macs, so you might already have one.

➤ **Jaz**—These disks hold 1GB or 2GB of data—that's 2,000MB. The drives have SCSI connectors.

➤ **CD-R or CD-RW**—A CD-RW drive can write to both CD-R (CD-ROM Recordable) and CD-RW (CD-ROM Rewritable) media. Either of these can be read in any computer's CD-ROM drive, but you need special software (such as Adaptec Toast, www.roxio.com/en/products/toast/) and a CD "burner" to write to CDs. CD-Rs can't be reused, but CD-RW discs can be erased and rewritten. If you have a newer iMac or Power Mac G4 (released in 2001) your built-in CD-ROM drive might actually be a CD-RW drive—check your Mac's documentation.

➤ **DVD**—Many newer Macs ship with DVD (Digital Versatile Disc) drives, but not all DVDs are created equal. To use DVDs for file transfer or storage—they can hold up to 5.2GB of data—your Mac must have a DVD-RAM drive, which can write to a DVD, rather than simply a DVD-ROM drive, which can only read them.

You Can Get There from Here

After you've chosen a disk format and gotten the drive installed, here's how you can copy a file from your hard drive to a removable disk:

1. Insert the disk in the appropriate drive.

2. Depending on your Dock & Desktop Preferences settings, the disk's icon might appear on the Desktop. If it doesn't, press Cmd+N to open a new Finder window, and then press Cmd+1 to view all the disks your computer has installed, including the one you just inserted (see Figure 16.1).

3. Double-click the disk's icon to see its contents.

4. Press Cmd+N to open a new Finder window and navigate through that window to the folder or file you want to copy.

Taking Control of Your Desktop

You can control whether disk icons appear on the desktop in the Dock & Desktop Preferences. See Chapter 20, "The Desktop and the Dock As You Like Them," for instructions.

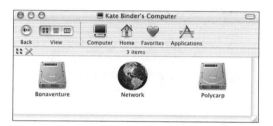

Figure 16.1

The Computer Finder window shows all the disks connected to your Mac, whether they're removable, internal, or network drives.

5. Drag the file or folder's icon into the window showing the removable disk's contents. Because this is a separate disk, the file or folder will be copied, rather than moved, and its icon includes a little plus sign to show that.

6. Press Cmd+1 to view your Mac's disks again.

7. Drag the icon for the removable disk on top of the Trash in the Dock to eject the disk.

Mary Had a Little LAN

When you first go from using sneakernet to transferring files on a network, it's like magic. Your files are on your computer, and poof! Now they're on another computer, too. Going back to using sneakernet is an unappealing prospect, so getting Mac OS X Macs working on an existing Mac LAN is a high priority for people with Mac networks.

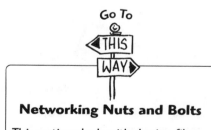

Networking Nuts and Bolts

This section deals with sharing files over a network, but if you're still at the stage of *creating* a network, see Chapter 11, "How to Succeed in Networking Without Even Trying," for more info.

Speaking the Same Language

Although Mac OS X uses AppleTalk networking, Apple's standard protocol for many years, the system speaks AppleTalk only when it's transmitted over *TCP/IP*. This means that some older Macs might not be able to share files with your OS X Mac. Here's what will work and what won't:

Lingua Franca

TCP/IP stands for Transmission Control Protocol over Internet Protocol. It's the way that your Mac connects to other computers over the Internet, and it's increasingly common as a way to network local computers. Unlike AppleTalk, TCP/IP is a cross-platform protocol, used by Macs, Windows PCs, and Unix computers, so using it brings OS X Macs one step further along the way toward being able to connect transparently with other platforms.

➤ If the OS X Mac has File Sharing turned on, Macs running Mac OS 8 and later can access its drives.

➤ If the OS X Mac has File Sharing turned on, Macs running System 7.5.3 and later can access its drives. To do so, however, they must be using Open Transport 1.1.2 or later and version 3.7 or later of the AppleShare Client.

➤ Mac OS X Macs can access shared drives or folders on other Mac OS X Macs and on Mac OS 9 Macs for which the Enable File Sharing Clients to Connect Over TCP/IP option is turned on in the File Sharing control panel.

➤ Mac OS X Macs can access shared drives or folders on Macs running systems as old as 7.5.5 with the use of a third-party product called ShareWay IP from Open Door Networks (www.opendoor.com). Installing ShareWay IP enables TCP file sharing on Macs running System 7.5.5 and later, allowing Mac OS X Macs to connect to them.

The Tools You'll Need

You can find both of the software components you need to connect to Mac OS X from System 7 Macs on Apple's Web site. Go to asu.info.apple.com and search for Open Transport and then for AppleShare Client.

What's the IP Address, Kenneth?

After you have all this software lined up and all your Macs are ready to talk to each other, you'll need to be sure each one has a different *IP address*. An IP address must have four segments, separated by periods, like this: 192.168.0.1. You can use any numbers you want for the third and fourth segments. The best numbers to use for the first and second segments are 192 and 168; those numbers signify that this is an internal address rather than one located out on the Internet somewhere.

To assign an IP address to a pre-OS X Mac, choose **Apple menu**, **Control Panels**, **TCP/IP** and fill in the IP Address field. To give a Mac OS X Mac an IP address, click the Desktop and choose **Desktop, System Preferences**. Click the Network button and fill in the IP address field in the Network pane (see Figure 16.2). (You might need to click the lock button and enter an Admin name and password first.)

Finally! Getting Connected

Now that you've assigned IP addresses to all the Macs concerned, you're ready to start sharing files. Here's how to connect to other Macs from your Mac OS X Mac:

Apple Gets Help from a Friend

ShareWay IP is a pretty neat product. So neat, in fact, that Apple licensed it for use in Mac OS 9—the TCP/IP file sharing option on Mac OS 9 Macs is actually made possible by a limited version of ShareWay IP.

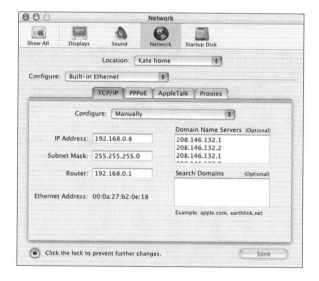

Figure 16.2

In the Network pane, you can assign your Mac an IP address so it can be located on a network by other computers.

1. Choose **Go, Connect to Server**.
2. In the left column of the Connect to Server dialog box, click **Local Network**. The other Macs on your network are listed in the right column (see Figure 16.3).
3. Click on a Mac's name and click **Connect**.
4. Now you'll be presented with a dialog box asking you for your user name and password. Enter those and click **Connect**.
5. In the following dialog box, choose a drive or shared folder from the list and click **OK** to *mount* it.

Figure 16.3

The Connect to Server dialog box lists Macs on your network.

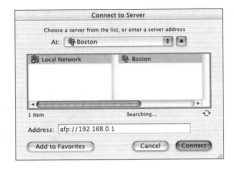

Network drives stay mounted on your Mac as long as they're running or as long as you're running. In other words, you'll lose contact if someone logs out, shuts down, or restarts the other Mac or if you do the same to your Mac.

Going the Other Way

Of course, networking is a two-way street. Here's how to connect to your OS X Mac running earlier systems:

1. Open the Network Browser (if it's not in your Apple menu, look for it in your Utilities folder).

Scaling Mount Macintosh

When you connect to another Mac's hard drive or to a shared folder on that Mac, the drive or folder appears on your Desktop or in a Finder window just as though it were part of your own Mac's system. A network drive to which you're connected in this way is referred to as being ***mounted*** on your Mac.

2. Click the first button (with the pointing finger) and choose **Go To Server** from the menu.

3. Enter the IP address of the Mac OS X computer to which you want to connect, and then click **Connect**. To find the IP address of your OS X Mac, check the Network Identity section of the Sharing pane in the Mac OS X System Preferences.

4. Enter your user name and password, and click **Connect**.

When you click Connect or OK, you'll be presented with a dialog box asking you for your user name and password. Enter those, or choose **Guest access**, and click **OK**. Then, you'll see a dialog box asking which drives or folders on the other Mac you want to *mount* on your own Mac. Click on the first one you want and Cmd+click on any others, and then click **OK**.

The Easy Way Out

Naturally, you don't want to have to remember and type in the IP address every time you mount a network drive from your pre-OS X Mac. Fortunately, there's a simple method to avoid this necessity: Make an alias of the drive by clicking the drive's icon and holding down Cmd+Option as you drag it. You can put the alias wherever you want it on your Mac. The next time you want to mount the network drive, just double-click the alias. You'll go directly to the login screen, where you can enter your name and password to use drives or folders on the other Mac.

Vintage Mac Software

Although it's not strictly a Mac OS X issue, the problem of software compatibility is definitely one that affects Mac users who upgrade to Mac OS X. The other Macsters you work with won't necessarily upgrade when you do, so you'll need to be sure that the software you're using with Mac OS X can save files that your friends' or co-workers' Macs can read. There are several steps you can take to ensure that:

➤ **Backsave your files**—When you save a file, choose **File**, **Save As** instead of just pressing Cmd+S. The Save dialog box in most programs has a Format pop-up menu that contains a variety of format options you can use. Sometimes these include the native formats of earlier versions of the software. For example, Photoshop 6 users can save files in a Photoshop native format that users of version 2.5 can open—yes, that far back!

➤ **Use alternative file formats**—Rather than a program's native file format, check the Save dialog box's Format pop-up menu for alternative formats (such as RTF, common in word processors) that aren't proprietary to any one program. For example, WordPerfect can't open Microsoft Word 2000 files, but it can open RTF files.

➤ **Invest in a translation program**—Programs such as MacLink (DataViz, www.dataviz.com) and DeBabelizer (Equilibrium Software, www.equilibrium.com) enable you to convert files from one format to another, and they typically cover dozens of applicable formats for any given kind of file.

➤ **Investigate crossgrade and upgrade deals**—Sometimes you just have to get you and your friends or co-workers on the same (software) page. If nothing else works, you might be able to save some money on the latest version of the software you're using. Software companies often offer discounts to users of older versions (upgrades) and to users of competing software (crossgrades).

Saving a Buck

A good place to find deals on Mac hardware and software, including the latest upgrade and crossgrade deals, is the DealMac Web site (`www.dealmac.com`).

The Least You Need to Know

➤ Sharing files with other Mac users requires one of two things: that you have a kind of removable disk drive in common or that you're on a network together. Removable disks are a handy way to get files to just about any Mac user, whereas file sharing over a network requires that both Macs have a network connection and be set up for TCP/IP networking.

➤ TCP/IP file sharing can be set up on any Mac running System 7.5.5 or later. Macs running System 7.5.3 can connect to shared folders on an OS X Mac, as long as they have a few free and easily downloadable software components installed. TCP/IP networking requires you to connect to another computer by entering its IP address, a string of numbers that gives a computer a unique identity on a network.

➤ When you're sharing files, another concern is software compatibility. You can keep your files compatible with older applications by saving in different formats, using translation software, or upgrading older apps to the latest versions.

Chapter 17

Interacting with Windows

In This Chapter

➤ Transferring files using removable disk drives

➤ Setting up file sharing with Windows PCs on a network

➤ Making sure your Mac files are Windows-compatible

➤ Sharing printers with Windows PCs

➤ Running Windows on your Mac

Sad to say, it's not an entirely Mac world (yet). And because there are so many more Windows PCs than Macs out there, Mac users have to learn how to get along with Windows, rather than vice versa. Macs make this job fairly easy, though, with built-in support for PC-formatted disks and platform-independent networking.

At some point in your life as a Mac user, you'll need to hand over a file to a Windows user. First, the file must be in a format the other system can use, and then you must figure out how to get it there. That can mean transferring files over a network or putting them on a disk the Windows computer can read.

Sharing printers with Windows users and running Windows software on our Macs are two other compatibility issues Mac users must contend with. Fortunately, third-party software vendors have taken up the challenge and supplied solutions to both these problems...read on for details!

Go To

◄THIS WAY►

Shopping at the Macintosh Mall

Any time you're looking for Mac software to perform a particular task, a good place to start is the Macintosh Products Guide (`guide.apple.com`), where you'll find thousands of programs that fulfill every possible need.

Moving Files with Sneakernet

On a sneakernet, you're the connection between one computer and the other—you put files on a disk and walk them to where they're going with your sneaker-clad feet. (Due to recent technological advances, you can now do this while wearing pumps or sandals as well.)

The first step in implementing sneakernet between a Mac and a PC is to find a disk format the two computers have in common. Here are some ideas:

➤ **Floppy disks**—Remember all those AOL floppies you got before they switched to CD-ROMs? I saved mine and reformatted them—and now I never use them because my G4 doesn't have a floppy disk drive. If your OS X Mac does have a floppy drive, you'll be able to use it to exchange files up to 1.2MB or so with most Windows PCs. Note, however, that some internal floppy drives won't work with Mac OS X, but most external ones will.

➤ **SuperDisk**—The same size as floppy disks, these disks hold a whopping 120MB. The drive also reads floppies, and it has a USB connector. These are not the same thing as the SuperDrive Apple introduced in early 2001, which is a DVD and CD-RW burner but has nothing to do with floppy disks.

➤ **Zip**—The newer Zip disks can contain 250MB of data, while the older ones hold only 100MB. The current version of the Zip drive uses USB.

➤ **Jaz**—With a capacity 20 times that of a Zip disk (2GB, or 2,000MB), Jaz disks are a good option for larger capacity needs. The drives are SCSI, which means you might need to get a SCSI add-on card if you have a newer Mac.

➤ **CD-R or CD-RW**—With your Mac's CD-ROM or DVD drive, you can read CD-R (CD-ROM Recordable) and CD-RW (CD-ROM Rewritable) media. To record them, you need special software (such as Adaptec Toast, `www.roxio.com`) and a CD burner. Many newer Windows computers and the latest Macs come with built-in CD-RW drives, so this can be a great option for transferring large quantities of data.

Doing the Floppy Hop

If you need to get files off a floppy disk and your Mac doesn't have a floppy drive, you have a couple options. First, if your Mac is connected to other computers either on a network or with an Internet connection, you can stick the floppy in some *other* Mac's floppy drive, copy the files, and transfer them to your Mac over the network or by e-mail. If you use floppies enough that this technique is starting to drive you crazy, you're best off picking up an Imation SuperDisk drive (**www.imation.com**), which costs only a few dollars more than a floppy drive and can read both floppies and SuperDisks.

When a PC-formatted disk is inserted in your Mac's drive, you'll see it on your Desktop or in a Finder window just as you would a Mac-formatted one. If you need to reformat a disk for use with a PC, you'll have to do that on the PC.

Moving Files Across a Network

Most networks use Ethernet cabling, and every Mac has an Ethernet port on the back—just plug in and go. Then, there are wireless networks, which require add-on cards and base stations. Regardless of the method chosen, putting together the hardware is simple. Getting PCs and Macs to talk to each other over a network, on the other hand, is a bit more complicated.

Peer-to-Peer with Windows

Like Macs, Windows can do *peer-to-peer* networking with other computers on a network. Unfortunately, Windows is not designed to do this with Macs. However, developers have created third-party cross-platform networking solutions that enable your Mac to talk to PCs and vice versa. These software packages are easy to install and come with explicit instructions for configuring both ends of the Mac-PC connection.

Networking Nuts and Bolts

This section deals with sharing files over a network, but if you're still at the stage of *creating* a network, see Chapter 11, "How to Succeed in Networking Without Even Trying," for more info.

Show Info

Two Faces of Networking

Computer networks are built on two different models: *peer-to-peer* networking and *server-based* networking. In the former, the networked computers talk to each other directly, whereas in the latter, interactions are regulated by a server computer that controls printing and file sharing on the network.

Read Me

Off with Its Head!

To save energy and space, server administrators often remove the monitors from their unattended servers, which are then called *headless servers*. Because these computers are intended to perform their assigned tasks, such as routing e-mail or backing up a network, without user intervention, the administrator doesn't need to see what's being displayed on their monitors. To use Timbuktu with a headless computer, you'll need to attach a video adapter to activate the computer's video functions.

Thursby Software (www.thursby.com) offers three Mac/Windows networking products: MacSOHO, DAVE, and TSSTalk. The first two products allow Windows and Mac to access files on each other's computers, whereas the software itself is installed only on the Mac side. DAVE is designed for larger networks and allows printer sharing, while MacSOHO is intended for small office and home office users and doesn't allow printer sharing. With either product, a Windows disk mounted over the network will look just like a Mac disk, and vice versa.

DoubleTalk (Connectix, www.connectix.com) is similar to MacSOHO; it prints to networked Windows PostScript printers, and you can create a peer-to-peer network with Macs and PCs.

If your network is primarily composed of Macs and you need to integrate one or a few PCs, you can use TSSTalk, also from Thursby Software. It allows both file sharing and printer sharing and is available for Windows 95/98, NT, and 2000. PC MacLAN from Miramar Systems (www.miramar.com) is a similar product that also allows printer sharing and is available for Windows 95/98, NT, and 2000.

A different tack is taken by Netopia's Timbuktu Pro (www.netopia.com), which puts the desktop of another computer (Mac or Windows) in a window on your Mac. You can control the other computer remotely and transfer files from your Mac to the remote computer. Timbuktu is popular with computer support people who must troubleshoot other people's computers from a network and with system administrators who are running *headless* servers.

On a Server-Based Network

If your OS X Mac is part of a Windows network that uses a server, you'll need to get the Mac to talk to the server, instead of directly to the other computers on the network. At least two products make this possible:

➤ **Sharity** (Objective Development, www.obdev.at) allows OS X Macs to act as clients in Windows networks. It allows your Mac to access Windows NT, Windows 95/98, OS/2, or other SMB-based (Server Message Block) file servers. It's simple to install and use, but you might need help from a network administrator to configure it before you can access the network.

➤ **Samba** (Samba Group, us1.samba.org/samba/samba.html) is a free utility that lets you set up Mac OS X as a server for Windows clients. Like Sharity, Samba uses the SMB protocol for sharing files, printers, and other resources on Windows networks.

File Format Compatibility

When you're creating files that need to cross from one platform to another, pay attention to the formats in which you save the files. The most commonly used applications on Mac and Windows are almost completely cross-platform compatible these days, including

➤ Microsoft Word, Excel, and PowerPoint

➤ Adobe InDesign, FrameMaker, Illustrator, and Photoshop

➤ QuarkXPress

However, other applications still have separate formats for Windows and Mac versions. And some applications exist on only one platform, which means there is no way to just open and use them. Before closing a file you plan to exchange with someone on a PC, choose **File**, **Save As** and see whether there's a Format pop-up menu (or one with a similar name) that contains different formats in which the file can be saved.

Here are a few specific tips:

➤ **Use the appropriate native file format—** When the program in question (for example, Microsoft Word's earlier versions) does have platform-specific formats, use them. So, if you're handing off a file to someone using Word 2 on Windows (unlikely, but possible), be sure you save that file from Word using the Word 2.x for Windows format available in the Save File as Type pop-up menu.

What's in a (File) Name?

When you double-click a document file on your Mac, its associated application starts up and opens the file, right? That's because Mac files contain information about the programs that created them right in the file format. PC files don't have this information, so you must include it in the filename by using a filename extension. For example, Microsoft Word files must have filenames ending with .DOC to be recognized on a Windows computer. So, be sure you learn and use the right filename extensions for the kinds of files you want to exchange with your Windows-using pals.

➤ **Investigate alternative file formats**—Rather than a program's native file format, find out whether the program can save in alternative formats, such as Rich Text Format (RTF) for text that can be read by many word processors, or TIFF, for images that can be read by almost any image editor.

➤ **Buy a translation program**—Programs such as MacLink (DataViz, www.dataviz.com) and DeBabelizer (Equilibrium Software, www.equilibrium.com) can convert files from one format to another. They can handle dozens of source and destination formats.

➤ **Turn your files into PDFs**—By converting your file to a *PDF* file, you enable anyone to view and print that file without having the original fonts or graphics. You can convert any printable file to a PDF in Mac OS X using the Print Preview feature. For instructions, see Chapter 12, "Printing Up a Storm."

Just Like the Real Thing

Adobe Systems introduced Acrobat and its PDF (Portable Document Format) in 1993. The idea was to create documents that would look the same on any computer platform and could be printed and passed along without the need to include fonts and graphics. The program you need to view PDF files, Acrobat Reader (**www.adobe.com/products/ acrobat/readermain.html**), is free. PDF is now so widely used that the U.S. Internal Revenue Service makes its forms and publications available on its Web site as PDF files that can be downloaded, printed, and used in filing tax returns. For more information about Acrobat and PDF, check out the PDFZone Web site (**www.pdfzone.com**).

Printing Both Ways

Sharing printers between Macs and Windows computers might or might not require special software, depending on how you want to do it. How you can accomplish this depends on whether your Mac and the PC are on a network together and what "languages," or protocols, the printer speaks.

Without a Network

If the Mac and PC are not networked, you're limited to printers that can use both the AppleTalk protocol and Windows printer protocols. You have two choices for setting up such a printer:

➤ Use a switchbox to alternate between connecting the printer to a Mac or Mac network and connecting it to a PC or a PC network. A device such as the 4-Port USB Switchbox from Belkin Components (www.belkin.com) allows you to share one printer among four different computers, and it works with both Macs and PCs.

➤ Connect the printer to the Mac and PC simultaneously without a switchbox. This works if the printer has multiple ports and can automatically switch between printing protocols. For example, with an inexpensive HP inkjet printer, you could plug the PC into the parallel port and the Mac into the USB port and print from either computer.

On a Network

When your Mac shares a network with one or more PCs, you have a few different options for printer sharing:

➤ Put the printer on the network (plugged into a network hub) and set up printer sharing with DAVE, TSSTalk, or MacLAN, explained earlier in this chapter in "Peer-to-Peer with Windows." In this case, the printer can be any kind of printer that you can use with an all-Mac or all-PC network.

➤ Connect the printer to a PC and use Windows' built-in printer sharing feature to make the printer available to your Mac using *TCP/IP* networking. For this to work, the printer must support TCP/IP, and you won't have access to the printer when the PC is turned off.

➤ Purchase LPR client software for the Windows PC that will allow it to print to any TCP/IP printer on the network. One example of this kind of software is INTELLIscribe from Brooks Internet Software (www.brooksnet.com).

➤ Buy a hardware print server that supports TCP/IP printing and connect it directly to the network. These devices are surprisingly inexpensive, and they have the added advantage of giving a printer that doesn't have one an Ethernet port. A good place to start shopping for a print server is Axis Communications' Web site (www.axis.com).

If you opt for any of the three TCP/IP options, you'll need to set up your printer in Mac OS X for TCP/IP printing. Instructions for setting up printers are found in Chapter 12, "Printing Up a Storm," and in this case the kind of printer connection you'll have is LPR.

Show Info

Lingua Franca

TCP/IP stands for Transmission Control Protocol over Internet Protocol. It's the way that your Mac connects to other computers over the Internet, and it's increasingly common as a way to network local computers. Unlike AppleTalk, TCP/IP is a cross-platform protocol, used by Macs, Windows PCs, and Unix computers, so using it brings OS X Macs one step further along the way toward being able to connect transparently with other platforms.

Running Windows Software

One of the coolest things Macs can do is—wait for it—run Windows! (You might not think this is so cool, but you gotta admit, Windows computers can't do the reverse.) That's right, with a software *emulator* you, too, can bring the Windows taskbar to a Mac near you. This lets you run software that doesn't come in Mac versions such as, for example, the Windows-only diagram and chart-creation program Visio.

See Me, Feel Me, Touch Me, Be Me

In the computer world, **emulation** means making one computer system act like (emulate) another one. Using various commercial and share-ware programs, your Mac can emulate everything from an Apple I to a VAX minicomputer to an arcade game such as the original Space Invaders.

When I want to run a Windows program, I use VirtualPC (Connectix Corporation, www.connectix.com). This program uses software to imitate the behavior of a PC, down to the smallest hardware characteristic. This makes it extremely compatible—you're unlikely to run into a Windows program that won't run on VirtualPC—but also slows it down, because everything it does happens in software rather than in hardware.

Doing anything with software is slower than doing it through a hard-wired function of a computer. That means that a Windows emulation program will always be slower than a real PC running Windows. But with today's blazingly fast G4s, iMacs, iBooks, and PowerBooks, using emulation is a very reasonable option for programs that don't place a heavy processing burden on the system. For example, Intuit TurboTax for Business (which unfortunately isn't available for the Mac) runs quite quickly on my Power Mac G4 in VirtualPC, but I wouldn't use the Windows version of Photoshop in VirtualPC to process large images. That's what I bought my Mac for!

The Least You Need to Know

➤ Sharing files with Windows users requires one of two things: You must have a kind of removable disk drive in common or you must be on a network together. With removable disks, you can get files to just about any Windows user, whereas file sharing over a network requires third-party software.

➤ When you're sharing files, another concern is software compatibility. You can be sure your files are Windows-compatible by saving in different formats or by using translation software.

➤ You can share printers between Macs and Windows in several ways, but most methods require that you either use third-party software or have a printer that can use TCP/IP networking.

➤ If you absolutely have to run a Windows program, you can do so on your Mac using a software emulator.

Chapter 18

Interacting with Unix

In This Chapter

➤ Transferring files using removable disk drives

➤ Setting up file sharing with Unix computers on a network

➤ File formats that work on Macs and Unix

➤ Accessing printers on a Unix network

➤ Running Unix programs on your Mac

The time has come, the author said, to talk of many things. Specifically, of Macs and Unix and what they have in common. When it comes down to it, a large portion of Mac OS X *is* Unix.

The idea of peeking at the Unix underpinnings of Mac OS X might make you nervous. And most of the time, you can just ignore the Unix side of Mac OS X. That's not the case, however, when you want to hook up with Unix users.

The good news is that exchanging files, printing, and using Unix applications on your OS X Mac are all pretty simple. The bad news is that (for the time being) there are no third-party products that simplify the process, like Dave or MacLAN Plus for integrating Windows computers and Macs on a network. The techniques you use to connect Unix and Macs are all Unix techniques—there's no easy way out.

Unix Geek Wanted

This chapter covers only the Mac side of the connection between Mac OS X and Unix. I'll let you know when the Unix side needs to be set up a particular way to work with your Mac, and you can pass that info along to your network administrator or the owner of the Unix computer in question.

Sharing Files with Sneakernet

The simplest option for exchanging files between two computers of any persuasion is to copy the files in question from the first computer onto a removable disk, pop the disk into a drive on the second computer, and copy them onto the second computer's hard drive. Because this "networking" method requires you to shlep the disk from one computer to the other, it's called sneakernet. True, it's an old joke, but it's still a good way to describe this method of file exchange.

For sneakernet to work, the two computers must be capable of reading the same disks. There are two ways for this to work on a Unix computer:

➤ Some versions of Unix, including some or all *Linux* distributions, have the native capability to mount Mac OS and DOS floppies by using the mount command. When a disk is mounted, it becomes part of the Unix file system, and you can format, read from, and write to it just as you would to your hard drive.

Blankie Not Included

Linux is a free version of Unix created by a Finnish university student, Linus Torvalds. It can run on almost any desktop computer, so it's used for Web and network servers or for any application that requires Unix but not a mainframe computer.

Most versions of Linux are released under the GNU licensing system, which gives users permission to use, revise, and redistribute software—but not sell it. For this reason, you can use any one of several distributions of Linux, each with slightly different features and varying levels of documentation and support from their creators.

➤ Most Unix installations (including Linux) have a suite of tools called mtools (see Figure 18.1). With mtools, Unix computers can format, write to, and read from DOS removable disks, including floppies and Zip disks. When you're using mtools, the disk in question is not mounted on your computer.

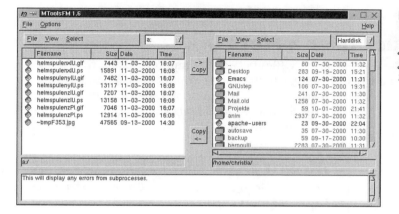

Figure 18.1

This is MtoolsFM, a program that provides a graphical interface for mtools.

mtools and Macs

Like most software in the Unix world, mtools is constantly being improved and updated. Its capabilities vary depending on the version of mtools installed on the Unix system you're using. Earlier versions might restrict you to the 8.3 naming convention. This means that file-names must use an eight-character name with a three-character extension after a period.

More on mtools

If you want more information about mtools, or to download the latest version, go to **www.tux.org/pub/knaff/mtools/**. The graphical interface for mtools (MtoolsFM, shown in Figure 18.1) is available at **www.core-coutainville.org/MToolsFM/**.

Whether a Unix user uses mtools or Unix's mount command to access a Zip or floppy disk is a matter of personal preference. If you mount a disk, you can use graphical tools to work with its files, the way you would on a Mac. If you don't mount it, you must use text commands—which, of course, is much cooler from a Unix geek's perspective.

Exchanging Files over a Network

Unix offers two basic ways of sharing files between computers. Using the first method, you mount a Unix *directory*, which enables you to work with its contents just as you would those of a shared folder on a networked Mac. Among Unix users, however, it's more customary to use *FTP* to retrieve the files you need.

Getting Directions to FTP

FTP stands for File Transfer Protocol, and it's a way to copy files over the Internet or over local networks.

In Unix-speak, a **directory** is the same thing as a Mac folder. A directory can contain files and other directories, just like a folder.

NFS Doesn't Mean "Not For Sale"

NFS stands for Network File System, a method developed by Sun Microsystems to allow computer users to access files across a network as though those files were located on the user's own computer.

Mount Disk

Before you can mount a Unix directory over a network, its owner must export it using a method called *NFS*. On other Unix computers, both exporting and mounting directories is done from a command line, meaning that the user must type in the appropriate commands. Of course, Mac users expect to be able to get things done with a graphical user interface, or GUI, and this task is no exception.

Although you can, if you prefer, mount and export directories from your own Mac OS X command line using the Terminal application, there are more Mac-friendly ways to accomplish the same thing. First is Apple's NetInfo Manager application, which comes with Mac OS X. This program is designed to administer a whole batch of network functions, so it's fairly complex to use. Be careful—NetInfo Manager is not a program you want to experiment with if you don't know what you're doing.

A second (and simpler) way to mount and export directories is to use a program called NFSManager (www.bresink.de/osx/), which provides easy access to the built-in NFS capabilities of Mac OS X. Using NFSManager, you can export your own folders and mount other people's directories with just a few clicks (see Figure 18.2). All that's required to mount another user's directory is to know the *pathname* for the directory.

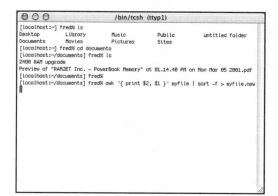

Figure 18.2

You can set up your shared folders for Unix network access using NFSManager.

Down the Garden Path

The ***pathname*** of a file or folder (or a directory, if we're speaking Unix) is the path you'd follow to access that file or folder from the top level of the computer it lives on. For example, the pathname for the first folder I exported is /Users/kbinder/Public. That's the Public folder inside my home folder, which in turn is inside the Users folder. The pathname for folders on another computer should also include the computer's name.

FTP

If the directory you need access to isn't exported, or if you're in a hurry, you can use FTP to move files from one computer to another across a Unix network.

Most Linux and other Unix computers have FTP servers on by default. You'll need to turn on Mac OS X's built-in FTP server if you want other people to be able to access your files through FTP. Here's how:

1. Click the Desktop and choose **Apple menu**, **System Preferences**.
2. Click the **Sharing** icon to open the Sharing pane.
3. If the lock button shows a locked padlock, click it and enter an Admin user name and password, and then click **OK**.
4. Click **Start** to begin sharing files.
5. Click **Turn On FTP Access** to make files available through FTP.

Now, before you do this, you should know that running an FTP server on computers with a direct Internet connection is not recommended by many security experts, because FTP passwords are not encrypted. This means that they can be intercepted and used to access your computer without your knowledge or permission. It's best to restrict your FTP serving to your local network.

Get Yourself a Client

The easiest way to access other computers through FTP is to use an FTP client program such as the venerable Fetch (**www.dartmouth.edu/pages/softdev/fetch.html**) or the thoroughly modern Transit (**www.panic.com**). You'll need to know the other computer's URL or IP address, and you'll need to enter your user name and password. Obviously, you'll have to have an account set up on the other computer.

File Formats

If you're planning to exchange files with Unix users, you'd probably like your Mac programs to be able to open the files you receive. Fortunately, most Unix file formats are based on plain text, which means that if you can't open them directly, you can import them into a file in the program you're using.

Here's a quick list of the file types you'll find most useful for exchanging files with Unix users:

➤ **Text files**—Unix word processors and text editors can save in ASCII text (plain text) and RTF (rich text formats). Any Mac text-editing program can open plain text files, but this format can't include any formatting, such as font, type size, or type styles. Documents that contain formatting should be saved as RTF files, which can be read by both Mac OS X's TextEdit program and standard word processors, such as Microsoft Word and the one in the free StarOffice suite (www.sun.com), which runs on Mac OS X, Windows, Solaris, and Unix.

➤ **Spreadsheets**—Almost any spreadsheet program can read and write files saved in DBF (dBASE File), DIF (Data Interchange Format), or SYLK (Spreadsheet Symbolic Link Format) formats.

➤ **Databases**—File formats for databases are fairly similar to those used for spreadsheets. In addition to DBF, DIF, and SYLK formats, database programs can export data in comma-separated and tab-separated text formats, which contain no formatting or special features, such as math formulas—just text.

➤ **Graphics**—Image file formats tend to be the same across all platforms. In other words, it doesn't matter whether your computer is using Mac OS, Windows, or Unix; a JPEG file is a JPEG file is a JPEG file and can be viewed on any platform. Standard graphics formats, such as GIF, JPEG, EPS, PNG, and BMP, are supported by both Mac OS X and Unix programs.

Sharing Printers

Printing is pretty much the easiest part of getting along with Unix. *TCP/IP* is the default communications protocol for Unix printers, and Mac OS X likes TCP/IP printing just fine. You can set up a Unix printer in the same way that you'd set up a TCP/IP printer on a Mac network.

The only information you'll need to set up a Unix printer is its IP address or its name, along with the name of the print queue (which allows you to distinguish between multiple printers attached to one print server), and the network administrator can give you that information. Instructions for setting up printers are found in Chapter 12 and, in this case, the kind of printer connection you'll have is LPR.

Running Unix Software

There are two kinds of Unix applications: terminal applications and X Window applications. The former are programs that run from a command line; in the case of Mac OS X, that means you need to start up the Terminal application to run them (see Figure 18.3). X Window applications, on the other hand, have a graphical user interface (GUI) and therefore look much more familiar to Mac users.

Read Me

PDFs Save the Day

If you run into a file that just can't be saved in a format available to both Unix and Mac computers, you can convert it to a PDF document. Anyone can view and print a PDF file without having the original fonts or graphics. You can convert any printable file to a PDF in Mac OS X using the Print Preview feature. For instructions, see Chapter 12, "Printing Up a Storm."

Show Info

Lingua Franca

TCP/IP stands for Transmission Control Protocol over Internet Protocol. It's the way that your Mac connects to other computers or printers over the Internet, and it's increasingly common as a way to network local computers.

To run terminal applications, you use a Terminal window. To run X Window applications, you'll need an X Window Server, such as Xtools (Tenon Intersystems, www.tenon.com). After you've installed Xtools, you can use it to run programs such as GIMP (GNU Image Manipulation Program), a free Unix image editing program that's nearly as powerful as Adobe Photoshop (which retails for about $600).

Figure 18.3

Mac OS X's Terminal program gives you access to the dreaded (or beloved, depending on your perspective) Unix command line.

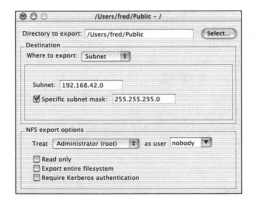

Unix by Remote Control

If the program you want to use isn't located on your own computer, the first thing you'll do is log in to the Unix computer where it's installed. The best way to do this is to telnet to the other computer, and the easiest way to do *that* is to use a *telnet* client such as MacTelnet (www.mactelnet.com).

Show Info

Long-Distance Love

Telnet is a way to interact with a networked computer through a terminal window just as though you were sitting in front of that computer. Using telnet, you can open a terminal window for a remote computer that works just like the Terminal application on your Mac. In this window, you can log in to the other computer and then enter Unix commands, such as instructions to run a program installed on the other computer.

After you've logged in, you have access to both terminal applications and X Window applications installed on the remote system, and you can run them just the way you would if you were sitting at the other computer.

Keeping It Local

Although Unix is generally network-oriented, you can also run Unix programs that are installed locally—that is, on your Mac. For this to be possible, though, the applications must be *compiled* to work on Mac OS X and Mac hardware. The reason for this is that there are many flavors of Unix, and Mac OS X uses as its base only one of them: FreeBSD Unix. Assuming the program you want to use has been compiled for use on FreeBSD Unix running on PowerPC, it should run fine on your Mac.

Compile On!

For a computer to understand the instructions contained in a program you're running, that program must be written in machine language. If you've ever seen machine language, though, you'll understand that no one could possibly write programs in it. The answer to this dilemma is for programmers to use programming languages that are more like human language, and then ***compile***, or translate, their programs into machine language using a utility called a compiler.

The Least You Need to Know

➤ Underneath its smooth, easy interface, Mac OS X is actually a version of Unix. That means that sharing files, programs, and printers with Unix computers is fairly easy, but it also means that accomplishing these things requires you to think the Unix way.

➤ Because Macs and Unix computers can both read and write several different disk formats, you can share files using removable disks. If your Mac is on a network with the Unix system in question, you can transfer files by mounting directories or by using FTP (file transfer protocol), the same method you can use to transfer files over the Internet.

➤ Setting up to print to Unix printers is a simple matter because Mac OS X's preferred printing method is TCP/IP, the same as Unix networks. To set up a printer, you just have to know its IP address or name and the name of its print queue.

➤ There are two kinds of Unix applications: terminal applications and X Window applications. You can run either of these right in Mac OS X, opening up the entire world of Unix software to you.

Part 5
Tweaking Mac OS X

Naturally, you want your Mac to be your Mac. Here's where you make that happen. In this part, you'll learn how to tweak Mac OS X to make it work the way you want it to work, with preferences, Finder viewing options, and even a selection of tips on making Mac OS X act more like Mac OS 9.

Chapter 19 covers Mac OS X's System Preferences in depth, with a section on what each preference pane means to you and what it can do. Moving on to the Desktop and the Dock, two of the most important aspects of Mac OS X's new interface, Chapter 20 includes a selection of ways to customize the look and feel of your Mac. In Chapter 21, you'll delve into the world of files, folders, and ways to move them around and get more information about them. Finally, Chapter 22 is for the retro types—it talks about techniques and third-party software you can use to put a more familiar face on this brand-new system.

Chapter 19

Setting System Preferences

In This Chapter

➤ Making systemwide settings

➤ Which settings require approval from an Admin user

➤ Which settings you can ignore if you're not online

Like all computers, your Mac is a complex set of different programs, all working together to accomplish whatever it is you want to do. Fortunately, as a Mac user you don't have to deal with most of that complexity. One way Mac OS X keeps things simple is by storing dozens of different system-level preference controls in one place, where you can get at them quickly. That place is the System Preferences. To get there, click on the Desktop or on the **Desktop** icon on the Dock, and then choose **Apple menu, System Preferences**.

To keep this chapter simple, I've grouped the different preference panes into categories that you'll see in the sections to follow. In the System Preferences dialog box, however, the panes are listed in alphabetical order rather than in groups of related panes. To use a pane, click its button; to switch panes, either click one of the buttons in the toolbar or click **Show All** and click the button for the pane you want (see Figure 19.1).

Figure 19.1

The System Preferences dialog box brings together settings that affect almost every function of your Mac.

Your Preferred Preferences

If you find yourself going back to a particular preferences pane often, you can add its button to the toolbar at the top of the System Preferences dialog box so that you can get there faster. To do that, just drag the button to the toolbar area. Drag buttons out of the toolbar area to remove them.

Getting Going

Getting your Mac up and running is, naturally, the most important thing you can do with System Preferences. The three panes covered here control how your Mac starts up and what it does while you're taking a break from using it.

Startup Disk

In the Startup Disk pane, you choose which system you want your Mac to start up from. In most cases, you'll have two choices: your Mac OS X system and your Mac OS 9 system. As soon as you click the **Startup Disk** button, System Preferences starts scanning your hard drives and removable disks for bootable systems. As it scans, it adds an icon for each system it discovers. When the one you want appears, click it. If the lock button shows a locked padlock, you might need to first click the lock button and enter an Admin user name and password, and then click **OK**. After the change has been authorized, just restart to use the system you've chosen.

Energy Saver

In some lines of work, it's a good idea to sleep whenever you can, because you never know when you'll be required to go without sleep for a long time. In the Energy Saver pane, you can make sure your Mac gets a chance to sleep when you're not using it. There are three settings, as follows:

➤ **System sleep**—This slider determines the amount of time before your Mac goes to sleep if it's not being used. Set the slider to Never if you don't want to use sleep, or choose a number of minutes between 30 and 60.

➤ **Display sleep**—If you want to set a different time for your monitor to go to sleep, check this box and adjust the slider.

➤ **Hard disk sleep**—If you want to set a different time for your hard drive to go to sleep, check this box and adjust the slider.

Screen Saver

Okay, so we all know that screen savers don't really save your screen. The image on most computer screens changes so often as you do different things with the computer that screen *burn-in* is very unlikely to happen. Nevertheless, Mac OS X includes a Screen Saver pane in System Preferences. And why is that? Because screen savers are fun, that's why!

Go To

This Way

You Can't Do That!

In Mac OS X, some system-level preferences can be locked so that changes to them must be approved by an Admin user. Startup Disk is one of them. See Chapter 6, "Sharing Your Mac with Multiple Users," to learn what an Admin user can do that others can't and how to find out which users of your Mac are Admin users.

Read Me

A Fresh Start

To restart your Mac, choose **Apple menu, Restart**. A quick alternative is to press your Mac's power button, which presents you with a dialog box containing Shut Down, Restart, Sleep, and Cancel buttons.

Show Info

Burn, Baby, Burn

You know how bank machine screens display ghost images of their initial login screens, no matter which screen you're actually on? That's *burn-in*—because the screen displays that image so much of the time, for such a long time, it's actually burned into the screen itself.

Sleeping MacBeauty

The two most common setups for the Energy Saver pane are to have the entire system sleep at a specified time or to have the system sleep set for a specified time but the hard disk sleep set to never. The reason for this is that it's hard on your hard drive—pun completely intended—to keep spinning up and down all the time. The safest way to use your hard drive is actually to just turn it on and leave it that way.

Saving Private Mac

A nice batch of screen savers comes with Mac OS X, but if you're like me, you want more, more, more! To download another funky batch of free screen savers, go to www.epicware.com/macosxsavers.html and follow the downloading and installation instructions.

There are three tabs on the Screen Saver pane:

➤ **Screen Savers**—The Screen Saver utility can display your choice of screen saver—one produces a floating Mac logo, for example. In this tab you can choose a screen saver, preview it, and configure any settings it might have, such as speed or color.

➤ **Activation**—Here you can use a slider to determine how many minutes of inactivity are required before your screen saver kicks in, and you can set the screen saver to require a password before turning off.

➤ **Hot Corners**—In this tab, you can designate corners of your screen to activate and disable the screen saver when the mouse is placed in those locations. Click once to put a check in a corner; click again to put a minus in a corner.

Nuts and Bolts

Here's a group of panes that control basic settings—things that will affect you every time you sit down in front of your Mac.

General

As you might guess from the name, the settings in the General pane are among the most basic (see Figure 19.2). Here you can choose an overall color scheme (Appearance) and a highlight color for selected menu options and text. You also can control whether clicking in the scrollbar moves you one window's worth up or down or to that specific point in the document.

Figure 19.2
The General pane controls some basic aspects of how your Mac's screen looks.

Dock

Love the Dock or hate it, here's where you can determine how it acts. Sliders enable you to set the size of the Dock and the amount each icon is magnified as you slide the mouse cursor over it, and a check box lets you turn magnification off and on. Two more check boxes control whether the Dock is always visible or sinks off the edge of the screen when you move the mouse away from it and whether program icons in the Dock bounce while the programs are starting up.

Software Update

This pane is the Mac OS X version of Mac OS 9's Software Update control panel. It enables you to check for and install updated software (system and selected applications) either on demand or on a schedule. You can click **Show Log** to see a report of what software it's downloaded and installed.

Classic

You probably know by now that Classic is the tool that enables you to run your legacy Mac OS 9 programs within Mac OS X. Classic requires you to have an entire Mac OS 9 System Folder, from which it boots up a Mac OS 9 environment that can run Mac OS 9 applications. You can have more than one Mac OS 9 System Folder on your Mac, and this preference pane is how you switch between them. It has two tabs:

➤ **Start/Stop**—Here you can choose a System Folder to be used with Classic, and you can click buttons to start, stop, restart, or force quit Classic. Check boxes allow you to start up Classic automatically when you log in and hide it while it's starting up.

➤ **Advanced**—If you need to troubleshoot your Classic system, here's where to start. With the Advanced Options pop-up menu, you can turn off system extensions or access the Classic system's Extensions Manager.

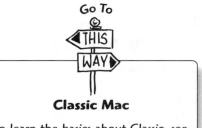

Classic Mac

To learn the basics about Classic, see Chapter 2, "Making Friends with Mac OS X." If you're ready to move on to more advanced Classic machinations, check out Chapter 8, "Using Third–Party Applications."

You can click **Rebuild Desktop** to—you guessed it—rebuild the Desktop for the Classic system. A slider enables you to set the amount of inactive time before Classic goes to sleep when you're not using it.

Users

If you're the only person who uses your Mac, you might never have occasion to see this pane. If you want to use Mac OS X's multiple users features, however, this is the place to start. Users are listed, along with their status as Admin or normal users, and you can click buttons to edit existing user accounts, delete users, or create new users.

Footprints on the Sands of Time

An **NTP server,** also called a network time server, is a computer that gives the current time to another computer that asks in the correct way. NTP stands for Network Time Protocol, the standard way for computers to request or supply the time over the Internet.

My Favorite Tip

No lie, this is one of my all-time favorite Mac tips. If you check Flash the Time Separators in the Menu Bar Clock tab, you'll always know whether your Mac is operating normally or frozen up. With Mac OS X, freezing up is an extremely unlikely thing for your Mac to do, so this isn't as good a tip as it used to be, but it's still useful.

Date & Time

If you have a computer, you have no excuse for not knowing what time it is, especially if you're online. The Date & Time pane lets you set the time, determine how the time is displayed, and connect to the Internet to keep your Mac's clock in step with the rest of the world.

➤ **Date & Time**—This tab displays the current date and time. You can manually change the time or date if Network Time Synchronization isn't on; you can turn it off in its own tab.

➤ **Time Zone**—Click on the world map or choose from the pop-up menu to set your time zone.

➤ **Network Time**—This is the cool part. If you click **Start** to turn Network Time Synchronization on, the Mac locates an *NTP server* on the Internet and sets your clock by it—a great way to make sure your computer's clock is always accurate. By default, Network Time Synchronization uses Apple's own server; if you'd like to use a different server, enter its address in the NTP Server field.

➤ **Menu Bar Clock**—If you need to know what time it is all the time, you'll want to check **Show the Clock in the Menu Bar** to have a digital clock displayed in the upper-right corner of your screen. Optional check boxes allow you to append seconds, AM or PM, and the day of the week to the time, as well as flashing the "time separators"—a fancy word for the colons that separate the hour from the minutes and the minutes from the seconds.

A Good Time Not to Bother

If you don't have a constant connection to the Internet, you should leave Network Time Synchronization turned off. When it's on, Mac OS X searches for an NTP server each time it boots up, which is a waste of your time if you're not online. To set the clock when you *are* online, just go to the Network Time tab of the Date & Time preferences and click **Start** to connect with the NTP server and set your clock (you might see the menu bar clock change when you do this), and then click **Stop** after a few seconds.

International

If you ordinarily use a language other than American English, the International pane is designed for you (see Figure 19.3). Here you can change the way dates, times, and numbers are displayed, as well as the language your Mac uses to talk to you and for keyboard layouts.

Figure 19.3

If you type in a language other than English, you might want to use a keyboard layout with special characters, such as different currency symbols.

➤ **Language**—Click and drag to specify your preferred languages in the upper part of the tab, and then choose a set of text behaviors to specify how things such as alphabetical order (which can vary depending on your language) are calculated.

➤ **Date**—Start here by making a choice from the Region pop-up menu. This changes the settings for all the other options to the most common ones for that region. Then you can customize the settings from there; the results of your choices appear at the bottom of the tab. The date format you choose is used in Finder windows, Inspector windows, and wherever the system displays a date.

➤ **Time**—As in the Date tab, the first action to take here is to choose a region. Then customize your settings to display the time to your liking. The results are displayed at the bottom of the tab.

➤ **Numbers**—Your choice from the Region menu determines the initial settings, but you can change the separators and currency symbols used by the system to suit yourself. The results are displayed at the bottom of the tab.

➤ **Keyboard Menu**—If you use different languages, you can switch among different keyboard layouts as you change languages. This ensures that all the appropriate special keys (such as currency symbols) are available as you type. To use more than one keyboard layout, click the check boxes next to the ones you want to use. If more than one is selected, you'll see a menu listing your choices to the right of the Help menu in any Mac OS X application (not in Classic applications).

Keeping Connected

Several preferences panes have to do with getting (and staying) connected with the Internet and with your local network (if you have one). Because your login name and password are the same whether you're accessing your Mac over a network or by sitting in front of it, I've included the Login panes here as well.

Internet

In this handy pane, you can control the basic settings for all your Internet applications, including your Web browser and e-mail client. There are four tabs:

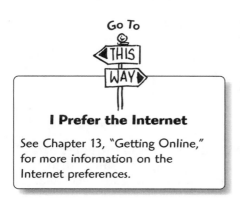

Go To

I Prefer the Internet

See Chapter 13, "Getting Online," for more information on the Internet preferences.

➤ **iTools**—Here, enter your iTools member name and your password if you have an iTools account. If you don't have one, you can click Free Sign Up to get one.

➤ **Email**—First, choose your e-mail program from the Email Reader pop-up menu. Then, enter your incoming and outgoing mail servers here, as well as your e-mail address, your user name, and your password.

➤ **Web**—Here you can choose your default Web browser and specify home and search Web pages. You also can specify a folder in which your Web browser should deposit downloaded files.

➤ **News**—If you like to read and post to newsgroups, here's where you should specify your preferred newsreader and enter your news server, user name, and password.

Network

The Network pane (see Figure 19.4) controls the nuts and bolts of how you connect to other computers, whether they're on a LAN (local area network) with your computer or on the Internet. Like some of the other panes, this one can be locked, requiring you to enter an Admin name and password before making any changes. There are four tabs:

➤ **TCP/IP**—These settings give your Mac an address on the network. The Configure pop-up menu enables you to choose different ways of configuring some or all of this information automatically. You'll need to get the correct information for this pane from your ISP (if you're a home user trying to get on the Internet) or from your IS staff (if you're trying to get set up on a local network).

TCP = To Connect People?

TCP/IP is now the standard networking protocol for Macs. You can learn more about how to set up a local network in Chapter 11, "How to Succeed in Networking Without Even Trying," and Chapter 13, "Getting Online," explains the Network preference settings that will allow you to connect to the Internet.

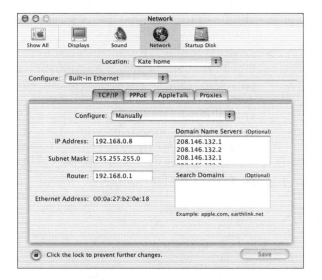

Figure 19.4
TCP/IP settings allow a computer to identify itself and communicate with other computers over local networks and the Internet.

➤ **PPPoE**—If you have a DSL connection, you might need to use this tab to specify your user name, password, and PPPoE server.

➤ **AppleTalk**—Here you can turn AppleTalk off and on and choose a name for your Mac; when other people connect to your computer using an AppleTalk network, this is the name they'll see. In Mac OS X, AppleTalk enables you to connect with Macs running Mac OS 9 or Mac OS X and with other computers that have AppleTalk capabilities, such as Windows NT servers.

➤ **Proxies**—If your network uses *proxies* (most common in the case of corporate or institutional networks), here's where you can enter the proxy information that will allow you to access the Internet.

Communication Breakdown

Mac OS X's version of AppleTalk can't communicate with Macs running systems older than Mac OS 9. For more information on how to share files with other Macs, see Chapter 16, "Interacting with Earlier Versions of Mac OS."

Login

The Login pane controls two separate things: how you log in and what happens when you do. It has two tabs, one of which requires Admin authorization:

➤ **Login Items**—Here you can set programs to start automatically when you log in. To add a program to the list, click **Add**, locate it in the dialog box, and click **Open**. To remove a program from the list, click it and click **Remove**. If you find yourself starting up the same applications every time you log in, such as your e-mail program and a Web browser, add them to this list and save yourself the trouble.

➤ **Login Window**—You might need to click the lock button and enter an Admin name and password to make changes here. After you've done that, you can click the check box and enter a name and password to skip the login screen when you start up your Mac. (This works only if you were logged in when the computer was shut down.) You can also set whether a password hint (entered in the Users pane) should be displayed when you enter your password incorrectly.

Internet by Proxy

A **proxy** is a computer and associated software, often part of a firewall system, that takes your computer's requests for information and passes them to the outside world, thus protecting your computer and its identity from "crackers" who might try to break in.

Sharing

To share files over a network, click **Start** to begin File Sharing. This allows other computer users to see your Mac's Public folders over a network. You also can control Web Sharing here by clicking **Start** to allow users to access Web pages stored in users' Sites folders.

The Sharing pane provides two additional ways for others to access your Mac. By clicking the Allow Remote Login check box, you enable *SSH* access, which allows people using Unix terminal applications to connect to your computer, and checking the Allow FTP Access check box turns on FTP access, enabling *FTP* clients to access files on your Mac. Don't check these boxes unless you don't have a direct Internet connection or you do have a good firewall in place, because people you don't know can sometimes use these services to gain unauthorized access to your Mac.

Playing with Peripherals

These three panes allow you to control the behavior of hardware attached to your Mac: your mouse (or trackball or trackpad), your keyboard, and your monitor (or multiple monitors).

Show Info

Alternative Netstyles

FTP stands for File Transfer Protocol, and it's a way to copy files over the Internet and over Unix networks. Because you're not viewing the files while they're transferred, as you do in a Web browser, FTP is often faster than using the Web to move files around, and it's the preferred way to transfer files to and from Unix computers. FTP clients include Fetch (**www.fetchsoftworks.com**) and Transmit (**www.panic.com**.

Mouse

The Mouse pane has only two controls: a slider to increase or decrease mouse speed, and another slider to control what's considered a double-click. When the slider is at the Fast end, you must click twice very quickly to double-click, while at the Very Slow end you can click more slowly. Use the text entry field to try out different settings.

Keyboard

If you let your finger rest too long on a key when you're typing, it repeats itself. This is a great feature when you actually want to type the same character over and over, but it's pretty annoying if you're just moving a little slowly. The Keyboard pane lets you set the amount of time before a key starts repeating, as well as the amount of time between repetitions.

Displays

The Displays pane enables you to set your monitor's *resolution* and *color depth*. To do this, click the **Display** tab, which offers you presets recommended by your monitor manufacturer. Click on a Resolution setting to change the monitor's resolution—higher numbers give you more space on your screen and make everything look smaller. Then, choose the color depth and refresh rate using the pop-up menus.

In the Color tab of the Displays pane, you can choose a device profile for your monitor, or click the **Calibrate** button to create your own custom profile.

Color Me Mac

The number of pixels your computer can display is referred to as its **resolution**. The more pixels shown on the screen, the more room you have to display different things, but the smaller they'll be. That's separate from the **color depth**, which is the number of colors your monitor displays. The human eye can see millions of colors, but for most images a depth of thousands of colors isn't distinguishable from a depth of millions of colors—and using the lower setting speeds up display a bit.

Middle Color Management

Using a device profile enables you to be sure that the color images you scan and see onscreen look the same when you print them. This is called "color management"—for more information, turn to Chapter 24, "Using Mac Technology to the Max."

Messing with Multimedia

Macs are all about multimedia: music, animation, video, images, speech, and text all rolled into a fun computer experience. This group of preference panes is a good place to start when you're exploring these different aspects of your Mac.

Sound

Divided into two areas, the Sound pane consists mainly of volume controls for the various sounds your Mac makes. The divisions are as follows:

➤ **System Volume**—In this area, you can set the basic volume level for your Mac's speakers. This volume is used for music and speech played by the computer. Drag the slider to increase or decrease the volume, and check **Mute** to turn sound off entirely. The second slider has no effect on built-in speakers, but if you're using external speakers it shifts the sound more to the left or right.

➤ **Alert Volume**—You can set the volume separately for alert sounds that signify a miskey or an error dialog box. The Alert Sound list enables you to choose the sound that you'll hear when your Mac wants your attention. If the Mute box is checked in the System Volume area, the menu bar will blink instead of a sound playing.

Speech

The Speech pane contains two tabs: Speech Recognition and Text-to-Speech. The first set of controls enables you to issue spoken commands to your Mac instead of using the mouse or keyboard. You can turn this feature off and on in the Off/On tab. In the Listening tab, you can give your computer a name or set a keyboard combination to let it know when you're talking to it, as opposed to just talking, and you can specify a microphone to use.

Some Mac applications can speak text that you enter, and the system reads error dialog boxes to you if you let them sit there for a few minutes without responding by clicking the appropriate button. To choose the voice and speed used for Speech, use the Text-to-Speech tab. Personally, I recommend Fred—he sounds fairly human.

QuickTime

QuickTime is Apple's sound-and-video technology. It's used in many places throughout Mac OS X, such as in the QuickTime Player and the QuickTime Web browser plug-in. In this preferences pane, you can make basic settings that allow QuickTime to run most efficiently on your Mac. There are five tabs:

➤ **Plug-In**—This tab contains settings for the QuickTime plug-in, used by Web browsers. You can set the plug-in to play movies automatically, as opposed to just saving them on your hard drive, and to save them after it plays them. You also can use kiosk mode, which removes some of the controls that the QuickTime player would ordinarily have when it's working within a Web browser.

➤ **Connection**—Indicating your Internet connection speed here enables QuickTime to choose the right version of a movie or sound file when more than one is available for playing on a Web page. If you choose one of the slower options, you can also choose whether to allow more than one movie or sound file to play at the same time, which can make the sound choppy.

➤ **Music**—If you work with digital music, you can use this tab to specify a software synthesizer with which to play music and *MIDI* files.

Go To

Quick Guide to QuickTime

To learn how to use QuickTime Player to play sound and video from the Internet, see Chapter 7, "Free Software! (Using Mac OS X's Built-In Apps)."

Show Info

Mac in the MIDI

MIDI stands for Musical Instrument Digital Interface, and it's a way for computers to communicate with synthesizers and other electronic music devices.

➤ **Media Keys**—Some Internet movies are password-protected. If you want to view these, and you have the password, you can enter it here to allow viewing of the protected files.

➤ **Update**—Similar to Software Update, this tab can update your QuickTime software automatically or whenever you ask it to.

ColorSync

Color management is a way of making sure that colors look consistent from the time you create or scan an image to the time you edit it onscreen and print it on a color printer. The building blocks of color management systems are *profiles*, and Apple's built-in ColorSync system enables you to specify a profile for each part of your system that's involved in reproducing color. Three tabs contain the ColorSync controls:

➤ **Profiles**—Here you can set the color profiles you want to use by choosing them from the menu. If you want to use a device profile that's not included in the list, you can download the profile from the manufacturer's Web site and put it in Library/ColorSync/Profiles on your hard drive; then it will appear in the pop-up menus.

➤ **CMMs**—Some third-party applications install their own color-matching methods; you can choose to use one of these, to use Apple's CMM, or to leave this set at automatic, in which case the CMM that's used will depend on what application you're using at the time.

➤ **Info**—Here you can name the settings you've just made. After they're named, the settings will appear in the Workflow pop-up menu at the top of the pane. This is a handy way to switch back and forth between two groups of settings you use often.

The Least You Need to Know

➤ System Preferences contains both nuts-and-bolts settings and more exotic preferences (such as the capability to allow terminal users access to your computer) that many people will never use (if they haven't read this book and don't know they exist!).

➤ Some of Mac OS X's services require you to be connected to the Internet. You can turn some of these off in System Preferences to save time and speed up your computer.

➤ System Preferences contain controls for some of the peripherals attached to your computer: the mouse or other input device, the keyboard, and the monitor.

➤ Multimedia settings enable you to control the quality and volume of sound and video playback as well as the color management settings that are used to keep color consistent on different devices.

➤ Network and Internet settings keep you connected with other users in your home, business, or school and let you get on the Internet.

Chapter 20

The Desktop and the Dock As You Like Them

In This Chapter

➤ Using the Dock to switch programs and store frequently used items

➤ What you can add to the Dock

➤ How you can customize the way the Dock works

➤ Changing the appearance of your Desktop

➤ Controlling where disk icons appear

The Desktop and the Dock are the first things you see every day when you start up your Mac using Mac OS X. Their design builds on lessons learned from earlier versions of the Mac system and incorporates new ideas about how your Mac can make your work—and play—easier. This chapter covers how to make the most of the Dock and the Desktop, so that you can truly make your OS X Mac your own. To give you some ideas, Figure 20.1 shows what my Mac OS X screen looks like.

Figure 20.1

On my Mac, I keep hard drives visible on the Desktop, use the Dock (at a small size, with magnification turned on) to access currently running applications, and store frequently used apps and files in a third-party docking program called DragThing, on the left.

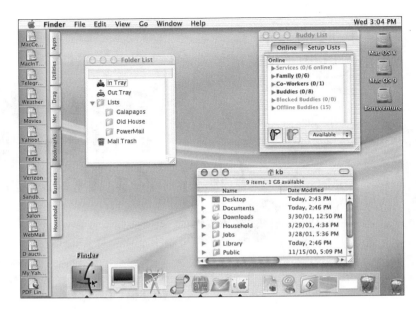

Hickory Dickory Dock

One of the most talked-about features of Mac OS X before its release was the Dock, an attractive platform at the bottom of your screen where you can stash stuff you want to get to quickly. When a program or document's icon has been added to the Dock, you just click it to start up the program or open the document. You can also press Cmd+Tab repeatedly to switch to any of the running items in the Dock; each time you press Tab, the next open Dock item is highlighted, and you can switch to it by releasing the Cmd key.

As you begin to work in Mac OS X, you'll want to add your own items to your Dock, perhaps remove some items that were placed there by default, and adjust the Dock's preferences so it works the way you want it to. Read on for ways to do all that—and more.

What Can You Put in the Dock?

The Dock can hold a lot of different things, each with its own characteristics. You may choose to use the Dock for certain kinds of items, or you might prefer to throw everything you've got into the Dock. Here's a list of what you can keep in your Dock (see Figure 20.2):

Read Me

Hide and Seek

If your screen is getting cluttered with document windows in too many applications, you can hide some of the applications to keep them from distracting you. The quickest way to do this is to Cmd+Option+click on the Dock icon of the application you want to use; all the other applications are hidden. If you just want to hide the application you're currently using as you switch to another, Cmd+click the new program's Dock icon. Hidden applications keep running; you can reveal them by clicking their icons in the Dock.

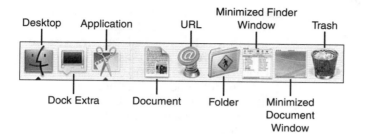

Figure 20.2

You can store all kinds of stuff in your Dock—if clutter's your thing, the Dock is for you.

➤ **Applications**—The "standard" way to start up an application is to find it in the Applications folder and double-click its icon. Alternatively, you can double-click a file created with that program. But the quickest way to start up an app is to click its icon in the Dock. You can add any application to the Dock by dragging it to the Dock's left side, and the system automatically places an icon for any currently running application in the Dock. To make this temporary icon stay in the Dock when you quit the program, Ctrl+click it, and then choose **Keep in Dock** from the contextual menu.

➤ **URLs**—To put your favorite Web site in the Dock, go to that site in any Mac OS X Web browser, be sure the Address or Location field is visible, and drag the address to the right side of the Dock. The icon for all URLs is a strange springy thing with an "@" sign on the top; one of the disadvantages of the Dock is that all URLs look alike. To find out where a particular URL will take you (or to learn the name of any Dock object), poise your mouse over it for a second.

➤ **Files**—If you find yourself using a particular document all the time, such as a letter or invoice template or a database, that document is a good candidate to place in the Dock. Just drag its icon to the right side of the Dock, and you'll be able to open the file whenever you want with a single click. The icon will be the generic document icon for the program in which the document was created, but you can tell one document from another in the Dock by holding your mouse over each one in turn to see its name.

Read Me

Picking It Up from Context

If you use contextual menus a lot, you might want to buy yourself a multibutton mouse. I use a two-button UniMouse from Contour Designs, with the right button set to emulate a Ctrl+click, so I just have to right-click any object to bring up its contextual menu.

Read Me

Switcheroo

To switch to any of the currently running applications, you can hold down the Cmd key and repeatedly press Tab. As you do so, the Dock highlights each application in turn; release the Cmd key when the application you want is highlighted.

231

Read Me

One of These Things Is Not Like the Others

Custom icons are a great way to make different folders distinguishable from one another in the Dock. See the "Icon Mania" sidebar later in this chapter for more info.

Read Me

I Dream of Genie Effects

When you minimize a window by clicking the yellow button, it swirls down into the Dock in a genie-like dance. The reverse happens when you click its icon in the Dock and it returns to full size. If you want to see this effect in slow motion, hold down the Shift key as you click.

➤ **Folders**—Folders can live in the Dock, too. While I was writing this book, I stored an icon for the folder in which I stored all the book's files in the Dock. That way I could open the folder with a single click and avoid having to locate it nested inside the Jobs folder in my home folder. Like URL icons, folder icons all look the same, so you'll have to get the name of each folder in the Dock by holding your mouse over it.

➤ **Minimized windows**—You can temporarily store a Finder or document window in the Dock without closing it by clicking the yellow button at the top-left corner of the window. This is a good way to hide a fantasy football Web page window, for example, when your boss walks by. A minimized window's Dock icon looks just like the window in miniature—they're actually kind of cute—so it's easy to identify the one you're looking for in the Dock.

➤ **Dock Extras**—If you liked the Control Strip of previous Mac systems, you're going to love Dock Extras. The contextual menus you see when you Ctrl+click Dock Extra icons (see Figure 20.3) are the Extras' entire reason for existing—they let you control your Mac's functions quickly and easily. The three Dock Extras included with Mac OS X live in a Dock Extras folder inside the Applications folder: Battery Monitor, Signal Strength, and Displays. To add them to the Dock, drag them onto the Dock's left side. More Dock Extras are on the way, such as the third-party AudioCD Player and Volume "docklings" from On-Core (www.on-core.com/pages/products.html).

Read Me

Life's a Drag

To drag a file (or another folder) into a folder you've placed in the Dock, hold down the Option key and drag the file over the folder's Dock icon. To open a file with an application in the Dock, drag the file over the application's Dock icon. If the app you want to use doesn't highlight when you drag the file over it, Cmd+drag it to force the application to open your chosen file.

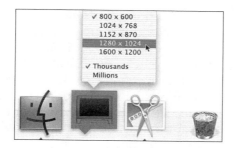

Figure 20.3

Dock Extras are intended for use directly from the Dock.

Now that you've added a whole bunch of stuff to the Dock, you might be ready to remove a few things. To delete icons from the Dock, just drag them off its edge—and watch them go "poof." Removing icons from the Dock doesn't delete the original objects, just their representations in the Dock.

Although some early adopters of Mac OS X had a hard time getting used to the Dock, it's indisputably a lovely piece of technology, from a visual standpoint. One of the impressive things about it is its capability to create dynamic icons of objects you add to it. For example, when the Clock program is running, its Dock icon is constantly updated with the correct time. For this reason, Clock runs, by default, with no window at all—the only place you see it is in the Dock. If you *want* a floating Clock elsewhere on your Desktop, you can have one, but you don't actually *need* one. More complex previews can live in the Dock, too; to see a good example, start up a QuickTime movie and then minimize its window by clicking the yellow button. You'll see the movie continue playing in the minimized window within the Dock. Now, that's impressive.

What you decide to add to and keep in the Dock will depend on how you want to work with your Mac. For some thoughts on ways to use the Dock, read "Dock Strategy," later in this chapter.

Having the Dock Your Way

In addition to changing what items live in the Dock, you can customize the way it acts. To change your Dock Preferences, choose **Apple menu**, **Dock**, **Dock Preferences**. Here's a list of the settings you can adjust:

➤ **Dock Size**—You can change the size of the Dock by dragging this slider. The size setting is variable, not absolute—if you have a lot of items in your Dock, the maximum size (at the Large end of the slider) won't be as big as if you had fewer items. This is to ensure that you won't make the Dock too big to fit across the bottom of your screen in its normal, unmagnified state.

Read Me

Little Big Dock

You can resize the Dock without visiting the Dock Preferences dialog box by dragging the thin line that separates the two sides of the Dock.

Read Me

Flawed Beauty

I just have one note regarding the Dock's beauty. You might notice that the Dock causes strange screen artifacts such as white patches if you activate it while you're using a Classic application. That's because Classic's drawing routines don't support the kind of sophistication that Mac OS X's do. It's purely cosmetic, though—nothing to worry about.

➤ **Magnification**—If you make your Dock small, you'll find this feature very useful. With Magnification on, Dock icons increase in size as you pass your mouse cursor over them and shrink again when you move the cursor away. You can set the amount of magnification that occurs, although if you have your Dock Size setting at the absolute maximum, you'll find that no magnification happens even at the Max end of the Magnification slider.

➤ **Automatically Hide and Show the Dock**—Neat freaks, this setting was designed for you. With this box checked, the Dock slides down off the bottom of your screen when you're not using it, only to return the second you mouse down to the screen's bottom edge. I love this effect and find it keeps the Dock from getting in the way of other things on my screen.

➤ **Animate Opening Applications**—Finally, this setting is for those who like a little touch of cuteness—really, just a tad—in their Mac experience. When this box is checked, Dock icons for programs bounce up and down when you click on them, and they stop when the program is fully launched. If the bouncing drives you crazy, turn it off here.

Dock Strategy

The Dock replaces several different aspects of previous Mac systems: the Apple menu, the Application menu, the Launcher, and the Control Strip. It's hard to pack so much functionality into one utility, and that fact has led to the development of multiple schools of thought on how best to use the Dock.

One group feels that the best way to use the Dock is to drag all your favorite applications into it, so that you can start them up quickly when you want them. Another advantage of this technique is that application icons stored in the Dock don't change their Dock positions when you start the programs up. That enables you to get used to seeing them in a specific order, which also increases your efficiency.

Another method is to remove everything from the Dock and use it purely for switching among applications that are currently running, whose icons appear in the Dock as soon as you start them up. Now, you're asking, how do you start programs up under this plan? The answer: a third-party utility such as DragThing (James Thomson, www.dragthing.com), shown in Figure 20.4, or PocketDock (Pocket Software, www.pocketsw.com). Like the Dock, these programs provide a floating palette or dock that can hold different kinds of items; unlike the Dock, they don't automatically add icons for running applications, and they don't change size without asking you.

234

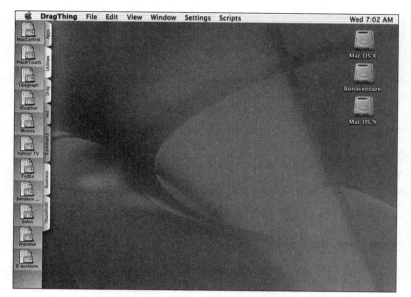

Figure 20.4

Because of its tabs, DragThing can store more items in the same amount of space as the Dock.

Orient Express

If you're mixing the Dock with other utilities, you might find it helpful to anchor the Dock somewhere other than at the bottom of your screen. Head right on over to **homepage.mac.com/isleep/** to download Docking Maneuvers (Austin Shoemaker), a little program that lets you do just this. As always, "hacking" the operating system in this way can result in unexpected problems, so make backups and proceed with caution.

The second method is the way I like to work, and DragThing was the first third-party program I installed after installing Mac OS X on my Mac.

That covers the Application menu and the Launcher functions of the Dock. If you are a big fan of earlier Mac systems' Control Strip or Apple menu, you can use the Dock to perform those functions as well, by placing Dock Extras and folders, respectively, in the Dock. You'll probably find, though, that the more things you put in the Dock, the harder it is to use. Experiment, find your own comfort level, and have fun!

Desktop Decisions

To really make your Desktop "as you like it," you're going to need to change the Desktop picture. Fortunately, doing so is about as easy as can be, and there are plenty of other things you can do to make your Desktop your own. Before you get started, check out the Mac OS X gallery (www.info.apple.com/usen/macosx/gallery/macosxgallery.html) to see how other people have transformed their Mac Desktops.

Finding the Way

Let's start with some things you can do right now to customize your Desktop. First, take a look at the Finder Preferences. To get there, click on the Desktop and choose **Finder**, **Preferences** (see Figure 20.5). Here's what you'll find there:

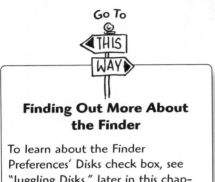

Finding Out More About the Finder

To learn about the Finder Preferences' Disks check box, see "Juggling Disks," later in this chapter. And for more info on the Keep the Same View check box, turn to Chapter 21, "File and Folder Boot Camp."

➤ **Desktop Picture**—You can change the Desktop Picture in two ways. First, click the **Select Picture** button and scroll through the list of pictures that come with Mac OS X. Or, if none of those is to your liking, install any picture you like by dragging its icon into the box. You can download a wide selection of desktop pictures from MacDesktops.com (www.macdesktops.com).

➤ **Icon Size**—This slider controls the size of icons on the Desktop, which can include any files you drag there from within folders, files you download to the Desktop, and disks (if you choose to show them on the Desktop).

➤ **Icon Arrangement**—Here's another one for the neat freaks (and that description includes me, because I always use this feature). If you click **None**, you can drop icons on the Desktop wherever you want them.

Figure 20.5

The Finder has its own preferences dialog box, separate from the System Preferences.

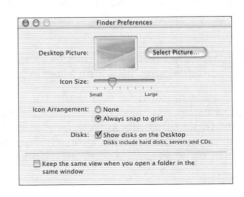

Icon Mania

Now that you've played with resizing icons, perhaps you're ready to move to the next level: custom icons. You can change the icon on any file or folder that belongs to you (meaning that you can't change icons for items created or downloaded by other users).

To change an icon, click an object that has the icon you want to use, press Cmd+I, and click the icon in the upper-left corner of the Inspector window. Press Cmd+C to copy the icon, and then click the object whose icon you want to change (without closing the Inspector window). Click the second object's icon in the Inspector window and press Cmd+V to paste the new icon into place.

You can find some fun icon collections at the Icon Factory (**www.iconfactory.com**), Xicons.com (**www.xicons.com**), and Icons.cx (**www.icons.cx**). As always, if you download and use any shareware icons, be sure to pay the shareware fee.

When you used icon view in earlier Mac systems, you could arrange icons in windows in whatever pattern took your fancy. Mac OS X likes to keep things tidy, so you might find that icons you've arranged in icon view end up in different configurations when you leave them for a while. Your best bet for keeping things the way you leave them is to use the **Always Snap to Grid** setting and tidy the icons yourself. To put icons back in neat rows, choose **View, Clean Up**. And if you want to realign icons in alphabetical order, choose **View, Arrange by Name**.

Appearances Count

Apple has stashed more fun settings in the General panel of the System Preferences. To get there, choose **Apple menu, System Preferences**. Here are the appearance settings you can change:

➤ **Appearance**—The original release of Mac OS X came with two color schemes, Blue and Graphite. The default setting is Blue; the Graphite scheme was added when Apple realized that graphic artists and others who work with color needed a neutral backdrop for their images. Items that are affected by this setting include the highlight color in menus, progress bars (to indicate progress in activities such as downloads), and the scrollbars in windows.

➤ **Highlight color**—Choose a color to indicate selected text and list items. The colors are all fairly light, which might seem annoying, but the idea is that the color shouldn't obscure the text or list item so that you can't read it.

The scrollbar setting at the bottom of the General panel is covered in the next chapter, "File and Folder Boot Camp."

Digging Deeper

If you *really* like to customize your Mac, you have even more options. Third-party utilities, such as TinkerTool (Marcel Bresink, `www.bresink.de/osx/`), can change a variety of settings such as the transparency of the Terminal window. And if you are comfortable using the Terminal's command line, you can use it to change all kinds of settings for which Apple hasn't seen fit to provide a graphical interface. That's how TinkerTool works, in fact—by giving you a graphical interface for a selected few of the settings available from the command line.

To investigate the settings you can change using Terminal, first start up Terminal. Click the Desktop, and then choose **Go**, **Applications**; Terminal is located in the Utilities folder inside the Applications folder.

Each component of Mac OS X and every application uses a text file called a plist, or property list, to store its settings. To modify system settings with Terminal, you use a program called defaults, like so:

```
defaults write com.apple.finder Desktop.HasTrash 1
```

Typing this string of text into the Terminal will tell the defaults program to write "Desktop.HasTrash 1" into the `com.apple.finder` file, which is the plist for the Finder. Making this particular change to the Finder's plist puts a Trash icon on your Desktop, in addition to the one that lives in the Dock.

For a list of other stuff you can change this way, check out `homepage.mac.com/pixits/defaults.htm`.

More Fun with the Finder

Normally, you can't change the icons for the default folders created by Mac OS X. However, if you're feeling adventurous, you can try a hack that's explained at Xicons.com (`xicons.macnn.com/articles/defaults.phtml`) that will allow you to put any icons you want on these folders. As always, be sure you have a current backup of your system before fiddling with it in this way.

The Wild Wild Web

If you really want to wreak havoc on your OS X Mac, you'll find lots of tips and tricks on the Web. A good place to start is ResExcellence (`www.ResExcellence.com/osx/`). Of course, you should take it slow, do lots of backups, and be prepared for unanticipated results when you use any system-level "hack" such as this.

Juggling Disks

Now that you've customized every inch of your Desktop, let's take a minute to look at your options for using and viewing disks in Mac OS X.

Users of earlier Mac systems are used to seeing their hard drives at the upper-right corner of their screens, with removable disks such as CDs, Zips, and floppies lined up below the hard drives. In Mac OS X, you can continue working that way if you like, or you can get rid of that clutter by removing drive icons from the Desktop. To set this option, click the Desktop and choose **Finder, Preferences**. Check the box labeled **Disks** to determine whether they show on the Desktop.

If you choose to leave your disks off the Desktop, how do you get to them to use their contents? Easy—click the Desktop and press Cmd+Option+C or choose **Go, Computer**. This opens a window showing everything at the top level of your computer, including hard drives, network drives, your *iDisk* (if you have one), and removable disks.

Here's how to accomplish a few other useful tasks with disks:

➤ To eject a disk, click it and choose **File, Eject**—or press Cmd+E, or drag the disk's icon to the Trash in the Dock, which will switch to an Eject icon when you're dragging a disk.

➤ To find out how much space is on a disk or what format it uses, click it and choose **File, Show Info**. This brings up the Inspector window, which contains a variety of information about the selected item.

➤ To erase and reformat a disk, you must use the Disk Utility program, which you'll find in the Utilities folder within the Applications folder. Start it up and click **Drive Setup** (see Figure 20.6), and then click the icon for the disk you want to erase. Click the **Partition** tab, and click **Partition** to erase the disk and reformat it.

I'm an iDisk

iDisks are part of Apple's iTools utility set for Mac owners. You can sign up for a free e-mail address, put up a Web page, and more. The iDisk itself is a storage space on Apple's servers that you can use to share files with friends, store backup files, and download software from Apple. If you didn't sign up when you installed Mac OS X, you can get in on this great deal now at `itools.mac.com`.

A Good Thing or a Bad Thing?

If you try to change disk icons (as suggested earlier in this chapter in the "Icon Mania" sidebar), they won't appear to change. But if you boot back into Mac OS 9, you'll see the new icons there, and there only.

Figure 20.6

Creating a disk with a single partition is the same thing as formatting the disk.

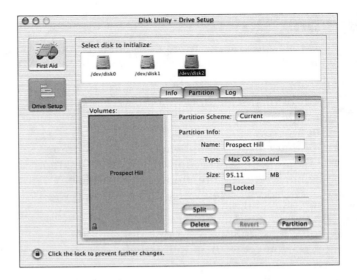

The Least You Need to Know

➤ The Dock is intended as an application launcher, an application switcher, and much more. You can store icons for applications, files, folders, URLs, Finder and document windows, and Dock Extras in the Dock, and you can use it to launch or open any of these items or switch to one that's already running or open.

➤ Because the Dock automatically adds an icon for any application that's running, it can get pretty crowded. Different users respond to this limitation in different ways. Adding a third-party application to your system to supplement the Dock can be helpful.

➤ You can customize your Desktop by changing the picture, setting different highlight and accent colors, applying custom icons to your files and folders, and other techniques. You can even use the Terminal's Unix command line to change settings that you can't access using Mac OS X's graphical interface.

➤ Manipulating disks (hard, network, and removable) is an important part of using your Mac, and to some extent you can customize that experience by determining whether disks appear on your Desktop.

Chapter 21

File and Folder Boot Camp

In This Chapter

➤ Viewing files and folders in single-window and multiwindow mode

➤ Switching window views: icons, columns, and lists

➤ Setting View options for one folder and setting Global options

➤ Customizing your Toolbar

➤ Using the Info window

No doubt you're familiar with that *other* operating system, the one with all the windows. It got its name because its creators "borrowed" the Mac window concept, which enables you to see what's inside each file, disk, or folder by double-clicking to open a "window" into it. Windows are a basic part of the Mac interface: You'll see one each time you double-click a document file, a disk, or a folder.

This chapter tells you just about everything you might want to know about viewing your files and folders in the Finder's windows, as well as how to get additional information about any item, such as its file size or the name of the application that created it.

Here a Window, There a Window

The two kinds of windows—document windows and Finder windows—have some things in common:

➤ The window's title appears at the top in the title bar, which you can click and drag to move the window around the Desktop.

➤ The three buttons at the left end of the window's title bar enable you to close the window (red), minimize it and place it in the Dock (yellow), and maximize it (green). If you've already maximized a window, clicking the green button restores it to its previous size.

➤ You can resize a window by dragging its lower-right corner.

Finder windows, however, have extra features designed to help you navigate within your Mac's disks more easily. The parts of a Finder window are described in Chapter 2. Here, we'll skip to the fun part: making the Finder jump through hoops for you.

One Window or Many Windows?

In the old Mac days, another window opened up every time you double-clicked a disk or folder. If you tend to be highly organized (or just have a lot of stuff), you might find yourself spawning windows all over the Desktop as you delve into a series of nested folders looking for something. Earlier Mac systems dealt with this by offering a keyboard shortcut: Hold down Option as you double-click an item, and the window containing that item closes as the new one opens.

Mac OS X offers a completely new way to navigate the Finder: single-window mode. When you operate this way, double-clicking a folder replaces the current contents of the window with the contents of the folder you're opening. As you work, you see only one window with constantly changing contents—similar to a Web browser window. To open more than one window, choose **File**, **New Finder Window** or press Cmd+N.

The interesting thing about Mac OS X is that you can work in more than one Finder mode at a time by setting different windows to different modes. The visibility of each window's Toolbar reflects which mode it's set for; windows with a Toolbar are in single-window mode, while windows without a Toolbar are in multiwindow mode. You can switch modes for a window by clicking the clear Toolbar button at the right end of the title bar or by choosing **View**, **Show/Hide Toolbar** (Cmd+B).

Read Me

Let's Get Inactive

Here's something new and cool: The Close, Maximize, and Minimize buttons are available in inactive windows. Try it out: Open multiple windows, and then pass your mouse cursor over these buttons on one of the windows behind the front window. The buttons are clear on inactive windows, but their color returns as your mouse passes over them. You can click to close, maximize, or minimize a window in the current program without bringing it to the front. If you're working in one program and you maximize a window that belongs to another application, that window does come to the front.

Go To

Finding Out About the Finder

To learn more about the Finder and the other parts of the Mac OS X interface, turn to Chapter 2, "Making Friends with Mac OS X."

Same As It Ever Was

As in earlier versions of the Mac OS, pressing Option as you double-click a folder will close the window that contains that folder. (As an incurable neat freak, I just love this keyboard shortcut.) In single-window mode (with the Toolbar showing), Option+double-clicking has the added effect of switching you to multiwindow mode (no Toolbar). To open a new window in multiwindow mode *without* closing the original window, press the Cmd key as you double-click.

Go Out the Window

Choices from the Go menu (such as **Go, Home** or **Go, Applications**) reflect your current window mode. If the uppermost window is in single-window mode, new contents appear in it; otherwise, a new window opens. The same is true even if you use the keyboard shortcuts to move to Go folders (such as Cmd+Option+H for your home folder or Cmd+Option+A for the Applications folder).

Which way you prefer to work can depend on your general preference or on what you're doing at a given time. Although single-window mode does help prevent clutter on your Desktop, it also makes it difficult to copy or move items from one folder to another. If you know you'll be working with a particular window for a while, such as when you're working on a project whose files are all located in the same folder, you'll probably want to switch that window to multiwindow mode so that it stays put.

Ch-ch-ch-changes

In earlier Mac systems, Cmd+N is the keyboard shortcut to create a new folder rather than a new Finder window. To create a new folder now, you can choose **File, New Folder** or press Cmd+Shift+N.

Read Me

List Columns, Not Column Columns

In list view, you can move the columns around to suit your needs by clicking on a column header and dragging it to a new position. (The only column you can't move is the Name column, which must always appear at the left side of the window.) You can also make columns wider and narrower by clicking and dragging the right ends of column headers.

Icons, Columns, and Lists, Oh My

Each window can display files in three different ways: Columns, Icons, and List view (see Figure 21.1). To switch among these, you can click the three buttons at the left end of the Toolbar, or you can choose from the options at the top of the Finder's View menu.

After you've chosen the view you want for a window, you can set viewing options by choosing **View, Show View Options** and clicking the **Window** tab. For List view, your viewing options include which columns to show, what format to use for displaying dates, what size to display icons, and whether to calculate folder sizes (the amount of disk space occupied by a folder's contents).

In Icon view, the choices are different; you can change the icons' sizes (but all icons in the window will have the same size), whether they snap to a neat grid, and whether the folder has a background color or image. If you choose Picture, you can place the picture in the folder's background by dragging it onto the white box in the View Options dialog box (see Figure 21.2), or click **Select** to locate a picture on your hard drive.

Figure 21.1

These three windows contain the same files shown in Column, Icon, and List view (from left to right).

Finally, your options for Column view are—nothing. You can't customize Column view windows.

Whichever view you choose for a window, you can maintain that view when you open a folder in single-window mode, or you can allow it to vary according to the settings you made for that particular folder's window. For example, suppose the current window is in single-window mode and uses List view. You double-click to open a folder that, when you last viewed its contents, was set to Icon view. To determine whether that folder's contents appear in Icon view or List view, choose **Finder, Preferences** and check or uncheck **Keep the Same View When You Open a Folder in the Same Window.**

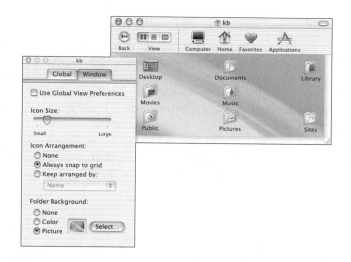

Figure 21.2
The View Options dialog box enables you to customize views (including window background images) on a window-by-window basis.

Another feature that takes effect no matter which view you're using is the way Mac OS X displays long filenames. If there isn't enough room to display the entire name, Mac OS X replaces the middle portion of the name with "...". To see the item's full name, hold your mouse cursor over the name for a second, or hold down the Option key as you move the cursor over the filename. This second method is most convenient when you're browsing a list of filenames.

We Do Windows

By now, you're probably amazed at the number of options you have for viewing windows. Hold onto your hat, because there are several more ways you can customize your Mac's windows. This section introduces you to View options and the Toolbar.

Custom Windows

Aside from choosing a window mode, you have some other choices to make about how your windows look.

First, if you're constantly changing windows to a specific set of viewing options, you can set the Global View options to reflect those choices. Choose **View**, **View Options** and click the **Global** tab. Choose **Global Icon** or **Global List** to set the icon or list preferences and make changes the same way you would in the Window tab. Then, if you want a window to use these Global preferences, choose **View**, **Show View Options**, click the **Window** tab, and click **Use Global View Preferences**. New windows always use the Global preferences.

Read Me

No Window Left Behind

Clicking a Mac OS X application's window will bring the application to the foreground, but any other open windows that belong to that application stay in the background. To bring all of an application's windows to the front, click the program's icon in the Dock.

Here are a couple other fun window facts:

➤ In the General preferences (choose **Apple menu**, **System Preferences** and click **General**), you can determine what happens when you click in a window's scroll-bar instead of dragging in it. Jump to Next Page moves the view down an entire page or screen, whereas Scroll to Here moves the view to the corresponding point in the window. For example, you'd click halfway down in the scrollbar to move to the halfway point in the document.

➤ You can display information about how many items are in each window and how much disk space is available by choosing **View**, **Show Status Bar**. The status bar is displayed in all windows or no windows, rather than on a window-by-window basis.

Off the Shelf

When you're in single-window mode, a row of useful buttons known as the Toolbar—or the shelf—appears across the top of each window. Do you love the Toolbar but find that your favorite destinations aren't in it? Click on a window, choose **View**, **Customize Toolbar**, and customize your Toolbar to your heart's content (see Figure 21.3). The buttons from which you can choose fall into three categories:

➤ **Window control buttons**—These buttons help you navigate within Finder windows. Back takes you to the previous contents of the current window, and Path shows you the folder path between the current folder and your Mac's top level. The View buttons enable you to switch among Icon, List, and Column views. The Eject button ejects the disk whose contents appear in the current window, Customize takes you back to the Customize Toolbar dialog box, and the separator can be placed on the Toolbar to separate groups of buttons.

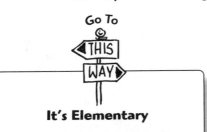

It's Elementary

Sherlock is the Mac's built-in file-finding and Internet-searching utility. To learn more about Sherlock, turn to Chapter 5, "Managing Your Files" (to find files with Sherlock) or Chapter 14, "Nothing but Net" (to search the Internet with Sherlock).

➤ **Function buttons**—These buttons are pretty self-explanatory; they save you a trip to the menu bar. New Folder creates a new folder, Delete sends selected items to the Trash, Connect opens the Connect to Server dialog box, and Find opens Sherlock.

➤ **Folders**—These buttons open the default folders created by Mac OS X, such as your home folder and the Applications folder.

After you have the Toolbar set up to your liking, you can click a button in it to open a folder or perform a function quickly. (And if you command-click on a folder in the Toolbar, that folder opens in a new window.) The Toolbar is most useful if you use single-window mode often, because it's not visible in multiwindow mode.

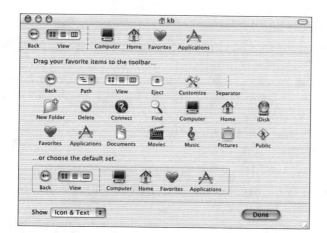

Figure 21.3
You can choose which buttons appear in your Toolbar.

Read Me

Rolling Your Own

You can also customize the Toolbar by dragging files, folders, disks, or programs directly onto it. The button you'll see will reflect the item's icon, so you might want to create custom icons for items you're adding to the Toolbar—see Chapter 20, "The Desktop and the Dock As You Like Them," for more information.

Info Overload

When you need to know more about a disk, folder, or file, what's the best thing to do? Ask for info, that's what.

If you've been using Macs for a while, you might be familiar with the old Get Info command in the File menu or its keyboard equivalent, Cmd+I. In Mac OS X, the keyboard shortcut is the same but the command name has changed. Now, you click on a file, folder, or disk and choose **File, Show Info**. The resulting window provides a variety of information about the selected item.

The specific information that is provided in the Info window varies depending on what kind of object is selected. You can choose from several panes within the Info box by choosing from the **Show** pop-up menu. Here's a list of the different panes you'll see for a document file:

➤ **General Information** (see Figure 21.4):

> ➤ **Kind**—What application created the file, if the selected item is a file, or "Volume" for disks and "Folder" for folders.

> ➤ **Size**—How much disk space the file or folder occupies (useful for knowing whether it will fit on a floppy disk, for example). This info doesn't show up if the selected item is a disk.

> ➤ **Where**—What folder and disk the file is in.

> ➤ **Created**—When the file was first created.

> ➤ **Modified**—What time the file was last changed by being saved.

> ➤ **Format**—What kind of formatting has been used (for disks only, not files or folders).

> ➤ **Stationery Pad**—Checking this box makes the file a template file; when you open it, it automatically will be duplicated and you'll open the duplicate.

> ➤ **Locked**—Check this box to lock the file so it can't be modified.

> ➤ **Comments**—Add comments about the file here, such as version control information or the author's name.

Figure 21.4

The General Information pane of the Info window for the manuscript version of this chapter.

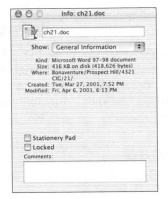

➤ **Application**—Here you can click a radio button to specify whether the originating application or another application should be used to open this particular file (see Figure 21.5).

➤ **Preview**—This pane shows an enlarged view of the file's icon (see Figure 21.6). In the case of many graphics and multimedia files, the icon is a thumbnail version of the image file itself, so the Preview is most useful in those cases. This pane doesn't appear in Info windows for disks and folders; only ones for files.

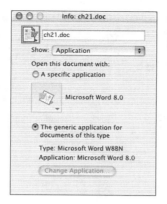

Figure 21.5

You can control what program opens when you double-click a file by changing the setting here.

Figure 21.6

The Preview information is most useful for image and movie files.

➤ **Application Files**—You'll see this option only if the selected item is a program. It can be used to see a program's optional components, add new ones, and delete unused ones (see Figure 21.7).

Figure 21.7

Because I use only English, I could delete the localized resources that allow the QuickTime Player to use other languages in its interface.

➤ **Privileges**—The file's owner can set access privileges for the file here by choosing from the pop-up menus (see Figure 21.8).

Figure 21.8

Each file can have different access privileges for its owner, the owner's group, and all other users.

Unlike earlier Mac systems, only one Info window can be open at a time. The Info window updates to show information for any file you select.

Information, Please

If you need to compare info for two or more files, you can open more than one window and set each window to Column view (click the appropriate button or choose **View, As Columns**). Then, click on the files you want to compare, each in a different window. The preview information shown in the right column includes much of what you'll see under General Information in the Info window.

The Least You Need to Know

➤ Mac OS X offers you two ways to use windows: a new window for every folder you open, or a single window that displays the contents of each folder you open in succession. You can switch a window from one mode to the other with a single click, and you can have windows in each mode open at the same time.

➤ Each window displays its contents in one of three views: Icon view, List view, or Column view. This third option is new to Mac OS X and enables you to see the contents of multiple nested folders at once.

➤ You can change a variety of settings to determine how your files and folders are arranged within windows, from adding and deleting columns in List view to putting a picture into a window as a background.

➤ The Toolbar is a handy place to store buttons that help you navigate windows, perform Finder functions such as creating new folders, and take you instantly to commonly used folders. You can use the default Toolbar or customize it to contain the buttons that you find most useful.

➤ The Info window displays information about a file, folder, or disk, and it enables you to set access privileges to determine which other users can view and change items.

Chapter 22

Making Mac OS X More Familiar

In This Chapter

➤ Restoring drive icons and the Trash to your Desktop

➤ Dealing with the loss of the Apple and Applications menus

➤ Third-party software that can supplement or substitute for the Dock

➤ Resurrecting the missing Launcher and Control Strip

➤ Finding familiar features under their new Mac OS X names

You've installed Mac OS X, or maybe it came on your new Mac. You like it pretty well so far—you're intrigued by its possibilities, and its new look appeals to you. But you're starting to get a little homesick. Maybe you're even having trouble getting work done because some of your favorite features are missing from Mac OS X. Perhaps the new system is just too new.

If this describes you, this chapter is what you've been waiting for. We'll look at ways to put the familiar Mac feel back into Mac OS X's *GUI*, so your transition to the new system will be smoother.

Gooey?

No, **GUI**—graphical user interface. This is the term for a computer/user interface that relies on graphics rather than textual commands. Macs and Windows PCs use a GUI, whereas DOS computers and Unix terminals use a "command-line interface" (CLI).

Getting Things Back Where They Belong

Where's your hard drive? And where'd the Trash go? Oh my gosh, that doesn't look like the Apple menu you know and love, and where the heck is the Application menu? You'll get answers to all these questions, and suggestions for coping with Mac OS X's differences from Mac OS 9, in this section.

Drive Icons and the Trash

One of the cool things about Mac OS X is that it enables you to completely clear your Desktop—no folders, no windows, no disk icons, no nothing (see Figure 22.1). On the other hand, this aspect of Mac OS X can be pretty disconcerting when you first start using the new system. Fortunately, you can put some "clutter" right on your Desktop where it belongs, if you're so inclined.

Figure 22.1

If you're into the clean, uncluttered look, Mac OS X is for you.

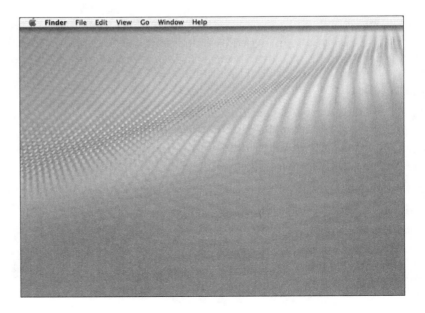

The first thing to do, if you haven't already, is choose **Finder**, **Preferences**. Check the box labeled **Show Disks on the Desktop** to put your hard drives and removable disks back on the upper-right corner of the Desktop, where you're used to seeing them.

Now, how about the Trash? Mac OS X stashes it in the Dock, which makes things very tidy indeed, but might also make it more difficult for you to find the Trash when you need it. If you prefer it on the Desktop, download a utility called TinkerTool (Marcel Bresink, www.bresink.de/osx/). With the help of this snazzy little program, you can put the Trash on the Desktop. You also can make several other changes to the way Mac OS X works, including

Climbing on Board the CLI

If you're the adventurous type, you might want to try changing system settings (such as the location of the Trash and the transparency of the Terminal) yourself using Mac OS X's command-line interface. Turn to the "Digging Deeper" section in Chapter 20, "The Desktop and the Dock As You Like Them," for more information.

➤ Disabling zoom rectangles when opening files

➤ Showing hidden files in the Finder

➤ Using transparent Dock icons to indicate hidden applications

➤ Indicating the active foreground application in the Dock

➤ Selecting the default fonts used in Mac OS X native applications

➤ Making Terminal windows transparent

A similar utility called Plus For X (Simon Wgzell, www.orcsoftware.com/~simon/plus/) can also let you position the Dock on any edge of your screen, rather than just on the bottom.

Missing Menus

Mac OS X's new Go menu definitely is a useful innovation, allowing you to navigate to the most-used folders in your system quickly and easily. And the new Apple menu is pretty handy, too, offering access to commonly used commands from any application. But the old Apple menu, which could contain anything you wanted to add, was the ultimate in customizability. If you miss it, there's good news and bad news.

The bad news is that there's currently no Mac OS X replacement for the old Apple menu. The good news is that I can offer some suggestions for ways to replicate some of its functionality using the Dock and other utilities. Here are a few ideas:

➤ **Add system utilities, such as the Print Center and System Preferences, to the Dock**—The Chooser might be gone, but the Print Center has taken its place. To ensure that you can access it any time, whether you're printing or not, drag it into the Dock from the Utilities folder inside the Applications folder. Do the same with System Preferences (if it's not already in the Dock) and any other utility programs you use a dozen times a day without even thinking about it.

Read Me

Keeping Time

Here's an example of how I use hierarchical folders. In my Mac OS 9 Apple menu was a folder called Timesheets, with folders within it called 1999, 2000, and 2001. Each of these folders contains my time-keeping records for that year, so I can access any of this information by navigating the hierarchical Apple menu rather than having to open each folder in turn starting with my hard drive icon. When I switched to Mac OS X, I dragged the Timesheets folder into my Dock.

➤ **Set up hierarchical folders in the Dock**—If you click on a folder in the Dock and hold down the mouse button for a second (or right-click, if you use a multibutton mouse), a pop-up menu appears listing the folder's contents, including submenus for folders within the folder, and so on. This functionality duplicates the hierarchical folder capability of the old Apple menu, one of its most beloved features.

➤ **Use the Classic Apple menu**—Yes, it's still there, and you can still use it to house whatever you want: applications (even Mac OS X ones), folders, and documents. Of course, you'll see it only when you're using a Classic application, but it's better than nothing, right?

➤ **Try out third-party launchers**—A wide variety of third-party utilities do what the Dock does in somewhat different ways. You can use these programs to provide quick access to items you used to store in the Apple menu. Read "Dock Alternatives," later in this chapter, for more information.

The other menu I keep reaching for in Mac OS X is the Application menu, which appears in the far-right end of the Mac OS 9 menu bar. It was intended to be used for switching applications, another function taken over by the Dock in Mac OS X. If you'd rather use a menu than the Dock to switch programs, well, as far as Apple is concerned, you're out of luck.

If you're running Classic, however, you might notice that the Application menu is still there whenever you're working in a Classic application. And if you head over to it and take a look, you'll also see that it includes not only the currently running Classic apps, but also whatever Mac OS X applications you're running at the moment (albeit with generic icons). So, you can still use the Classic Application menu to switch from a Classic app to another Classic app or a Mac OS X app, although it disappears again when you get to the Mac OS X program.

More Third-Party Help

No operating system works, out of the box, just the way everyone wants it to—which means there's always room for third-party software developers to create programs to fulfill all those unmet needs. The Mac is no exception to this rule, and developers began offering enhancement utilities as soon as the Public Beta of Mac OS X was released. Since then, the field has widened as more developers have released new products and Mac OS X versions of old favorites. Read on for a selection of third-party ways to enhance your Mac OS X experience.

Dock Alternatives

Whether you like the Dock or not, you can't deny that it gets crowded pretty quickly when you start adding things to it. It's beautiful, and the way it can retract into the bottom of your screen is a wonderful feature, but let's face it: The Dock can use some help.

Fortunately, you can download any of a variety of alternatives to the Dock that you can use either to replace the Dock (although it's always running, you don't have to use it) or to supplement it. My preference is to use the Dock for switching applications and to use a third-party dock to access frequently used files and programs. Read on for some suggested Dock alternatives (see Figure 22.2).

DragThing (James Thomson, www.dragthing.com) provides multiple customizable docks that can contain files, folders, disks, and servers. You also can have a *process dock*. You can have as many different docks as you want, and each one can have different settings for things such as the size of icons displayed and whether the names of the items appear. Also—and this is my favorite part—docks can have multiple layers, each with a tab so you can switch among them.

Go To

Gooey Excellence

ResExcellence is a Web site devoted to modifying Mac software (including the system) to suit your own taste. Its archive of Mac OS X GUI utilities (www.resexcellence.com/archive_software/index7.shtml) contains lots of useful programs, some of which will restore Mac OS 9 functions—and others of which will give you help in areas where you didn't even know you needed help.

DragThing   PocketDock

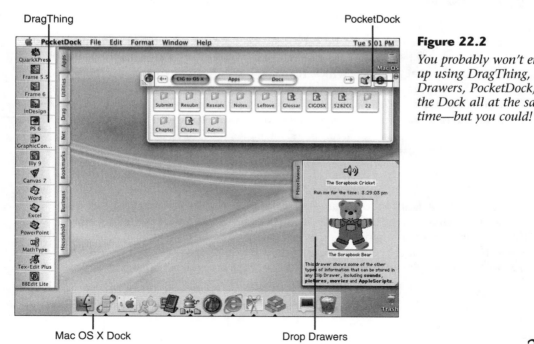

Mac OS X Dock   Drop Drawers

Figure 22.2

You probably won't end up using DragThing, Drop Drawers, PocketDock, and the Dock all at the same time—but you could!

257

Read Me

Out of My Way, Dock!

If you don't use the Dock, you want to get it out of your way. Even if you do use it, you might want it to show up only when you need it. The answer is to choose **Apple menu**, **Dock**, **Turn Hiding On** to hide the Dock until you move your mouse all the way to the bottom of your screen.

Show Info

It's All About the Process

A *process dock* shows you the processes that are taking place on your computer at the moment—in other words, the programs that are running. You also can have process menus—that's what Mac OS 9's Application menu was (and still is, in Classic).

Drop Drawers (Sig Software, `www.sigsoftware.com`) enables you to put drawers along the edges of your screen in which you can store icons for almost any item you can think of: documents, text snippets, Web links, e-mail addresses, applications, pictures, and sounds. Its special process drawers can contain icons for all running programs. The drawers retract into the edges of the screen, showing only their handles, when they're not needed.

PocketDock (Pocket Software, `www.pocketsw.com`) is a utility for organizing and launching applications, documents, and Web links. Its tab-based user interface enables you to store lots of stuff without taking up lots of screen space. PocketDock supports drag and drop of links and tabs and multiple floating dock windows.

Missing in Action

Two more components of the Mac OS that bit the dust in the move to Mac OS X are the Launcher, a very early incarnation of the Dock, and the Control Strip, a favorite of PowerBook and iBook users because of its capability to pack so many functions into so small a space. Fortunately for fans of these utilities, third-party developers have released versions of both that work in Mac OS X.

The very first "click here to start your favorite program" utility in the Mac system software was the Launcher, which first saw the light of day when System 7 was released. Although the Dock and its third-party alternatives have wooed most users away from the Launcher, it's available once more for those who still love it (Brian Hill, `personalpages.tds.net/~brian_hill/launcher.html`).

The Control Strip, on the other hand, has a hardcore following of fanatic users who collect CSMs (Control Strip modules) like trading cards. Control Strip certainly is a useful utility; it retracts into a tiny handle on the side of your screen when you don't want it, and its modules are self-contained utilities that perform an incredible variety of functions, ranging from changing monitor resolution to offering you a tiny slot machine game. If you can't bear to lose the Control Strip now that you've switched to Mac OS X, try OpenStrip (Joe Strout, `www.strout.net/info/coding/macdev/openstrip/`).

Ripley's Launcher or Not

Believe it or not, I still use the Launcher on my PowerBook 2400, because it's a fine way to access a relatively small number of frequently needed programs and documents all in one place. And because it's part of the system software and doesn't require any extensions to work, it's pretty much crashproof and conflictproof.

Familiar Faces, New Names

Although Mac OS X has a slew of new features, it also has almost all the features of earlier Mac systems. But many of them have changed their names, and a lot of them have changed their locations as well. Table 22.1 lists some common Mac functions under their Mac OS 9 names and their Mac OS X names.

Table 22.1   What Went Where in Mac OS X

Feature	New Location/Name
About This Computer	It's still under the Apple menu, but now it's called About This Mac. You'll find the version number of your system software there. To find out how much memory the currently active programs are using, use Process Viewer, which you'll find in the Utilities folder within the Applications folder.
Chooser	It's been replaced by Print Center (in the Utilities folder within the Applications folder).
Control panels	Their functions all exist in System Preferences (choose **Apple menu**, **System Preferences**).
Disk First Aid	It's been renamed Disk Utility (in the Utilities folder within the Applications folder).
Drive Setup	It's now part of Disk Utility (in the Utilities folder within the Applications folder).
Get Info	It's still under the File menu, but it's now called Show Info.
SimpleText	Its replacement is called TextEdit (in the Applications folder).
Startup Items	Choose **Apple menu**, **System Preferences**, click **Login**, and then click **Add** on the Login Items tab.

As you use Mac OS X more, you'll get used to the way things work in the new system, and you might even find that you no longer want to use the add-ons and workarounds detailed in this chapter. That's been the experience of most people who were taken aback by the changes Mac OS X made in our Mac experience—including me.

The Least You Need to Know

➤ Mac OS X offers a clean, uncluttered Desktop, but you can add drive icons and the Trash to the Desktop to make Mac OS X feel more like Mac OS 9 if the new system is a little *too* clean for you.

➤ The Apple menu and Application menu are gone in Mac OS X, as well, but their functionality is duplicated to some extent by the Dock. Third-party software and workarounds allow you to accomplish their tasks using Mac OS X's capabilities. Other third-party software can supplement the Dock, restore the Launcher, and bring back the Control Strip familiar to Mac OS 9 users.

➤ Some of Mac OS 9's functions remain in Mac OS X, but in new places or under new names. Table 22.1 lists some of these features and tells you where to find them.

Part 6

Becoming a Mac OS X Power User

Many people can use their Macs quite happily for years just the way they came out of the box. If you want more from your Mac, this part is for you—stick around and you'll be using your Mac to the max.

Diving right in, Chapter 23 introduces AppleScript, an easy-to-learn scripting language that enables you to automate tasks by writing simple programs. (Trust me, it's even easier than it sounds.) Chapter 24 introduces three more Mac features you might not have run into before: ColorSync color management, for ensuring that your printed images look the same as they do on your monitor; Text-to-Speech, for making your Mac read you bedtime stories and more; and Speech Recognition, for controlling your Mac with spoken commands. And, if you've always been intrigued by the power and mystery of Unix, Chapter 25 will bring you face-to-face with the Unix at the core of Mac OS X—and you'll find out it's less mysterious (and more useful) than you might have believed.

Chapter 23

Automating Your Work with AppleScript

In This Chapter

➤ What AppleScript is and what it's good for

➤ Writing and recording new AppleScripts

➤ Different ways to activate scripts

➤ Software that makes scripting easier

Most of us spend an amazing amount of time doing things that our Macs can do all by themselves—if we take the time to tell them what to do. That's what scripting is all about. You can give your Mac instructions by creating AppleScripts: custom programs written in a language that's pretty close to plain English.

Why Should You Care About AppleScript?

Unlike many programming languages, AppleScripts use simple, clear English-like words and phrases, and they don't have to be *compiled* before you can use them. They're easy to create, and they enable you to get more done in less time.

Using scripts is faster than working manually, for several reasons. Most importantly, when running a script, the Mac can use its top speed in issuing and reacting to commands, instead of having to wait for you to get around to giving it the next command in the series at your slow human speed. You must think the sequence of commands through as you write a script, but after that all you need to do is start it up and let it run.

Programming Prep

Programmers write their programs in programming languages that look like human languages (to one degree or another). But for computers to understand the instructions they're getting, those programs must be translated—or **compiled**—into a mathematical "machine language." Scripts, on the other hand, run in their native, text-based form.

Of course, if you're using a script to perform a series of actions, you can do something else while it's running. And finally, scripts can do some things you can't, and they're smart—they can include conditions so that one action happens under some circumstances and another happens under other circumstances.

No matter what you do with your Mac, AppleScript can give you a hand. Here are a few examples:

➤ When you're about to delve into your finances, you can use a script to start up TurboTax, Quicken, and Calculator with a single click.

➤ Desktop publishing pros can use AppleScript to place a text box over each graphic in a page layout document that contains the filename of that image.

➤ If you connect to the Internet with a dial-up account, a script can dial in, check all your e-mail addresses, and close the connection.

These ideas just begin to scratch the surface of what you can accomplish with scripts. Expert scripters have created games and other complex applications, even a system to automate programming grids for a publisher of newspaper TV listings. If you can think of it, your Mac can probably do it with a script.

Cooking Up Scripts

AppleScript was introduced at the same time as the Mac's System 7. Since that time, Mac users have written millions of AppleScripts, and some of them are kind enough to share the fruits of their labors with the rest of us. You can download shareware and freeware scripts from sites all over the Web.

Other People's Scripts

MacScripter.Net archives hundreds, maybe thousands, of cool AppleScripts at its ScriptBuilders subsite (`macscripter.net/script-builder.html`), and Apple offers a few useful AppleScripts on its Web site (`www.apple.com/applescript/scripts/scripts.00.html`). The MacScripters.Net main site (`www.macscripters.net`) also offers links to script archives, tutorials, and other AppleScripting resources.

If you're ready to try creating your own scripts, read on to learn about writing and recording AppleScripts and what to do with them when they're finished.

Writing Scripts in Script Editor

The easiest way to get started scripting is to jump right in, and you'll find the "pool" into which to jump in the Applications folder. Double-click **Script Editor** to start it up. The untitled window that opens is where you'll type your first script (see Figure 23.1). Click in the window's lower text field and enter the following:

```
tell the application "Finder" to make new folder in home
➥with properties {name:"My Scripts"}
```

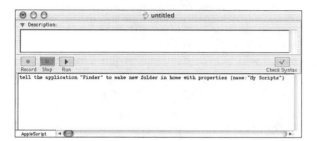

Figure 23.1

The lower text field in a Script Editor window contains the script, and you can put optional information about the script in the upper field.

After you've typed in this short script, click the **Check Syntax** button to be sure everything's typed correctly. If you make a typo, Script Editor lets you know about it in a dialog box; fix the typo and click **Check Syntax** again. If the script checks out okay, Script Editor formats the text to make it easier to read by indenting some lines, making commands bold, and so on. Now the script is ready to run—so click **Run**.

As you'd expect, the script creates a new folder in your *Home folder* that's called My Scripts. If you like, you can store the scripts you write in this folder while you're working on them. If you want to save your script, skip to "Saving Scripts," later in this chapter—but come on back, because there's more good stuff here.

Show Info

Going Home Again

Your **Home folder** is where all your personal files are stored. To see its contents, including the new folder created by the example script, click the Desktop and press Cmd+H. For more information about what's in your home folder, see Chapter 5, "Managing Your Files."

Each line of an AppleScript is a statement. You can write simple statements or compound ones. The previous example is a simple statement; a compound statement that performs the same function is

```
tell app "Finder"
make new folder in home with properties {name:"My Scripts"}
end tell
```

265

Taking Shortcuts

Notice that the second version of the script eliminates "the" and "to." You can use "the" anywhere in a script to make your statements read more naturally, but it doesn't have a function. "To" isn't needed because the command that we're giving the Desktop application is on a separate line.

Each statement includes commands that target objects; in this case, the command is "make" and the object is "new folder." To find out which objects and which commands you can use to work with a given application, including the Finder, you can open that application's dictionary from the Script Editor. Choose **File**, **Open Dictionary** and choose the application from the list or click **Browse** to locate an application that isn't listed.

The dictionary opens in a window with two sections (see Figure 23.2). On the left are listed the objects (italic text) and commands (plain text) that you can use with this application. If you click on one, details about it show up in the area on the right.

Definitions for commands show what kind of object they can be applied to and what the result of the command will be. For example, when I run the sample script shown earlier, the result is a reference, which in this case is the pathname of the object that was created:

```
folder "My Scripts" of folder "kbinder" of folder "Users"
➥of startup disk of application "Finder"
```

Figure 23.2

The Desktop's dictionary shows Finder commands and objects that you can work with in scripting.

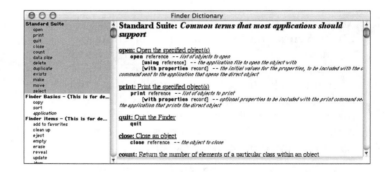

Definitions for objects list their elements (the things they can contain, such as words and pages in the case of text documents) and their properties (their characteristics, such as the name of a folder).

All this gives you just a taste of how scripting works. If you want to learn more about AppleScripting, two Web sites are all you need to get started:

➤ **Apple's AppleScript Web site**—www.apple.com/applescript/

➤ **MacScripter**—www.macscripter.net

From there, you can move on to reading books, working through tutorials, and even subscribing to e-mail discussion lists where you can learn from your fellow AppleScripters.

Recording Scripts

You can record AppleScripts by performing the actions you want included in a script in the right sequence. As you work, Script Editor translates your actions into the script commands needed to reproduce them. Recording scripts is both faster and more accurate than typing them in yourself.

There are a few drawbacks to recording scripts. For one thing, you can record only actions, not decision-making processes. If your script needs to make decisions (such as "If this is true, then do this; otherwise, do that"), recording can only get you started—you'll need to add the decision-making statements in Script Editor. Also, Script Editor doesn't necessarily record actions in the most efficient way, so you might need to prune and consolidate the statements that result from recording your actions. Finally, not all applications are recordable—sad, but true.

That said, recording scripts is a great way to get started with scripting—it helps you get a sense of how statements relate to the actions that result from them. To record a script, just open Script Editor, click in the lower text area, click **Record**, and go about your business. When you're finished performing the actions you want to record, go back to Script Editor and click **Stop**. Congratulations—it's a baby script!

Saving Scripts

You can save a script with different options, depending on how you want to use it. To save an AppleScript, choose **File**, **Save As**. In the Save dialog box (see Figure 23.3), first enter a name for the script, and then choose a format from the pop-up menu:

➤ **Text**—Use this format if you don't plan to run the script from any program other than Script Editor; usually, you use this choice when a script is incomplete or when you're going to send it to another person to look over.

➤ **Compiled Script**—This format allows the script to be used by another application, such as your e-mail program. When you double-click the script in the Finder, though, it will open in Script Editor instead of running.

Read Me

Getting Results

Any time you use AppleScript commands to create, move, copy, or otherwise handle an item, you'll get a result showing you what that item is and where it is after you're done. To see the result as you work in Script Editor, choose **Controls**, **Show Result** or press Cmd+L.

Read Me

Keeping Your Scripting Secrets

If you don't want other users (or yourself!) to be able to open the AppleScript in Script Editor and modify it, choose **File**, **Save As Run-Only**. Always be sure you have a backup copy of the run-only script in another format.

Figure 23.3

Depending on how you want to use it, you can save an AppleScript in one of four different formats.

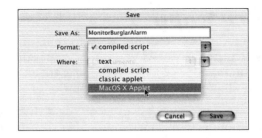

➤ **Classic Applet**—To make the script into a program that you can run in the Classic environment by double-clicking its icon, choose this option. Do this when you want the script to run in Mac OS 9.

➤ **Mac OS X Applet**—If you want the script to run natively in Mac OS X when you double-click its icon, choose this option. With this option, the script will run only on OS X Macs.

If you choose either of the applet options, two check boxes appear: Stay Open, which keeps the script running after it has executed its commands, and Never Show Startup Screen, which, if left unchecked, adds a startup dialog box to the script that enables you to cancel it before it runs. Most of the time, you'll leave Stay Open unchecked and Never Show Startup Screen checked, which are the default settings.

Putting Your Scripts to Work

Almost as important as what a script does is how you invoke it. You can start up a script in several ways; the best method to use usually depends on what the script will do. For a script that you want to run each day before you start working, saving it as an applet and making it a login item is appropriate. If you will be using a script several times a day on different groups of files, maybe making it a droplet is a better bet. Read on for more info.

Using Scripts Within Applications

All Mac applications are *scriptable*, but some are more scriptable than others. And some have direct support for using AppleScripts, while others don't.

To use an AppleScript from within an application, you should save it as a compiled script. What you do with it then depends on how the application will use it. Some programs can run scripts automatically, such as an e-mail client that runs an AppleScript on each e-mail message that meets certain criteria. In this case, you'll have to put the script into a specific folder where the application can find it and set up the application to use it (see the documentation for the program in question).

If you want to start the script running yourself each time you use it, you can use Script Runner to do the job. This is a handy utility that you'll find in the AppleScript folder within your Applications folder (click the Desktop and press Cmd+A). You can launch any script from Script Runner, as long as you've put the script into Script Runner's Scripts folder.

To open the Scripts folder, double-click **Script Runner**. The program presents you with a small floating palette containing just one button. You can click the button to see a pop-up menu of AppleScripts. The first time you try this, you won't see anything but the Open Scripts Folder command, because you haven't put any scripts in the Scripts folder. So, choose the command to open the folder and drag your scripts into the folder. Click the close button at the upper-left corner of the palette to quit Script Runner, and then double-click its icon in the Finder to start it up again. Now, if you click the button, you'll see the scripts listed; choose one to run it, or press the Command key and choose one to open it in Script Editor so you can edit it.

Getting Off the Ground

Apple includes some sample AppleScripts with Script Runner to get you started. They're in the Example Scripts folder that you'll find in the same folder as Script Runner. Open the Example Scripts folder, select all the contents, and drag them into the Scripts folder. You'll find that each folder within the Scripts folder has turned into a hierarchical menu in Script Runner; choose a folder name, and then slide the mouse over to choose one of the scripts the folder contains.

Dragging with Droplets

Droplets are scripts that you operate using drag-and-drop. When you drag files or folders on top of a droplet icon, the script starts up, does its work, and quits—all nice and neat. Because they work by opening the files or folders you drop on top of them, droplets must start with on open. For example, a droplet that sends items to the Trash looks like this:

```
on open theFiles
tell application "Finder"
move theFiles to trash
end tell
end open
```

In this script, theFiles is a variable that represents whichever files you drag onto the droplet. The Finder is told to move those files to the Trash and then stop. By using a variable, you don't have to rewrite the script to insert individual filenames each time you want to use it—that would make the script less efficient than just trashing the files yourself.

To make this script into a droplet, you'd save it as an applet with Stay Open unchecked and Never Show Startup Screen checked. What would you need it for? It's not much good as it is, because dragging the objects to the Trash instead is just as easy. But you could add statements that would, say, check the date of the objects dragged onto the droplet and trash only the ones that were last modified before your preferred "freshness date," leaving the others where they are or moving them to a folder of your choice. That's just one idea—I'm sure you can come up with lots more.

Creating Login Items

If you want a script to run when you start up or log in to your Mac, you can save it as an application (see "Saving Scripts," earlier in this chapter) and make it a login item. To add a login item:

1. Choose **Apple menu**, **System Preferences** and click the **Login** button (if you don't see it, click **Show All**).

2. Click the **Login Items** tab to display the list of current login items.

3. Click **Add** and navigate to the file you want to add to the list, and then click **Open**.

A Hint from (Not) Heloise

The first AppleScript-related item I added to my login items was Script Runner. Its floating palette appears in front of any window I have open, allowing me to choose and run scripts from within any application.

From now on, the file you chose will open every time you log in to your Mac. For example, a script could check the contents of your Drop Box folder and notify you with a dialog box if anything new is in the folder. If you want to get more elaborate, the script could copy the new files to a different folder, invoke an application to convert them to a new format, and rename them to your specifications—all automatically. The possibilities are mind-boggling!

The Least You Need to Know

➤ AppleScripts enable your Mac to perform simple or complex sequences of actions without your intervention. They're a way to automate processes, thereby saving time and helping to ensure accuracy.

➤ AppleScript is an English-like language that's easy to learn because commands use natural vocabulary and grammar. Although its building blocks of commands and objects are simple to learn, AppleScript is a very powerful scripting language because it can control everything your Mac does, even some functions you can't control directly yourself.

➤ You can implement your AppleScripts in several ways, including as standalone applications, from within other applications, and as folder actions. Which method you use depends on how you want the script to be triggered.

Chapter 24

Using Mac Technology to the Max

In This Chapter

➤ What color management is and why you should care

➤ How to set up Apple's ColorSync color management system

➤ How to create a custom ColorSync device profile for your monitor

➤ Getting your Mac to read text to you

➤ Teaching your Mac to respond to spoken commands

Apple has always been there first with the coolest, most appealing technologies. This chapter introduces you to three useful and innovative functions that are built right into your Mac: color management, text-to-speech, and speech recognition. Using these features, you can keep your color images looking the same from scanner to monitor to printer; you also can tell your computer what to do by talking to it and have it read you a bedtime story. Don't believe me? Keep reading....

Color Management: Not Labor-Intensive

If you scan photos, you might notice that the image you see onscreen doesn't look quite the same as the image lying on your scanner bed. So, you fiddle with it a bit, and then you print it—only to discover that the printout doesn't look like the onscreen image *or* the original. How frustrating!

Colorful Language

When color is reproduced with light, you must combine all colors to get white—so this type of color reproduction is called **additive color**. **Subtractive color**, on the other hand, requires you to remove all colors to get white. Monitors use additive color, also referred to as RGB color (for red, green, and blue, the three additive primary colors), whereas printers use subtractive color, which is often called CMYK (for cyan, magenta, yellow, and black, the subtractive primaries). RGB has a larger **gamut**, or range of possible colors, than CMYK.

Why does this happen? Mainly, it's because your monitor uses *additive color* to create colors onscreen, but your printer uses *subtractive color* to create colors on paper—and never the twain shall meet. The range of colors that your monitor can display—its *gamut*—is different from the range of colors that can be created by mixing your printer's different ink or toner colors. Then, there's the fact that your monitor, scanner, and color printer haven't been calibrated to work together, which means that they each can have a different idea of the correct color mix needed to reproduce a specific color in your documents.

Color Whatsis?

The answer to all this color confusion is color management. It's a way of translating colors into a universal color language, so all your hardware devices can agree on what colors they're talking about, and then modifying the way those colors are printed or displayed based on the special characteristics of each device.

Apple's color management system is called *ColorSync*. It uses device profiles to characterize the way each device in your color system reproduces color. For example, ColorSync can use a scanner profile and a monitor profile to refine an image's color based on its knowledge of how the scanner "sees" the image and how the monitor displays it. The idea is that what you see is what you'll get, all the way through the image-editing process.

For color management to really work, though, you must have the right profiles. Some profiles are included with Mac OS X, and your color devices might have come with color profiles; check the installation CD-ROMs that came with your monitor, scanner, and printer.

If you're really in pursuit of perfect color, you might want to consider creating your own color profiles. For monitors, you can create profiles using the Display pane in the System Preferences; instructions appear later in this chapter. To create profiles for scanners and digital cameras, you'll need to spend a little money on a third-party product. Two color profiling applications that you can use are Color Encore ICC Input ($169, Southwest Software, www.swsoft.com) and WiziWYG Deluxe ($599, Praxisoft, www.praxisoft.com). Although these products are not yet available in Mac OS X versions, you can use them in Classic.

Profiles in Color

If you don't already have the profiles you need, you might be able to download them from manufacturers' Web sites. If you still can't find the profiles you're looking for, here are a few more places to try:

➤ Profile Central (**www.profilecentral.com**)

➤ PANTONE ColorReady profiles (**www.pantone.com/support/ colorready_profiles.asp**)

➤ Epson inkjet printer profiles (**www.inkjetmall.com/store/ profilechooser1.html**)

Making Color Management Work for You

After you have obtained or created profiles for your scanner, monitor, and color printer, you're ready to set up your ColorSync preferences. Here's how:

1. Open System Preferences by clicking its icon in the Dock or by choosing **Apple menu**, **System Preferences**.

2. Click the **ColorSync** button, and then click the **Profiles** tab (see Figure 24.1).

3. Choose a scanner or monitor profile from the Input Profile pop-up menu. Use a scanner profile if you intend to work with scanned images, and a monitor profile if you create digital images from scratch.

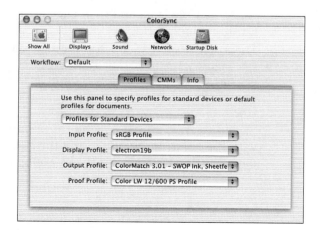

Figure 24.1

ColorSync uses profiles to determine how each device that's part of your Mac system handles color.

273

4. Choose a monitor profile from the Display Profile pop-up menu. You can create your own custom monitor profile; for instructions, see "Mixing Your Own," later in this chapter.

5. Choose a printer profile from the Output Profile pop-up menu.

6. Choose a *proofing* printer profile from the Proof Profile pop-up menu. If you have only one printer, don't worry about setting a proofing printer.

7. Click the **Info** tab and enter a name for the profile set you've created. You might want to use different groups of profiles for different situations (perhaps you use different color printers at home and at work, for example), so giving this "workflow" set a distinctive name will enable you to distinguish it from other groups of profiles you might use.

The Proof Is in the Profile

If you have more than one color printer—say, an inkjet and a dye-sublimation printer—you'll probably want to use the less expensive printer for initial prints, because its paper and colorants are probably cheaper, too. In the design world, this is called **proofing**.

When you're choosing profiles, be sure you come as close as you can to the exact profile for your device. Using an Epson inkjet profile won't do you much good if your printer is a Hewlett-Packard model, for example.

Mixing Your Own

The easiest way to get started with color management is to create your own custom monitor profile. You can do this using the Display Calibrator utility. Follow these steps:

1. Open System Preferences by clicking its icon in the Dock or by choosing **Apple menu, System Preferences**.

2. Click the **Displays** button to show the Displays preferences.

3. Click the **Color** tab, and then click the **Calibrate** button.

4. The Apple Display Calibrator Assistant starts up (see Figure 24.2). Click the right-arrow button to get started, and then follow the instructions on each screen.

5. When you've completed the steps, give the new profile a name. I usually name a new profile with the name of the device and the current date (electron19blue 3/26/01, for example).

Profile Prerequisite

For the profile creation process to work, you'll need to locate your monitor's brightness and contrast controls and know how to use them. If you're not sure where they are or how they work, check the monitor's manual before starting to create your profile.

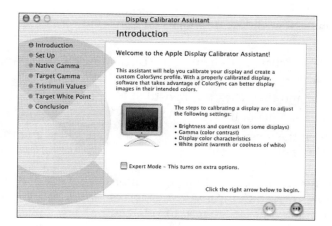

Figure 24.2

The Apple Display Calibrator Assistant helps you create a profile for your monitor, step by step.

You also can start up the Display Calibrator by opening the Applications folder (click the Desktop and choose **Go, Applications**), and then looking for Display Calibrator in the Utilities folder. After you've created your profile, you can select it as your Display Profile (see "Making Color Management Work for You," earlier in this chapter).

Speaking in Tongues

If Chatty Cathy was your favorite toy as a kid (or Speak and Spell, depending on your generation), boy, have I got a feature for you. Mac's Text-to-Speech function allows Mac OS X and some applications to speak to you—more specifically, to read text to you.

The first place you can use Text-to-Speech is in Mac OS X's alert boxes. For example, if you push the power button on your Mac, you'll see a dialog box asking you whether you want to shut down, restart, log out, or cancel the operation. And if you're like me, sometimes you've already turned away from your computer and you don't see the dialog box immediately. Well, with Text-to-Speech, if you don't respond right away your Mac starts reading the dialog box's message to you—a great way to get your attention and remind you that something still needs doing!

Try, Try Again

If you don't see the profile you just created in the Display Profile pop-up menu, log out and log back in (choose **Apple menu, Log Out**). The new profile should show up when you're logged in again.

Hearing Voices

Which voice you prefer your Mac to use is up to you. I think that Bruce, Fred, and Kathy are the most intelligible, and I like to turn the Rate up a notch or two past normal—but then I'm a New Englander, and we do speak more quickly than most Americans.

To set up Text-to-Speech, you need to choose the voice you want your Mac to use. Here's what to do:

1. Open System Preferences by clicking its icon in the Dock or by choosing **Apple menu**, **System Preferences**.

2. Click the **Speech** button, and then click the **Text-to-Speech** tab.

3. Click on a voice to hear a sample of it.

4. Adjust the speed at which the voice talks by dragging the Rate slider, and then click **Play** to hear another sample speech.

In addition to dialog boxes, Text-to-Speech works in applications designed to use it, such as iCab, a new Web browser (iCab Company, `www.icab.de`). When you're viewing a Web page in iCab that you want your Mac to read to you, choose **View**, **Speak All**. Other applications that have speech functions might put the command in a different menu, but it's always that simple.

I Like iMic

iMacs and PowerBooks have built-in microphones, but you might get better results with an external third-party microphone. A USB microphone such as the iMic (Griffin Technology, `www.griffintechnology.com`) will run you about $35.

Working from a Script

Some useful AppleScripts are included with Mac OS X, and many more can be downloaded from the Web. If you learn AppleScript—and it's pretty easy to get started—you can write them yourself. For more info, turn to Chapter 23, "Automating Your Work with AppleScript."

Talking Back to Your Mac

I bet you talk to your computer all the time, right? I know I do. But is your Mac listening to you? With Speech Recognition turned on, it can respond to your spoken commands and even tell you the current time, today's date, or a knock-knock joke. And this feature is built right into Mac OS X. All you need to add is, perhaps, a microphone, and many Macs ship with microphones.

Speak to Me

After you have your microphone in place, you can start up speech recognition by opening the System Preferences (click its icon in the Dock or choose **Apple menu**, **System Preferences**). Click the **Speech** button, and then click the **Speech Recognition** tab (see Figure 24.3).

Now, before you start making any settings, let's take a minute to go over exactly what you can make your Mac do using speech recognition. Most of the commands that Speech can understand are called Speakable Items. They're really AppleScripts—little programs that you can write to control the functions of your Mac. Even simpler, though, is to create speakable items by dragging files, folders, or aliases into the Speakable Items folder.

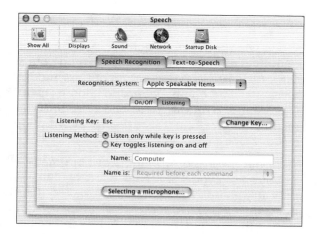

Figure 24.3
You can choose when and how your Mac listens for your speech.

Here's how to turn on Speech Recognition:

1. Open System Preferences by clicking its icon in the Dock or by choosing **Apple menu**, **System Preferences**.

2. Click the **Speech** button, and then click the **Speech Recognition** tab.

3. In the On/Off subtab, click **On** to start up Speech Recognition. The first time you turn on Speech Recognition, you'll see an explanation of how it works.

4. In the Listening subtab, choose a method of telling your Mac to listen to your commands.

> ➤ **Listen only while key is pressed—**
> This option requires you to hold down a key on your keyboard to make your Mac listen to your commands. Click **Change Key** to change the key that you need to hold down; by default, it's the Escape key in the upper-left corner of your keyboard.

> ➤ **Key toggles listening on and off—**
> This option allows your Mac to listen for your commands all the time; you can press the key to turn listening off when you'll be talking on the phone and don't want to accidentally give your Mac a command. Choose from the pop-up menu to determine how often you have to say the Mac's name, and enter a new name in the Name field if you like.

Keep Your Hands on the Keyboard

I like to use the "Key Toggles" option to trigger listening. Because I use a lot of keyboard shortcuts for efficiency's sake, I don't want to lift my hands from the keyboard unless I really have to. So, my Mac is listening for my commands most of the time. If you move your hands around more as you work, using a key to trigger listening might work well for you.

Checkmate!

The speakable commands available to you vary depending on the program you're working in. To see a good example of application-specific speakable commands, open the Applications folder (click the Desktop and choose **Go**, **Applications**) and start up the Chess game. When it's running, a new "Chess" entry appears in the Speech Commands window; click the triangle next to it to see the available commands.

Now, what can you tell your Mac to do?

When you turned on Speech Recognition, a small round microphone window appeared on your screen. Click the triangle at the bottom of the window to reveal a small pop-up menu, and choose **Open Speech Commands Window**. This window records the commands you give, and it lists the available options (see Figure 24.4).

Try it out by saying, "Computer, what time is it?" As you speak, you'll see the window's volume level indicator go up and down; try to speak so that the indicator stays green, rather than going up to the red area. If the computer doesn't understand your command the first time, repeat it three or four times. When it's recognized, the text of the command appears above the microphone window, you hear a sound (by default, the "Whit" sound), and the command is executed.

Figure 24.4

The Speech Commands window keeps track of what you've told your Mac to do.

Cutting New Orders for Your Mac

Now that your Mac is listening for your orders, tell it, "Open the Speakable Items folder." This folder contains the AppleScripts and other items that you can use as speakable commands. To add an item to the list, just drag it into the folder; after you've done this, speaking the item's name opens it. If it's an AppleScript, the script is executed; if it's a folder, the folder is opened; and if it's an alias of a program, the program is started up.

What's in a Name?

You can change the text of a command by changing the name of an item in the Speakable Items folder. For example, you might change the "Log me out" item to simply "Log out." Then, you have to say only "Log out" to execute the command. To change an item's name, click the name, wait a second, and type a new name.

The Least You Need to Know

➤ Color management provides a way to ensure that color images look the same on your screen and when you print them. Apple's ColorSync color management system uses device profiles to translate color from one hardware device's terms to another's.

➤ You can create your own custom profile to reflect the way your monitor reproduces color, using Mac OS X's Display Calibrator utility.

➤ Text-to-Speech allows your Mac to speak to you by reading text in document windows and in dialog boxes. You can choose the voice and the rate of speech that are used.

➤ With Speech Recognition, you can control your Mac with spoken commands. A set of useful commands is included with Mac OS X, and you can create your own commands.

Chapter 25

Harnessing the Power of Unix

In This Chapter

➤ What Unix is and where it came from

➤ What makes Unix useful

➤ How you can get a peek at the Unix within Mac OS X

➤ How Unix programs work

➤ What you can do with Unix software and where to get it

As a Mac OS X user, you have two choices: Ignore the Unix underneath, or take advantage of it. Either way, you get the stability and power of Unix. If you elect to venture further into the Unix deeps, you'll have the opportunity to learn new ways of computing. This chapter will give you a taste of Unix—just enough to whet your appetite.

What's Unix, Anyway?

Unix is a mature and very robust operating system that grew out of experiments at Bell Labs in the 1960s. It first was used in 1970 on a minicomputer made by Digital Equipment Corporation (DEC). Today it's used by major ISPs, telephone companies, banks, scientific institutions, utilities, manufacturers, and so on. Your ISP probably is running Unix. America Online, for example, is hosted on a network of several hundred Unix machines made by DEC (now Compaq). The basic Unix architecture, with *protected memory* and *preemptive multitasking*, hasn't changed for 30 years, and as a result the system is remarkably crash-free.

Peter Picked a Peck of Protected Preemptive Processing

Protected memory means that the system software sets up a special area in its memory for each program you start up. Although the OS can resize that area to give you more memory if you need it, no other program is affected by what goes on there. So, if that program crashes, it doesn't affect the rest of what's in memory at the time—any other programs and, best of all, the system software itself. ***Preemptive multitasking***, on the other hand, allows the system to allocate processing power for each task as it comes up, alternating jobs so quickly that to you, it seems as though everything's happening at once.

Although some Unix applications use a GUI (almost always the X Window System), these are not part of the system itself. Applications (called *commands* and *utilities*) that are part of the system are primarily designed to handle text files, and they're mostly very compact and highly specialized. For example, one common text-editing program called *sed* is about 65KB in size. Almost all of these programs are operated from a command-line interface.

Repeat After Me: QWERTY

A ***command-line interface*** (CLI) is text-based rather than graphical. You don't get icons, and you can't use your mouse; you just type in commands at a text prompt.

Using a Command-Line Interface

The first thing to know about a command-line interface is that you shouldn't be intimidated by it—it's just another way to get things done. In many cases, typing commands in a text-based interface can be faster than using the icons and menus of a GUI, just as using keyboard shortcuts often is faster than pulling down menus. And if you've ever used DOS, you've already used some commands that look and work a lot like Unix commands.

You're Going to Need a Clue

Unix is very friendly. In fact, it's so friendly that it'll quite happily let you shoot yourself in the foot. For example, you can type the command `rm *` (or "remove everything") at the command prompt, and the Unix system won't ask whether you really want to remove the 1,485 files in the folder you're currently working in; it'll just do it. This means that you must be careful to not make typos—at best your instructions won't be carried out, and at worst they'll be carried out in an unanticipated and possibly disastrous way.

Peeking Under the Hood

If you're ready to take a look at what's underneath that gorgeous Desktop you're looking at, fire up the Terminal application and let's go exploring. There might be an icon for Terminal in your Dock; if not, click the Desktop and choose **Go**, **Applications**. Then, open the Utilities folder and double-click **Terminal** to start it up.

You'll see a window containing something similar to the following text:

```
[localhost:~] kbinder%
```

[localhost] is the name of the computer you're using, and ~ signifies that the *working directory* (Unix-speak for folder) is the home directory for the current user. Of course, the text that follows is the login name of the current user—in this case, kbinder.

Now type ls in the window, and press Return. Hey! It's a list of the files in the folder you're currently working in, which by default is your home folder. If you enter ls public, you'll see a list of the files in the Public folder within your home folder (see Figure 25.1). Most Unix commands are pretty cryptic at first, but after you get to know them you can enter them quickly and turn series of commands into scripts.

Where Am I?

The **working directory** is the folder in which you're currently working. When you're working in a terminal window, the name of the working directory is part of the command prompt.

Figure 25.1

The Terminal window provides a peek into the text-based Unix system that underlies Mac OS X.

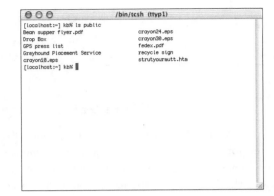

Doing More, Going Further

When Mac OS X was released as a public beta, a Unix geek named Simon Slavin wrote a primer on using the Unix command line. It's a great little text document that explains how to perform a few simple tasks using the Terminal application. You can find it at **www.hearsay.demon.co.uk**. A good place to start learning more about Unix is the Resources for Newbies page at FreeBSD.org (**www.freebsd.org/projects/newbies.html**). Free BSD is the flavor of Unix that forms the basis of Mac OS X. And if you're the structured type, you can learn more about Unix by reading a book such as *Sams Teach Yourself UNIX in 24 Hours.*

Turning Commands into Scripts

If you take the time to learn *shell scripting*, you'll discover the true power of Unix. The first thing to know is that Unix is built along the lines of a Tinkertoy set, in the sense that many of the commands you can give a Unix system aren't built in. They invoke tiny programs such as sed, mentioned previously. As an example, here's a very short script that you could type at the command line. It takes a list of names that are entered first-last and prints them last-first, sorted by last name.

She Sells Shell Scripts

Shell scripting is similar to writing macros. You're learning shell scripting just by using a command-line interface because you're talking to a shell, also known as a command interpreter, at the command prompt. A shell script is simply a series of the same kind of commands you normally type in one at a time, saved as a text file and invoked all at once. Shell scripting is one of the things that makes Unix so powerful.

```
awk '{ print $2, $1 }' myfile | sort -f > myfile.new
```

This script strings together requests for two different programs, sending the results of one program's actions to another program. That's called a pipeline, and the character that makes it happen is called a pipe. (It's the vertical bar that you get by pressing Shift+\.) Here's what the script is really saying:

> Program "awk," take the file called "myfile," swap the first and second words on each line, and send the result down the pipeline to Program "sort." Program "sort," take the text you receive from program "awk" and sort it alphabetically, without regard to capitalization, and then put the results in a new file called "myfile.new."

Admittedly, using this kind of language doesn't come naturally to most people, but when you get the hang of it you can do a lot with very little effort.

Turning a Script into a Reusable Command

To use the script once, you type it at the command prompt. If you decide that you want to use it again, you can make a few small changes, save it as a text file, and reuse it. Here's how:

1. In the Terminal window, type `pico nameswap`. This starts up a text editor called, you guessed it, pico, with an empty text file called `nameswap`.

2. In the pico window, type the following:

```
#! /bin/sh
awk '{ print $2, $1 }' $1 | sort -f > $1.new
```

The first line tells the system that the rest of the file is a command that should be executed. The second line is just like the original pipeline command, except that in place of `myfile` you've entered `$1` (see Figure 25.2). This enables you to specify the filename to process when you use the command, rather than having to edit the script again each time you want to process a different file.

Figure 25.2

pico is a Unix text editor that might cause you to flash back to your pre-Mac experiences with DOS or Apple II computers.

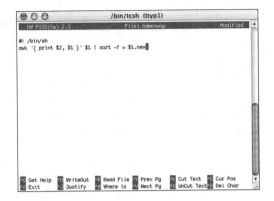

3. Press Ctrl+X, which is pico's Quit command.

4. When pico asks whether you want to save your changes, press Y. Then, press Return to quit pico.

5. Back at the shell prompt, enter the following command to make the script executable:

```
chmod +x nameswap
```

Processing Prerequisites

To use this script to process a file that's not in your working directory, you must include its entire pathname (meaning the list of folders within folders that contains the file), and you must have permission to access the directory in which the file is located.

This command makes the script executable and allows any user to access it.

6. To execute the command, type `nameswap` *filename*. In place of *filename*, enter the actual name of a file you want to process that's located in your working directory. The system runs the script on the file and dumps the results into a new file called *filename.new*.

At this point, `nameswap` is functionally equivalent to the other commands you can use on the command line. And *that's* why geeks love Unix—because you can build your own commands this easily.

Creating a real script often would be more complex than the example given here; for example, error checking should be included. As you can see from this example, you're not going to learn shell scripting in a day.

But it's also apparent that if you do learn how to create scripts such as this one, you'll be able to accomplish a lot with minimal effort.

Using Unix Applications

There's a whole world of Mac software out there, so why would you need Unix software? Well, most of the time Unix programs aren't producing graphical output, and they're very streamlined, with none of the bells and whistles of the Mac programs we're used to. That means they're fast, and they're reliable. Plus, you can find a Unix program to do just about anything you can imagine. And the world of Unix geeks is a friendly one in which people share their expertise and the results of their experimentation. So, you won't be on your own.

What Can Unix Do for Me?

Maybe you need to use Unix applications, and maybe you don't—it depends on what you want to do with your Mac. If you're interested in messing around with networks, then Unix was made for you. If you need to do complex things to a whole lot of text files, such as HTML or SGML, you'll love the range of tools Unix provides. And Web designers can use Unix tools to do such things as write *CGI programs* and run the fastest, most reliable Web servers around.

Although you can find Unix software to do almost anything you want to do with a computer, from playing games to faxing, Unix excels in several areas, including

➤ **Web serving**—The most widely used Web server program on the Internet is Apache, a Unix program. (By the way, Apache is included with Mac OS X—click on the Desktop, choose **Help**, **Mac Help**, and search for Apache for more info.) Because of its stability and speed, Unix is popular as a platform for Web serving in general; several commercial vendors, including Netscape, also offer Unix servers with varying levels of features.

Show Info

CGI Me to the Moon

Common Gateway Interface programs (**CGI programs**) are programs running in conjunction with Web servers to create dynamic content, usually Web pages, in response to a Web user's input. For example, a search engine such as AltaVista or Google (**www.altavista.com** and **www.google.com**) uses a CGI program to build a brand-new page of search results each time you perform a search. The program that builds that page is a CGI program. Another good example is Web counters—the programs that track how many times Web pages have been accessed and insert that number at the bottom of the page. Most of these use CGI scripts.

➤ **Text processing**—If you need to massage large amounts of text—rearrange it, search and replace stuff, change formatting codes conditionally, whatever—Unix is where you want to be. Although some of the available utilities exist on other platforms, they all originated on Unix—we're talking about things such as awk, sed, grep, join, and sort (you can get an idea of how these things work by reading the sed FAQ at www.cornerstonemag.com/sed/sedfaq.html).

Express Yourself

If you've ever used wildcards to search and replace text in Microsoft Word, you've glimpsed a tiny bit of the power of regular expressions. Some Mac applications, including Word and the text editor BBEdit (Bare Bones Software, **www.barebones.com**), can use them. Virtually all Unix text utilities use them. "A Tao of Regular Expressions" (**sitescooper.org/tao_regexps.html**) is a good introduction.

➤ **Networking**—Although there are Mac programs for telnet, FTP, and news, these all originated in Unix text-based versions, and they're all still there. Unix also offers all kinds of utilities for creating and troubleshooting networks.

Text In, Text Out

Most Unix command-line programs work on and produce plain text files rather than word processing files, spreadsheets, or other formatted files. Although some Unix programs can produce "styled" text, they do so by using input that has user-visible formatting commands in it, such as **.nr po 1i** to produce a one-inch left margin in a program called *nroff*.

How to Use Unix Apps

There are two kinds of Unix applications. You've already seen a couple of examples of the first kind: command-line applications. These include awk, sort, and ls, all of which appear earlier in this chapter. You start using a command-line program by typing its name, sometimes followed by other text that indicates things such as what file the program should work on and what optional settings it should use.

The second kind of Unix app is not text-based. These have real-live *GUIs* and almost invariably require you to use a graphical environment called an *X Window server*. X Window allows you to use applications installed on your computer as well as those running on Unix computers with which your computer is networked. Xtools (Tenon Systems, www.tenon.com) is an X Window server that runs on Mac OS X.

Unlike Mac or Windows applications, X applications (referred to as X clients) don't follow the interface and display conventions of the underlying operating system, because Unix doesn't *have* any display conventions. The advantage of this is that X clients look and act the same no matter what computer you use them on.

Although X Window applications have GUIs, they aren't necessarily as easy to start up and work with as Mac OS applications, because they don't have more than 15 years of hard-and-fast interface guidelines determining how they work the way Mac programs do.

Where to Find Unix Software

Unix software is all over the place, and most of it's free.

Many Unix commands and utilities are distributed in source form, which means that you get the C language program just as the programmer wrote it and you actually have to build the executable copy

Don't Tell Me, Show Me

A graphical user interface, or **GUI**, is what we Mac users are used to. It's a graphical representation of what's going on inside a computer's brain, instead of a textual one.

More About X Window

Oregon State University's Web site contains a great practical Unix tutorial called "Coping with Unix, a Survival Guide" that includes a section on how to use the X Window system. You can find it at **nacphy.physics.orst.edu/ coping-with-unix/book.html**.

that is going to run on your system. It's not for the neophyte or for the faint of heart, but it's not all that difficult, either. The source usually comes with a "makefile" that drives the Unix make command. The make command knows how to invoke the right tools and utilities to process the source files into executable program files.

An advantage of source-form distribution is that users like you (if they care to learn the ins and outs of programming) can modify the programs. Most programs distributed this way are distributed under the *GNU* license, originated by the Free Software Foundation, and people who make improvements give those improvements back to the community, which results in better software for everybody. Just like the helpful Mac community!

Some Gnu Information

GNU is what's known as a recursive acronym, meaning that it refers to itself. It stands for "GNU's Not Unix," and it's pronounced "guh-NEW." There's more information about GNU, and how its originators want free software to work, at **www.fsf.org**, as well as a bunch of—you guessed it—free software.

Here are a few Web sites with links to Unix software to get you started:

➤ X.org (the group that maintains the X Window standard): www.x.org

➤ Garbo Unix archives: garbo.uwasa.fi/unix/

➤ Online Unix Software Repository: amp.nrl.navy.mil/code5595/online-software/

➤ Unix System Administrator's Resources: www.stokely.com/unix.sysadm.resources/

➤ The Internet Goodies List: www.ensta.fr/internet/unix/

The Least You Need to Know

➤ Unix is a network-oriented operating system that's been around for a long time and, therefore, has had a lot of its bugs worked out. It's fast, it's stable, and it's what's at the core of Mac OS X.

➤ By nature, Unix uses a command-line interface, in which you type textual commands and receive textual output and feedback. Graphical interfaces are available for Unix, but they don't have the consistency of the Mac interface.

➤ If you use the same Unix commands often, you can create shell scripts that string various commands together in a reusable form. This is similar to, but more powerful than, recording macros.

➤ Unix software often is free and usually rather utilitarian, although there are games for Unix. To use it, however, you need a little know-how; you might even have to turn a Unix program from source code into an executable form yourself.

Part 7
Keeping Mac Happy

Wonderful as Mac users tend to think their computers are, we do need to remember that they're only, well, computers. That means we must take good care of them with regular maintenance and emergency help when it's needed.

In Chapter 26, you'll learn how to maintain your Mac so it's always running at peak performance. Chapter 27 shows you why it's important to back up your files and explains how backups work and ways you can set up a backup system. Closing out this part, Chapter 28 offers a few troubleshooting techniques in case you run into problems with your Mac's hardware or software.

Good MacHousekeeping

In This Chapter

➤ Updating your system and other software to stay current

➤ Preventing virus infections

➤ Maintaining your Classic system

➤ Defragmenting your hard drive

➤ Uninstalling software

➤ Using disk scanning software to diagnose and repair problems on your drives

Even when your Mac is using a brand-new, shiny-bright operating system—Mac OS X—things sometimes go wrong. Problems can be caused by software bugs, software conflicts, electrical fluctuations that cause the computer to shut down or restart unexpectedly, and even just normal use. This chapter covers ways to maintain your system so you can catch and repair any problems before they start causing trouble.

Go To

Help!

If you're already in trouble, skip to Chapter 28 for troubleshooting procedures that will help you figure out what's wrong with your Mac and how to fix it.

Periodic Mac Maintenance

Housekeeping isn't usually much fun, but it's important—if you keep up with the cleaning and maintenance chores in your home, you'll be more comfortable, you'll be able to find things when you need them, and you'll deal with problems such as leaky pipes and rattling windows before they become disasters.

Taking good care of your Mac is a good idea, too, for the same reasons. If you keep up with the maintenance tasks explained in this section, your Mac will reward you by running smoothly at top speed. You'll also avoid the frustration of time-wasting system crashes and software conflicts. So, put down the feather duster and the oil can, and pick up that mouse!

For Optimal Performance

The installer for the initial release of Mac OS X skipped a step in setting up the system—just a tiny step, but completing it can speed up your Mac. You can take care of this in several ways: Install the Developer Tools CD that came with Mac OS X; update your system to the latest version of Mac OS X using the Software Update System Preferences pane (see "Update Your System," later in this chapter); or download Xoptimize (`softrak.stepwise.com`; search for Xoptimize), a program that will perform this housekeeping task for you.

The details: The installer skipped a step called "prebinding," in which the system catalogs various software components so it can load them quickly when they're needed. More recent updates, as well as the Developer Tools installer, perform this step.

Update Your System

Apple software engineers are constantly improving Mac OS X, as well as Apple's other software products. While you're working away on your Mac, those kind souls in Cupertino, California are adding new features, fixing problems, and making compatibility changes in Mac OS X. Periodically, you can reap the benefits of their labors by downloading new versions of the system software.

To be sure your software is always up to date, you can use Software Update (choose **Apple menu**, **System Preferences** and click **Software Update**). This utility checks for software updates over the Internet, either whenever you tell it to or at scheduled intervals. When it finds a newer version of a system component or a bundled utility program (such as Mail or QuickTime Player), it lets you know, and if you choose, it downloads and installs the new software. It's a good idea to check for updated software at least every few weeks, either automatically by choosing **Update Software Automatically** or manually by clicking **Update Now**.

An oddity of System Update is that it sometimes must install one update before it can "see" others. So, after you run it, it's a good idea to go back and run it again until it finds no more needed updates.

Update Other Software

Along with beingsure your system software is up to date, you should keep an eye on updates to the other software you're using. If you're having trouble with a program, an update can eliminate the bug or conflict that's causing your problems. It might also bring new features (sometimes ones you like, sometimes not). Mostly, though, updating your software will help ensure that it continues to work right with the other applications you're using and with your system software. This is a concern because changed features in updated system software occasionally "break" other programs; as a result, you'll often see a flurry of program updates released shortly after a new system update comes out.

These days, because most computer users have at least some access to the Internet, the most common way to update software is to download an updater posted on the company's Web site. If you have a CD-R or CD-RW drive, you can use it to make a collection of updaters so that you don't need to track them down again if you should have to reinstall the software from scratch. Installing an update usually requires you to simply double-click the installer, which is a special program that puts everything in the right place and makes any system configuration settings that the new software requires.

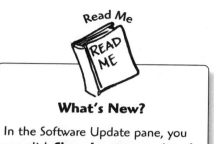

What's New?

In the Software Update pane, you can click **Show Log** to see a list of what you've updated recently.

Keeping Track of Everything

A great place to find the latest version of just about any Mac software is VersionTracker (`www.versiontracker.com`). You can search by title, developer, or keyword, and the site tracks both Mac OS X and Classic software—everything from new versions of the most obscure shareware programs all the way up to the latest upgrades for Adobe Photoshop and the most recent virus information files for virus checkers (see "Check for Viruses," later in this chapter).

Before installing an update to a program, be sure you can go back to the older version if you need to. This can mean simply locating the original CD-ROM, if you're using a version that hasn't been updated since you originally installed it, or it might require you to back up all the program's files by copying them onto another disk—or even just make a note of where you can download an older installer if you need it. Don't forget to include preference and other "customized" files in that backup—you'll find them in the Library folder within your home folder, either in a special folder all their own (such as the Fire folder put there by the instant messaging application Fire) or inside the Preferences folder.

Update with Care

Sometimes it's not a good idea to install the latest and greatest software, either system software or other programs. If your Mac is "mission-critical," meaning that you can't make a living if it's out of order or if certain programs are disabled, you'll probably want to be a bit more cautious about installing updates, just in case the updated software causes problems with your system. I often wait to install major updates until I see what problems other users report.

You can keep track of potential problems with major software updates (especially system software updates) at two highly respected Mac Web sites: MacinTouch (`www.macintouch.com`) and MacFixit (`www.macfixit.com`). These sites track software conflicts, bugs, and other problems and report readers' solutions for them.

The Macro View

One category of virus that Mac users have had to worry about in the last few years has been macro viruses, which are written in Microsoft's Visual Basic programming language and used to control Microsoft applications, especially the e-mail programs Outlook and Outlook Express. Some of these critters can affect Mac users who don't use Outlook for e-mail, but they can't be spread unless you're an Outlook user, and many of them have no effect at all unless they're received in Outlook.

Check for Viruses

Viruses—now there's a fun topic! Mac users have been lucky over the years to avoid the incredible number of viruses that affect Windows PCs. This is due mostly to the undeniable fact that there are many more computers running Windows out there, which means both that there are more programmers who know how to create Windows viruses and that creating and spreading a Windows virus is more entertaining for malign programmers because it affects more users than a Mac virus would. Of course, there have been some Mac viruses over the years, and there will undoubtedly be more to come. Some viruses are relatively benign, while others can make your life miserable by doing things such as erasing vital files.

Now, you might be asking yourself (or me) the following: What about Unix viruses? The answer is threefold. First, there are far fewer Unix viruses—perhaps a dozen at this writing. Second, they are far more difficult to write than are viruses for Windows or Mac OS. Finally, built-in Unix security is quite capable of preventing virus activity or, in some cases, strictly limiting the damage. For the moment, Unix viruses aren't a concern for Mac OS X users.

You can protect your Mac from contracting a virus by diligent use of an antivirus program such as Sophos Anti-Virus (Sophos, www.sophos.com) or Virex (McAfee, www.mcafee.com). These programs check files that you download or copy onto your system and also scan removable disks that you use with your Mac. They can also run scans on demand. When they find a virus, they can usually remove it; at the very least, they can warn you about infected files so that you can get rid of them.

There are two keys to using antivirus software. First, *use* it. This means refraining from turning the virus scanner off or canceling scans when you need to get some work done in a hurry and don't want to wait while disks or files are scanned. Second, be sure you download and install the periodic virus information files that developers release. Without these files, virus scanners can't recognize and deal with new viruses.

Go To

More Things to Keep Track Of

In addition to application and system updates, VersionTracker (**www.versiontracker.com**) keeps track of the latest virus information files. Check the site around the first of each month for the most recent updates.

Take Good Care of Classic

Because Classic is like a whole other system within your Mac OS X system, it requires some special care. The Classic pane of the System Preferences enables you to take care of Classic maintenance with the following functions found in the Advanced tab (see Figure 26.1):

➤ **Rebuild Desktop**—This is a maintenance function that helps ensure that files have the correct icons and that the right program starts up when you double-click a file. You should click this button to rebuild the Desktop every week or two if you use Classic every day.

➤ **Restart with Extensions Off**—You can prevent problems with Mac OS 9 extensions that are causing trouble with your Classic software by turning off extensions. Choose this option from the pop-up menu at the top of the tab to restart Classic with extensions turned off.

➤ **Open the Extensions Manager upon Restarting**—If you need to have some extensions active (such as QuickTime if you want to view QuickTime movies), you can deactivate just the ones that are causing trouble with the Mac OS 9 Extensions Manager. Choose this option from the pop-up menu to restart Classic and open the Extensions Manager.

Figure 26.1

Classic is a whole Mac system-within-a-system, so it needs occasional maintenance.

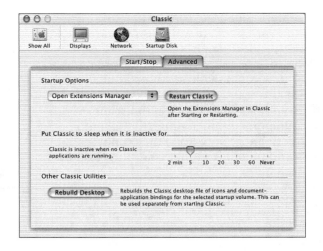

Defragment Your Hard Drive

As you use your Mac, you save files to the hard drive, copy them, download more files, delete them, and so on. All this file shuffling leads to files scattered all over your hard drive; sometimes single files even end up in pieces—fragmented—on different sections of the drive. Disk fragmentation can slow down your Mac—logically enough, because it has to go looking all over the place for each file you open. You can use software utilities to defragment your drive, or you can use the good old-fashioned method of copying all your files onto another drive, reformatting your hard drive, and copying all your files back onto it.

Speed Demon

Another way to speed up your Mac is to decrease the video resolution (the number of colors your monitor displays). Unless you're doing image editing, chances are that you won't be able to tell the difference between the "Thousands of colors" and "Millions of colors" settings in the Monitors pane of the System Preferences.

If you opt to use a defragmenting utility, two options are PlusOptimizer (Alsoft, www.alsoft.com) and Norton Utilities (Symantec, www.symantec.com/mac/). They include optimizer modules that not only defragment your files but also arrange frequently used files on your hard drive for the most efficient access.

As I write this, neither utility runs under Mac OS X, either natively or in Classic, but both come with CD-ROMs that will boot your Mac. To use the software, you pop in the CD, choose it in the Startup Disk pane of the System Preferences, and reboot. By the time you read this, of course, these products may well be available in native Mac OS X versions.

When It's Time to Go

It's a rare program that lasts forever on your Mac. Eventually, most applications are replaced by competing products or are no longer useful to you, for whatever reason. When you're finished using a program, permanently, you might want to uninstall it to reclaim the disk space it's taking up (or just because you are, like me, a tidy soul).

When you're sure you won't need a program any more, even to open the files you created with it in the past, you can get rid of it in one of two ways. If it appears to be a single file (a "package"), you can just drag it to the Trash. If the application uses multiple files stored throughout your system, though, you'll be better off if you use an uninstaller.

Sometimes, the installer you used to install the program in the first place has an uninstall module. You can try popping in the CD-ROM, starting up the installer, and looking for a pop-up menu with an Uninstall option. If you don't find one, you might be a good candidate for a handy program called Spring Cleaning (Aladdin Systems, www.aladdinsys.com). Created by the makers of the perennial file compression fave StuffIt, Spring Cleaning performs a number of clean-up functions—it primarily uninstalls software, but it can also do useful jobs such as cleaning out your Web browser's cache folder.

A Few Useful Tools

In addition to the useful programs mentioned throughout this chapter, it's a good idea to keep at least one general disk repair and maintenance utility around. Fortunately, one comes with Mac OS X: Disk Utility (in the Utilities folder within the Applications folder). It's a boring name for a vital program.

Read Me

Deleting Files Is a Privilege

You might find that you don't have the right access privileges to move or delete applications you no longer need. If this happens, log out and log back in using an Admin user name and password. Turn to Chapter 6, "Sharing Your Mac with Multiple Users," for more information about the Admin account.

OS Tension

Don't Be Too Quick to Trash Files

Be careful when you're uninstalling software—it's all too easy to delete files that are necessary to your system or to other applications. When I'm ready to delete files, I put them in a folder I've named Temporary Backup and leave them there for at least a few weeks before trashing them. That way, I can easily put them back where they belong if it turns out that I need them after all.

Disk Utility contains two modules: Drive Setup and First Aid. The former is used to format both removable disks and hard drives, and the latter is used to repair the disk and file structures on your drives (see Figure 26.2). It's very easy to use; just click the icon for the drive you want to scan and click either **Verify** (to scan without making any changes) or **Repair** (to scan and fix any problems found). You can verify your startup disk, but you can't repair it, so if you find problems with it, you'll need to reboot from the Mac OS X CD-ROM and run First Aid again to fix the problems.

Figure 26.2

First Aid can fix small problems on your disks before they become large ones.

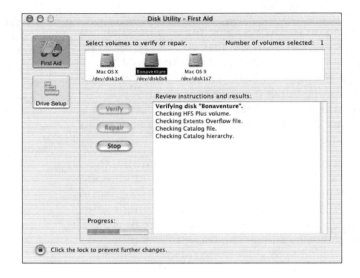

It's a good practice to run First Aid when your computer crashes and must be restarted, when a power failure causes a restart, and when you notice any strange behavior related to saving, copying, or moving files, such as an error message telling you that you can't save a file because it's already open (which, of course, is nonsense). It also never hurts to run First Aid every once in a while just to catch any creeping problems that you might not have noticed. Most of the time, it will tell you it found nothing—which is a good thing!

You might have noticed that I've said you should have "at least one" program of this kind. Several third-party utilities offer features that Disk Utility doesn't have; here are a few you might want to check out:

➤ **Drive10** (Micromat, www.drive10.com) comes from Micromat, the makers of the highly respected Mac utility TechTool. It was the first disk repair and utility recovery product released for Mac OS X. Although you can use Drive10 to repair drives and recover data, the program also provides automatic, regular backups of important volume structure data, which can make data and drive recovery easier and more reliable.

➤ **DiskWarrior** (Alsoft, www.alsoft.com) is a very safe method of repairing damaged drives and recovering files. Its DiskShield feature prevents damage by checking the validity of any data being read from or written to the directory to let you know of any anomalies. When you use Disk Warrior to repair a damaged disk directory, it actually builds a whole new directory instead of patching the original.

➤ **Norton Utilities** (Symantec, www.symantec.com/mac/) is the granddaddy of Mac disk repair utilities. It can be used for regular maintenance as well as repair, and it includes both a disk optimizer and an "unerase" feature.

What You'll Fix, and How Many Times

When you run any disk repair utility, it won't be looking for physical damage to the disk, but rather corruption in the disk's formatting or directory of files. These elusive errors can accumulate over time, as a disk is used, and can cause files to get lost or become corrupted so that you can't open them. Whenever you find errors using a disk repair program, allow them to be repaired, and then run the scan again until the program reports no errors found.

Any of these three products is a good idea to have around, and many hard-core Mac geeks (like yours truly) install and use more than one. Check the Read Me files first, though, to be sure that the programs' automatic scanning and protection components don't conflict with each other; you might need to skip installation of some components.

You'll find Apple System Profiler useful in a completely different way from these disk utilities. This little program, located in the Utilities folder within your Applications folder, scans your Mac and provides you with tons of information about how it's set up, including

➤ **System Profile**—In this tab, you'll see your system software version and basic information about your Mac's hardware and your network.

➤ **Devices and Volumes**—Here, Apple System Profiler lists all the devices, such as mice, keyboards, scanners, and hard drives, that are attached to your Mac, along with information about the interfaces those devices use.

➤ **Frameworks**—This list shows the version number of each framework installed in your system; these files enable applications to access system services ranging from file sharing to help.

➤ **Extensions**—The files whose version numbers appear in this tab are mostly hardware drivers that enable the system software to work with your Mac's hardware, including devices such as hard drives, network cards, modems, and digital cameras.

➤ **Applications**—All your installed programs are listed in this tab.

Use Apple System Profiler when you need to know which model of SCSI card your Mac has, what drivers your USB devices are using, and how much video RAM you have. It can answer all these questions and more. You'll find this program particularly useful when you need to contact technical support about a problem with your hardware or software. To create a report that you can e-mail to someone who's helping you, choose **File**, **New Report**. When the report window is complete, choose **File**, **Save** to put the report information into a file that you can attach to an e-mail.

The Least You Need to Know

➤ Computers need regular maintenance, just like houses and cars. You can do several things to take care of your Mac, including making sure that you're using the latest versions of your system and other software, scanning for viruses, maintaining Classic like any other Mac OS 9 system, and defragmenting your hard drive.

➤ Uninstalling unneeded software in Mac OS X is usually simpler than in Mac OS 9, because many programs are distributed in "packages"—bundles of files that look like single files in the Finder. To uninstall such a program, you can just drag it to the Trash.

➤ For more complex software, an uninstaller program can help round up all the little bits and pieces that the program used and get rid of them. Some application installers work as uninstallers, and a third-party product called Spring Cleaning can uninstall any application.

➤ Apple's Disk Utility program contains a First Aid module that can scan your disks for problems and repair them before they cause you to lose any data. Third-party programs can perform a similar function, as well as other useful tasks, and several include additional utilities that monitor the health of your disks as you use them and warn you immediately when a problem crops up.

➤ Apple System Profiler gives you all the information you might need to know about makes and models of cards and devices that your Mac uses. This can be especially helpful when troubleshooting problems or conflicts.

Chapter 27

Preparing for the Worst

In This Chapter

➤ The importance of backing up your Mac's files

➤ Deciding what kind of backup you need

➤ Backing up over a LAN

➤ Backing up to the Internet

There are two kinds of people, they say: those who've experienced a hard drive crash—and those who *will* experience a hard drive crash. If you're in the first group, you already know how important it is to back up your important files. If you're still a member of the second group, congratulations! You're a lucky Mac user—and you *probably* have time to back up your files before it's too late.

Of course, I'm not saying that your hard drive is really about to crash—a complete failure of your drive actually is fairly rare. But it's still a good idea to be prepared, and there are lots of other good reasons for keeping a backup. For example, I got serious about backing up after pulling an all-nighter to re-create a project that was due the next day—I'd accidentally deleted it that afternoon.

The Tao of Backup

If you're not sure that backing up your Mac is important, surf on over to the Tao of Backup (www.taobackup.com) and read the story you'll find there, along with the associated information. If that still doesn't convince you, you're on your own!

Backup Strategies

For many Mac users, backing up can be as easy as dragging their most important files onto a removable disk once a week or so. The kinds of files you'd want to copy might include

➤ Work projects in progress

➤ Data files for your financial software (such as Quicken)

➤ Your e-mail address book and Web browser bookmark file

If you do have trouble with your Mac, restoring your files is as simple as copying them back onto your hard drive from the removable disk. One disadvantage of this system is that removable disks are limited in size—2GB Jaz disks are the largest available at the moment, and that's probably only a fraction of the size of your Mac's hard drive. Another downside is that if you end up having to rebuild your entire hard drive with a new system, you'll need to reinstall all your applications, which will take you quite a while, and there are sure to be files such as preference files, custom templates, and archived e-mail that you won't have backed up.

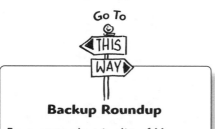

Backup Roundup

For a comprehensive list of Mac backup products, ranging from free to shareware to sophisticated commercial apps, see the Macintosh Products Guide (`guide.apple.com`).

That's why backup software came into existence. Programs such as Retrospect (Dantz Development, `www.dantz.com`) automate backups, copying all your files to removable disks, tapes, or another hard drive at specified intervals. Incremental backups mean that after the first backup, the software copies only new or changed files, saving time and storage space. There are also less expensive options, some of which are available for Mac OS X.

Here are some points to consider when you're designing your own backup system:

➤ **What kind of backup medium will you use?** You can use anything from floppy disks to an extra hard drive, in addition to tapes or one of the many higher-capacity removable media such as Zips or Jaz disks.

➤ **Will you use one or multiple backup sets?** Alternating your backups to multiple disks (or whatever media you use) gives you near-duplicates as well as allowing you to retrieve files that were deleted or corrupted before your latest backup but after the one before that.

➤ **How often will you back up?** If you use your computer only a couple of times a week, maybe weekly backups will work for you. If you're Mac-ing away all day, every day, you'll want to back up *at least* every day.

➤ **Where will you store your backups?** It's a good idea to keep a complete backup someplace other than your house or office. You can trade backups periodically with a friend or neighbor if you go this route, or store offsite backups in a safe place you visit regularly.

Have You Backed Up Today?

TidBITS, a weekly e-mail newsletter about the Mac, has published a great series of articles that provide an extensive discussion of backup strategies and methods. You'll find it at `http://db.tidbits.com/getbits.acgi?tbser=1041`.

Backing Up on a LAN

Whether you use backup software or go the "copy important files" route, you can create a backup system for a *LAN*. One of the simplest ways to back up files with two Macs is to keep a folder on each Mac to which you copy important files from the other Mac. You also can use a portable drive to move from one Mac to the other and copy files onto a removable disk. Or, if you like automation as much as I do and have as little time to waste, you can invest a little money in backup software and have everything taken care of for you while you're away from your computer.

Retrospect, the most widely used Mac backup software, is also the best solution for backing up Macs over a LAN. Although a few other programs can perform similar functions, this section covers how Retrospect works in order to keep things simple. Similar programs work pretty much the same way.

Typically, network backup requires both client and server software, meaning that (in the case of Retrospect) while Retrospect runs on one networked computer, the other computers have Retrospect Client software. The client software identifies the computer to Retrospect and lets Retrospect know when it needs to be backed up. The drives on computers running Retrospect Clients look just like local drives to Retrospect, and you can back them up the same way.

You have two choices for creating automated backups with Retrospect. You can set up a regularly scheduled backup, usually set to happen overnight, or you can set up a backup server, which runs during specified intervals and backs up any of a group of computers that show up on the network during that time.

A LAN in Your Neighborhood

A *LAN* is a local area network, meaning a group of computers in the same building or nearby buildings that are linked together on a network. Of course, that brings up the question: What if your network isn't local? The answer: Then it's a WAN, a wide-area network. That's a network that links computers that are more than a kilometer or so apart, perhaps even in different cities.

This is a great way to back up laptops; when you connect to the network with a PowerBook, iBook, or PC laptop, Retrospect senses the laptop's presence and backs it up right away.

You can get Retrospect Clients for both Mac and Windows computers, so Retrospect can back up mixed networks as well as all-Mac ones.

Real-World Backup

All this "strategy" stuff might seem kind of abstract until you start doing it yourself. To give you an idea of how backing up works in one small office with several Macs, here's how I do it:

➤ **Media**—I use DAT tapes that hold 12GB of uncompressed data. Because my system uses both software and hardware compression, the tapes end up holding 18GB–20GB of data. I erase a tape and start filling it up from scratch after about three months of use, and I buy new tapes every several months to be on the safe side.

➤ **Software**—I have Retrospect (Dantz Development, www.dantz.com), which backs up changed and new files from my network's four Macs to the tape drive on my G4.

➤ **Frequency**—Every night, Retrospect backs up to one of three tapes. Each Monday, one tape is taken offsite to a friend's office, and he gives me one of his backup tapes to store. I alternate the two tapes I have left, using tape 1 one night and tape 2 the next. That way I always have three backups: one day old, two days old, and less than a week old.

If my entire hard drive crashes (this has happened only once), I can restore everything, from the system software to yesterday's e-mail. I just boot from the system CD and reformat my drive, pop in last night's tape, and take a nap for a couple hours while Retrospect puts my files back where they belong. If my drive is physically dead, I restore my most vital files to an external hard drive and keep working while I wait for a new internal drive to arrive via mail order. Without a backup, I'd have to reinstall all my software from the original CDs, and I'd lose all my data files. And if I've simply accidentally deleted or mistakenly modified a file, my backup strategy ensures that I can retrieve yesterday's version of the file within a few minutes.

Backing Up to the Net

Internet backup services have sprung up all over the place in the last couple of years. The idea is to copy your important files to free or rented space over the Internet. Depending on the amount of data you want to back up and the speed of your Internet connection, this might or might not be a viable option for you. For some users, Internet backup can serve as part of a larger backup system. There are a few advantages to backing up to the Net:

➤ You can back up and retrieve files from any location where you can round up a Net connection.

➤ The files are offsite and therefore protected from office disasters such as fire or burglary.

➤ You don't need to buy additional hardware, such as a tape drive.

Retrospect, in all its versions, can back up to the Internet—you just choose "Internet" as a destination and enter the location, user name, and password for your storage space. You must locate storage space separately, but Dantz maintains a list of recommended providers on its Web site (www.dantz.com/sp/ftpproviders.html). An alternative is a service such as BackJack (www.backjack.com), which charges a monthly fee and offers free software to automate the backup process. Both options use encryption to ensure that your data stays private as it travels across the Internet.

iBackup

If you just want to back up a few files, you can copy them to your iDisk. It's not big enough or fast enough to accommodate your entire system, however.

For most people, bandwidth limitations and Internet storage costs will prevent Internet backup from being a standalone backup system. But it provides a good supplement for especially critical files, files that you'll need to access when you're away from your own computer, and files that you need to back up while you're traveling.

The Least You Need to Know

➤ If your Mac contains files you don't want to lose, you should be backing those files up. Period.

➤ You can back up important files simply by copying them to a removable disk. If you can afford backup software and some kind of removable media, though, you'll be better off in the long run with an automated backup that you can just forget about—until you need to restore your files.

➤ Backing up networked computers usually requires backup software. It's best done overnight or at another time when the computers aren't being used, and backups can include Windows computers as well as Macs.

➤ Internet backups are a good backup to your backup system—you can use these services to store copies of your most vital files or files to which you need access from places other than your office.

Chapter 28

Troubleshooting

In This Chapter

➤ Figuring out what's causing a Mac problem

➤ Techniques to fix problems

➤ Specific issues you might encounter

➤ Troubleshooting resources

For every computer user, the day eventually comes when something goes wrong—really wrong. And Mac users are no exception. With Mac OS X, your Mac should be more stable than ever before, but the physical design of computers in general ensures that problems will crop up occasionally. When they do, this chapter can help you figure out what's causing the problem and how to fix it.

Read Me

Caveat Lector

Reading this chapter won't teach you everything there is to know about fixing problems with your Mac, and it won't turn you into a real-life Mac mechanic. It's my hope that this chapter will show you how to analyze your Mac's problems, fix many of them, and be able to describe the rest to a real expert so they can be repaired.

Analyzing the Problem

The first thing to do when your Mac starts acting strangely is to take your hands off the mouse and the keyboard, sit back, and think about what's happening. You might need to experiment some with the Mac to figure that out, but go slowly and be careful. Here are some questions to ask yourself about the problem you're seeing:

Periphery

Peripherals are devices that connect to your Mac, such as scanners, printers, and so on.

➤ What do you know about the problem?

➤ Does it appear only when you're using certain programs?

➤ Does it affect only certain *peripherals*?

➤ Does it act like a hardware problem or a software issue? This can be hard to pin down, but take a guess. For example, if your hard drive is making strange noises, it's probably a hardware problem. If your files have bizarre icons, you're mostly likely looking at a software issue.

➤ Did it show up after you installed new software or hardware?

To figure out the cause of the problem, you must narrow down the possibilities. You can do that in several ways:

➤ First, make a note of any unusual dialog boxes or error messages, and log the problematical behavior so you can look this information up or explain it to tech support later on if necessary.

➤ Quit all applications but the one that's causing problems; choose **Apple menu**, **Force Quit** to quit programs that don't respond to a normal Quit command.

➤ Log out and log back in. This forces all applications and the Desktop to quit, which often can straighten things out.

Scuzzy Peripherals?

SCSI devices use the Small Computer System Interface, a connection system for peripherals such as scanners and external drives. You can connect one SCSI device to another in a "daisy chain" and connect the first device in the chain to your Mac.

➤ Reboot. All manner of strange behaviors can simply disappear when you reboot your computer.

➤ If you've recently installed new software, try uninstalling or deactivating it to see whether the problem disappears.

➤ Try the same thing with new or rearranged hardware. For example, if you have multiple SCSI peripherals, the order in which they're connected to each other and then to your Mac can affect their operation and even whether the Mac boots.

➤ Shut your Mac down and check all the hardware connections: mouse, monitor, external drives, scanner, and so on. Unplug everything and plug it back in again—but don't try this with the Mac running.

When you think you have an idea what kind of problem you're dealing with, you can figure out where to start fixing it. If possible, now is a good time to run Apple System Profiler so you have a snapshot of all the hardware and software in your system that you can use to answer questions from tech support if needed. (See Chapter 26 for instructions.)

What Goes There?

Problems with your Mac fall into four basic categories. First, your Mac could have a hardware failure or the system software could be corrupted in some way. In this case, you'll need to take the Mac to a repair shop (for a hardware failure) or reinstall Mac OS X (for corrupted system software). It's more common for new hardware or software to conflict with the rest of your Mac's system. In this case, the first line of defense is to remove the hardware device or uninstall the software and contact the manufacturer or the developer for an updated version that won't conflict with your system.

Sometimes, a hardware device or a program has an actual bug, in which case you have two choices: Work around the problem, if possible, by avoiding the specific feature in question, or contact the manufacturer or the developer for an updated version. Now also is a good time to recheck any Read Me files that came with the device or program to see whether you're running into a known issue that you didn't notice at installation.

And finally, though most of us usually hate to admit it, some problems can be attributed to good old user error, which means that you're not using the software or hardware correctly. In this case, read the instructions and try again; if you still can't get things to work right, call the manufacturer or the developer for technical support.

The following sections cover several common problems you might encounter with your Mac and offer suggestions for fixing them.

Your Mac Won't Boot

In this case, what actually happens when you press the Power button can include the following:

➤ **Nothing at all**—You hear no startup chime, you see no lights flash. In this case, check the power cable; if it's plugged in, your Mac needs professional repair help.

Surfing for Updates

When you run into a software bug or conflict, you often can find an updated version of the software on the developer's Web site. And with conflicts, remember that at least two programs are involved, so either developer (or both developers) might release updates that fix the problem. VersionTracker (**www.versiontracker**) is a good place to look for updates, too.

➤ **Chimes of Doom**—This poetic term refers to a sound I fervently hope you never hear: several successive chimes that actually are the individual notes in your Mac's usual startup chord, played separately—or, if you have a newer Mac, the equally chilling sound of breaking glass. These sounds indicate a severe hardware failure. Turn the Mac off immediately. If the Mac was very hot or cold when you heard the Chimes of Doom, wait until the computer returns to room temperature and try again. If you still hear the Chimes, take the Mac in for professional service.

➤ **Sad Mac**—If you see a strange, frowning Mac symbol on your Mac's screen, instead of the usual smiling Mac that indicates the beginning of the boot process, you've met the Sad Mac. The most common cause for the Sad Mac is damage to the formatting of your hard drive, which means you might be able to start up from a CD-ROM with a system installed on it. Try your Mac OS 9 or Mac OS X installation CDs. If you succeed in booting the Mac, use First Aid to try to repair the damage to the drive. If the drive can't be repaired (and even if it can, if you're as conservative as I am), back up any data it contains, reformat it, and reinstall your system software.

Read Me

Back to Backups

If you haven't gotten the idea by now, let me spell it out: Backups are a good thing. Although Mac OS X is a very stable operating system, and modern computers don't have nearly as many hardware failures as older ones, disasters still happen. When one happens to you, you want your important files to be backed up so you don't have to worry about them as you try to fix your Mac. Turn to Chapter 27, "Preparing for the Worst," for more coverage of how and when to back up your Mac.

➤ **Blinking question mark**—This symbol looks like a floppy disk with a question mark inside it, and it indicates that the Mac can't find valid system software. Its appearance might indicate that the hard drive formatting has been damaged, or it might indicate that the system software has been corrupted. Follow the same course of action as for the Sad Mac, previously.

➤ **Kernel panic**—If you've never seen a kernel panic, don't worry—you'll know it when you see it. The visible sign is a screen full of white text that includes the word "panic" along with a lot of other stuff that probably doesn't make much sense to you. In the background, you'll see an image of the screen as it looked right before the panic. Generally, restarting will get you out of this situation. If not, jot down the information on the screen and try booting from the Mac OS X installer CD. If you can get that far, you're probably best off reinstalling the system software.

➤ **Partial boot**—When your Mac begins the boot process normally, with the Happy Mac and then the Mac OS X logo and boot progress bar, and then freezes, there might be a problem with the system software. A possible solution is to boot into single-user mode, which loads the Unix components of Mac OS X but not its graphical interface. To get there, hold down S as the Mac boots. When you see the command line, type /usr/fsck -y. This runs the Unix fsck (file system check) utility, which can make repairs similar to Disk First Aid. When it's done, type logout to continue starting up. If you can't get to single-user mode, you'll need to reinstall Mac OS X from the CD; pop it in and hold down the C key while the Mac boots to start up from the CD.

➤ **Complete boot with freeze at end**—This can happen if one of your *login items* develops problems. The answer is to reboot from your Mac OS X CD and delete the offending program or document.

Stacking Login Items

If you use certain programs or documents every time you log in to your computer, make them login items by choosing **Apple menu**, **System Preferences** and clicking the **Login** button. Click the **Login Items** tab, and then drag the programs or documents into the window so that they'll open automatically when you log in.

It's a good idea to keep your Mac OS X system CD near your Mac, because it's often the first line of defense when the Mac won't boot. Third-party disk repair utilities, such as Drive10 (Micromat, www.drive10.com) and DiskWarrior (Alsoft, www.alsoft.com), also often come with bootable CDs that you can use to start up your Mac and make repairs.

313

Maximum Verbosity

Holding down the V key as your Mac boots into Mac OS X starts the Mac up in verbose mode. You'll see a black screen with white text that describes what's happening as the system boots, before switching to the normal Mac OS X startup screen. Sometimes, booting this way will allow you to start up your Mac when it won't boot normally.

Unexpected Quits or Freezes

With Mac OS X, it's much less likely than with earlier systems that your Mac will just freeze up. Although the current application might stop working, you should almost always be able to click on another application's window or use the Dock to switch to another program. If this doesn't work, you can choose **Apple menu**, **Force Quit** to quit the offending program and keep on using your Mac. If you can't get any response from the Mac at all, press the reset button to reboot. Then, when the Mac is back in action, use Disk Utility's First Aid module or a third-party disk repair utility, such as Drive10 or DiskWarrior, to repair any damage resulting from the freeze and restart.

Applications still might quit unexpectedly in Mac OS X, but this is a matter of much less concern than with earlier versions of the Mac OS. Because Mac OS X uses *protected memory*, you can continue using other programs or the Finder after an unexpected quit with no adverse consequences—you no longer need to restart your Mac when a program unexpectedly quits.

Memory of a Mac

Protected memory is an *operating system* feature that blocks off the area of your Mac's memory (RAM) used by each program so that, if the program crashes, the system and any other programs that are running are unaffected.

As for what's causing freezes or unexpected quits, sometimes it's a temporary glitch that doesn't show up again when you restart the program, and sometimes it's a more serious problem. If it happens more than once, try to figure out the sequence of events that triggered the freeze or quit. For example, does it always happen when you try to paste text from your Web browser, or does it occur only when you're running a backup and surfing the Web at the same time? Such circumstances might indicate a conflict between the two programs involved.

314

New software often is the culprit in problems like this. Have you installed anything new lately? Be sure to check the Software Update log to see whether something new has been installed while you weren't paying attention. (Choose **Apple menu**, **System Preferences** and click on **Software Update**, and then click the **Show Log** button.)

Erratic Behavior

When an application or the system software doesn't work the way you expect it to, there could be several reasons. It might be that the right thing is happening, even though it's not what you expected to happen. Or, under Mac OS X, it could be that certain functions don't work unless you enter an *Admin* password or are logged in as an Admin user.

Another reason for erratic behavior—including features that don't work, document elements that change or shift position unexpectedly, or strange redrawing behavior—can be missing components that the application or the system needs. Have you dragged any mystery files to the Trash lately, or did you have a hard drive crash or power failure that might have deleted files? In this case, you'll need to reinstall the program in question, or reinstall Mac OS X if the system software is acting up.

Strange behavior can also be due to a software bug or conflict, which you're most likely to encounter when you've recently installed or upgraded software. If you don't remember changing any of your software, choose **Apple menu**, **System Preferences** and click **Software Update**, and then click the **Show Log** button. This will tell you what, if any, software has been updated recently by Mac OS X's Software Update utility. After you've figured out what the culprit probably is, head to the developer's Web site or VersionTracker (www.versiontracker.com) to see whether a more recent version that might fix the bug or conflict is available.

Show Info

Adding Admins

An **Admin** user is a user who has greater access to files and settings under Mac OS X. The first account you created when you started up or installed Mac OS X is automatically an Admin user, and you can make other users Admin users in the Multiple Users pane of the System Preferences (choose **Apple menu**, **System Preferences**).

Missing or Jumbled Files

When files are missing or have strange names, it's often an indication that something's wrong with the catalog information Mac OS X uses to keep track of what's on your hard drive. Try running Disk Utility's First Aid module (Disk Utility is in the Utilities folder within the Applications folder) to fix the problem. Third-party utilities, particularly DiskWarrior (Alsoft, www.alsoft.com), can be even more effective in remedying this situation. If you can't fix them, you'll be best off restoring the files from a backup—you do have a current backup of all your important files, don't you?

Missing or Malfunctioning Peripherals

If your Mac can't "see" a peripheral, such as a printer, scanner, or external drive, first check the connection. Because some connections (primarily SCSI, and, of course, power) shouldn't be broken while your Mac is running, your best bet is to shut everything down, unplug all the connectors in question, and plug them back in firmly. For SCSI devices, check to be sure that all the devices connected to your computer are using different SCSI IDs—two devices with the same ID can really upset your Mac—then, if that doesn't help, try some SCSI voodoo. Then, be sure the peripheral is getting power (check its indicator lights and listen for its fan, if it has one) and be sure it's turned on before the Mac is.

Hoodoo Voodoo

If you have SCSI peripherals, *you'll* be the one doing SCSI voodoo at some point. SCSI is a quirky protocol that responds to changes in cables, cable lengths, device positioning, order of the devices in the daisy chain, and so on. When you run into SCSI problems, switch things around, hold your breath, cross your fingers, and see whether the problem has been solved. Many times, everything will be hunky-dory after this kind of voodoo.

If the Mac still doesn't recognize it when you try to use it, the driver probably has been deleted, become corrupt, or been disabled by a conflicting piece of software. Head to the manufacturer's Web site to see whether you can find a more recent version of the driver, and install that.

On the other hand, when the peripheral just doesn't work correctly, such as a printer that sits there forever without printing, the problem could lie either with the device itself or with the system. First, shut down, turn off the peripheral, and reboot. If that doesn't make the problem disappear, consider that the problem might be a driver conflict, and try to locate an updated driver. From this point, your best recourse is to try to locate a specific description of the same problem you're seeing in either the manufacturer's Web site support area or from user reports on the Web (see the next section for some places to start looking).

Other Helpful Resources

This chapter hits the high points of troubleshooting problems with your Mac, but there's a lot more info out there that will help you through a bad patch. The following are good places to start searching for information:

➤ **MacFixIt** (www.macfixit.com) is where you'll find any and all information about known software and hardware problems that affect Mac users. Bringing together the collective knowledge and experience of thousands of Mac users, as well as the considerable expertise of site owner Ted Landau and his colleagues, MacFixIt is the place to go to find out whether others have experienced the same problem you're having—and discover what they've done to fix it.

➤ **MacInTouch** (www.macintouch.com) features daily news updates and an impressive collection of special reports collated from reader e-mail on subjects ranging from what backup drives provide the best value to what versions of major Mac programs you need to install to ensure compatibility with system software upgrades.

➤ **Mac-Mgrs** (www.mac-mgrs.org) is a community of people who manage Macs, whether at work or at home. It's a knowledgeable group that interacts through an e-mail list and has little tolerance for time-wasting questions that can be easily answered by reading documentation—so be sure you *RTFM* before going to Mac-Mgrs with your questions.

Show Info

The *What* Manual?

If you're polite, **RTFM** stands for "Read the Fine Manual." It's a standard geek abbreviation used to suggest that you read the instructions before asking how to do something.

➤ **Apple Support** (www.apple.com/support/) offers, naturally, the most definitive information about maintaining and troubleshooting your Mac. No information is available about third-party software or hardware, but that aside, Apple's technical library is quite impressive. Head here when you want the official word.

➤ **Your local dealer** might surprise you, in this day of mail-order mania. Check your local business directory for a nearby Apple dealer; if you can establish a good relationship with these people, you'll have found a good source of expertise and assistance that has a human face—which can be a big plus when you're panicking over your broken Mac.

➤ **Geek friends** are, naturally, a computer user's best asset. Cultivate them, reward them for their help with pizza and chocolate, and have some respect for them—geeks are human, too, and most of us are geeks of one kind or another when it comes right down to it.

➤ **Mailing lists** (lists.apple.com) are for you if you like to have information come right to your Mac without being asked. The list of lists you'll find on Apple's Web site includes those sponsored by Apple as well as independent lists, and it spans a wide variety of topics, from one devoted to Apple's long-since defunct eMate device to those targeted toward people who use Macs in particular professions (such as MacAccounting, MacArtists, and MacAttorney).

The Least You Need to Know

➤ The first step to take when you're having trouble with your Mac is to analyze what's happening for clues that will help you determine whether the issue is hardware-related or software-related and what's causing it.

➤ The kinds of problems you might encounter over time include your Mac's refusal to start up, unexpected quits or freezes on the part of applications, erratic behavior by the system or applications, missing or jumbled files, and missing or malfunctioning peripherals.

➤ You'll find a lot of help for misbehaving Macs on the Web, through e-mail lists, and from friends and local Apple dealers who are familiar with the Mac's quirks and tendencies.

Useful Web Sites

If you want to know more about anything, chances are that the information you're looking for is out on the Web somewhere. More and more information is being added every day, too, in the form of both new content and archived old content that's gradually being converted for use on the Web. I've listed some of my favorite Mac- and computer-related Web sites, and each of those sites will undoubtedly lead you to even more sites. So, get surfing!

The Best Mac Sites

These Web sites cover the Mac in all its glory, from news about Apple's latest products to troubleshooting information and specifications for every Mac ever sold. Some you'll visit when you need specific info; others are all-around sites that you'll want to stop by every day or every week.

TidBITS: www.tidbits.com

TidBITS is a weekly newsletter distributed through e-mail and also accessible through this site. Published for more than a decade, it provides some of the most comprehensive and most useful Mac-related information anywhere in the world. Its sister mailing list, TidBITS Talk, offers intelligent, focused discussion about topics that have already appeared in TidBITS, topics that readers would like to see covered, and topics that the editors are researching before publishing articles about them. TidBITS is proof that some of the best things in life really are free.

MacInTouch: *www.macintouch.com*

Ric Ford knows the Mac—and he's ready and willing to share his knowledge with you. The MacInTouch Web site is updated daily with news about new Mac software and hardware, updated information about existing products, and coverage of the Mac world in general. E-mailed information from readers is collated into comprehensive reports about issues of interest to the Mac community, such as software compatibility with new system updates. MacInTouch is the first Web site I visit every morning. (All right, sometimes I check the weather first, but you know what I mean.)

MacFixit: *www.macfixit.com*

If you've got a Mac problem, MacFixit can probably help. This site tracks bugs, conflicts, and hardware problems as well as readers' solutions to them. When my mouse isn't tracking, when my fax software conflicts with the driver for my CD-R drive, when I want to know whether updating my system software or firmware will cause problems, I surf directly to MacFixit.

MacCentral: *maccentral.macworld.com*

This is a site for news junkies—Mac news junkies, that is. Whether it's a new Mac, an important announcement from a major software developer such as Adobe, or Apple's quarterly earnings report, you'll find the news here first—with lots of detail. MacCentral has merged with *MacWEEK*, for many years the best print source of Mac news, so you can access the *MacWEEK* archives here as well.

Macworld: *www.macworld.com*

If you want to subscribe to a print magazine about the Mac, *Macworld* is the one. Of course, who knows how much longer that will be true? Print is certainly not dead, but many niche magazines are going down hard as the Internet offers more content faster and more often. As *Macworld* the magazine gets thinner each month, Macworld.com the Web site is going strong, offering content from the magazine accompanied by content from several Web partners and stories that the magazine doesn't have room for. You can also search the archives to find Mac news from years gone by—such as an article heralding the release of Microsoft Word 6 (which turned out to be a problematical upgrade that seriously annoyed a lot of its users).

MacSpeedZone: *www.macspeedzone.com*

Here you'll find everything you ever wanted to know about how fast your Mac is and how you can make it faster. MacSpeedZone clocks the speed of each new Mac model, as well as every third-party processor upgrade, so you can see how your Mac stands up to others, both past and present. The site also advises users on ways to make their Macs faster, such as adding RAM and installing processor upgrades.

EveryMac: www.everymac.com

So, you're thinking of buying a used PowerBook, but the seller hasn't got a clue as to the speed of the machine's Ethernet port. The answer you're looking for—and much, much more—is to be found at EveryMac, where you'll find hardware specifications and secondhand price ranges for every Mac model, and every Mac clone ever sold.

Low End Mac: www.lowendmac.com

Although Low End Mac contains Apple and Mac news briefs, how-to articles, and opinion columns, its reason for being is to teach readers how to best use their older and less expensive Mac models. You'll find profiles of Mac models dating all the way back to the Mac's immediate predecessor, the Lisa. If you want to know whether a used Mac is worth buying, or if you already have an old Mac and wonder what you can get it to do, this is the place to find out.

MacNN: www.macnn.com

It's CNN for the Macintosh world—that's all you need to know.

MacAddict: www.macaddict.com

OK, so maybe *Macworld* isn't the only print magazine about the Mac. There's *MacAddict*, too—it has a little more attitude than *Macworld*, and it also has a useful Web site that contains some of the magazine's content and much more. Here you'll find hardware and software reviews, features, editorials, and fun articles (such as one that explains a way to make your Mac OS X Desktop icons big—*really* big).

Clan MacGaming: www.clanmacgaming.com/macosx.php

If you're into games, you'll find the info you want at Clan MacGaming. I have to admit that the faux Scottish name is part of why I love this site. The other reason I love it is its comprehensive coverage of the latest games and gaming hardware, including what works with Mac OS X. You'll also find a calendar of upcoming releases and interviews with top game designers.

dealmac: www.dealmac.com

Want a deal? Head on over to dealmac, where you'll find the best sales, rebates, exchanges, and just plain lowest prices on Macs, Mac software, and peripherals. The site is updated constantly; you can even receive a daily report of new deals via e-mail.

321

Macintosh Products Guide: guide.apple.com

If you really want to know what's up with Macs, what better place to find out than Apple's Web site? The Macintosh Products Guide lists thousands of products, both software and hardware, that work with or on your Mac. You can search the database by product name, developer, or category, and each listing links to the developer's Web site. Some listings even contain ad links that allow you to buy the products immediately.

Apple Support: www.apple.com/support/

You'll find a huge library of technical support information at Apple's Web site, including downloadable software updates, detailed TIL (Technical Information Library) notes, and tutorials. Turn to this site for formal support and definitive information rather than funky workarounds and user reports.

Mac Software Archives

Although you usually can find downloadable software at developer Web sites, who wants to go tracking all over the Web when you can find everything you need in one or two places? The Web sites listed here provide searchable archives of Mac software.

VersionTracker: www.versiontracker.com

Here you'll find the latest version of everything, from virus definition files to tiny patches and point upgrades, as well as the latest shareware programs and even some commercial demos. If you want to keep your system up to date, VersionTracker is the tool you need. It includes listings for both Classic Mac OS and Mac OS X.

MacDownload: www.macdownload.com

When you're looking for Mac software to do a particular job, and you don't even know if there *is* such a program, try a search at MacDownload. You'll find a wide selection of shareware and commercial software that's likely to contain what you're looking for.

The Mac Orchard: www.macorchard.com

If you're looking specifically for Mac Internet software, there's no better place. From Web browsers to FTP clients, from servers to e-mail and news clients, the Mac Orchard tracks the best shareware and freeware Internet programs, along with capsule reviews from both the site's maintainer and its readers. Some commercial software is included in the site's listings, but only if it's fully downloadable.

MacScripter.net: `www.macscripter.net`

Pretty much everything you ever wanted to know about using AppleScript can be found here, including a large archive of scripts, script snippets, and scripting additions that allow your scripts to access new functions. MacScripter.net also reports the latest scripting news and reviews AppleScript books.

Learning About Unix

Mac OS X is a pretty clever operating system. Although it's founded on Unix, you'll be able to use it for years without ever encountering any evidence of that fact. On the other hand, if you want to experiment with Unix, you can start up the Terminal program and jump right in. Here are a few Web sites to get you started with Unix.

Unix Primer: `www.hearsay.demon.co.uk`

As its author Simon Slavin says, "This is for anyone who understands the Macintosh side of Mac OS X and is wondering how to get started in learning about the Unix part of it. It's a Rich Text file designed to be read by the TextEdit application included with Mac OS X." Simon's primer will walk you through your first Unix baby steps.

Resources for Newbies: `www.freebsd.org/projects/newbies.html`

"The following resources are some of those which FreeBSD newbies have found most helpful when learning to use FreeBSD," according to this site's author. Of course, FreeBSD is the flavor of Unix on which Mac OS X is built. The topics covered here include learning FreeBSD, learning Unix in general, learning the X Window System, and ways you can contribute to the FreeBSD community.

GNU Project: `www.fsf.org`

The GNU Project's mission is the development of a free Unix version called the GNU system. The most common use of GNU is in conjunction with the Linux kernel created by Linus Torvalds; GNU supplies the elements that a kernel needs to form a complete Unix system. What you'll find here is Unix documentation and software.

Tao of Regular Expressions: `sitescooper.org/tao_regexps.html`

Regular expressions—what a beautiful concept! A regular expression is a formula for matching text that follows a pattern; it's an expanded version of the wildcard searches that word processors allow. Using regular expressions, which were originated on Unix systems, you can massage your text within an inch of its life—which comes in handy when working with HTML, databases, and lists of just about anything.

323

sed FAQ: *www.cornerstonemag.com/sed/sedfaq.html*

sed is a Unix utility that uses regular expressions. Yes, it's included with Mac OS X, so you can use it from a Terminal command line. If you're a Unix scripting geek, you're drooling right now. If you're *not* a Unix scripting geek, this FAQ (frequently asked questions) list will start you on your way to being one.

Coping with Unix: *nacphy.physics.orst.edu/coping-with-unix/book.html*

This is a great site that contains some of the content from the book *A Scientist's and Engineer's Guide to Workstations and Supercomputers* (John Wiley & Sons, 1993). It contains just enough information to walk an academic user through a project conducted on a Unix mainframe, which is a common setup on college campuses. But it's also a great way for Unix newbies in general to learn a bit about Unix from a user's perspective instead of from a technical perspective. Topics from the introductory section, for example, include "Logging In," "Logging Off," "Unix Commands, Generalities," "Specific Unix Commands," "Setting Up Files and Directories," and "Your Home Directory."

X.org: *www.x.org*

X.org is the group that maintains the X Window standard, a way of using Unix applications with graphical interfaces. You can use the X Window system to run applications such as Gimp, a completely free Unix cousin of Adobe Photoshop.

All-Around Useful Sites

I surf the Web pretty much all day, every working day. Now, I know you're not interested in where I check the weather forecast or where I buy supplies for my greyhounds. But I do want to mention a few Web sites that I find perennially useful.

Google: *www.google.com*

Google is my all-time favorite search engine. It's so smart about figuring out what I'm looking for that it's even a bit spooky. And the developers are always adding new features; with Google, you can view the text from PDF documents, translate found pages into your native language, and read cached versions of pages that have been moved or removed from the Web. In early 2001, Google added a huge database of Usenet postings to its assets, which means it can now search newsgroups as well as the Web. When I need to search the Web, my fingers start typing "google" almost before my Web browser opens up.

AltaVista: www.altavista.com

Every once in a while, Google doesn't work out for me. I like AltaVista for those times because it can perform Boolean searches, which means it can use terms like "and," "not," and "near" to narrow down your search results. This means that I can do searches like this: "greyhound NOT bus NEAR adopt" to find sites about greyhound adoption and avoid ending up with a list of Greyhound bus schedules.

Outpost.com: www.outpost.com

When it comes to mail order, Outpost.com is one of the best. Although the company no longer offers free overnight shipping (my idea of heaven), it still has a wide selection of Mac-related merchandise, great customer service, and excellent prices.

PDFZone: www.pdfzone.com

If you're interested in Adobe Acrobat, this Web site offers weekly news updates and a database of Acrobat add-ons and other software. Full disclosure: I'm one of the editors of this site. I won't get paid any more if you visit it, but you'll definitely find the Acrobat and PDF information you're looking for.

Tao of Backup: www.taobackup.com

If you think you don't need to back up your Mac, think again. The only time you don't need to back up a computer's data is if you don't have any files on it that can't be replaced and if you have unlimited time to rebuild your system in case of a disaster. Now that we've gotten past that little issue, if you want to study backup philosophy, this is the place to do it. You'll learn simple rules about how and why to back up that you'll thank me for when the day comes that your hard drive crashes, that you accidentally delete a bunch of files you still need, or that a power surge fries your Mac.

Coalition Against Unsolicited Commercial E-Mail: www.cauce.com

You say you like spam? You enjoy receiving tons of unsolicited e-mail promoting debt consolidation, multilevel marketing schemes, and gray-market prescription drugs? Then stay away from this Web site, where you'll find ways to fight the onslaught of spam, which most of us don't enjoy.

Speak Like a Geek

128K Macintosh   The very first Mac, which made its debut in 1984. Its 128 kilo-bytes of memory, or *RAM*, amounted to one five-hundredth of the minimum RAM in most new Macs sold today.

access privileges   Settings that determine who can read, write, or move a file or folder.

additive color   Color made up of light, as on a computer monitor or television; so called because you must add all three of its primary colors (red, green, and blue) together to form white. See also *subtractive color*.

Admin   An administrative user of Mac OS X. A user who can read, write, and move some files that do not belong to him or her and who can change locked system prefer-ence settings and install new software.

AirPort   An Apple combination of hardware (AirPort cards and the AirPort base sta-tion) and software that allows Macs to form a network and communicate with each other without wires.

Apple menu   The menu at the left end of the Mac's menu bar. In Mac OS 9 and ear-lier versions of the system, this menu was customizable. In Mac OS X, it is not cus-tomizable; it contains commands such as Shut Down that can be used no matter which application you're using.

AppleScript   A scripting language (simpler than a programming language) that's built into the Mac system and enables you to automate tasks.

AppleTalk   Apple's proprietary system for network communication, used primarily by Macs and Mac-compatible devices such as printers.

Aqua   The visual aspect of Mac OS X's new user interface, so named because of its slick, fluid appearance.

boot   To start up a computer. Short for "bootstrap," as in to pull oneself up by one's bootstraps, because computers can start themselves one step at a time from a dead stop.

burn-in   An image permanently formed on the surface of a computer monitor because the display has been left on with no changes for too long.

cable modem   A high-speed Internet connection that operates over your cable television line, but at a different frequency from the TV transmission; you can watch TV and remain connected to the Internet at the same time.

Carbon   The collection of system capabilities shared by Mac OS X and Classic Mac OS; applications that use only these capabilities can run under both operating systems. See also *Classic* and *Cocoa*.

CD-R   Compact Disc Recordable; a CD-R drive can record data on discs similar to CD-ROMs. Once written, a CD-R disc cannot be erased or reused.

CD-RW   Compact Disc ReWritable; a CD-RW drive can record data on disks similar to CD-ROMs. CD-RW discs can be erased and reused.

CGI   Common Gateway Interface, a system for communicating with a Web server. In response to user requests, CGI programs collect content from databases and display it as Web pages. Search engines use CGIs to build their results pages.

Classic   An operating system within a system that can run old Mac OS programs that won't run under Mac OS X. When Classic is active, you can run almost any Mac OS 9 program just as if you had booted your computer with Mac OS 9. See also *Carbon* and *Cocoa*.

Cocoa   A new programming system that works only with Mac OS X. Cocoa programs can take advantage of all of Mac OS X's new capabilities. See also *Carbon* and *Classic*.

color depth   The number of colors displayed on a computer monitor at one time.

color management   The science of translating and adjusting scanned, displayed, and printed colors to produce consistent color from original art to final printout.

command-line interface   A way of interacting with a computer by typing in commands and receiving textual feedback. See also *graphical user interface (GUI)*.

compiled   Converted from a programming language to a machine language. Programmers must compile their programs before the software will run on a computer. Many Unix programs are distributed in their uncompiled state because so many versions of Unix require different compiled versions of the programs.

compression   A way of shrinking computer files by encoding their data differently.

consumables   The materials consumed by printers, including ink, toner, and paper.

contextual menus   Menus that pop up wherever you click if you use a *modifier key*—specifically, the Ctrl key. Their commands vary according to the context in which you're working.

dialog box   A *graphical user interface* (GUI) element in which you can click buttons, enter text, choose from pop-up menus, and drag sliders to determine the settings you want to make in a program or your system software. See also *sheet*.

directory   The *Unix* word for *folder*.

DNS   Domain Name Server; a program that converts a typed *URL* into a numerical *IP address* where your Web browser can find the Web page you're looking for.

Dock   The panel at the bottom of your Mac OS X Desktop that contains an icon for every running program, as well as icons for any other programs you want to access quickly.

drag and drop   A method of choosing a file on which to perform an action by clicking the file's icon and dragging it into a dialog box, on top of an application's icon, into the Dock, or elsewhere, depending on what you're doing.

Drop Box   A folder within your Public folder that other users can use to give files to you; you are the only person who can see the contents of the Drop Box folder.

DSL   A high-speed Internet connection that operates over your phone line, but at a different frequency from your voice; you can talk on the phone and remain connected to the Internet at the same time.

dual-boot system   A computer system that contains system software for more than one system; in the case of Mac OS X, a dual-boot system might be able to boot from either Mac OS X or Mac OS 9.

e-mail   Electronic mail that travels from your computer to another computer across the Internet or over a local network.

emulator   A program that imitates the behavior of an operating system, such as Microsoft Windows. Using an emulator such as Virtual PC, you can run Windows (and Windows programs) on your Mac.

Ethernet   A networking technology that enables you to transfer data at high speeds; all Macs sold today have built-in Ethernet interfaces.

file sharing   A system feature that enables you to transfer files from your Mac to other computers and vice versa, and can also enable other users to access your files if you allow it.

filename extensions Three-letter (usually) codes that are placed at the end of filenames to signify the type of file; for example, TIFF graphics files use a .tif or .tiff filename extension.

Finder The part of Mac OS X that displays the contents of your hard drives and other drives in windows on your Desktop.

firmware Information stored within your Mac (and within some other devices such as printers and modems) that allows it to *boot*.

folder A system-level equivalent of a real-world file folder, in which you can store files and other folders to help you organize them.

font The software that enables your Mac to represent a particular typeface.

FTP File Transfer Protocol, a system of copying files from one computer to another that's widely used on the Internet and in the *Unix* world.

gamut The range of colors that a particular device, such as a scanner, monitor, or printer, can reproduce.

GNU A recursive acronym for Gnu's Not Unix. GNU is a free version of Unix that's widely used to form a large part of the Linux system.

graphical user interface (GUI) A way of interacting with a computer by moving icons around and receiving visual feedback. See also *command-line interface*.

headless A computer that doesn't have a monitor attached; usually, headless systems are servers that don't require user interaction very often.

home folder The folder in your Mac OS X system in which you can store all your personal files.

hot-swappable Capable of being connected to or disconnected from your Mac without shutting the computer down; usually refers to disk drives.

HTML HyperText Markup Language, the coding language used to create Web pages.

hub A device that connects all the cables forming an Ethernet network (or, in some cases, all the cables for your Mac's USB devices).

iDisk A storage space on Apple's Web site that's available to any Mac user who registers for the free *iTools* service.

IP address A numerical code that identifies the location of each computer on the Internet, including your Mac.

ISP Internet Service Provider; a company that provides access to the Internet.

iTools A free service available to any Mac user that includes an e-mail address and Web storage space.

LAN   Local Access Network; a small network enclosed entirely within one building.

Linux   A Unix system created by Finland's Linus Torvalds.

LocalTalk   A proprietary Apple networking system that uses standard telephone cable to connect Macs with each other and with printers. It's very slow compared to *Ethernet*.

log in   To identify yourself as a particular user by entering a user name and a password. You must log in to use Mac OS X, but you can set the system to log you in automatically so that you bypass the login screen. This is the default setting.

memory   See *RAM*.

minimized   A folder or document window that has been stored in the Dock, where you can see a thumbnail view of it.

modem   A device that allows your computer to connect to the Internet over a standard phone line, a DSL line, or a cable line, depending on the type of modem.

modifier keys   Special keys that enable you to give commands to your Mac by holding them down at the same time as you press letter or number keys. The Mac modifier keys are Shift, Option, Command, and Control.

mount   To place a disk drive on your Mac's Desktop so you can access its files. You can mount drives connected to your Mac and drives connected to computers on a network.

MP3   A compressed music file that's very small and therefore can be transferred easily over the Internet.

multithreading   The capability of an *operating system* to alternate between multiple tasks so quickly that it appears to be doing them at the same time.

NAT   Network Address Translation; a system for allowing multiple networked computers to access the Internet using a single Internet connection.

newsgroups   Online discussion groups that cover thousands of subjects; the main newsgroup system is called Usenet. You can subscribe to and read newsgroups using a newsreader program.

NFS   A system that enables a computer to access files over a network as if they were on its own disks.

NTP server   See *timeserver*.

operating system (OS)   The software that enables a computer to run.

outline font   See *printer font*.

pane   A separate "page" in a dialog box, usually accessible by choosing from a pop-up menu or (in the case of System Preferences) clicking a button.

pathname   The location of a file or folder as expressed by naming the successive folders in which the item is stored.

PDF   See *Portable Document Format.*

peer-to-peer   A decentralized system in which information is transferred from one computer to another without going through a central server.

peripheral   A device that connects to your Mac, such as a printer, scanner, tape backup drive, or digital camera.

pixel   Picture element; a square on the screen made up of a single color.

plug-ins   Software add-ons that give programs additional capabilities.

Point-to-Point Protocol (PPP)   The most common system of creating an Internet connection over a standard phone line.

pop-up menu   A menu that appears in a dialog box or other interface element rather than dropping down from the menu bar at the top of the screen.

Portable Document Format   The file format used by Adobe Acrobat Reader and its related software. When viewed onscreen and printed, a PDF document looks just like the original document from which it was created, regardless of whether the user has the original fonts or artwork.

PostScript   A printer language and font format (used primarily by laser printers and very high-end printing devices) that enables printers to output type and graphics at any size and maintain the same high quality.

preemptive multitasking   An *operating system* feature that allows your Mac to allocate varying amounts of its processing power to the different processes it's working on to meet your perceived needs at any given time.

printer font   The component of font software that is used to print the font at any size.

process dock   A dock, or floating palette, that shows the currently running programs.

profiles   Data files that characterize how a device reproduces color. See also *color management.*

proofing   Printing a document on a high-end printer with a view toward seeing how it will look when reproduced on a printing press.

protected memory   An *operating system* feature that places barriers around the areas of a computer's memory (or *RAM*) that are being used by each program, such that if one program crashes, the other programs will be unaffected.

RAM   Random Access Memory; the part of a computer that stores the currently running programs and the currently open documents so you can work with them.

resolution   The number of pixels per inch contained in a graphic or displayed on a monitor.

root   A "superuser" account that can move, modify, or delete any file or folder on your Mac. By default, the root account is disabled; to use it, you must first enable it using the NetInfo Manager utility.

RSIs   Repetitive strain injuries; the kind of injury that results from too much typing, too much mousing, or other repetitive work.

sans serif   A font that does not have *serifs* at the end of its strokes.

screen font   The component of font software that is used to display the font onscreen.

scriptable   An application whose functions can be controlled with *AppleScript*.

search engine   A Web site that searches the Web for terms you specify and returns a list of Web pages that contain those terms.

serif   A short, often tapered line at the end of a font's letters.

server-based   A centralized system in which information is transferred from one computer to another by being moved through a central server.

sheet   A dialog box that's attached to the title bar of the document to which it relates, such as a Save or Print dialog box.

shell scripting   A method of controlling Unix computers by stringing together lists of commands in text files that can then be executed like programs.

Sherlock   The Mac OS's built-in utility for searching both your Mac system (to locate missing files) and the Internet.

snail mail   Mail sent using the real-world postal service, as opposed to e-mail, which usually reaches its destination almost instantaneously.

subtractive color   Color made up of pigments, as on a printed page; so called because you must add all three of its primary colors (cyan, magenta, and yellow) together to form black. See also *additive color*.

system software   See *operating system (OS)*.

TCP/IP   Transmission Control Protocol over Internet Protocol; the networking method Mac OS X uses, which is an industry standard also used by Windows PCs and *Unix* computers.

Telnet   A method of connecting to a *Unix* computer so that you can control it by entering commands in a *Terminal* window on your computer.

Terminal   A utility (located in the Utilities folder within Mac OS X's Applications folder) that enables you to give Unix commands and use Unix programs.

timeserver   A computer on the Internet that transmits a time signal that your Mac can use to set its clock automatically.

top level   A *Finder* view of your Mac that shows the hard drives, removable drives, and network drives to which it has access.

Trash   The holding location for files or folders you want to delete. Dragging items into the Trash does not delete them (double-click the Trash to open it and retrieve items). you must choose **Finder**, **Empty Trash** to permanently remove them from your hard drive.

TrueType   A font technology that allows type to be output on any printer at any size and maintain high quality.

Unix   A powerful *operating system* that is controlled through a *command-line interface*. Mac OS X's foundation is a Unix system, and you can access the Unix command-line interface using the *Terminal* program.

URL   An alphanumeric address that points to a specific location on the Internet, such as www.apple.com for Apple's Web site.

working directory   The directory, or folder, you're currently working in when you're using the *Unix command-line interface* through Mac OS X's *Terminal* program.

WYSIWYG   What You See Is What You Get; a term that describes the capability of modern graphic design programs to create an onscreen image of the pages being designed.

Index

Symbols

4X4 EVO game (Mac OS X), 110
10Mbps Ethernet, 120
100Mbps Ethernet, 120

A

AAAClipArt.com Web site, 182
About This Mac command, 259
access privileges, file sharing, setting, 123-125
accessing
 folders
  Finder, 31
  privileges, 65
 Mac OS 9, 63
accessories (games)
 Harman/Kardon SoundSticks, 113
 Racing Simulator, 113
accounts (e-mail), configuring (Mail), 164-165

Acrobat Reader
 downloading, 27-28
 PDFZone.com, 325
action games
 4X4 EVO, 110
 Oni, 109
 Quake 3 Arena, 109
ADB (Apple Desktop Bus), 54
Add to Favorites command (Font panel), 132
adding
 icons to Dock, 29
 printers (Print Center), 134
 speakable commands (Speech Recognition), 278-279
 special effects to video footage (iMovie), 101
 system utilities (Dock), 255
 users, 77-78
additive colors (monitors), 271-272
Address Book, 167
 categories, 167-168
 entries, typing, 167-168
 pictures, 168

Admin user, 315
Admo.net Web site, 183
Adobe Acrobat Reader, 138
 PDF (portable document format), development of, 200
Adobe Photoshop, 182
Adobe Systems Web site, 27-28
 Acrobat Reader application, 138
Adrenaline Entertainment Web site, 109
ADSL (asynchronous DSL), 146
AirPort (wireless networking), 150
 advantages over cabled networks, 122
 base station, 122
 installing, 122
Aladdin Systems Web site, 299
aliases
 creating, 69-70
  via dragging (Option+Cmd), 70
 uses, 69

AltaVista Web site, 325
  search engine facilities,
  156
analog modems, 142
animation of opening applications (Dock), 234
antivirus software
  McAfee Virex, 297
  proper use of, 297
  Sophos Anti-Virus, 297
Apache Web Server, 287
Apple channel (Sherlock),
  160
Apple Computer
  introduction of original
    Macintosh, 7, 11
  Jobs, Steve, 11
  Mac OS X, evolution of,
    11
Apple Donuts Web site,
  Sherlock plug-ins, 163
Apple menu
  commands
    About This Mac, 259
    Control Panel, 19
    Dock Preferences, 233
    Force Quit, 314
    Log Out, 76
    Restart, 17, 94, 217
    Shut Down, 17
    System Preferences, 20,
      77-78, 142-143
  Desk accessories, 82
    Calculator, 82
    Clock, 83
    Key Caps, 83
    Stickies, 84
  old version, recovering
    functionality of, 255-256
Apple Movie Gallery, iMovie
  productions, 101
Apple Phone Support, offline
  help, 41-42
Apple Store Web site, 101

Apple Support Web site, 317,
  322
Apple System Profiler
  devices and volumes, 301
  extensions, 301
  frameworks, 301
Apple Web site
  AppleWorks resources, 96
  Classic applications list-
    ings, 95
  Hardware Guide, 113
  Help Center connections,
    39
  help tools
    Discussions Area, 43
    Knowledge Base, 42
    Software Updates Area,
      43
    Support Area, 42
    Technical Information
      Library (TIL), 42
  iDisk, 87
  iMovie
    camcorder ratings, 103
    Gallery, 101
  iTunes
    downloading, 98
    hardware compatibility
      listings, 102
    third-party apps listings,
      90
AppleScript, 263
  applications, using with-
    in, 268-269
  introduction of, 264
  MacScripters.Net Web site,
    264
  recording, 267
  saved formats, 267
    Classic applet, 268
    compiled script, 267
    Mac OS X applet, 268
    text, 267

ScriptBuilders Web site,
  264
Speech Recognition, com-
  mand additions, 278-279
uses, 264
AppleTalk protocol, 190-191
  networked printers, con-
    necting to, 127
AppleWorks, 96
applications
  Carbon, 34-35
    Mac OS X and earlier
      platforms, 90-91
  Classic, 33-34
    Apple Web site listings,
      95
    installing, 94
    Mac OS 9 platform
      only, 93
  Cocoa, 34
    Color panel, 91
    Font panel, 91
    Mac OS X platform
      only, 91-92
    Print Preview com-
      mand, 92
    Services feature, 92
  conflict/bug resources
    MacFixit Web site, 296
    MacInTouch Web site,
      296
  deleting, 299
  erratic behavior, trou-
    bleshooting, 315
  freezes, troubleshooting,
    314-315
  graphic design
    Stone Super Seven
      Suite, 95
    TIFFany, 95
  hiding on Dock, 230
  opening animation
    (Dock), 234

scripts, using within, 268-269
sources (Mac Orchard Web site), 160
storing in Dock, 230-231
switching (Cmd+Tab), 231
third-party, Apple Web site listing, 90
Unix, 282
  CGI programs, 287
  command-line interface, 288
  GUIs, 289
  networking programs, 288
  text processing programs, 287
  Web serving programs, 287
updating, 295-296
version tracking, 295-296
Applications command (Go menu), 81, 144
Applications folder, 60
  Calculator, 82
  Clock, 83
  restrictions, 61
  Stickies, 84
  System Administrator, managing, 61
  TextEdit, 84-85
  viewing, 60
Aqua, screen elements, 27
arcade games
  Native Assault, 109
  SNES9X, 109
  TheCowCatchingGame, 109
arranging Desktop icons, 236-237
assigning IP addresses (networks), 190-191
asynchronous DSL. *See* ADSL
audio music. *See* iTunes

auto-racing game controllers, 51
automatic hide/show option (Dock), 234
automatic online connections (PPP), 144
Axis Communications Web site, hardware print servers, 201

B

back arrow button (Finder), 30
background windows in applications, clicking on, 245
BackJack, Internet backup service, 307
backups
  DAT tapes, 306
  design guidelines, 304
  frequency of, 306
  Internet services, implementing, 307
  LANs, implementing, 305-306
  resources, TidBITS newsletter, 305
  software
    Macintosh Products Guide Web site, 304
    Retrospect, 304
  strategies
    file types, 304
    removable disk media, 304
  Tao of Backup Web site, 303, 325
Bare Bones Software Web site, 288
Barry's Clipart Server Web site, 182

basic installation of Mac OS X, 15
BBEdit text editor, 288
Belkin Components Web site, printer switchboxes, 201
Bell Labs, Unix development, 32, 281
Beseen Web site, 183
bitmap fonts, 130
blinking question mark, non-boot troubleshooting alert, 312
Blizzard Entertainment Web site, 108
bookmarks in Web browsers, 157
booting
  troubleshooting non-boots, 311
    blinking question mark, 312
    Chimes of Doom, 312
    kernel panic, 313
    partial freezes, 313
    Sad Mac, 312
  verbose mode, 314
Brooks Internet Software Web site, LPR client software, 201
bugs in software, repair updates, 311
Bungie.com Web site, 109
burning MP3s to CD-Rs or CD-RWs, 99
buttons
  dialog box controls, 26
  Finder
    back arrow, 30
    clear, 30
    green, 30
    red, 30
    yellow, 30

C

cable modems
high-speed access, 145
manual connection settings, 146-147
cabled networks
disadvantages, 123
versus wireless networks, 121
cabling
Ethernet
hubs, 118
RJ-45 connectors, 119
LocalTalk, 118
caffeineSoft.com Web site, 95
Calculator, copying/pasting functions, 82
camcorders, connecting to iMovie
footage edits, 101
footage imports, 101-102
canceling print jobs, 138
Carbon applications, 34-35
games, installing, 107-108
Mac OS X and earlier platforms, 90-91
Carrot Software Web site, 107
Casteel.org Web site, 111
CAUCE (Coalition Against Commercial Email), 164
CD-Rs (CD-ROM Recordables), 99, 188, 196
summary features table, 52-53
CD-RWs (CD-ROM Rewritable), 99, 188, 196
summary features table, 52-53
CDs, burning MP3s to (iTunes), 99
CGI programs (Common Gateway Interface), 287
CH Products Web site, 112

changing Desktop pictures, 236
channels (Sherlock)
Apple, 160
creating, 163
editing, 163
Entertainment, 161
Files, 160
Internet, 160
News, 161
People, 160
Reference, 161
selecting, 161
Shopping, 161
characters (Key Caps application), 83
chatting, 169
check boxes and dialog box controls, 26
Chess game, 111
Chimes of Doom, non-boot troubleshooting alert, 312
Chooser, replaced by Print Center, 259
Clan Lord game, 108
Clan MacGaming Web site, 106, 321
Classic environment
Apple menu, utilizing, 256
applications, 33-34
Apple Web site listings, 95
crash potential, 93
Help menu contents, 38
identifying, 93
installing, 94
Mac OS 9 platform only, 93
fonts, installing, 131
games, installing, 106-107
Mac OS 9, 13, 18
accessing, 63
installations, 62-63

maintenance
Desktop Rebuilds, 297
restarting with extensions off, 297
Classic pane, System Preferences dialog box, 219
clear button (Finder), 30
client programs (FTP)
Fetch, 208
Transit, 208
clip art resources
AAAClipArt.com, 182
Barry's Clipart Server, 182
Clips Ahoy!, 182
ClipArtConnection, 182
GifArt.com, 182
ClipArtConnection Web site, 182
Clips Ahoy! Web site, 182
Clock, placing on Dock, 83
Close button (windows), 241-242
Cmd+C (Copy) keyboard shortcut, 68
Cmd+N (new window) keyboard shortcut, 25
Cmd+O (open file) keyboard shortcut, 25
Cmd+P (Print) keyboard shortcut, 133
Cmd+V (Paste) keyboard shortcut, 68
Cmd+X (Cut) keyboard shortcut, 68
Coalition Against Unsolicited Commercial E-Mail (CAUCE) Web site, 325
Cocoa applications, 34
games, installing, 107-108
Mac OS X platform only, 91-92
tools
Color panel, 91
Font panel, 91

Print Preview command, 92
Services feature, 92
coding Web pages, sample code (HTML), 178
Collections list (Font panel), 131
color
  additive, 272
  images, number of, 180
  management. *See* ColorSync
  Stickies notes, 84
  subtractive, 271-272
  Web pages, browser preferences, 159
Color command (Font panel), 133
color depth
  monitors, 226
  scanners, 49
Color panel, Cocoa application tool, 91
ColorSync
  device profiles, 272-273
    applications, 272
    Inkjet Mall Web site, 273
    PANTONE Web site, 273
    Profile Central Web site, 273
  preferences, setting, 273-274
  profiles (Library folder), 62
Column view (files), 244-245
command-line interfaces (Unix), 10, 254, 282, 288
  commands, entering, 282-283
commands
  Apple menu
    Dock Preferences, 233
    Force Quit, 314

Log Out, 76
Restart, 17, 94, 217
Shut Down, 17
System Preferences, 20, 77-78, 142-143
dialog box options, 25
ellipsis (...) indicator, dialog box options, 25
File menu
  Copy, 83
  Duplicate, 67
  Eject, 239
  Make Alias, 69-70
  Move to Trash, 74
  New Finder Window, 30-31
  New Folder, 66, 243
  New Note, 84
  Open Enclosing Folder, 74
  Open Movie, 86
  Page Setup, 134-135
  Paste, 83
  Print, 133, 136
  Print Item, 74
  Save As PDF, 86, 137
  Show Info, 239, 247
  Show Original, 74
Finder menu, Preferences, 236
Font panel
  Add to Favorites, 132
  Color, 133
  Edit Collections, 132
  Edit Sizes, 133
  Get Fonts, 133
Format menu, Font, 84
Go menu
  Applications, 81, 144
  Connect to Server, 191-193
  Go to Folder, 31
  Recent Folders, 31

Security menu
  Disable Root User, 78
  Enable Root User, 78
selecting (menu bar), 24
Special menu, Restart, 19
View menu
  Customize Toolbar, 246
  Show Status Bar, 246
  Show View Options, 244
compiled programs versus scripts, 264
compiling Unix applications (FreeBSD Unix), 210-211
composing Stickies notes, 84
compound script statements (Script Editor), 265
computer viruses. *See* viruses
configuring
  computers for file sharing, 123
  e-mail accounts (Mail), 164-165
  hardware routers, Internet connection sharing, 150
  Internet access, DHCP option, 126
  iTools, 174-175
  Mac OS X
    country information, 16
    Internet connections, 16
    keyboard layout, 16
    System Preferences, 20, 77-78, 142-143
    time zone information, 16
    user accounts, 16
  phone modem connections (PPP), 142-143
  PPPoE, DSL services, 148-149
  Text-to-Speech, 275-276

Connect to Server command (Go menu), 191-193
connecting
    networked printers
        AppleTalk, 127
        TCP/IP, 127
    networks, Ethernet components, 121
    peripheral devices, 53-55
    printers
        local, 47
        networks, 47
Connectix Web site, 198
console emulators (games), 109
contextual menus, 50, 231
    opening, 27
Control Panel (Apple menu), 19
    Software Update, 14
Control Strip, CSMs (control strip modules), 258
controllers (games)
    P5 glove, 112
    PoolShark, 112
controlling access for file sharing, 125
conventional videotape, exporting to iMovie, 102
converting audio CDs to MP3 format (iTunes), 99
Coping with Unix Web site, 324
Copy command (File menu), 83
copying
    files, 67
    folder icons to other folders, 61
    folders, 67
    hard drive files to removable disk drives, 188-189
    numbers (Calculator), 82

copyrights and MP3 controversy, 103-104
CounterGuide Web site, 183
counters resources
    Admo.net, 183
    Beseen, 183
    CounterGuide, 183
    Hitometer, 183
    theCounter, 183
    Zcounter, 183
countries, Mac OS X configuration, 16
crashes, troubleshooting (Disk Utility), 299-300
creating
    aliases, 69-70
        via dragging (Option+Cmd), 70
    folders, 66, 243
    login items with scripts, 270
    new channels (Sherlock), 163
    Web pages
        HomePage (iTools), 175-177
        textual content (HTML), 178-180
custom installations, 15
Customize Toolbar command (View menu), 246
customizing
    Desktop preferences, 236-237
    Toolbar, 247
    window view options, 245-246

D

Dantz Development Web site, 304
Date & Time pane (System Preferences dialog box)

    Menu Bar Clock tab, 220
    Network Time tab, 220
    Time Zone tab, 220
date/time timeservers, 142
deactivating login screens, 76
DealMac Web site, 194, 321
DeBabelizer, file format translation program, 193
DEC (Digital Equipment Corporation), Unix development, 281
defragmenting hard drives, 298
Deja.com Web site, Usenet newsgroups, 169
deleting
    Dock items, 29, 233
    files, 299
Delta Tao Software Web site, 108
descreening (scanners), 49
designing Web pages, 179
desk accessories (Apple menu, pre-Mac OS X systems), 82
    Calculator, 82
    Clock, 83
    Key Caps, 83
    Stickies, 84
Desktop
    appearance
        cluttered versus uncluttered, 254-255
        setting preferences, 254-255
    color schemes, 237
    customizing utilities
        Plus For X, 255
        TinkerTool, 255
    drive icons, removing, 239
    icons
        arrangement of, 236-237
        custom, 237
        sizes, 236

multiple users and home folders, 79

pictures

changing, 236

launch appearance, 16-17

Mac OS X Gallery, 236

MacDesktops, 236

preferences, setting, 236-237

rebuilding (Classic maintenance), 297

Trash, location of, 255

Desktop folder (Users folder), 64

Developer Tools CD, prebinding fix, 294

devices, malfunctions, troubleshooting, 316

DHCP (Dynamic Host Configuration Protocol), 126

Diablo II game, 108

dialog boxes

controls

buttons, 26

check boxes, 26

pick lists, 26

pop-up menus, 26

radio buttons, 26

tabs, 26

text entry fields, 26

function of, 25

Open, 25

Page Setup, 133

Print, 133, 136

Save, 25

System Preferences, 20, 215-216

View Options, 244

digital cameras, Image Capture utility, 86

digital music, MP3 compression information, 98

digital subscriber line. *See* DSL

directories (Unix), mounting, 206

Disable Root User command (Security menu), 78

disabling root account, 78

Discussions area, Apple Web site, 43

disk defragmentation, 298

Disk First Aid, replaced by Disk Utility, 259

disk repair utilities (thirdparty)

DiskWarrior, 313

Drive10, 313

Disk Utility

missing files, troubleshooting, 315

modules

Drive Setup, 299-300

First Aid, 299-300

replacement for Disk First Aid, 259

disks

drive icons, removing from Desktop, 239

ejecting, 239

erasing, 239

icons, changing, 239

iDisks, 239

information, viewing, 239

reformatting, 239

DiskWarrior disk utility, 301, 313

Display Calibrator, color profiles, creating, 274-275

displaying image files (Preview utility), 86

Displays pane (System Preferences dialog box), 225-226

DNS (domain name servers), 147

Dock

Apple menu, replacement strategies, 255-256

application icons, 81

as replacement for previous Mac menus, 234

Clock icon, 83

Docking Maneuvers program, 235

document windows, hiding, 230

dynamic icons, 233

Extras

Battery Monitor, 232

Displays, 232

Signal Strength, 232

files, dragging into folders, 232

hiding, 258

hierarchical folders, setting up, 256

icons

adding, 29

deleting, 29

dragging mouse across, 28

Magnification feature, 28

opening programs, 28

items

launching, 230

removing, 233

switching (Cmd+Tab), 230

Late Breaking News, Mac OS X topics, 40-41

minimized windows, 28

screen appearance, 16-17

settings

animate opening applications, 234

automatic hide/show option, 234

size, 233

storage items
applications, 230-231
Dock Extras, 232
files, 231
folders, 232
minimized windows, 232
URLs, 231
strategies, 234-235
system utilities, adding, 255
third-party utilities
DragThing, 234, 257
Drop Drawers, 258
PocketDock, 234, 258
use guidelines, 234-235
versus third-party launchers, 256
white patches, troubleshooting, 234
Dock pane (System Preferences dialog box), 219
Dock Preferences command (Apple menu), 233
Docking Maneuvers program, 235
document windows, 23, 241-242
hiding (Dock), 230
documents
opening (Dock), 230
print options (Page Setup dialog box), 134-135
mini-printouts, 137
number of copies, 136
page ranges, 136
previewing, 137
Documents folder (Users folder), 64
domain name servers (DNS), 147
domain names, registering/purchasing (InterNIC), 182

Down & Out game, 108
downloading
Adobe Acrobat Reader, 27-28
iMovie, 101
iTunes, 98
screen savers, 218
Sherlock plug-ins, 163
Web pages, browser preferences, 159
drag-and-drop action, droplet scripts, 269-270
dragging files
alias creation (Option+Cmd), 70
into Dock folders, 232
DragThing (Dock third-party utility), 234, 257
drive icons, removing from Desktop, 239
Drive Setup (Disk Utility), 299-300
hard drive reformatting, 14
Drive10 disk utility, 300, 313
Drop Drawers (Dock third-party utility), 258
droplets (scripts), sample code, 269-270
DSL (digital subscriber line), 145
ADSL service, 146
hardware routers, 150
Linksys, 150
MacSense, 150
high-speed access, 145
manual connection settings, 146-147
PPPoE, configuring, 148-149
dual booting in Mac OS 9/X, 17-20
Duplicate command (File menu), 67

DVD (Digital Versatile Disc), 188
iMovie, exporting to, 102
removable disk drive, 188
Dynamic Host Configuration Protocol. *See* DHCP
dynamic icons (Dock), 233
dynamic range of scanners, 49

E

e-mail
accounts, setting up (Mail), 164-165
Address Book, 167
categories, 167-168
entries, typing, 167-168
pictures, 168
CAUCE Web site (Coalition Against Unsolicited Commercial E-mail), 325
messages
reading, 165
receiving, 165-166
sending, 166-167
sorting, 165
spam, 164
Edit Collections command (Font panel), 132
Edit Sizes command (Font panel), 133
editing
footage in iMovie, 101
new channels (Sherlock), 163
users, 77-78
Eject command (File menu), 239
ejecting disks, 239
emulation software (VirtualPC), 202

Emulation.net Web site, 109
Enable Root User command
    (Security menu), 78
enabling root account, 78
Energy Saver pane (System
    Preferences dialog box)
    display sleep option,
        217-218
    hard disk sleep option,
        217-218
    system sleep option,
        217-218
Entertainment channel
    (Sherlock), 161
Epicware.com Web site,
    screen saver resources, 95,
    218
erasing disks, 239
erratic behavior in applica-
    tions, troubleshooting, 315
Essential Reality Web site, 112
Ethernet, 197
    10Mbps, 120
    100Mbps, 120
    final connections, 121
    Gigabit, 120
    hubs, 118
        number of ports, 119
        typical cost, 119
    peripheral interface, 55
    RJ-11 connectors, 119
    RJ-45 connectors, 119
EveryMac Web site, 321
executing searches
    (Sherlock), 161-162
exiting Mac OS X, 17
exporting footage from
    iMovie, 102
Extended format (HFS Plus),
    minimum installation
    requirements, 13
extensions, disabled, restart-
    ing (Classic maintenance),
    297

F

Family list (Font panel), 131
Fetch, FTP client program,
    208
file backups. *See* backups
File menu commands
    Copy, 83
    Duplicate, 67
    Eject, 239
    Make Alias, 69-70
    Move to Trash, 74
    New Finder Window,
        30-31
    New Folder, 66, 243
    New Note, 84
    Open Enclosing Folder, 74
    Open Movie, 86
    Page Setup, 134-135
    Paste, 83
    Print, 133, 136
    Print Item, 74
    Save As PDF, 86, 137
    Show Info, 239, 247
    Show Original, 74
file sharing
    access levels
        None, 125
        Read and Write, 125
        Read Only, 125
        Write Only, 125
    access privileges, setting,
        123-125
    IP addresses, assigning,
        123
File Transfer Protocol. *See* FTP
filename extensions, 68-69
files
    aliases, creating, 69-70
    copying, 67
    deleting, 299
    Dock storage type, 231
    dragging into Dock fold-
        ers, 232

exchanging with Unix
    computers, 204-209
format compatibility
    across platforms,
    199-200
    Unix compatibility,
        208-209
icons, 24
information
    Application Files pane,
        249
    Application pane, 248
    General Information
        pane, 248
    Preview pane, 248
    Privileges pane, 250
    viewing, 247-250
Library folder examples,
    62
lost, locating (Sherlock
    utility), 70-73
missing, troubleshooting,
    315
moving, 67
name extensions, 68-69
networks, sharing,
    189-193, 197-200
new appearance of in
    home folder, 65
removable disk drives
    CD-R, 188
    CD-RW, 188
    copying to, 188-189
    DVD, 188
    Jaz, 188
    SuperDisk, 188
    Zip, 188
renaming, 68
sharing, 79-80
    System Preferences dia-
        log box, 224-225
window display options
    Column view, 244-245
    Icon view, 244-245
    List view, 244-245

Files channel (Sherlock), 160
Finder
    buttons
        back arrow, 30
        clear, 30
        green, 30
        red, 30
        yellow, 30
    folders, access methods, 31
    hard drive contents, navi-
        gating, 29
    hidden pop-up menus, 30
    title bar, 30
    versus previous versions
        of Mac OS, 29
    windows, 23, 241-242
        button indicators, 30
        folder display, 24
        opening, 30-31
        resizing, 30
        scrollbars, 30
Fire, instant messaging appli-
    cation, 95
FireWire, peripheral inter-
    face, 54
firmware, 13
First Aid (Disk Utility),
    299-300
    hard drive formatting, 14
flatbed scanners, 48
Flight Sim Yoke USB LE
    flight controller, 51, 112
floppy disks, removable disk
    drives, 196-197
FLY! II game, 108
folders
    access privileges, 65
    aliases, creating, 69-70
    automatic creation, 65
    copying, 67
    creating, 66, 243
    Dock storage type, 232
    Finder
        access methods, 31
        navigating, 29

hard drive
    Applications, 60-61
    Library, 60-62
    System, 60, 64
    Users, 60, 64-65
hierarchical, setting up
    (Dock), 256
icons, 24
    moving, 67
    opening, 24
    opening (multiwindow
        mode), 242-243
    opening (single-window
        mode), 242-243
    renaming, 68
    restrictions on creation of
        subfolders, 66
    top-level, creation of, 66
Folders buttons (Toolbar),
    246
Font command (Format
    menu), 84
Font panel, 131
    Cocoa application tool, 91
    Collections list, 131
    commands
        Add to Favorites, 132
        Color, 133
        Edit Collections, 132
        Edit Sizes, 133
        Get Fonts, 133
    Family list, 131
    Size list, 132
    Typeface list, 132
fonts
    bitmap, 130
    installation methods, 130
    Library folder, 62
    OpenType, 130
    outline, 130
    PostScript, 47
    PostScript Type 1, 130
    sans serif, 159
    serif, 159

TrueType, 130
Web pages, browser pref-
    erences, 159
Force Quit command (Apple
    menu), 314
Format menu commands,
    Font, 84
formats, file compatibility
    across platforms, 199-200
    Unix compatibility,
        208-209
formatting text (TextEdit),
    84-85
free page stuff
    clip art
        AAAClipArt.com, 182
        Barry's Clipart Server,
            182
        ClipArtConnection, 182
        Clips Ahoy!, 182
        GifArt.com, 182
    counters
        Admo.net, 183
        Beseen, 183
        CounterGuide, 183
        Hitometer, 183
        theCounter, 183
        Zcounter, 183
Free Software Foundation
    Web site, Unix software,
    290
FreeBSD Unix, compiling
    applications, 210-211
FreeBSD.org Web site, Unix
    resources, 284
freezes, troubleshooting,
    314-315
fsck utility, non-boots, trou-
    bleshooting, 313
FTP (File Transfer Protocol),
    169, 182
    client programs
        Fetch, 208
        Transit, 208

client software, Web page uploads, 182
files, exchanging with Unix computers, 206-208
Web upload protocol, 169
Function buttons (Toolbar), 246

G

game controllers
    auto-racing devices, 51
    flight controllers, 51
    gamepads, 51
    joysticks, 51
GamePad Pro USB Joystick, 112
gamepads, 51
games
    accessories
        Harman/Kardon SoundSticks, 113
        Racing Simulator, 113
    action
        4X4 EVO, 110
        Oni, 109
        Quake 3 Arena, 109
    arcade
        Native Assault, 109
        SNES9X, 109
        TheCowCatchingGame, 109
    Carbon, installing, 107-108
    Clan MacGaming Web site, 106
    Classic, installing, 106-107
    Cocoa, installing, 107-108
    console emulators, 109
    controllers
        Flight Sim Yoke USB LE, 112
        P5 glove, 112
        PoolShark, 112
        Pro Pedals, 112

WingMan Gaming Mouse, 112
    joysticks, GamePad Pro USB, 112
    logic/puzzle
        Down & Out, 108
        MegaMinesweeper, 107
    networks, 110
    real world
        Chess, 111
        Klondike, 111
        Maximum Pool, 110
        Video Poker, 111
    ROMs, 109
    shareware, 108
    strategy
        Clan Lord, 108
        Diablo II, 108
        FLY! II, 108
        Tropico, 108
General pane (System Preferences dialog box), 218
genie effects, windows, minimizing, 232
Get Fonts command (Font panel), 133
GIF (graphic interchange format) images, 180
    interlacing, 181
    lossless compression, 180
    progressive, 181
GIFArt.com Web site, 182
Gigabit Ethernet, 120
GIMP (GNU Image Manipulation Program), 209
GNU license, Unix software, 289
GNU Project Web site, 323
Go menu commands
    Applications, 81, 144
    Connect to Server, 191-193
    Go to Folder, 31
    Recent Folders, 31
Go to Folder command (Go menu), 31

Google Web site, 324
    search engine facilities, 156
Grab utility, screen shots, printing, 136
graphic design applications
    Stone Super Seven Suite, 95
    TIFFany, 95
graphical user interface (GUI), 8, 254
graphics tablets, 51
Gravis Web site, 112
green button (Finder), 30
Greyhound Project Web site, 161
Griffin Technology Web site, microphones, 276
GUI (graphical user interface), 8, 254
GUI applications (Unix), 289

H

hard drives
    contents, navigating (Finder), 29
    defragmenting, 298
    Drive Setup, 14
    Extended format (HFS Plus), 13
    files, copying to removable disk drives, 188-189
    First Aid, 14
    folders
        Applications, 60-61
        Library, 60-62
        System, 60, 64
        Users, 60, 64-65
    iMovie large space requirements, 103
    indexes, creating (Sherlock utility), 72

minimum space, installation requirements, 13
partitions, installation requirements, 13
reformatting, 14
repairing (Disk Utility), 299-300
hardware
compatibility listings, Apple Web site, 113
DealMac Web site, 194
devices, troubleshooting functions, 316
games, WingMan Gaming Mouse, 112
iMovie requirements, 102-103
iTunes requirements, 102
keyboard preferences (System Preferences dialog box), 225
monitor preferences (System Preferences dialog box), 225-226
mouse preferences (System Preferences dialog box), 225
networks
Internet routers, 121
LocalTalk-to-Ethernet adapters, 120
Outpost.com, 119, 325
peripheral devices, 46
game controllers, 51
graphics tablets, 51
interfaces, 53-55
mouse, 50
port connections, 50
portable hard drives, 53
printers, 46-47
removable storage devices, 51-53
scanners, 48-49
troubleshooting category, 311

hardware print servers, 201
hardware routers
Internet connection sharing, configuring, 150
Linksys, 150
MacSense, 150
Harman/Kardon SoundSticks, 113
headless servers, 198
Help Center
Apple Web site connection, 39
data file storage, 62
navigation buttons, 39
Quick Clicks, 40
topics, searching, 38
Help menu
Classic applications, 38
contents, program-dependent, 37
Help Viewer, opening, 37
helper applications, Web pages, browser preferences, 159
hidden pop-up menus (Finder), 30
hiding Dock, 230, 258
hierarchical folders, setting up (Dock), 256
high-speed access
cable modems, 145
manual connection settings, 146-147
DSL, 145
manual connection settings, 146-147
PPPoE configuration, 148-149
Hitometer Web site, 183
holding print jobs, 138
home folder
Documents folder, 79
Library folder, 79
new files, appearance of, 65

organization, 66
Public folder, 79
user privileges, 79
HomeFree Web site, wireless networks, 122
HomeLine Web site, wireless networks, 122
HomePage (iTools), 170
creating, 175-177
iDisk storage, 177
templates, 175-176
hosting services
HostMe.com, 182
Web sites, 181-182
HostMe.com Web site, 182
hot-swappable devices, 53
HTML (HyperText Markup Language)
tags, 158, 178
tutorial site, 179
Web pages
browser code interpretation, 156-159
sample code, 178
textual content display, 178-180
hubs
Ethernet, 118
number of ports, 119
typical cost, 119
USB type, 119
HyperText Markup Language. *See* HTML

I

iCab Web browser, 95, 158
Text-to-Speech capability, 276
iCards service (iTools), 170
Icon Factory Web site, 237
icons
Applications folder, copying to other folders, 61

Desktop
  arranging, 236-237
  customizing, 237
  sizing, 236
disks, changing, 239
Dock
  adding, 29
  deleting, 29
  dragging mouse across, 28
  Magnification feature, 28
  opening programs, 28
  removing, 233
dynamic nature (Dock), 233
files, 24
folders, opening, 24
sources
  Icon Factory, 237
  Xicons.com, 237-238
Icon view (files), 244-245
id Software Web site, 109
identifying Classic applications, 93
iDisk (iTools), 170, 239
  Apple Web site, 87
  Web pages, storage of, 177
iMacs, 9
Image Capture utility,
images, transferring from digital cameras, 86
images
  colors, number of, 180
  editors (Adobe Photoshop), 182
  formats, saving as (Preview utility), 86
  GIF, 180
  interlaced, 181
  JPEG, 180
  line art, 49
  lossless compression, 180
  lossy compression, 180

PDF format, 27-28
progressive, 181
scanners
  color depth, 49
  descreening, 49
  dynamic range, 49
  interpolation, 49
  ppi (pixels per inch), 49
  prescans, 49
  resolution, 49
  selection criteria, 48
  uses, 48
viewing (Preview utility), 86
iMovie
  Apple Movie Gallery, 101
  camcorder compatibility ratings, 103
  cost, 101
  disk space considerations, 103
  downloading, 101
  footage
    editing, 101
    exporting, 102
    importing from source, 101-102
    special effects additions, 101
  hardware requirements, 102-103
  interface
    Clip Viewer, 100
    Monitor area, 100
    Shelf, 100
    Timeline, 100
  iTools service, Web page display options, 102
implementing backups
  Internet services, 307
  LANs, 305-306
importing footage to iMovie, 101-102
indexes, hard drives, creating (Sherlock utility), 72

Inkjet Mall Web site, 273
inkjet printers, consumable supplies, 46-47
installing
  AirPort wireless networks, 122
  Classic applications, 94
  fonts, 130
  games
    Carbon versions, 107-108
    Classic versions, 106-107
    Cocoa versions, 107-108
  Mac OS 9, 62-63
  Mac OS X, 12
    basic installation, 15
    custom installation, 15
    Extended format (HFS Plus), 13
    hard drive partitions, 13
    installer icon, 14-15
    minimum hard drive space, 13
    minimum RAM, 13
    recent firmware updates, 13
    Software Update panel, 14
    troubleshooting, 15
    video card requirements, 13
  new printers (Print Center), 134
instant messaging applications, 169
  Fire, 95
intellectual property, MP3 controversy, 103-104
interfaces (peripheral devices), 53
  ADB, 54
  Ethernet, 55

347

FireWire, 54
LocalTalk, 55
SCSI, 54
USB, 54
interlaced images, 181
International pane (System Preferences dialog box), 221-222
Date tab, 222
Keyboard Menu tab, 222
Language tab, 221
Numbers tab, 222
Time tab, 222
Internet
backup services
BackJack, 307
implementing, 307
connections, Mac OS X configuration, 16
gaming, 110
network access (DHCP), 126
Internet channel (Sherlock), 160
Internet Connect, online connections, launching, 144
Internet connection sharing
hardware routers, configuring, 150
NAT (network address translation) software, 149-150
IPNetRouter, 150
SurfDoubler, 150
wireless networking (AirPort), 150
Internet Explorer preferences, 158
colors, 159
downloads, 159
fonts, 159
helper applications, 159
identity, 159
Internet Goodies List Web site, 290

Internet pane (System Preferences dialog box), 222-223
Internet Radio Tuner (iTunes), 99
Internet routers, 121
Internet service providers. *See* ISPs
InterNIC Web site, domain name registration, 182
interpolation (scanners), 49
IP addresses
LAN file sharing, configuring, 123
networks, assigning, 190-191
IPNetRouter, Internet connection sharing software, 150
ISPs (Internet service providers), 142
Internet Connect option, 144
phone modem connections, PPP (Point-to-Point Protocol), 142-143
iTools, 169
Internet information repository, 151-152
services
HomePage, 170
iCards, 170
iDisk, 170
KidSafe, 170
Web pages, creating (HomePage), 102, 175-177
Web sites
free space, 173
signing up, 174-175
iTunes
CDs, converting to MP3 format, 99
compatibility listings, 102

copyright and intellectual property issues, 103-104
downloading, 98
features, 98
hardware requirements, 102
interface, miniature versus full size, 100
launching, 98
library listings, viewing, 98
MP3s (Library collection), 99
older version support for CD burning, 99
Radio Tuner, station categories, 99

J - K

Jaz drives, 188, 196
summary features table, 52-53
Jobs, Steve, merging NeXT technology into Apple Computer, 11
joysticks
GamePad Pro USB, 112
Macally Airstick, 51
JPEG (Joint Photographic Experts Group) images, 180

kernel panic, non-boot troubleshooting alert, 313
Key Caps, special characters, 83
Keyboard pane (System Preferences dialog box), 225
keyboard shortcuts
Cmd+C (Copy), 68
Cmd+N (new window), 25
Cmd+O (open file), 25
Cmd+V (Paste), 68
Cmd+X (Cut), 68

Option+Cmd (alias creation), 70
Option+Cmd+A (Applications folder), 81
keyboards, layout, 16
KidSafe service (iTools), 170
Klondike game, 111
Knowledge Base, Apple Web site, 42

L

LANs (local area networks), 118
  backups, implementing, 305-306
  cabling
    Ethernet, 118-121
    hubs, 119
    LocalTalk, 118
  file sharing
    access privileges, setting, 123-125
    IP addresses, 123
  files, sharing, 189-193
  Internet routers, 121
  LocalTalk-to-Ethernet adapters, 120
laser printers
  consumables, 46-47
  PostScript fonts, 47
Late Breaking News, Mac OS X topics (Dock), 40-41
Launcher, third-party utility replacements, 258
launching
  installer for Mac OS X, 14-15
  iTunes, 98
  Mac OS X, screen appearance, 16-17
  programs (Dock), 230
  Script Runner, 269
  Sherlock, 160

Speech Recognition, 276-277
Terminal application (Unix), 283
Library collection, MP3 storage (iTunes), 99
Library folder, 60
  file types, 62
  fonts, installing, 130
licensing agreements, 14
line art, 49
Linksys Web site, DSL hardware routers, 150
Linux, free version of Unix, 204
Liquid Information Web site, Usenet newsgroups, 169
List view (files), 244-245
local area networks. *See* LANs
local connections (printers), 47
LocalTalk, 55, 118
LocalTalk-to-Ethernet adapters, 120
Log Out command (Apple menu), 76
logging in multiple users, 76
logging on to networks, 191-193
logic/puzzle games
  Down & Out, 108
  MegaMinesweeper, 107
login items, 313
  scripts, creating, 270
login names, System Administrator, identifying, 61
Login pane (System Preferences dialog box), 224
login screens, deactivating, 76
Logitech Web site, 112
lossy compression, JPEG images, 180

lost files, locating (Sherlock utility), 70-73
Low End Mac Web site, 321
LPR client software, INTELLIscribe, 201

M

Mac Orchard Web site, 160, 322
Mac OS 9
  accessing, 63
  Classic applications
    games, installing, 106-107
    installing, 94
    requirements, 18
  crashes, 93
  dual booting with Mac OS X, 17-20
  font installations, 131
  installing, 62-63
  rebooting, 94
  Software Update panel, 14
Mac OS X
  action games
    4X4 EVO, 110
    Oni, 109
    Quake 3 Arena, 109
  arcade games
    Native Assault, 109
    SNES9X, 109
    TheCowCatchingGame, 109
  Carbon games, installing, 107-108
  Cocoa games, installing, 107-108
  configuration
    country information, 16
    Internet connections, 16
    keyboard layout, 16

time zone information, 16

user accounts, 16

crashes in Classic environment, 93

dual booting with Mac OS 9, 17-20

evolution of, 11

frivolous benefits, 12

graphic design applications

Stone Super Seven Suite, 95

TIFFany, 95

inability to run on older Mac systems, 9

installation, 12

basic, 15

custom, 15

Extended format (HFS Plus), 13

hard drive partitions, 13

installer icon, 14-15

minimum hard drive space, 13

minimum RAM, 13

READ BEFORE YOU INSTALL.pdf, 14

recent firmware updates, 13

Software Update panel, 14

troubleshooting, 15

video card requirements, 13

instant messaging applications, 95

launching, screen appearance, 16-17

licensing agreement, 14

logic/puzzle games

Down & Out, 108

MegaMinesweeper, 107

networks, sharing with older Macs, 190

possible program conflicts, 12

practical benefits, 11

real world games

Chess, 111

Klondike, 111

Maximum Pool, 110

Video Poker, 111

shutting down, 17

software compatibility solutions

alternative file formats, 193

crossgrade/upgrade deals, 193

translation programs, 193

strategy games

Clan Lord, 108

Diablo II, 108

FLY! II, 108

Tropico, 108

supported models

iMacs, 9

Power Mac G3, 9

Power Mac G4, 9

PowerBook G3, 9

PowerBook G4, 9

system software updates, 294-295

Unix foundation, 8

Web browser selection, 95

Mac OS X Gallery, Desktop picture sources, 236

Mac-Mgrs Web site, troubleshooting resources, 317

Mac-related reference sites

Apple Support.com, 322

Clan MacGaming.com, 321

dealmac.com, 321

EveryMac.com, 321

Low End Mac.com, 321

MacAddict.com, 321

MacCentral.com, 320

MacFixIt.com, 320

Macintosh Products Guide.com, 322

MacInTouch.com, 320

MacNN.com, 321

MacSpeedZone.com, 320

Macworld.com, 320

TidBITS.com, 319

MacAddict Web site, 321

Macally Airstick (joystick), 51

MacCentral Web site, 320

MacDownload Web site, 322

MacFixIt Web site, 316, 320

Macintelligence Web site, 111

Macintosh

appeal of GUI, 7

introduction of, 7

system software, 11

Macintosh Products Guide Web site, 196, 322

backup software, 304

MacInTouch Web site, 320

hardware router sources, 150

troubleshooting resources, 317

MacLink, file format translation program, 193

MacNN Web site, 321

MacScripter.net Web site, 323

MacSenseTech Web site, 150

MacSpeedZone Web site, 320

MacTelnet, telnet client program, 210

Macworld magazine Web site, 320

magnification settings (Dock), 234

Mail

accounts, setting up, 164-165

messages
    reading, 165
    receiving, 165-166
    sending, 166-167
    sorting, 165
mailing lists, troubleshooting resources, 317
maintenance
    Classic environment
        desktop rebuilds, 297
        restarting with extensions off, 297
    Disk Utility, 299-300
    files, deleting, 299
    hard drives, defragmenting, 298
    reasons for, 293-294
Make Alias command (File menu), 69-70
managing colors. *See* ColorSync
MANs (metropolitan area networks), 118
Maximize button (windows), 241-242
Maximum Pool game, 110
McAfee Virex, 297
MegaMinesweeper game, 107
memory (protected), 9-10
memos, writing (TextEdit), 84-85
menu bar
    commands
        keyboard shortcuts, 25
        selection, 24
    screen appearance, 16-17
    versus pop-up menus, 24
menus
    Apple menu, replacement strategies, 255-256
    commands
        keyboard shortcuts, 25
        selecting, 24

contextual, 27, 50, 231
pop-up, 24
submenus, 24
text highlight colors, 238
messages (e-mail)
    reading, 165
    receiving, 165-166
    sending, 166-167
    sorting, 165
metropolitan area networks (MANs), 118
Miacomet Web site, 112
microphones, 276
Microsoft Word, text files, HTML export feature, 180
MIDI (Musical Instrument Digital Interface), 227
Minimize button (windows), 241-242
minimized windows
    Dock, 28, 232
    genie effects, 232
Miramar Web site, 198
missing files, troubleshooting, 315
modems
    analog, 142
    connection problems, troubleshooting, 145
    Hayes Compatible, 145
    phone
        ISP connections, 142
        popularity of, 142
modifier keys, keyboard shortcuts, 25
modifying Desktop icons, 237
monitoring print jobs, 138
monitors
    additive colors, 271-272
    color depth, 226
    display preferences (System Preferences dialog box), 225-226

headless servers, 198
resolution, 226
video resolution, system speed tips, 298
mount command (Unix), 204
mounted drives (networks), 192
mounting Unix directories (NFS export), 206
mouse
    multibutton, 50
    port connections, 50
    repetitive strain injuries (RSIs), 50
    versus
        trackballs, 50
        trackpads, 50
    WingMan Gaming Mouse, 112
Mouse pane (System Preferences dialog box), 225
Move to Trash command (File menu), 74
movies, playing (QuickTime Player), 86
Movies folder (Users folder), 64
moving
    files, 67
    folders, 67
    windows, 24
MP3s
    burning to CD-Rs or CD-RWs (iTunes), 99
    compression information, 98
    converting audio CDs (iTunes), 99
    copyright and intellectual property rights, 103-104
    Library collection, organizing (iTunes), 99
    playing, 98
    Rio Player, 98

mtools (Unix), 205
multibutton mouse, 50
multimedia
 ColorSync preferences
 (System Preferences dia-
 log box), 228
 digital camera images
 (Image Capture utility),
 86
 QuickTime Player, 86
 System Preferences dia-
 log box, 227-228
 sound preferences (System
 Preferences dialog box),
 226-227
 speech preferences
 (System Preferences dia-
 log box), 227
multiple programs, preemptive multitasking, 9
multiple users
 adding, 77-78
 editing, 77-78
 files, sharing, 79-80
 home folders, contents of,
 79
 login/logout procedures,
 76
 passwords, 76
 user names, 76
multithreading programs, 10
multiuser environment, folder access restrictions, 66
multiwindow mode, files,
 opening, 242-243
Music folder (Users folder),
 64
music. *See* iTunes
Musical Instrument Digital
 Interface (MIDI), 227

N

NAT (network address trans-
 lation), 149-150
 software
 IPNetRouter, 150
 SurfDoubler, 150
Native Assault game, 109
navigating Help Center, 39
Netopia Web site, 198
Netscape Communicator, 95
Netscape Navigator, 158
Network pane (System
 Preferences dialog box),
 223-224
 AppleTalk tab, 224
 PPPoE tab, 223
 Proxies tab, 224
 TCP/IP tab, 223
networks
 AppleTalk protocol,
 190-191
 cabling
 Apple versus conven-
 tional, 119
 Ethernet, 118-119
 LocalTalk, 118
 versus wireless, 121
 data transfer rates, deci-
 sion criteria, 120
 Ethernet, 197
 final connections, 121
 hubs, 119
 file sharing
 access privileges, set-
 ting, 123-125
 IP addresses, 123
 files
 exchanging with Unix
 computers, 206-209
 possible sharing prob-
 lems with older Macs,
 190
 sharing, 189-193,
 197-200

hardware
 Internet routers, 121
 LocalTalk-to-Ethernet
 adapters, 120
 headless servers, 198
 Internet access (DHCP),
 126
 Internet connection sharing, NAT (network
 address translation) software, 149-150
 IP addresses, assigning,
 190-191
 logon connections,
 191-193
 mounted drives, 192
 peer-to-peer, 197-198
 printers
 AppleTalk, 127
 connections, 47
 sharing on both PC/
 Mac platforms, 201
 TCP/IP, 127
 proxies, 224
 server-based, 198-199
 ShareWay IP, 190-191
 versus sneakernet, 187,
 196-197
New Finder Window com-
 mand (File menu), 30-31
New Folder command (File
 menu), 66, 243
New Note command (File
 menu), 84
News channel (Sherlock), 161
newsgroups
 troubleshooting resources,
 317
 Usenet, 152
 Deja.com, 169
 Liquid Information,
 169
NeXT computers, 11

NFS (Network File System), Unix directories, mounting, 206

None access (file sharing), 125

Norton Utilities
disk defragmenter, 298
repair utility, 301

notes (Stickies)
composing, 84
sizes, 84

NTP server (Network Time Protocol), 220

numbers, copying/pasting (Calculator), 82

O

objects, scripts (Script Editor), 266

office applications, AppleWorks, 96

offline help
Apple Phone Support, 41-42
resources, 41-42

OmniWeb Web browser, 95, 158

On-Core Web site, Dock Extras, 232

Oni game, 109

online connections
automatic settings, 144
launching (Internet Connect), 144

online help
Apple Web site, 39, 42
Late Breaking News (Dock)
Issues, 40-41
Tips, 40-41
updates, 40-41

Online Unix Software Repository Web site, 290

Open dialog box, 25

Open Enclosing Folder command (File menu), 74

Open Movie command (File menu), 86

OpenDoor Networks Web site, 190-191

opening
contextual menus, 27
Finder windows, 30-31
folders, 24
multiwindow mode, 242-243
single-window mode, 242-243
Help Viewer, 37

OpenStrip, as replacement for defunct Control Strip, 258

OpenType fonts, 130

operating systems, function of, 8

Option+Cmd keyboard shortcut (alias creation), 70

Option+Cmd+A keyboard shortcut (Applications folder), 81

Oregon State University Web site, Unix tutorial resources, 289

organizing home folders, 66

outline fonts, 130

Outpost.com Web site, Mac mail order, 119, 325

P

P5 game controller, 112

Page Setup command (File menu), 134-135

Page Setup dialog box, 134-135

PageSpinner (HTML editor), 182

panes
System Preferences dialog box
Classic, 219
ColorSync, 228
Date & Time, 220
Displays, 225-226
Dock, 219
Energy Saver, 217-218
General, 218
International, 221-222
Internet, 222-223
Keyboard, 225
Login, 224
Mouse, 225
Network, 223-224
QuickTime, 227-228
Screen Saver, 217-218
Sharing, 224-225
Software Update, 219
Sound, 226-227
Speech, 227
Startup Disk, 216-217
Users, 220

PANTONE Web site, 273

passwords
root account, selection guidelines, 78
users, 76

Paste command (File menu), 83

pasting numbers (Calculator), 82

PCs
Mac files, sharing with, 196-200
printers, sharing with Macs, 200-201

PDF (Portable Document Format), 27-28, 138, 200

PDFZone Web site, 200, 325

peer-to-peer networks, 197-198

crossplatform products
  DoubleTalk, 198
  PC MacLAN, 198
  Thursby Software, 198
  Timbuktu Pro, 198
People channel (Sherlock),
  160
performance, video resolution adjustments, 298
peripheral devices, 46
  color profiles
    applications, 272
    creating (Display
      Calibrator), 274-275
  ColorSync, 272-273
    preferences, setting,
      273-274
  game controllers
    auto-racing devices, 51
    flight controllers, 51
    gamepads, 51
    joysticks, 51
  graphics tablets, 51
  interfaces, 53
    ADB, 54
    Ethernet, 55
    FireWire, 54
    LocalTalk, 55
    SCSI, 54
    USB, 54
  malfunctions, troubleshooting, 316
  mouse
    alternatives, 50
    port connections, 50
    repetitive strain injuries
      (RSIs), 50
  portable hard drives, hot-swappable, 53
  printers, 46
    inkjet, 46-47
    laser, 46-47
    local connections, 47

network connections,
  47
PostScript fonts, 47
removable storage devices,
  51-52
  CD-Rs, 52-53
  CD-RWs, 52-53
  Jaz drives, 52-53
  SuperDisk, 52-53
  Zip drives, 52-53
scanners
  color depth, 49
  descreening, 49
  dynamic range, 49
  interpolation, 49
  ppi (pixels per inch), 49
  prescans, 49
  resolution, 49
  selection criteria, 48
  uses, 48
personal information, concealing on Web pages, 159
phone modems
  connection problems,
    troubleshooting, 145
  Hayes Compatible, 145
  ISP connections, PPP
    (Point-to-Point
    Protocol), 142-143
  online connections,
    launching (Internet
    Connect), 144
  popularity of, 142
pick lists, dialog box controls, 26
pico text editor (Unix),
  285-286
pictures
  Address Book, 168
  Desktop, changing, 236
  Mac OS X Gallery, 236
  MacDesktops, 236
Pictures folder (Users folder),
  65

placing Desktop icons,
  236-237
platforms
  Carbon applications, 90-91
  Classic applications, 93
  Cocoa applications, 91-92
playing
  movies (QuickTime
    Player), 86
  sound files (QuickTime
    Player), 86
plug-ins
  Library folder, 62
  Sherlock
    downloading, 163
    function of, 162
Plus For X utility, Desktop
  customizing tool, 255
PlusOptimizer, disk defragmenter utility, 298
Pocket Software Web site, 258
PocketDock, Dock third-party utility, 234, 258
Point-to-Point Protocol. *See*
  PPP
PoolShark game controller,
  112
pop-up menus
  dialog box controls, 26
  versus menu bar, 24
PopTop Software Web site,
  108
portable hard drives, hot-swappable, 53
ports, mouse connections, 50
PostScript fonts, laser printers, 47
PostScript Type 1 fonts, 130
Power Mac G3, 9
Power Mac G4, 9
PowerBook G3, 9
PowerBook G4, 9
PowerMail, e-mail client, 95
ppi (pixels per inch), 49

PPP (Point-to-Point Protocol), 142-143
  automatic connection options, 144
  ISP/phone modem connections, configuring, 142-143
PPPoE (PPP over Ethernet), 148-149
prebinding fix (Developer Tools CD), 294
preemptive multitasking, 9-10, 281-282
Preferences command (Clock menu), 83
Preferences command (Finder menu), 236
prescans (scanners), 49
Preview pane, files, viewing, 248
Preview utility, images
  formats, 86
  saving as, 86
  viewing, 86
previewing print jobs, 137
Print Center, 133
  Chooser successor, 259
  print jobs
    canceling, 138
    holding, 138
    monitoring, 138
  printers, adding, 134
Print command (File menu), 133, 136
Print dialog box, 133, 136
Print Item command (File menu), 74
print jobs
  canceling, 138
  holding, 138
  monitoring, 138
  previewing, 137
Print Preview command, 92
Print Setup dialog box, 133

printers
  adding (Print Center), 134
  ColorSync system preferences, 228
  definitions (Library folder), 62
  fonts
    bitmap, 130
    OpenType, 130
    outline, 130
    PostScript Type 1, 130
    TrueType, 130
  inkjet, consumables, 46-47
  Inkjet Mall Web site, 273
  laser
    consumables, 46-47
    PostScript fonts, 47
  local connections, 47
  network connections, 47
  networked
    AppleTalk, 127
    TCP/IP, 127
  Page Setup dialog box, 134-135
  print jobs
    canceling, 138
    holding, 138
    monitoring, 138
    previewing, 137
  print locations, 133
  proofing role, 274
  subtractive colors, 271-272
  switchboxes, 201
  TCP/IP networking
    hardware print servers, 201
    LPR client software, 201
    Unix, sharing with Macs, 209
printing
  across PC/Mac platforms
    on network, 201
    without network, 200-201

documents
  mini-printouts, 137
  number of copies, 136
  page ranges, 136
  Page Setup dialog box, 134-135
  screen shots (Grab utility), 136
privileges, folder access, 65
Privileges pane, files, viewing, 250
process dock, 257
Profile Central Web site, 273
profiles
  color, creating (Display Calibrator), 274-275
  ColorSync, preferences, setting, 272-274
programs
  Dock, 28
    opening, 28
    removing, 233
  multithreading, 10
  preemptive multitasking, 9-10
progressive images, 181
proofing (printers), 274
protected memory, 9-10, 281-282, 314
proxies (networks), 224
Public folder (home folder), file sharing capabilities, 64, 79-80
publishing Web pages to servers, 181-182

Q

Quake 3 Arena game, 109
Quartz, screen display
  PDF image format, 27-28
  translucent/transparent objects, 27-28

Quick Clicks (Help Center), 40

quick letters, writing (TextEdit), 84-85

QuickTime pane (System Preferences dialog box), 227-228

QuickTime Player
iMovie, exporting to, 102
movies, playing, 86
sound files, playing, 86

R

racing controllers, Pro Pedals, 112

Racing Simulator, 113

radio buttons, dialog box controls, 26

Radio Tuner (iTunes), station categories, 99

RAM (random access memory), 9
minimum installation requirements, 13
protected memory, 9, 314

random access memory (RAM), 9, 13

Read and Write access (file sharing), 125

Read Only access (file sharing), 125

reading e-mail messages (Mail), 165

real world games
Chess, 111
Klondike, 111
Maximum Pool, 110
Video Poker, 111

rebooting Mac OS 9, 94
Classic game installations, 106-107

rebuilding desktop (Classic maintenance), 297

receiving e-mail messages (Mail), 165-166

Recent Folders command (Go menu), 31

recording scripts (Script Editor), 267

red button (Finder), 30

Reference channel (Sherlock), 161

reformatting
disks, 239
hard drive, 14

registering domain names (InterNIC), 182

regular expressions (Unix), 288

removable disk drives
CD-R, 52-53, 188, 196
CD-RW, 52-53, 188, 196
DVD, 188
files
copying to, 188-189
sharing, 196-197
floppy disks, 196-197
Jaz, 52-53, 188, 196
repairing (Disk Utility), 299-300
SuperDisk, 52-53, 188, 196
Zip, 52-53, 188, 196

removing items from Dock, 233

renaming
files, 68
folders, 68

repair utilities (third-party)
DiskWarrior, 301
Drive10, 300
Norton Utilities, 301

repetitive strain injuries (RSIs), 50

ResExcellence Web site, 238, 257

resizing
Desktop icons, 236
Dock, 233

Finder windows, 30
windows
Close button, 241-242
Maximize button, 241-242
Minimize button, 241-242

resolution
monitors, 226
scanners, 49

Resources for Newbies Web site, 323

Restart command (Apple menu), 17, 94, 217

Restart command (Special menu), 19

restarting with extensions off (Classic maintenance), 297

Retrospect software, LAN backups, 304-306

Rio MP3 Player, 98

RJ-45 connectors (Ethernet), 119

root account
dangers of, 78
enabling, 78
locking, 78

router software, 121

RTF (Rich Text Format), 84-85

S

Sad Mac, non-boot troubleshooting alert, 312

Samba, server-based network product, 199

sans serif fonts, 159

Save As PDF command (File menu), 86, 137

Save dialog box, 25

saving
images (Preview utility), 86
scripts
Classic applet format, 268

compiled script format, 267

Mac OS X applet format, 268

text format, 267

scanners
  color depth, 49
  descreening, 49
  dynamic range, 49
  flatbed, 48
  interfaces
    FireWire, 48
    SCSI, 48
    USB, 48
  interpolation, 49
  ppi (pixels per inch), 49
  prescans, 49
  resolution, 49
  selection criteria, 48
  slide, 48
  uses, 48

screen
  elements
    Aqua appearance, 27
    Quartz, 27-28
  launch appearance, 16-17
  translucent/transparent objects (Quartz), 27-28

Screen Saver pane (System Preferences dialog box), 217
  Activation tab, 218
  Hot Corners tab, 218
  Screen Saver tab, 218

screen savers, downloading, 218

screen shots, printing (Grab utility), 136

Script Editor
  objects, 266
  recording scripts, 267
  syntax checks, 265
  writing scripts, 265-266

Script Runner
  launching, 269
  scripts, automatic execution, 268-269

scripts
  advantages, 263
  AppleScript
    introduction of, 264
    MacScripters.Net Web site, 264
    ScriptBuilders Web site, 264
    uses, 264
  applications, using within, 268-269
  compound statements (Script Editor), 265
  droplets, sample code, 269-270
  freeware, 264
  login items, creating, 270
  objects (Script Editor), 266
  recording (Script Editor), 267
  saving
    Classic applet format, 268
    compiled script format, 267
    Mac OS X applet format, 268
    text format, 267
  shareware, 264
  syntax checks (Script Editor), 265
  versus compiled programs, 264
  writing (Script Editor), 265-266

scrollbars, 30, 246

SCSI peripheral interface, 54

search engines
  AltaVista, 156, 325
  Google, 156, 324

searches (Sherlock)
  dragging results to new windows, 162
  executing, 161-162

lost files, 70-73
  results, 162

security, file sharing in multiple user environment, 79-80

Security menu commands
  Disable Root User, 78
  Enable Root User, 78

sed FAQ Web site, 324

selecting
  commands from menus, 24
  Desktop pictures, 236
  scanners, guidelines, 48
  Sherlock channels, 161

Selection command (Capture menu), 136

sending e-mail messages (Mail), 166-167

serif fonts, 159

server-based networks, 198-199
  products
    Samba, 199
    Sharity, 199

Services feature, Cocoa application tool, 92

setting
  Desktop preferences, 236-237, 254-255
  Web browser preferences, 158
    colors, 159
    downloads, 159
    fonts, 159
    helper applications, 159
    identity, 159

shareware, 108

ShareWay IP, TCP file sharing, 190-191

sharing
  files
    multiple user environment, 79-80
    networks, 189-193, 197-200

removable disk drives, 196-197
  with Unix computers, 204-209
printers
  across PC/Mac platforms, 200-201
  across Unix/Mac platforms, 209
Sharing pane (System Preferences dialog box), 224-225
Sharity, server-based network product, 199
shell scripting (Unix), 284-286
Sherlock
  channels
    Apple, 160
    creating, 163
    editing, 163
    Entertainment, 161
    Files, 160
    Internet, 160
    News, 161
    People, 160
    Reference, 161
    selecting, 161
    Shopping, 161
  hard drive indexes, creating, 72
  launching, 160
  lost files
    searching for, 70-73
  multiple channels, 70-71
  plug-ins
    downloading, 163
    function of, 162
  searches
    criteria, 71-73
    dragging URLs to browser window, 162
    initiating, 161-162
    results, 162
    terms, 161-162

Shopping channel (Sherlock), 161
Show Info command (File menu), 239, 247
Show Original command (File menu), 74
Show Status Bar command (View menu), 246
Show View Options command (View menu), 244
Shut Down command (Apple menu), 17
shutting down Mac OS X, 17
Sierra Attractions Web site, 110
Sig Software Web site, 258
signing up for iTools, 174-175
SimpleText, replaced by TextEdit, 259
single-mode window
  buttons
    Folders, 246
    Function, 246
    Window control, 246
  files, opening, 242-243
Sites folder (Users folder), 65
size list (Font panel), 132
sizing
  Desktop icons, 236
  Dock, 233
  Stickies notes, 84
slide scanners, 48
snail mail, 167
sneakernet
  files
    exchanging with Unix computers, 204-206
    sharing, 196-197
  versus real networks, 187, 196-197
SNES9X game, 109
software
  applications
    updating, 295-296
    version tracking, 295-296

backups (Retrospect software), 304
bug fixes, repair updates, 311
compatibility solutions, 193
  alternative file formats, 193
  backsaving files, 193
  crossgrade/upgrade deals, 193
  translation programs, 193
conflicts/bugs resources
  MacFixIt, 296
  MacInTouch, 296
DealMac Web site, 194
deleting, 299
emulation (VirtualPC), 202
erratic behavior, troubleshooting, 315
Macintosh Products Guide Web site, 196
troubleshooting category, 311
Unix
  compiling, 210-211
  executing, 209
  GNU license, 289
  remote execution (telnet), 210
  terminal applications, 209
  X Window applications, 209
updates
  automatic, 294-295
  manual, 294-295
software routers, 121
software sites
  Mac Orchard.com, 322
  MacDownload.com, 322
  MacScripter.net, 323
  VersionTracker.com, 322

Software Update pane
(System Preferences dialog
box), 219
Software Update utility, 16
Software Updates Area
(Apple Web site), 43
Sophos Anti-Virus, 297
sorting e-mail messages
(Mail), 165
sound files
Library folder, 62
playing (QuickTime
Player), 86
Sound pane (System
Preferences dialog box),
226-227
SP Engineering Web site, 113
spam (CAUCE Web site), 164
Speech pane (System
Preferences dialog box), 227
Speech Recognition, 276
commands window, 278
launching, 276-277
listening options, setting,
277
speakable commands,
adding (AppleScript),
278-279
volume controls, 278
Spring Cleaning program,
clean-up functions, 299
start pages in Web browsers,
158
Startup Disk pane (System
Preferences dialog box),
216-217
Stickies
colors, 84
composing, 84
Stone Super Seven Suite,
graphic design applications,
95
storing Dock items
applications, 230-231
Dock Extras, 232

files, 231
folders, 232
minimized windows, 232
URLs, 231
strategy games
Clan Lord, 108
Diablo II, 108
FLY! II, 108
Tropico, 108
streaming video, playing
(QuickTime Player), 86
submenus, command indica-
tors, 24
subtractive colors (printers),
271-272
SuperDisk, 52-53, 188, 196
Support Area (Apple Web
site), 42
SurfDoubler, Internet connection sharing software,
150
Sustainable Softworks Web
site, NAT software, 150
switchboxes (printers), 201
switching
applications (Cmd+Tab),
231
between Mac OS 9 and
Mac OS X, 17-20
Symantec Web site, Norton
Utilities, 298
symmetric multiprocessing,
10
System Administrator
Applications folder, man-
aging, 61
identifying, 61
system crashes, troubleshooting (Disk Utility), 299-300
System folder, 60
access controls, 64
system freezes, troubleshooting, 314-315
system maintenance, reasons
for, 293-294

System Preferences com-
mand (Apple menu), 20,
77-78, 142-143
System Preferences dialog
box, 20
General panel
Appearance tab, 237
Highlight Color tab,
238
panes, 215-216
Classic, 219
ColorSync, 228
Date & Time, 220
Displays, 225-226
Dock, 219
Energy Saver, 217-218
General, 218
International, 221-222
Internet, 151-152, 156,
222-223
Keyboard, 225
Login, 224
Mouse, 225
Network, 223-224
QuickTime, 227-228
Screen Saver, 217-218
Sharing, 224-225
Software Update, 219
Sound, 226-227
Speech, 227
Startup Disk, 216-217
Users, 220
system software updates
automatic, 294-295
manual, 294-295
system utilities, adding
(Dock), 255

T

tabs, dialog box controls, 26
tags (HTML), 178
Tao of Backup Web site, 303,
325

Tao of Regular Expressions
 Web site, 323
TCP/IP (Transmission
 Control Protocol/Internet
 Protocol), 146
 AppleTalk protocol,
 190-191
 cross platform protocol,
 printer sharing, 201
 networked printers, con-
 necting to, 127
 Unix/Mac printer sharing,
 209
Technical Information
 Library (TIL), Apple Web
 site, 42
telnet
 client program
 (MacTelnet), 210
 Unix software, 169
 remote execution, 210
Tenon Systems Web site, 289
Terminal application (Unix),
 209
 documentation resources,
 284
 launching, 283
Terminal Reality Web site,
 108-110
Terminal window, customizing (TinkerTool), 238
text
 dialog box controls, 26
 formatting options
 (TextEdit), 84-85
 manipulation, keyboard
 shortcuts, 68
 Web pages, HTML displays,
 178-180
Text-to-Speech
 iCab Web browser pages,
 reading, 276
 voice samples, selecting,
 275-276

TextEdit
 documents, RTF (Rich
 Text Format), 84-85
 Font menu commands, 84
 memos, writing, 84-85
 SimpleText successor, 259
 text formatting options,
 84-85
theCounter Web site, 183
TheCowCatchingGame
 game, 109
third-party apps, Apple Web
 site listing, 90
third-party microphones, 276
third-party repair utilities
 DiskWarrior, 301, 313
 Drive10, 300, 313
 Norton Utilities, 301
third-party Finder utilities,
 256
 Control Strip alternative,
 258
 Dock alternatives, 257
 DragThing, 257
 Drop Drawers, 258
 PocketDock, 258
 Launcher alternatives, 258
Thursby Software Web site,
 198
TidBITS Web site, 305, 319
TIFFany, graphic design
 applications, 95
time zones, Mac OS X con-
 figuration, 16
timeservers, 142
TinkerTool utility, customiz-
 ing Mac OS X with
 Desktop, 255
 Terminal window, 238
title bar (Finder), 30
Toolbar
 customizing, 247
 single-mode window but-
 tons
 Folders, 246
 Function, 246
 Window control, 246

top-level folders, creation of,
 66
topics (Help Center), 38
trackballs, 50
trackpads, 50
transferring digital camera
 images to hard drive, 86
Transit, FTP client program,
 208
translation programs
 DeBabelizer, 193
 MacLink, 193
translucent/transparent
 objects, screen appearance
 (Quartz), 27-28
Transmission Control
 Protocol/Internet Protocol.
 See TCP/IP
Trash, placing on Desktop
 (TinkerTool), 255
Tropico game, 108
troubleshooting
 analysis guidelines,
 310-311
 categories
 hardware failures, 311
 software corruption,
 311
 user errors, 311
 disk repairs (Disk Utility),
 299-300
 Dock, white patches, 234
 erratic behavior, 315
 Internet resources
 Apple Support, 317
 Mac-Mgrs, 317
 MacFixIt, 316
 MacInTouch, 317
 mailing lists, 317
 missing files, 315
 non-boots, 311
 blinking question
 mark, 312
 Chimes of Doom, 312
 kernel panic, 313

partial freezes, 313
Sad Mac, 312
peripheral device malfunctions, 316
phone modems, connection problems, 145
system freezes, 314-315
TrueType fonts, 130
Typeface list (Font panel), 132

U

Uniform Resource Locators. *See* URLs
Unix
advantages
free software, 32
large user base, 32
stability, 32
application types
command-line, 288
CGI, 287
GUIs, 289
networking, 288
text processing, 287
Web serving, 287
X Windows, 289
command line interface (CLI), 10, 254, 282
command entry, 282-283
development at Bell Labs, 32, 281
directories, pathnames, 206
file formats
database exchange guidelines, 208
graphics exchange guidelines, 209
spreadsheet exchange guidelines, 208

text exchange guidelines, 208
foundation for Mac OS X, 8
GUIs, 282
lack of viruses, 296
Linux incarnation, 204
Mac files, sharing with, 204-209
mount command, 204
mtools, 205
pico text editor, 285-286
preemptive multitasking, 281-282
printers, sharing with Macs, 209
protected memory, 281-282
regular expressions, 288
resource sites
Coping with Unix Web site, 324
FreeBSD.org Web site, 284
GNU Project Web site, 323
Oregon State University Web site, 289
Resources for Newbies Web site, 323
sed FAQ Web site, 324
Tao of Regular Expressions Web site, 323
Unix Primer Web site, 323
X.org Web site, 324
shell scripting, 284-286
software
compiling, 210-211
executing, 209
remote execution (telnet), 210

terminal applications, 209
X Window applications, 209
software resources
GNU license, 289
Internet Goodies List Web site, 290
Online Unix Software Repository Web site, 290
X.org Web site, 290
Terminal application, launching, 283
working directory, 283
Unix Primer Web site, 323
updating
application software, 295-296
system software
automatic, 294-295
manual, 294-295
patches, 311
URLs (Uniform Resource Locators), 157
address syntax
ftp, 157
http, 157
mailto, 157
news, 157
clippings, 158
Dock storage type, 231
pronunciation, 157
typing in Web browsers, 156
USB (Universal Serial Bus), 54
hubs, 119
Usenet newsgroups, 152
Deja.com, 169
Liquid Information, 169
users
accounts, Mac OS X configuration, 16
adding, 77-78

Admin, 315
  privileges, 76
  editing, 77-78
  errors, troubleshooting, 311
  files, sharing, 79-80
  home folder contents, 79
  login screens, deactivating, 76
  multiple, login/logout procedures, 76
  passwords, 76
  root account
    capabilities, 78
    enabling, 78
    locking, 78
  user names, 76
Users folder, 60
  Desktop folder, 64
  Documents folder, 64
  home folder, 64
  Library folder, 64
  Movies folder, 64
  Music folder, 64
  Pictures folder, 65
  Public folder, 64
  Sites folder, 65
Users pane (System Preferences dialog box), 220
utilities (third-party Finder customization), 256
  Control Strip alternatives, 258
  Dock alternatives, 257-258
  Launcher alternatives, 258

V

verbose mode (booting), 314
VersionTracker Web site, 322
  software patches/fixes, 311
  software resources, 295-296
  virus updates, 297

Vicom Technology Web site, NAT software, 150
video cards, installation requirements, 13
video footage
  editing in iMovie, 101
  exporting from iMovie, 102
  importing to iMovie, 101-102
  special effects, adding (iMovie), 101
Video Poker game, 111
video resolution, monitors, speed tips, 298
View menu commands
  Customize Toolbar, 246
  Show Status Bar, 246
  Show View Options, 244
View Options dialog box, 244
viewing
  Applications folder, 60
  disk information, 239
  files
    Application Files pane, 249
    Application pane, 248
    General Information pane, 248
    information, 247-250
    Preview pane, 248
    Privileges pane, 250
  images (Preview utility), 86
VirtualPC software emulator, 202
viruses
  antivirus software
    McAfee Virex, 297
    proper use of, 297
    Sophos Anti-Virus, 297
  Macintosh
    versus Unix, 296
    versus Windows, 296

macro transmissions, 296
VersionTracker monthly updates, 297
voice samples, selecting (Text-to-Speech), 275-276

W

WANs (wide area networks), 118
Web browsers
  bookmarks, 157
  function of, 156-159
  HTML interpretation, 156-159
  iCab, 95, 158
    Text-to-Speech capability, 276
  Internet Explorer, 158
  Microsoft Internet Explorer, 95
  Netscape Communicator, 95
  Netscape Navigator, 158
  OmniWeb, 95, 158
  preferences, setting, 158-159
  Sherlock site results, dragging to new window, 162
  start pages, 158
  URLs
    addressing, 156
    clippings, 158
Web pages
  bookmarks in Web browsers, 157
  browser interpretation, 156-159
  clip art
    AAAClipArt.com, 182
    Barry's Clipart Server, 182
    Clip's Ahoy!, 182

ClipArtConnection, 182
GifArt.com, 182
counters
Admo.net, 183
Beseen, 183
CounterGuide, 183
Hitometer, 183
theCounter, 183
Zcounter, 183
design applications, 179
HTML
sample code, 178
tutorial site, 179
images
GIF, 180
interlaced, 181
JPEG, 180
lossless compression, 180
lossy compression, 180
number of colors, 180
progressive, 181
iTools, creating with HomePage, 175-177
links, 156
start pages, 158
textual content, creating (HTML), 178-180
Web servers, pages, publishing to, 181-182
Web sites
Adobe Systems, 27-28
Acrobat Reader application, 138
Adrenaline Entertainment, 109
Aladdin Systems, 299
AltaVista, 156, 325
Apple
Classic applications listings, 95
Discussions Area, 43
Hardware Guide, 113

Help Center connections, 39
iDisk, 87
iMovie Gallery, 101
iMovie camcorder compatibility ratings, 103
iTunes downloads, 98
Knowledge Base, 42
Software Updates Area, 43
Support Area, 42
Technical Information Library (TIL), 42
third-party apps listing, 90
Apple Donuts, Sherlock plug-ins, 163
Apple Support, 322
BackJack Internet Backup Service, 307
Bare Bones Software, 288
Belkin Components, 201
Blizzard Entertainment, 108
Bungie, 109
caffeineSoft, 95
Carrot Software, 107
Casteel.org, 111
CH Products, 112
Clan MacGaming, 106, 321
clip art
AAAClipArt.com, 182
Barry's Clipart Server, 182
ClipArtConnection, 182
Clips Ahoy!, 182
GifArt.com, 182
Coalition Against Unsolicited Commercial E-mail (CAUCE), 325
Connectix, 198
Coping with Unix, 324

counters
Admo.net, 183
Beseen, 183
CounterGuide, 183
Hitometer, 183
theCounter, 183
Zcounter, 183
Dantz Development, 304
dealmac, 321
Deja.com, 169
Delta Tao Software, 108
domain names, purchasing, 182
Emulation.NET, 109
Epicware.com, screen savers, 95, 218
Essential Reality, 112
EveryMac, 321
Free Software Foundation, 290
FreeBSD.org, 284
GNU Project, 323
Google, 156, 324
Gravis, 112
Greyhound Project, 161
Griffin Technology, 276
HomeFree, 122
HomeLine, 122
hosting services, 181-182
iCab, 95
Icon Factory, 237
id Software, 109
Inkjet Mall, 273
Internet Goodies List, 290
InterNIC, 182
iTools
free space, 173
signing up, 174-175
Linksys, 150
Liquid Information, 169
Logitech, 112
Low End Mac, 321
Mac Orchard, 160, 322
Mac OS X Gallery, 236

363

MacAddict, 321
MacCentral, 320
MacDesktops, 236
MacDownload, 322
MacFixIt, 320
Macintelligence, 111
Macintosh Products
    Guide, 196, 322
MacInTouch, 150, 320
MacNN, 321
MacScripters.Net, 264,
    323
MacSenseTech, 150
MacSpeedZone, 320
Macworld Magazine, 320
Miacomet, 112
Miramar, 198
Netopia, 198
OmniWeb, 95
On-Core, 232
OpenDoor Networks,
    190-191
Oregon State University,
    Unix resources, 289
Outpost.com, 119, 325
PANTONE, 273
PDFZone, 200, 325
Pocket Software, 258
PopTop Software, 108
PowerMail, 95
Profile Central, 273
ResExcellence, 238, 257
Resources for Newbies,
    323
ScriptBuilders, 264
sed FAQ, 324
Sierra Attractions, 110
Sig Software, 258
software fixes
    MacFixIt, 296
    MacInTouch, 296
SP Engineering, 113
Sustainable Softworks,
    NAT software, 150

Symantec, 298
Tao of Backup, 303, 325
Tao of Regular
    Expressions, 323
Tenon Systems, 289
Terminal Reality, 108-110
Thursby Software, 198
TidBITS, 319
troubleshooting
    Apple Support, 317
    Mac-Mgrs, 317
    MacFixIt, 316
    MacInTouch, 317
    mailing lists, 317
Unix Primer, 323
VersionTracker, 311, 322
Vicom Technology, NAT
    software, 150
Webmonkey, HTML tutor-
    ial resources, 179
X.org, 290, 324
Xicons.com, 237-238
YardSale.net, Sherlock
    plug-ins, 163
Webmonkey Web site, HTML
    tutorial resources, 179
white patches, troubleshoot-
    ing (Dock), 234
wide area networks (WANs),
    118
Window control buttons
    (Toolbar), 246
windows
    applications in back-
        ground, clicking on, 245
    document, 23
    file display options
        Column view, 244-245
        Icon view, 244-245
        List view, 244-245
    Finder, 23
        button indicators, 30
        opening, 30-31
        resizing, 30

icons, file folders, 24
minimizing genie effects,
    232
moving, 24
multiwindow mode,
    242-243
resizing buttons
    Close, 241-242
    Maximize, 241-242
    Minimize, 241-242
single-window mode,
    242-243
types
    document, 241-242
    Finder, 241-242
view options
    customizing, 245-246
    scrollbars, 246
    status bar information,
        246
WingMan Gaming Mouse,
    112
wired networks, disadvan-
    tages, 123
wireless networks
    AirPort, 150
        advantages over cabled
            networks, 122
        base station, 122
        card, 122
        creating, 122
    versus cabled networks,
        121
working directory (Unix),
    283
Write Only access (file shar-
    ing), 125
writing
    memos (TextEdit), 84-85
    scripts (Script Editor),
        265-266
WYSIWYG (What You See Is
    What You Get), 97-98
    Web page creation, 179

X - Y - Z

X Window Systems applications (Unix), 209, 289
X.org Web site, 290, 324
Xicons.com Web site, 237-238
Xtools (Unix), 209, 289

YardSale.net Web site, Sherlock plug-ins, 163
yellow button (Finder), 30

Zcounter Web site, 183
Zip drives, 188, 196
   summary features table, 52-53

Easy Adobe Photoshop 6

by Kate Binder

Another excellent book by Kate Binder, *Easy Adobe Photoshop 6* uses a simple and friendly approach to teach you the basics of Photoshop 6. This book is based completely on visual learning. You don't have to read text to complete a given task. In addition, the book is focused on the topics and tools that are most frequently used for the most common Photoshop tasks and avoids the complex tasks of higher-level users. Some of the tasks covered include interface basics, selection tools, color, editing and manipulation, filters, printing, and using Photoshop for the Web.

ISBN: 0-7897-2423-5   *$24.99 USA/$37.95 CAN*

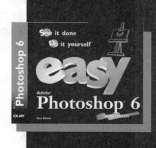

The Complete Idiot's Guide to iMovie 2

by Brad Miser

A quick and easy way to learn more about producing professional-looking digital video with your iMac, *The Complete Idiot's Guide to iMovie 2* is a must-have guide to learning everything there is to know about shooting and editing your own movies with iMovie 2. Brad Miser's light-hearted approach and down-to-earth advice will have you off and running with iMovie 2 in no time.

ISBN: 0-7897-2477-4   *$19.99 USA/$29.95 CAN*

Special Edition Using Mac OS X

by Brad Miser

Now that you have a handle on the basics of running Mac OS X, you're ready for *Special Edition Using Mac OS X*. This in-depth look at Mac OS X goes way beyond the typical reference book by providing expert advice on making Mac OS X work for you by including coverage of iTools, Mail, security, networking and customizing your system with Mac OS X, and much more. Plus, you get handy keyboard shortcuts and helpful troubleshooting tips in almost every chapter!

ISBN: 0-7897-2470-7   *$39.99 USA/$59.95 CAN*

The Scanning Workshop

by Richard Romano

With all of Max OS X's cool tools and features at your fingertips, you no doubt will be moving into the realm of working with digital images—if you haven't already! Richard Romano's *The Scanning Workshop* takes you through the journey of becoming the master of your digital world. Begin by learning what scanner is right for you, how to set up and prescan your images, edit those images on your computer, and create a Web photo album with all those fantastic shots.

ISBN: 0-7897-2558-4   *$29.99 USA/$44.95 CAN*

THE **COMPLETE** **IDIOT'S** **GUIDE** TO

| Arts & | Business & | Computers & | Family | Hobbies | Language | Health & | Personal | Sports & | Teens |
| Sciences | Personal Finance | the Internet | & Home | & Crafts | Reference | Fitness | Enrichment | Recreation | |

IDIOTSGUIDES.COM

Introducing a new
and different Web site

Millions of people love to learn through *The Complete Idiot's Guide*®
books. Discover the same pleasure online in **idiotsguides.com**–part of
The Learning Network.

Idiotsguides.com is a new and different Web site, where you can:

✳ Explore and download more than 150 fascinating and useful mini-guides—FREE!
Print out or send to a friend.

⊕ Share your own knowledge and experience as a mini-guide contributor.

● Join discussions with authors and exchange ideas with other lifelong learners.

🏛 Read sample chapters from a vast library of *Complete Idiot's Guide*® books.

✗ Find out how to become an author.

✂ Check out upcoming book promotions and author signings.

🏠 Purchase books through your favorite online retailer.

Learning for Fun. Learning for Life.

IDIOTSGUIDES.COM • LEARNINGNETWORK.COM

Copyright © 2000 Pearson Education